Face, Communication and Social Interaction

Face, Communication and
Social Interaction

Edited by
Francesca Bargiela-Chiappini
and Michael Haugh

LONDON   OAKVILLE

Published by
Equinox Publishing Ltd
UK: Unit 6, The Village, 101 Amies Street, London SW11 2JW
USA: DBBC, 28 Main Street, Oakville, CT 06779

www.equinoxpub.com

First published 2009

British Library Cataloguing-in-Publication Data

A catalogue record for this book is available from the British Library.

ISBN   978-1-84553-291-8   (hardback)

Library of Congress Cataloging-in-Publication Data

Face, communication and social interaction / edited by Francesca Bargiela-Chiappini and Michael Haugh.
    p. cm.
  Includes bibliographical references and index.
    ISBN 978-1-84553-291-8 (hb)
    1. Interpersonal communication. 2. Social interaction. 3. Identiry (Psychology) 4. Intercultural communication. I. Bargiela-Chiappini, Francesca. II. Haugh, Michael.
    P94.7.F33   2008
    153.6—dc22
                        2008017427

Typeset by S.J.I. Services, New Delhi
Printed and bound in Great Britain by Lightning Source UK Ltd, Milton Keynes

Contents

Part II: Face, identity and self

Foreword

Linguists' interest in the notion of 'face' has been closely tied to linguistic politeness research. While Goffman introduced the concept of 'face' to the intellectual arena, it drew unprecedented attention in linguistics when Brown and Levinson gave it the central role in their universal theory of politeness. Three decades have passed since the first publication of their work in 1978, and numerous studies supporting, opposing, and redefining the issues have ensued. The sixteen chapters in this book, *Face, Communication and Social Interaction*, reflect the diverse paths that research on linguistic manifestations of 'face' have taken.

Brown and Levinson's work on linguistic politeness was innovative and inspirational in many ways: it was the first comprehensive study of linguistic politeness after Robin Lakoff's seminal work; it showed how degrees of politeness can be expressed and determined in a principled way using the concept of 'face'; and it explained seemingly disparate phenomena found in various languages by universally valid principles. Brown and Levinson postulated that all Model Persons ('willful fluent speakers of a natural language') are endowed with the qualities of 'rationality' and 'face', and, according to rational reasoning, choose linguistic strategies to satisfy communicative and face-oriented ends. They explained their universal notion of 'face' as being derived from that of Goffman and from the English folk term. They identified two aspects of 'face' representing 'basic wants': 'negative face' and 'positive face', and they described linguistic strategies used to redress face threatening acts.

Like all innovative and ambitious work, Brown and Levinson's work generated debate and criticism. Their postulation of a Model Person with 'face' wants was reminiscent of the ideal speaker postulated by Chomsky in the theory of Generative Grammar, which also claimed universality. While abstract models of this sort and the postulated universal principles may provide us with a great sense of order, they tend not to account for all of the phenomena. Indeed, such unaccounted instances in the putatively universal model will often be the most crucial to understanding the functions and uses of a language, which will serve to refine and redefine the proposed universals. Neither a Model Person, nor an ideal speaker exists in a real situation of verbal communication, but rather there are actual speakers who interact and negotiate with one another, responding to the changing contexts. Assuming universality of a fundamental concept such as 'face' risks overlooking important variability within and across languages and their users. After Brown and Levinson's work, a number of studies addressed this and related limitations, including my work two decades ago which reexamined the universality claim of the concept of 'face' defined by Brown and Levinson, highlighting some examples from Japanese that show the relational aspect of 'face', and that do not easily fit into the universality claim. Examples that do not readily accord with the universality hypothesis do not have to be from Japanese or any 'exotic' language, but could have been from any natural language. The fact that 'face' is a concept people think they know and understand also presents challenges. The intuitive appeal is an important aspect of the explanatory power of 'face', yet it creates difficulties in using the concept of 'face' as an analytical tool to explain other interactional phenomena such as politeness.

Questions regarding 'face' are undeniably multi-dimensional. This fundamental property of 'face' is best illustrated in the context of verbal interaction, and is the central issue of this book, too. The context of verbal interactions is where interlocutors negotiate their 'face' in relation to others as conversations unfold, based on their understanding of the immediate and larger context of interaction, on their knowledge and sense of what may be at stake as a person or a member of a group in the society, and on their understanding of who they are. While observations are made about the many aspects of 'face' in interaction, it is important not to forget that each aspect is part of a whole. All dimensions yield insights that are not captured by any single theoretical stance. *Face, Communication and Social Interaction*, thoughtfully conceived of and edited by Francesca Bargiela-Chiappini and Michael Haugh, does a magnificent job in providing us with a wealth of studies on 'face' that provide a multi-dimensional understanding of the issues, and that will motivate further progress in this important intellectual inquiry.

Yoshiko Matsumoto
Stanford University, CA

1
Face and interaction

Michael Haugh

1.1. The rise of face in research on communication and social interaction

It is an enduring theme of humanity that people are concerned about what others think of them. Studies focusing on this concern about what others think of us have, following the seminal work of Goffman (1955, 1967), often come under the rubric of 'face(work)' in academic work. Recourse has been made to face, for instance, in the study of politeness, compliance-gaining strategies, impression management, negotiation and conflict management, courtroom discourse, management practice and organisational behaviour, and second language learning. The notion of face has thus become firmly established as a means of explaining various social phenomena in a range of fields within the social sciences.

The concept of face was first introduced into academic discourse by Goffman (1955, 1967), who defined face as 'the positive social value a person effectively claims for himself by the line others assume he has taken during a particular contact' (Goffman, 1955: 213). However, it was really only through the highly influential work of Brown and Levinson (1978, 1987) on politeness that face became a major focus of attention for researchers working on communication and social interaction. Face was defined by Brown and Levinson as 'the public self-image that every member wants to claim for himself', encompassing the want to be unimpeded (negative face) and the want to be appreciated and approved of (positive face) (Brown and Levinson, 1987: 61). Yet while face has become seemingly indispensable in the discussion of various aspects of social interactions, particularly politeness, its conceptualisation and application in research has been the subject of considerable debate, as figurative usages of the term face have continued to proliferate in academic research.

Two key issues have emerged in regards to face, in particular Brown and Levinson's notion, over the past thirty years. The first is the claim that face has been grounded in a 'western' perspective on interaction and so is ultimately ethnocentric. It has long been argued, for instance, that Brown and Levinson's approach to face is overly individualistic and unnecessarily focused on the avoidance of imposition (see, for example, Bargiela-Chiappini, 2003, 2006; Haugh, 2005a; Ide, 1989; Lim, 2004; Mao, 1994; Matsumoto, 1988). In neglecting the rich socio-cultural milieu from which the metaphor of face originally emerged (Ervin-Tripp, Nakamura and Guo, 1995), Brown and Levinson have created 'the impression that face is an *a priori attribute of individuals* that stands to be *threatened* in interaction, and must thus above all be safeguarded' (Terkourafi, 2007: 320, original emphasis). Numerous studies indicate, however, that face goes beyond such threats to the individual's self-image in three important ways. Firstly, face can involve an awareness of one's position within a network of relationships (Haugh, 2007a; Hernández-Flores, 1999; Hu, 1944; Koutlaki, 2002; Ruhi and Işık-Güler, 2007; Ukosakul, 2003, 2005). Secondly face can be associated with groups as well as individuals (Haugh, 2005b; Ho, 1976; Nwoye, 1992). And thirdly, face may be given or gained as well as sacrificed among other things, rather than simply being lost or saved (Ervin-Tripp, Nakamura and Guo, 1995; Gao and Ting-Toomey, 1998; Hinze, 2005). In surveying the rich tapestry of work on folk conceptualisations of face, then, it becomes apparent that Brown and Levinson have perpetuated a somewhat impoverished notion of face and facework.

A number of scholars have thus attempted to neutralise these charges of ethnocentrism by developing alternative theoretical conceptualisations of face, with a particular focus on broadening the distinction between positive and negative face to accommodate cross-cultural variation. Lim and Bowers (1991: 420), for instance, propose that positive face actually involves two distinct wants – 'the want to be included' (fellowship face) and 'the want that one's abilities be respected' (competence face) – which complement negative face, or 'the want to be unimpeded' (autonomy face). Mao (1994: 472), on the other hand, proposes in his theory of Relative Face Orientation that positive and negative face should be reconceptualised as 'ideal social identity [or] total communion with others' and 'ideal individual autonomy [or] separate and almost inviolable space' respectively, which should be understood as opposing forces towards which various societies orient differently. Similarly, O'Driscoll (1996, 2007) has proposed in Face Dualism theory that positive face be redefined as 'connection and belonging', akin to Lim and Bower's (1991) 'fellowship face', while negative face be redefined as 'separation and individuation' (O'Driscoll, 2007: 474). Terkourafi (2007, 2008) has more recently claimed that a universal notion of face, or face2, be conceptualised as grounded in the dimension of approach/withdrawl. Finally, Arundale (1993, 2006) has proposed in Face Constituting Theory that what underlies face is the dialectical opposition of connectedness (encompassing unity, interdependence, solidarity, association, congruence and so on) and separateness (encompassing differentiation, independence, autonomy, dissociation, divergence and so on) (Arundale, 2006: 204). The distinction between connection and separateness, or variants thereof, appears to have remained central in attempts to develop alternatives to Brown and Levinson's notion of face to date. What distinguishes these different proposals, then, is the broader framework from which they emerge. While most of these proposals are grounded in a broadly Gricean approach to communication (Arundale 2008), Arundale's (1999, 2006) Face Constituting Theory is perhaps the most truly alternative line of enquiry to date in being grounded within a radically different conceptualisation of communication.

The second key debate has centred on the claim that face and facework should be a focus of research in their own right, as they involve issues broader than simply politeness (see, for example, Arundale, 1999, 2006; Domenici and Littlejohn, 2006; Locher and Watts, 2005; Spencer-Oatey, 2000, 2005; Ting-Toomey, 1988, 2005; Watts, 2003). The expansion of research on face and facework beyond a narrow focus on politeness has developed concurrently in two fairly independent fields. The first group encompasses scholars from the North American school of communication studies. Within this school, the conceptualisation of face has been shifted towards a more general concern for identity (Cupach and Imahori, 1993; Domenici and Littlejohn, 2006; Ting-Toomey, 2005). Work on individualism and collectivism has also been incorporated in distinguishing between facework that involves a focus on self-face identity concern, other-face identity concern, and mutual-face identity concern (Ting-Toomey and Kurogi, 1998; Ting-Toomey, 1988, 2005), or alternatively facework at the level of personal, relational, and community identities (Domenici and Littlejohn, 2006). This move towards conceptualising face as concern for identity, however, raises the question of how such research on face can be distinguished in a meaningful way from broader work on identity.

Within European-Continental pragmatics, a second group of scholars has been recently calling for a shift back to Goffman's original conceptualisation of face in the study of social interaction (Bargiela-

Chiappini, 2003). In the discursive approach to politeness within the broader framework of relational work (Watts, 2003; Locher and Watts, 2005), as well as Rapport Management Theory (Spencer-Oatey, 2005, 2007), Goffman's (1955: 213) original definition of face as 'the positive social value a person effectively claims for himself by the line others assume he has taken during a particular contact' has been adopted for analysis. This move back to Goffman's original notion of face certainly circumvents many of the criticisms that have dogged Brown and Levinson's conceptualisation of face. However, such a move has not been without its own problems. While Bargiela-Chiappini (2003) called for a re-visiting of Goffman's work on face, she went on to point out that Goffman's face was intended for examining interaction in North American contexts, and so is rooted in a view of social actors that are concerned with their own self-image and self-preservation (p.1463). Such a conceptualisation, however, is not necessarily appropriate as an analytical tool in other socio-cultural contexts. Although Goffman's notion of face has been invoked as salient in analysing interactions, such a move may (inadvertently) impose analytical understandings of interactions which are not consonant with the understandings of participants, thereby potentially leading to a loss of focus on the phenomenon researchers set out to analyse in the first place (Haugh, 2007b: 301-302). Thus, while a return to a more interactionally-grounded notion of face certainly holds much promise, in light of the wealth of studies on folk conceptualisations of face that have been alluded to in this discussion, a more careful examination of the implications of this proposed shift back to Goffman's notion of face is clearly warranted.

While developments in research on face and facework over the past fifty years since Goffman first introduced the notion of face into academic discourse have certainly led to a richer theoretical and analytical tapestry within which researchers can work, a number of key controversies remain to be resolved, as this brief survey has indicated. At the heart of these continuing debates about face has arguably been an underlying tension between various theoretical conceptualisations of face as a cognitive state of individuals that motivates certain social behaviours, and folk conceptualisations of face as a kind of shared cultural construct that constrains social behaviour. The debate about the cross-cultural validity of Brown and Levinson's (1978, 1987) notions of positive and negative face, for instance, arguably turns on broader disputes about the validity of explanations of social behaviour rooted in the cognition of individuals versus explanations that make recourse to norms shared across socio-cultural groups.

Mirroring the distinction between first-order and second-order politeness (Eelen, 2001: 30-48; Watts, Ide and Ehlich, 1992: 3-4), then, we might say that a key issue facing researchers making recourse to face in their analyses is the progressive dichotomisation of second-order (or face2) and first-order (or face1) notions of face. However, it is worth noting that while face1 is often equated with folk or emic notions of face (Haugh and Hinze, 2003: 1582; Haugh, 2007b: 302; O'Driscoll, 1996: 8; Ruhi and Iṣɪk-Güler, 2007: 684; Terkourafi, 2007: 315-316), face can also be conceptualised as being grounded in the participant's perspective, as opposed to that of the analyst. In other words, in applying the first-order/second-order distinction we need to ensure we do not conflate a finer distinction, namely that between (first-order) *emic* perspectives, where the aim is to 'understand speech practices which make sense to the people concerned, i.e., in terms of indigenous values, beliefs and attitudes, social categories, emotions, and so on' (Goddard, 2006: 2), and (first-order) *participant* perspectives, where the aim is to understand 'the participants' orientations to meanings, interpretations and evaluation of utterances' (Piirainen-Marsh, 2005: 214). For example, while the notion of *wakimae* (translated as 'discernment') invoked by Ide (1989) in place of Brown and Levinson's (1987) etic (or 'universal') notion of face to account for politeness in Japanese is culture-specific and so emic in nature, Ide makes no claim that her analyses would be understood as such by the participants in interactions. In fact, Ide seems to not consider the participant's perspective at all, apparently comfortable with her status as a 'cultural-insider' to justify her analyses.[1] However, to make recourse to folk or emic notions of face without proper consideration of their (ultimate) grounding in interaction may simply led to a reification of such first-order notions. What has been missing in much work to date, therefore, is a deeper consideration of the intervening level of interaction. In this volume, then, it is proposed that by placing interaction at the centre of the analysis of face – echoing Bargiela-Chiappini's re-opening of discussion about face in her 2003 article – (new) insights may be gained into these (old) debates.

1.2. Face as co-constituted in and constitutive of interaction

The working premise of the contributors to this volume has been, to a greater or lesser extent, that face is fundamentally interactional. In invoking interaction in the study of face, however, it is important to clarify exactly what is meant in claiming that face is an interactional phenomenon. We propose that face is interactional in a number of different senses. In its most basic sense, face is interactional in that it presupposes evaluation by others of the behaviour of individuals as well as groups (Arundale, 1993, 1999; Haugh and Hinze, 2003; Ho, 1976, 1994). Without interaction there can be neither behaviour to evaluate nor others to make those evaluations. Consequently, all research on face and facework must ultimately deal with social interaction and communication in some way or another. While this may seem something of a truism, it does have implications for the kinds of data that are allowable in analyses of face and facework. Many of the contributors in this volume, for instance, although not all, make recourse to natural, interactional data in their analyses.

Face is interactional in a more technical sense as well in that it emerges through interaction as a joint accomplishment of interlocutors (Arundale, 2006; Chen, 1990/91; Dippold, 2006; Golato and Taleghani-Nikazm, 2006; Haugh, 2007a; Lerner, 1996; MacMartin, Wood and Kroger, 2001; Piirainen-Marsh, 1995, 1996). In other words, we can say that face is *co-constituted* in interaction. Lerner (1996), for instance, has shown how face and facework might be treated as an interactional achievement from the perspective of conversation analysis. Lerner (1996) first defines face as 'the ongoing and ever-changeable level of regard that accrues to persons engaged in interaction' (p.303), and then goes on to argue in relation to threats to face that 'both the possibility and terms of the disregard as well as the resources available to deal with it are part of the sequential organisation of talk-in-interaction' (p.316). In other words, facework is 'recognisable not by reference to individual desire but by reference to common practices that demonstrate that desire' (p.319). In the example below, the response to an emerging request across turns 1–2 is treatable as an instance of facework according to Lerner (1996: 315).

(1)

1	J:	Okay, you c- I just uh thought if you uh- .hh en I'll take the book in so we c'n kind'v exchange packages
2	P:	hhh Oh I have – I have yer <u>book</u> but if you don't mind I'd [like tuh keep it awhile,
3	J:	[OH please. No if you'd like to yer perfectly welcome

(Lerner, 1996: 315)

In turn 1, J has proposed they exchange packages. Within this proposal, however, is embedded a request for P to return a book. This embedded request is oriented to by P in turn 2, where P responds by asking to keep the book for longer. In turn 3, J's initial (embedded) request is recast by herself 'as a premature request for the return of the book, or at least as a request made *without regard* to whether P has finished with it or not' (Lerner, 1996: 316, emphasis added). In other words, turn 1 is treated by J as a potential face-threat. In order to recast her initial face-threatening request, J draws upon the local sequential environment with a turn-initial 'Oh please' that is 'designed to interrupt an emerging action…and to show that the projected (imposing) request by P is actually regarded as perfectly suitable or is even viewed with favour' (Lerner, 1996: 316), following by a 'No' which 'specifically rejects the request *as* an imposing request' (p.316, original emphasis). As Heritage (1998) has demonstrated more generally across interactions in English, 'oh-prefacing responses to inquiry work to treat the inquiry to which they respond as 'unexpected' or inapposite' (Heritage, 1998: 313). The 'facework' accomplished in this instance has therefore arguably been achieved through drawing upon more general features of sequential organisation of talk-in-interaction.

The treatment of face as co-constituted in interaction, however, raises the crucial issue of how we might determine whether face or facework is actually involved in particular interactions. As MacMartin, Wood and Kroger (2001) argue, identifying face(work) in interactional data always involves making a judgement.

> The identification of some utterance in terms of face requires a judgment, that is, it must be recognised as face threat in order to be interpreted as doing face threat. The question, is, 'whose judgment?' (MacMartin, Wood and Kroger, 2001: 229)

While theoretical notions of face and facework have often been invoked in seeking to make sense of data, for instance, in much of the work on 'politeness' inspired by Brown and Levinson's theory (1987), the warranting of the analyst's interpretation of a particular sequence within an interaction as involving face(work) is not as straightforward as might first appear. To justify the attribution of face or facework to a particular sequence based on an 'operational' definition of face, for example, arguably leads to ontological circularity in that the 'analyst claims that talk shows evidence for the existence of a particular psychological state or process', such as face in the sense proposed by Brown and Levinson (1987), and then 'explains the production of that talk in terms of the existence of [that particular psychological state or process]' (Antaki, Billig, Edwards and Potter, 2003: 13). In order to avoid such ontological circularity, it is incumbent upon the analyst to demonstrate that his or her interpretation is consistent with that of the participants for that particular interaction. If the analyst's interpretation deviates from that of the participants and so imposes an understanding of the interaction that is not consistent with that of the participants themselves, the analysis itself runs the risk of losing sight of the object of analysis, as long argued by ethnomethodologists, for instance (Garfinkel, 1967; Heritage, 1984), and more recently by Eelen (2001) in his groundbreaking critique of politeness theories.

> A situation in which the scientific account contradicts informants' claims and dismisses them as being 'wrong' does not represent a healthy situation. Such a practice immediately leads to a rupture between scientific and commonsense notions, causing the theory to lose its grasp on the object of analysis. In an investigation of everyday social reality informants can never be 'wrong,' for the simple reason that it is their behaviour and notions we set out to examine in the first place. (Eelen, 2001: 253)

Such a position is also consistent with that of conversation analysts who caution against the imposition of theoretical categories, such as face, on participants' actions (MacMartin, Wood and Kroger, 2001: 225; Schegloff, 1988: 95, 1991: 48, 1992a: 106, 1992b: 194–195; Sidnell, 2005: 165; Wilson, 1991: 29). The onus is thus on the analyst to demonstrate that his or her analysis is somehow consonant or analogous – although not necessarily synonymous – with the understandings of the participants (Arundale, forthcoming; Haugh, 2007b: 310).

In the discursive approach to politeness and more broadly relational work (Locher and Watts, 2005; Watts, 2003), this issue is essentially sidestepped by only tentatively identifying utterances which are 'open to interpretation' or warrant '*potential* evaluation by the participants (or others)' as instances of facework (Locher and Watts, 2005: 17; Watts, 2003: 220).[2] However, as argued by Haugh (2007b: 303), if the analyst is not able to identify with a certain degree of certainty that face(work) is involved, then it is questionable what indeed has been accomplished through such an analysis. Moreover, as Piirainen-Marsh (2005) points out, the discursive approach 'directs the analyst towards identifying pre-established institutional structures which determine expectations for face and appropriate conduct' rather than seeking to 'demonstrate how participants recognise and display particular understandings of utterances as meaningful, situated actions' (p.199). Thus, while the discursive approach explicitly advocates rejecting the imposition of theoretical categories by the analyst (Watts 2003: 11), the epistemological status of the categorisation of actions as either 'marked' or 'unmarked', for instance, is ambiguous, as it is unclear whether such a categorisation is consonant with the understandings of participants (cf. Haugh, 2007b: 300).

In the following extract discussed by Locher and Watts (2005: 25-26), the compliments made at the beginning of a dinner party by an older married couple, Kate and Roy, about the hosts' 15 year old daughter Debbie are claimed to be a 'marked case of relational work' (p. 26).

(2)

1	Roy:	nice to see you how are you? nice to <u>s</u>ee you.
2	Deb:	nice to see you ( )
3	Kate:	<u>G</u>od does she look gorgeous.
4	Roy:	there you go lady.
5	Deb:	thank you.
6	Kate:	Deb? <u>E</u>verytime I see you, you're <u>m</u>ore beautiful. and <u>I</u> don't know how much more <u>b</u>eautiful you can get?
7	M:	((laughter))
8	Kate:	it's <u>un</u>believable. [it <u>d</u>oesn't] <u>s</u>top does it.
9	Deb:	[thank you.]
10		thank you ((laughter))
11	Kate:	it <u>d</u>oesn't <u>s</u>top.
12	Deb:	((laughter))
13	Kate:	she looks absolutely <u>g</u>orgeous.

(Locher and Watts, 2005: 25)

Such an analysis, however, raises the question of how the analyst can legitimately establish that the facework involved here is indeed 'marked'. In justifying their interpretation of compliments made to Debbie as being marked, which they characterise as giving 'more than they need to give' (Locher and Watts, 2005: 25), their analysis focuses on the compliment-givers, particularly Kate, whose contribution 'in its emphatic and enthusiastic form seems to be a marked case of relational work' (p.26). The response of the target of the compliments, Debbie, on the other hand, is simply characterised as 'laughing acceptance' (p.26). The question remains, therefore, does Debbie herself consider these compliments to be 'marked'? Locher and Watts (2005) go on to claim that 'whether the participants see the compliments as realisations of politeness remains debatable, but it is clearly open to polite interpretation by the participants concerned' (p.26). Thus, while the analysts are apparently willing here to characterise the compliments as 'marked' instances of relational work (and thus facework), whether they are understood by the participants, in particular, the person receiving the compliments as 'marked' (and thus polite) is left an open question. The discursive approach, at least as applied in this particular analysis, is thus left open to the charge of invoking the notions of marked and unmarked relational work (and thus facework) without adequately justifying their analysis in terms of the understandings of the participants themselves.

As Schegloff (1991, 1992a, 1992b) has argued more generally in relation to the analysis of social structures in interaction, it is not enough to simply invoke such social structures in discussing interactions.

> A solution must be found to the analytic problems which obstruct the conversion of intuition, casual (however well-informed) observation, or theoretically motivated observation into demonstrable analysis. For without solutions to these problems, we are left with 'a *sense* of how the world works,' but without its detailed explication. (Schegloff, 1991: 48)

We, as analysts, therefore need to show that face is indeed 'demonstrably relevant *to* the participants' (Schegloff, 1991: 50). This involves, from a conversation analytic perspective, explicating how participants themselves display their orientation to utterances as matters of face through their uptake (Lerner, 1996: 319; MacMartin, Wood and Kroger, 2001: 229; Terkourafi, 2005: 244-256), or by establishing what can be termed 'procedural consequentiality' (Arundale, forthcoming; cf. Haugh, 2007b: 310). In focusing on the '*participants' analyses of one another's verbal conduct* – on the interpretations, understandings, and analyses that participants themselves make, as displayed in the details of what they say' (Drew, 1995: 70, original italics), then, the analyst can establish that (1) the interaction does involve the participants making such evaluations, and (2) these evaluations are procedurally consequential for the flow of the discourse.

However, since (ordinary) participants themselves may not describe such evaluations using metapragmatic terms such as face or facework, the analyst needs to take an additional step in demonstrating that the identification of face(work) has validity within the theoretical framework in which the analysis is undertaken, or what is termed 'conceptual consequentiality' (Arundale, forthcoming; cf. Haugh, 2007b: 310), in order to establish that the (social) actions are relationally consequential, and thus face has indeed been co-constituted in that particular interaction. This could involve recourse to what the participants might say about the interaction, although such an analysis is limited by the fact that participants often do not have the metalinguistic skills to articulate such evaluations (O'Keefe, 1989), and furthermore, consulting participants inevitably creates 'another text, another conversation, only this time the interaction is with the analyst' (Mills, 2003: 45). Establishing conceptual consequentiality, then, requires recourse to non-sequential as well as sequential aspects of talk, which may include 'aspects of the currently invoked identity of the participant' and 'the history of their particular relationship, not only within the course of, but also prior to the conversation being examined' (Haugh, 2007b: 311; cf. Arundale, forthcoming). While such an approach is generally eschewed by conversation analysts (Antaki, 1998; Schegloff, 1997, 1999; see McHoul, Rapley and Antaki 2008 for a recent discussion), ethnographic analyses that widen 'the context of the interaction – e.g. adding prior or subsequent talk, visual documentation, background information about participants' (Duranti, 1997: 275) may add 'a new, and in some respects, richer analytical dimension' (Duranti, 1997: 273). In the case of face, such details are arguably crucial to warranting a detailed explication of how face has been co-constituted in interaction, since face exists not only as a theoretical construct that is of interest to analysts, but has very real import for 'ordinary' folk as well. As Schegloff (1988) admits, the study of 'normative' aspects of vernacular culture – including, we submit, folk notions of face – is important in its own right.

> Like the grammarians' intuition of grammaticality, it may be a real object in its own right, even if it is not, and does not describe, the way people actually conduct themselves. Because it may itself inform people's conduct, and because it casts an omnipresent shadow on empirical analysis, it is an important object for inquiry in its own right. (Schegloff, 1988: 133, fn.6)

While the reification of such folk or vernacular notions of face in analyses is not advocated here, the wealth of ethnographic studies of face in different socio-cultural settings outlined in the previous section attests to the omnipresence of such notions in many interactions. To ignore such non-sequential aspects of talk thus arguably leads to an impoverished understanding of face and facework in interaction.

In invoking these broader aspects of discourse, then, we propose that the analysis of face in interaction should move beyond the constraints of conceptualising interaction as situated and bounded to a consideration of the broader socio-cognitive, as well as the historical and socio-cultural dimensions of face and facework (Blommaert 2005: 56, 2007: 16). As Blommaert (2005, 2007) has argued, discourse is subject to what he describes as 'layered simultaneity'.

> It occurs in a real-time, synchronic event, but it is simultaneously
> encapsulated in a several layers of historicity, some of which are
> within the grasp of participants while others remain invisible but
> are nevertheless present. (Blommaert, 2005: 130)

This means broadening our understanding of interaction to seeing it
as a 'polycentric and stratified' environment where 'people continuously
need to observe 'norms' – orders of indexicality – that are attached to a
multitude of centres of authority, local as well as translocal, momentary
as well as lasting' (Blommaert, 2007: 2; cf. Silverstein, 2003). The ways
in which face may either be invoked by interlocutors to influence interactions, or alternatively presupposed as part of the interpretative frame(s)
brought to interaction (Goffman, 1974), are indicative of the orders of
indexicality implicit in any consideration of face. In order to analyse
face we need to not only consider the horizontal distribution and spread
of the orders of indexicality that face evokes (across communities, socio-
cultural groups and the like) (cf. Agha, 2003), but also the 'processes of
hierarchical ordering, in which different phenomena are not juxtaposed,
but layered and distinguished as to the scale on which they operate
and have value and validity' (Blommaert, 2007: 1). In other words, we
can say that face is not only co-constituted in interaction, but is also
constitutive of interaction. The inherent reflexivity of norms and the
broader context has long been argued by ethnomethodologists
(Garfinkel, 1967; Heritage, 1984), as well as by some scholars in
European-Continental pragmatics (Mey, 2001, 2006).

> Social context not only constrains language use, but is itself
> constructed through the use of appropriate language: social norms
> are (re)-instituted through the use of language. (Mey, 2006: 53)

In the way same way, as an often salient aspect of the 'social context',
face is arguably not only 'constructed through the use of appropriate
language' (that is, face is co-constituted in interaction), but also 'constrains language use' (that is, face is constitutive of interaction). In exploring the ways in which face is constitutive of the horizontal and
vertical layers of interaction, then, the underlying tensions between
'micro' and 'macro' perspectives can perhaps be reconciled (cf. Bargiela-
Chiappini, 2006: 423).

The ways in which face can be invoked in interactions has been the
subject of considerable research, particularly in societies where face
itself can become the subject of metapragmatic discourse (Gao, 1996;
Haugh, 2005b; Koutlaki, 2002; Lim, 2004; Ruhi and Işık-Güler, 2007;
Ukosakul, 2003). However, while metapragmatic discourse about face

is often associated with East Asian societies, apparent from the advice frequently directed at Westerners about the importance of 'saving face' in Asia (Cardon and Scott, 2003; Hodgson, Sano and Graham, 2000; Lewis, 2000), for instance, the invoking of face in interactions is not necessarily restricted to such societies (Haugh and Hinze, 2003: 1597; cf. Ervin-Tripp, Nakamura and Guo, 1995: 45). In the following example, face is invoked in English in the context of competitive sports.

(3) Brisbane AM radio station 612 4QR, June 2001
The loss awoke us. We had to save face after such a defeat.
(Haugh and Hinze, 2003: 1598)

This was said by an Aussie Rules player, Alastair Lynch, who was referring to the loss of Brisbane Lions to Carlton, an Aussie Rules team based in Melbourne.[3] In this particular context, face refers to their reputation as a team that can compete with the best of them. However, while face is invoked here in a particular interaction, namely an interview broadcast on a Brisbane radio station, it also invokes a kind of historicity in that the reputation or 'face' of the Brisbane Lions is something that is established over a number of seasons. It also invokes the broader discourse of defending the collective honour of one's team that is commonly associated with metapragmatic invocations of face in English.

In a pilot survey of the appearance of the phrase 'save face' in print media found in the Factiva database over the three month period from May to July 2001, for example, out of the 59 relevant tokens of 'save face' located, 21 were related to sporting contexts, with 17 of those being the collective face of either the team itself, or the country the team represents, as seen in Table 1.1 below.[4]

From this survey, it appears that the phrase 'save face' is invoked in sporting contexts where either a team has shown greater ability and 'toughness' in subsequent matches to compensate for previous perceived

Table 1.1 Tokens of 'save face' in print media, May–July 2001

	Personal	*Collective*	*TOTAL*
Sports	4	17	21
Politics	14	12	26
Business	1	5	6
Celebrity	3	0	3
Personal	3	0	3
TOTAL	26	33	

Source: Factiva database

weakness or failures (collective face), or an individual has left a team
without undue shame (personal face) (cf. Haugh and Hinze, 2003: 1598).
In other words, the phrase 'save face' can be deployed in order to invoke a sports team's ongoing history of successes (and failures), and
the broader emotive dimensions implicated in defending the collective
honour or 'face' of the community or country which the team
represents.

The way in which face is constitutive of interaction is not limited to
metapragmatic invokings of face. It may also arguably be presupposed
as part of the interpretative frame(s) brought to certain interactions. In
the following interaction taken from the Tokyo University of Foreign
Studies Corpus of Spoken Japanese (Usami, 2005), there is evidence
that the face of Lin as a competent speaker of Japanese is being presupposed (at least by Lin), and so constitutes part of the interpretative
frame in this particular excerpt

(4) Lin, a learner of Japanese, is chatting with her teacher, Kimura

1   Lin: *Hômusuteii, Nihon no,* (Kim: *un*) *Nihon-ryôri ga suki desu kara,*
            (Kim: *un un*) *daitai, un, Nihon no tabemono ga* (Kim: *un*) *zenbu*
            heiki da to [*omoi-masu.*
            'Homestay, Japanese, (Kim: mm) I like Japanese cuisine so (Kim:
            mm, mm) basically I think all Japanese food is okay (for me)'
2   Kim: [*A, hontôni? Sokka sokka, yoku kiku no wa ne, chotto shoppai tte*
            kiku n desu yo, watashi.
            'Oh really? Okay, okay. I often hear it, I often hear that it is a bit
            salty'
3   Lin: *Shoppai...*
            Salty...
4   Kim: *Daijôbu?*
            '(Is that) okay?'
5   Lin: *Iya, daijôbu desu.*
            No, that's okay'
6   Kim: *A, hontô ne, sokka sokka.*
            'Ah, yeah, okay, okay'

(see Haugh, 2007a: 674—675 for a fuller morphological gloss of this example)

After listening to Lin's views about Japanese cuisine, Kimura goes on to
comment that Japanese food is often said to be salty in turn 2. The
trailing-off repetition of the word *shoppai* ('salty') by Lin in turn 3 projects
possible uncertainty about the meaning of the word, and so Kimura
expresses concern as to whether Lin has really understood the word in
turn 4. Lin's somewhat curt response in turn 5 (particularly the down-
shift to the casual form of 'no', *iya*) is evidence of Lin's discomfort that

Kimura has brought attention to her uncertainty about the meaning of the word. In doing so, Kimura has brought into question Lin's competence as a speaker of Japanese, thereby potentially threatening her face.

However, in order to sustain such an interpretation of a potential loss of face on the part of Lin, it becomes apparent that both the participants are presupposing that Lin expects to maintain positive perceptions of her competence as a second language speaker of Japanese. Such a presupposition can arguably be warranted by the analyst in a number of ways. First, the way in which Kimura initiates the repair sequence in line 4, leaving room for Lin to self-correct or 'remember' the meaning of the word herself rather than immediately providing correction, is indicative of her orientation towards maintaining such positive perceptions (and thus Lin's face). Kimura's ready acceptance of Lin's claim that she does indeed know the meaning of the word in line 6 confirms this orienting. Second, the emotive reaction of Lin, evident from her somewhat curt response in line 5, indicates that Lin is also orienting towards maintaining positive perceptions of her competence in Japanese (and thus her face). Third, from an examination of the longer interactional sequence from which this extract is taken it is apparent that Lin demonstrates a very high level of proficiency in Japanese, and so it is expectable that if Lin's proficiency lapses in some manner this may adversely affect Lin's image. Fourth, findings from previous studies on the salience of face in Japanese interactions more generally (Haugh, 2005b, 2007; Sueda, 1995; Tanaka and Kekidze, 2005; Yabuuchi, 2004) also suggest such a presupposition is not unwarranted. If Lin's face in the sense of this assumed competence is presupposed by the interactants, and there is evidence to indicate this is indeed the case, then Lin's face is arguably constitutive of the interaction, as well as being constituted in the interaction.

It is suggested here, therefore, that, by broadening the focus of analysis of face to include ways in which it is both co-constituted in as well as constitutive of interaction, the problem of the emerging gap between first-order and second-order perspectives on face might be addressed in two senses. It avoids divergence between the analyst's interpretation (second-order) and that of the participants (first-order). And it also helps reconcile etic or cross-culturally applicable frameworks (second-order) with emic or culture-specific perspectives (first-order) on face. An investigation of the ways in which face is *co-constituted in* as well as *constitutive of* interaction thus lies at the heart of this collection. In this way, then, we are proposing that research on face and facework be shifted to an epistemology grounded in social constructionism

(Berger and Luckmann, 1996; Garfinkel, 1967), 'where meaning comes into existence in and out of our engagement with the realities in our world' (Crotty, 1998: 8), and an ontology grounded in interpretivism (Goffman, 1967, 1974; Sacks 1992), 'where social reality is regarded as the product of processes by which social actors negotiate the meanings for actions and situations' (Crotty, 1998: 11). This volume represents an attempt to broaden this debate beyond those who might be *prima facie* conducive to such a move.

1.3. Overview of the volume

In placing interaction at the centre of analyses of face it is not the aim of this volume to diminish the value of cognitive or socio-cultural perspectives on face. Levinson (2005, 2006a, 2006b) has recently argued, for example, that in order to understand complex notions such as 'culture' and 'language' three interdependent ontological levels are necessary.

> (1) The individual level: this is the level inhabited by my 'interaction engine', 'grammatical competence', and other cognitive beasts.
>
> (2) The interactional level: this is the level where we can talk about recurrent sequence types, the overall structure of conversations, the co-production of extended turns, etc., each of which is an emergent structure....
>
> (3) The sociocultural level: this is the level where we can talk about the social organization of institutions, and the constraints they place on language use in specific activity types or speech events. (Levinson, 2006a: 91)

Levinson (2005) goes on to claim in an interchange with Schegloff (2005) that 'one doesn't have to be a realist about these entities – one can treat them as analytical fictions' (p.449). We submit that such an approach in relation to face gives us a useful framework in which to structure, at least initially, further discussion of the multitude of perspectives on face that presently exist. However, we use this framework to structure this volume with the proviso that ultimately such a categorisation is arguably only relevant to the extent that these categories are *oriented to* by participants in interaction (Schegloff, 1992b). For example, participants may orient in interaction towards 'what I think you think of me' as a representation of what is going inside of people's minds (individual level), or alternatively orient towards shared understandings of a particular notion of face as a means of categorising membership in broad groups such as 'Chinese' or 'Turkish' (socio-cultural level) (Hester and Eglin, 1997; Sacks, 1992; Schegloff, 2007). In such cases, the participant orientations toward a particular categorisation can be analysed as emerging through interaction.

In relation to face, then, at the 'individual level' we find the (socio-)cognitive processes underlying person perception, action interpretation, and the attributing and inferring of evaluations of self (or self's group) and other (or other's group), for instance (Ames, Knowles, Morris, Kalish, Rosati and Gopnik, 2001; Holtgraves, 1992, 2005). While work on (socio-)cognitive processes often adopts a positivist epistemological stance, this is not to say that work on such processes cannot be reconceptualised within an alternative framework (for example, Arundale and Good's (2002) notion of 'dyadic cognizing' or Kecskes's (2008) 'dynamic model of meaning'). At the 'interactional level' we can examine the emergence of implicit and explicit displays of evaluations (of self or other, or their groups), interpretings of those evaluations displayed through subsequent responses, and thus the joint accomplishment or conjoint co-constitution of emergent understandings of those evaluations, or what is termed face (Arundale, 2006; Haugh, 2007a, 2007b; Lerner, 1996). Finally, at the 'socio-cultural level' we can analyse the ways in which the evaluations underlying face are constrained by orders of indexicality, and so are subject to what Blommaert (2005: 130, 2007: 3) terms 'layered simultaneity.' In other words, at the socio-cultural level we can study the interconnections of face with events over longer spans of time, including those beyond the person or group whose face is at issue. Once again, such work does not necessarily have to entail a positivist epistemological stance.

In placing interaction at the centre of analyses of face, then, we are not endorsing a move to attempt to explain social structures solely in terms of a purported 'interactional level' (cf. Schegloff, 1991, 2005). Indeed, in preparing this volume, we have assumed that analysis of face is necessarily interdisciplinary. The contributions are thus illustrative of a range of approaches to interaction. This is not to say that all these approaches are ultimately compatible in terms of their underlying epistemological and ontological assumptions. But in exploring these different approaches to interaction and their implications for our understanding of face and facework, we believe there is value in teasing out such underlying assumptions.

In proposing a shift to grounding research on face in interaction, it is perhaps natural to begin with a closer examination of face as it is co-constituted in interaction. Part I, 'Face in interaction' thus encompasses contributions that deal with face as it arises in various kinds of institutional and non-institutional interactions. It opens with a bold challenge to the epistemological assumptions underlying Goffman's conceptualisation of face by Robert Arundale. He argues that while Goffman's approach to face and facework has been enormously influential, its commitments to positivist social psychology and a Parsonian view of the individual mean that Goffman's conceptualisations are not compatible with subsequent developments in social constructionism, ethnomethodology and communication studies. He thus argues that an alternative theory of face and facework that is grounded in these findings is required to advance the field. His argument is illustrated by way of contrasting a Goffmanian analysis of a compliment/request exchange with an analysis grounded in his own Face Constituting Theory. From the latter analysis it becomes apparent that face can be re-conceptualised as an emergent and non-summative achievement in the particular, local social environment co-created through the actions of persons in interaction, thereby grounding research on face(work) in the perspective of social constructionism and conversation analysis/ ethnomethodology.

In the two chapters that follow, an analysis of face(work) drawing from insights in conversation analysis and ethnomethodology is undertaken in different intercultural settings. In Chapter 3, Rosina Márquez Reiter examines how facework is dynamically co-constructed in the context of telephone calls by Montevidean Spanish speaking telemarketing agents to Bonaerense Spanish speaking clients. In particular, Márquez Reiter shows how issues of power emerge as salient in the emergence of face in such contexts. In doing so, she illustrates how multiple data collection procedures – including actual recordings of the calls, field notes and informal interviews with the agents themselves – can be integrated in the analysis of how face is interactionally achieved through an intercultural telephone conversation in a business context. Her integration of context internal (i.e., how face unfolds in the call) and context external (i.e. cultural factors influencing the facework strategies pursued by participants) explanations echoes the call for an analysis of face as both co-constituted in and constitutive of interaction.

This theme is further explored in Michael Haugh and Yasuhisa Watanabe's chapter which analyses how face arises in an intercultural business meeting involving Japanese and non-Japanese members of a Japanese firm based in Australia. Four key incidents in an meeting where the faces of different members of the firm were demonstrably oriented to by participants are used as a means of gaining insight into interactional and normative dimensions of facework in Japanese. In particular, they argue that a theory of face(work) needs to be grounded in an approach that draws upon participant understandings as a resource, and thus does not neglect emic notions of face (such as *kao* in Japanese), yet is ultimately not constrained by them either. Echoing the claims made in the preceding two chapters, the analysis draws from both conversation analysis and ethnography to explicate the interactional achievement of face, as well as projectings and interpretings of face that can arise in interaction, or what they term 'face-in-interaction'.

The technical sense in which interaction is conceptualised in the first three chapters, namely as 'index[ing] the conjoint, non-summative outcome of two or more factors' (Arundale, 2006: 196), lies in contrast to the more general sense of interaction which is drawn upon in the final two chapters in the first part of the volume. Both Anchimbe's discussion of political face-saving in broadcast interviews and Koutlaki's analysis of facework and politeness in more ordinary, interpersonal settings draw from data that is interactional. However, their analyses are not explicitly oriented towards the understandings of participants *per se*, and are thus perhaps closer in their underlying epistemological and ontological stances to the work of Goffman.

In Chapter 5, Anchimbe elucidates the key face-saving strategies exploited by the former British prime minister, Tony Blair, and the former French president, Jacques Chirac, in interviews that were broadcast internationally at the beginning of the second war in Iraq. In particular, Anchimbe shows how such political face-saving goes beyond the face demands of individuals to encompass their 'political face', which in this context includes the face of the party they represent, the face of their country, and the face of international alliance towards which they are aligned. In this way, Anchimbe's contribution is consonant with Blommaert's (2005, 2007) call to conceptualise discourse, in which face among other things arises, as involving multiple socio-linguistic scales that have different orders of indexicality, as the face-saving work attempted by Blair and Chirac is not only oriented towards the interviewer, but also the broader audience, which includes not only their domestic constitutents, but also the political leaders of other countries.

In the following chapter, Koutlaki shifts the focus of analysis to how facework occurs in non-institutional settings amongst Persian speakers. She integrates the emic notions of *šæxsiæt* and *ehteram* in her analysis of interpersonal encounters amongst her acquaintances that she recorded. Drawing from these analyses Koutlaki argues that Persian face is oriented towards the wants of groups, rather than simply the wants of individuals, and also may involve face enhancement, rather than just face-saving. Koutlaki also draws out the normative orientations of participants in proposing three principles of politeness in Persian that align her work with Leech's (1983) approach to politeness rather than that of Brown and Levinson (1987). The way in which detailed ethnographic analyses can complement interactional analyses thus becomes apparent in this chapter.

Part II, 'Face, identity and self' shifts to an exploration of how face is also constitutive of interaction. While the contributions draw on interactional data, their analyses centre on more cognitively-grounded dimensions of face(work), including the related notions of identity and self. This section leads with a contribution by Helen Spencer-Oatey who investigates the relationship between face and identity through self. Spencer-Oatey draws from recordings of intercultural business meetings arising when a (mainland) Chinese firm visited a British engineering company supplemented by interviews with members of both firms. Echoing other recently published work, she proposes that analyses of face(work) also need to incorporate an identity perspective. Drawing from research on identity and self in social psychology, then, she argues that in much of the politeness literature thus far the face needs of others have been stressed over the face needs of self. Her analyses of a number of incidents in which participants were oriented to the face needs of themselves thus moves towards redressing that imbalance.

The move to analysing self face rather than exclusively focusing on the face of others is also evident in the following two chapters. In Chapter 8, Şükriye Ruhi builds on self-presentation theory in an analysis of how emic face idioms in Turkish arise in recordings of conversations in institutional and family settings, supplemented by analyses of popular dramas. Ruhi's work echoes that of Spencer-Oatey's, as well as Goffman, in her explicit focus on face as an interactionally claimed self-image. Her analysis indicates that face idioms in interactions are used to project or evaluate self or other with respect to behavioural expectations and norms, in particular those relating to relationships and interactional goals. An important finding to emerge from this analysis is that self- and other-face management is oriented not only toward local, situated interactional goals, but also toward future interaction. Ruhi's finding thus supports Spencer-Oatey's earlier claim that the analysis of face needs to move beyond the constraints of the local, situated context to encompass analysis across longer spans of time.

In Ge Gao's chapter on communication strategies associated with facework in Chinese the theme of face as an image of self is once again prominent. Drawing from survey data, Gao argues that there is a close relationship between face and the social self (that is, social position, status, reputation, prestige etc.), on the one hand, and the relational self (that is, mutual respect, goodwill, affection, friendship etc.) on the other. The way in which face is most salient in public settings was reflected in the kinds of communication strategies that were found to be associated with 'giving face' (*gei mianzi*) and 'saving face' (*liu mianzi*), such as not revealing others' mistakes in public, or covering up others' embarrassment. Gao also explores how to better distinguish between the two most important emic notions of face in Chinese, namely *mianzi* and *lian*, an issue which has troubled numerous studies of face in Chinese to date. In using survey data, Gao's data is one step removed from interaction, being metapragmatic reflections *about* interaction. Yet it is worth remembering that such research has the advantage of being able to access a broader data set thereby lending her conclusions potentially greater generalisability.

In the final two chapters in this section, the connections between face and self are pushed in different directions, reflecting the diversity of approaches that exist in the field. In Chapter 10, Thomas Holtgraves gives a succinct overview of more than twenty years of research on face and facework grounded in social psychology. Holtgraves also takes the position that face is essentially the public display of a subset of one's identity, and so is inevitably interactional, at least in the broader sense of involving two or more persons. He explores through a review of experimental research how perceptions of self, and thus face, are influenced by interpersonal variables such as perceived power or social distance. Holtgraves suggests that such findings point to the need to explain both individual and cultural variability in processes of person perception, language production and language comprehension, and argues that Brown and Levinson's notion of face is indeed amenable to exploring such issues across different cultures.

In Chapter 11, on the other hand, Alexander Kozin explores the resonances and dissonances between Goffman's work on face, and the work of the French phemonologist Emmanuel Levinas. While the latter work has to a large extent been untouched by researchers working on face(work), Kozin's chapter opens up new avenues for face researchers to explore in Levinas' notion of face as the self represented in the social world by and in the Other. Kozin explores the very limits of what it means to be human through an analysis of traumatic situations in which people are unable to manage their face. In doing so, Kozin reminds us that face has a moral or ethical dimension that reaches to very core of the human self.

While the theme of culture is touched upon in many of the contributions, it is in Part III, 'Face, norms and society', which consists of four chapters dealing with face in its broader historical and socio-cultural context, that this theme really comes to the fore. Each contributor, however, approaches differently the problem of how to validate our intuition that there are important links between individual interactions (the so-called 'micro') and the broader socio-cultural expectations or 'norms' that interactants bring to interactions (the so-called 'macro'). This section opens with Stella Ting-Toomey's chapter, which draws from her Conflict Face-Negotiation Theory in exploring a case study of an incident of intercultural facework collision that occurred at the annual sales conference of a Japanese multimedia subsidiary in the United States. Invoking the broader socio-cultural norms outlined in the Corporate Values' Cultural Grid, Ting-Toomey shows how the face threat implicit in the Japanese vice-president's speech and the response of the American sales manager reflected underlying differences in their orientation to these norms. In discussing these underlying norms, Ting-Toomey illustrates how facework may involve confusion or misunderstanding, particularly in intercultural settings.

The theme of broader socio-cultural norms is also explored in the following chapter by Tae-Seop Lim, whose approach is similar to that of Gao in drawing from a data set that is one step removed from interaction, in being based on respondents reflections *about* face in interactions. Lim argues that the traditional individualism-collectivism distinction is inadequate for characterising how facework is conceptualised in Korea. He draws parallels between what he terms the relativistic and holistic cognition that underlies perceptions of self and other on the one hand, and the holistic and relativistic characteristics of face on the other. Lim argues, for instance, that one's face in Korea is always given relative to one's respective position within a broader social network, and so cannot be viewed as the possession of an individual *per se*. In linking face with a broader social network, face is conceptualised as something more global and long-term in contrast to the moment-by-moment emphasis of interactional analyses of facework in the first section.

Yet another approach to exploring the relationship between broader socio-cultural norms and face is proposed in Marina Terkourafi's work on the situated conceptualisation of face in Greek society. Terkourafi invokes the sociological distinction between the macro-level notions of *gemeinschaft* and *gesellschaft* in exploring the relationship between the emic or first-order notion of face in Greek society, and a universal, second-order notion of face, which she characterises in terms of intentionality (i.e. in the sense of 'aboutness') and the biologically-grounded dimension of approach versus withdrawal. The *gemeinschaft* element of Greek society is seen in a type of social organisation that minimises the need for being explicit, and emerges in local interpretations in the importance placed on acknowledging the in-group in facework in Greek. The *gesellschaft* element, on the other hand, is reflected in the use of diminution, for instance, which lowers the speaker's commitment toward the performed speech act. Terkourafi also explores how such understandings inevitably change over time in discussing changes in the usage of the greeting term *na'sai kala* (lit., 'a wish') from being restricted to the ingroup (a *gemeinschaft* orientation) to being used with a wider range of addressees (a *gesellschaft* orientation).

In the final chapter in this section, Margaret Ukosakul argues that politeness in Thai society involves maintaining one's face. Ukosakul claims that consideration and respect for the ego and feelings of others, which are achieved through orienting to norms of indirectness, avoidance of confrontation and criticism, and suppression of negative emotions, are central to maintaining good interpersonal relations in interactions, and thus politeness. Her study analyses the rich array of face idioms found in Thai, drawing from insights in cognitive linguistics, to establish the underlying link between face and (avoiding) feelings of shame. It is argued by Ukosakul that the large number of face idioms to be found in Thai reflects the salience of maintaining honour and avoiding shame in social interactions. In drawing upon idioms, then, Ukosakul presupposes that idiomatic meanings can be viewed as 'shared understandings', that emerge across societies over time.

The chapters in this volume thus represent a wide range of approaches to engaging with social interaction in research into face and facework. As the epistemological and ontological commitments of these approaches are fundamentally different, we are not trying to suggest that all these approaches fit with the approach to interaction that has been suggested in this chapter. But in proposing a shift towards a talk-in-interaction analytical approach to face and facework, perhaps in the guise of conversation analysis or more broadly ethnomethodology, we hope to move beyond some of the dichotomies that have plagued the field to date, such as the ever-popular emic/etic, east/west, individualism/collectivism distinctions, and thereby push the field forward in new directions. At the very least, we believe such an approach opens the field to those who wish to push the boundaries even further. As will be seen in the final concluding chapter by Francesca Bargiela-Chiappini, our purpose here has not been to advance another 'new' theory of face, but has instead been rather more modest. Ultimately, in drawing these contributions together, we have been aiming to draw upon the existing wealth of studies of face(work) in order to work towards formulating new perspectives on face and so continue deepening our understanding of face and facework.[5]

Endnotes

1. In the introduction to a recent collection of politeness papers, for instance, Lakoff and Ide (2005: 11) claim that 'each of us can probably speak with some confidence about the workings of her own culture's politeness system.'
2. It is worth noting that in earlier work, Locher (2004) does not hedge her analysis of facework in this manner, but the issue of the analyst's vis-à-vis the participants' understandings is not addressed in any detail.
3. Aussie Rules is a team game, similar in some ways to Rugby Union or Rugby League, that is played in Australia.
4. Other contexts in which the phrase 'save face' appeared in this period included personal and collective face in politics (26 tokens), and to a lesser extent face in business (6 tokens), the face of celebrities (3 tokens), and face in cross-cultural situations (3 tokens).
5. I would like to thank my co-editor, Francesca Bargiela-Chiappini, as well as Bob Arundale for insightful, and at times penetrating, comments on earlier drafts of this chapter.

References

Agha, A. (2003) The social life of cultural value. *Language and Communication* 23: 231–273.
Ames, D., Knowles, E., Morris, M., Kalish, C., Rosati, A. and Gopnik, A. (2001) The social folk theorist: insights from social and cultural psychology on the contents and contexts of folk theorising. In B. Malle, L. Moses and D. Baldwin (eds.) *Intentions and Intentionality. Foundations of Social Cognition* 307–329. Cambridge, MA: MIT Press.
Antaki, C. (1998) Identity ascriptions in their time and place: 'Fagin' and 'the terminally dim'. In C. Antaki and S. Widdicombe (eds.) *Identities in Talk* 71–86. London: Sage.

Antaki, C., Billig, M., Edwards, D. and Potter, J. (2003) Discourse analysis means doing analysis: a critique of six analytic shortcomings. *Discourse Analysis Online* 1. Available at <http://extra.shu.ac.uk/daol/previous/v1_n1.html>.

Arundale, R. B. (1993) Culture specific assumptions and the concept of face: a proposal toward a cultural universal for studying face management in using language. Paper presented at *International Pragmatics Association Conference*, Kobe, Japan.

Arundale, R. B. (1999) An alternative model and ideology of communication for an alternative to politeness theory. *Pragmatics* 9: 119–154.

Arundale, R. B. (2006) Face as relational and interactional: a communication framework for research on face, facework, and politeness. *Journal of Politeness Research* 2:193–216.

Arundale, R. B. (2008) Against (Gricean) intentions at the heart of human interaction. Intercultural Pragmatics 5: 231–260.

Arundale, R. B. (forthcoming) Relating. In M. Locher and S. Lambert Graham (eds.) Interpersonal Pragmatics. Berlin: Mouton de Gruyter.

Arundale, R. and Good, D. (2002) Boundaries and sequences in studying conversation. In A. Fetzer and C. Meierkord (eds.) *Rethinking Sequentiality. Linguistics Meets Conversational Interaction* 121–150. Amsterdam: John Benjamins.

Bargiela-Chiappini, F. (2003) Face and politeness: new (insights) for (old) concepts. *Journal of Pragmatics* 35: 1453–1469.

Bargiela-Chiappini, F. (2006) Face. In Keith Brown (ed.) *Encyclopedia of Languages and Linguistics* 421–423. Amsterdam: Elsevier.

Berger, P. and Luckmann, T. (1966) *The Social Construction of Reality*. New York: Doubleday.

Blommaert, J. (2005) *Discourse. A Critical Introduction*. Cambridge: Cambridge University Press.

Blommaert, J. (2007) Sociolinguistic scales. *Intercultural Pragmatics* 4: 1–19.

Brown, P. and Levinson, S. (1978) Universals in language usage: politeness phenomena. In E. Goody (ed.) *Questions and Politeness* 56–311. Cambridge: Cambridge University Press.

Brown, P. and Levinson, S. (1987) *Politeness. Some Universals in Language Usage*. Cambridge: Cambridge University Press.

Cardon, P. and Scott, J. (2003) Chinese business face: communication behaviours and teaching approaches. *Business Communication Quarterly* 66: 9–22.

Chen, V. (1990/1991) *Mien tze* at the Chinese dinner table: A study of the interactional accomplishment of face. *Research on Language and Social Interaction* 24: 109–140.

Crotty, M. (1998) *The Foundations of Social Research*. Crows Nest, NSW: Allen and Unwin.

Cupach, W. and Imahori, T. (1993) Identity management theory: communication competence in intercultural episodes and relationships. In R. Wiseman and J. Koester (eds.) *Intercultural Communication Competence* 112–131. Newbury Park, CA: Sage.

Dippold, D. (2006) Face in L2 argumentative discourse: psycholinguistic constraints on the construction of identity. In R. Kiely, P. Rea-Dickins, H.Woodfield and G. Clibbon (eds.) *Language, Culture and Identity in Applied Linguistics* 163–179. London: Equinox.

Domenici, K. and Littlejohn, S. (2006) *Facework. Bridging Theory and Practice.* Thousand Oaks, CA: Sage.

Drew, P. (1995) Conversation analysis. In J. Smith, R. Harre and L. van Langenhove (eds.) *Rethinking Methods in Psychology* 64–79. London: Sage.

Duranti, A. (1997) *Linguistic Anthropology.* Cambridge: Cambridge University Press.

Eelen, G. (2001) *A Critique of Politeness Theories.* Manchester: St. Jerome.

Ervin-Tripp, S., Nakamura, K. and Guo, J. (1995) Shifting face from Asia to Europe. In M. Shibatani and S. Thompson (eds.) *Essays in Semantics and Pragmatics* 43–71. Amsterdam: John Benjamins.

Garfinkel, H. (1967) *Studies in Ethnomethodology.* Englewood Cliffs, NJ: Prentice-Hall.

Gao, G. (1996) Self and other: a Chinese perspective on interpersonal relationships. In W. Gudykunst, S. Ting-Toomey and T. Nishida (eds.) *Communication in Personal Relationships across Cultures* 81–101. Thousand Oaks, CA: Sage.

Gao, G. and Ting-Toomey, S. (1998) *Communicating Effectively with the Chinese.* Thousand Oaks, CA: Sage.

Goddard, C. (2006) Ethnopragmatics: a new paradigm. In C. Goddard (ed.) *Ethnopragmatics. Understanding Discourse in Cultural Context* 1–30. Berlin: Mouton de Gruyter.

Goffman, E. (1955) On facework: an analysis of ritual elements in social interaction. *Psychiatry: Journal for the Study of Interpersonal Processes* 18: 213–231.

Goffman, E. (1967) *Interaction Ritual: Essays on Face-to-Face Behavior.* New York: Pantheon Books.

Goffman, E. (1974) *Frame Analysis: An Essay on the Organisation of Experience.* New York: Harper & Row.

Golato, A. and Taleghani-Nikazm, C. (2006) Negotiation of face in web chats. *Multilingua* 25: 293–321.

Haugh, M. and Hinze, C. (2003) A metalinguistic approach to deconstructing the concepts of 'face' and 'politeness' in Chinese, English and Japanese. *Journal of Pragmatics* 35: 1581–1611.

Haugh, M. (2005a) The importance of 'place' in Japanese politeness: Implications for cross-cultural and intercultural analyses. *Intercultural Pragmatics* 2: 41–68.

Haugh, M. (2005b) What does 'face' mean to the Japanese? Understanding the import of 'face' in Japanese business interaction. In F. Bargiela-Chiappini and M. Gotti (eds.) *Asian Business Discourse* 211–239. Berlin: Peter Lang.

Haugh, M. (2007a) Emic conceptualisations of (im)politeness and face in Japanese: implications for the discursive negotiation of second language learner identities. *Journal of Pragmatics* 39: 657–680.

Haugh, M. (2007b) The discursive challenge to politeness theory: an interactional alternative. *Journal of Politeness Research* 3: 295–317.

Heritage, J. (1984) *Garfinkel and Ethnomethodology*. Cambridge: Polity Press.

Heritage, J. (1998) Oh-prefaced responses to inquiry. *Language in Society* 27: 291–334.

Hernández Flores, N. (1999) Politeness ideology in Spanish colloquial conversations: the case of advice. *Pragmatics* 9: 37–50.

Hester, S. and Eglin, P. (eds.) (1997) *Culture in Action: Studies in Membership Categorization Analysis*. Boston, MA: International Institute for Ethnomethodology and University Press of America.

Hinze, C. (2005) Looking into 'face': The importance of Chinese *mian* and *lian* as emic categories. In F. Bargiela-Chiappini and M. Gotti (eds.) *Asian Business Discourse(s)* 169–210. Berlin: Peter Lang.

Ho, D. (1976) On the concept of face. *American Journal of Sociology* 81: 867–884.

Ho, D. (1994) Face dynamics: from conceptualization to measurement. In Stella Ting-Toomey (ed.) *The Challenge of Facework* 269–285. Albany, New York: State University of New York Press.

Hodgson, J., Sano, Y. and Graham, J. (2000) *Doing Business with the New Japan*. Lanham: Rowman and Littlefield.

Holtgraves, T. (1992) The linguistic realization of face management: implications for language production and comprehension, person perception, and cross-cultural communication. *Social Psychology Quarterly* 55: 141–159.

Holtgraves, T. (2005) Social psychology, cognitive psychology, and linguistic politeness. *Journal of Politeness Research* 1: 73–93.

Hu, X. (1944) The Chinese concept of face. *American Anthropologist* 46: 45–64.

Ide, S. (1989) Formal forms and discernment: two neglected aspects of universals of linguistic politeness. *Multilingua* 8: 223–248.

Kecskes, I. (2008) Dueling contexts: a dynamic model of meaning. *Journal of Pragmatics* 40.

Koutlaki, S. (2002) Offers and expressions of thanks as face enhancing acts: *tae'arof* in Persian. *Journal of Pragmatics* 34: 1733–1756.

Lerner, G. (1996) Finding 'face' in the preference structures of talk-in-interaction. *Social Psychology Quarterly* 59: 303–321.

Lakoff, R. and Ide, S. (2005) Introduction: broadening the horizon of linguistic politeness. In R. Lakoff and S. Ide (eds.) *Broadening the Horizon of Linguistic Politeness* 1–20. Amsterdam: John Benjamins.

Leech, G. (1983) *Principles of Pragmatics*. London: Longman.

Levinson, S. (2005) Living with Manny's dangerous idea. *Discourse Studies* 7: 431–453.

Levinson, S. (2006a) Cognition at the heart of human interaction. *Discourse Studies* 8:85–93.

Levinson, S. (2006b) On the human 'interaction engine'. In N. Enfield and S. Levinson (eds.) *Roots of Human Sociality. Culture, Cognition and Interaction* 39–69. Oxford: Berg.

Lewis, R. (2000) *When Cultures Collide: Managing Successfully across Cultures.* London: Nicholas Brealey.

Lim, T. (2004) Towards an Asian model of face: the dimensionality of face in Korea. *Human Communication* 7: 53–66.

Lim, T. and Bowers, J. (1991) Facework. Solidarity, approbation, and tact. *Human Communication Research* 17: 415–450.

Locher, M. 2004. *Power and Politeness in Action.* Berlin: Mouton de Gruyter.

Locher, M. and Watts, R. 2005. Politeness theory and relational work. *Journal of Politeness Research* 1: 9–34.

MacMartin, C., Wood, L. and Kroger, R. (2001) Facework. In P. Robinson and H. Giles (eds.) *The New Handbook of Language and Social Psychology* 221–237. Chichester, West Sussex: John Wiley.

Mao, L. (1994) Beyond politeness theory: 'face' revisited and renewed. *Journal of Pragmatics* 21: 451–486.

Matsumoto, Y. (1988) Reexamination of the universality of face: politeness phenomena in Japanese. *Journal of Pragmatics* 12: 403–426.

Mey, J. (2001) *Pragmatics. An Introduction* (2nd edn). Oxford: Blackwell.

Mey, J. (2006) Pragmatics: overview. In K. Brown (ed.) *Encyclopedia of Language and Linguistics, Volume 10* (2nd edn) 51–62. Amsterdam: Elsevier.

McHoul, A., Rapley, M. and Antaki, C. (2008) You gotta light? On the luxury of context for understanding talk in interaction. *Journal of Pragmatics* 40: 42–54.

Mills, S. (2003) *Gender and Politeness.* Cambridge: Cambridge University Press.

Nwoye, O. (1992) Linguistic politeness and socio-cultural variations of the notion of face. *Journal of Pragmatics* 18: 309–328.

O'Driscoll, J. (1996). About face: A defence and elaboration of universal dualism. *Journal of Pragmatics* 25: 1–32.

O'Driscoll, J. (2007) Brown and Levinson's face: how it can – and can't – help us to understand interaction across cultures. *Intercultural Pragmatics* 4: 463–492.

O'Keefe, B. (1989) Communication theory and practical knowledge. In B. Dervin (ed.) *Rethinking Communication* 197–215. Sage: Newbury Park.

Piirainen-Marsh, A. (1995) *Face in Second Language Conversation.* Jyvaskyla: University of Jyvaskyla.

Piirainen-Marsh, A. (1996) Face and the organization of intercultural interaction. In T. Hakukioja, M. Helasvuo and E. Karkkainen (eds.) *SKY 1996 Yearbook of the Linguistic Association of Finland* 93–133. Jyvaskyla: University of Jyvaskyla.

Piirainen-Marsh, A. (2005) Managing adversarial questioning in broadcast interviews. *Journal of Politeness Research* 1: 193–217.

Ruhi, Ş. and Işık-Güler, H. (2007) Conceptualizing face and relational work in (im)politeness: revelations from politeness lexemes and idioms in Turkish. *Journal of Pragmatics* 39: 681–711.

Sacks, H. (1992) *Lectures on Conversation.* Edited by G. Jefferson. Oxford: Blackwell.

Schegloff, E. (1988) Goffman and the analysis of conversation. In P. Drew and A. Wooton (eds.) *Erving Goffman. Exploring the Interaction Order* 89–135. Boston: Northeastern University Press.

Schegloff, E. (1991) Reflections on talk and social structure. In D. Boden and D. Zimmerman (eds.) *Talk and Social Structure* 44–70. Oxford: Polity Press.

Schegloff, E. (1992a) On talk and its institutional occasions. In P. Drew and J. Heritage (eds.) *Talk at Work: Interaction in Institutional Settings* 101–134. Cambridge: Cambridge University Press.

Schegloff, E. (1992b) In another context. In A. Duranti and C. Goodwin (eds.) *Rethinking Context. Language as Interactive Phenomenon* 191–227. Cambridge: Cambridge University Press.

Schegloff, E. (1997) Whose text? Whose context? *Discourse and Society* 8: 165–187.

Schegloff, E. (1999) Discourse, pragmatics, conversation, analysis. *Discourse and Society* 9: 413–416.

Schegloff, E. (2005) On integrity in inquiry...of the investigated, not the investigator. *Discourse Studies* 7: 455–480.

Schegloff, E. (2007) A tutorial on membership categorisation. *Journal of Pragmatics* 30: 462–482.

Sidnell, J. (2005) Advice in an Indo-Guyanese village and the interactional organisation of uncertainty. In S. Mühleisen and B. Migge (eds.) *Politeness and Face in Caribbean Creoles* 145–168. Amsterdam: John Benjamins.

Silverstein, M. (2003) Indexical order and the dialectics of sociolinguistic life. *Language and Communication* 23: 193–229.

Spencer-Oatey, H. (2000) Rapport management: a framework for analysis. In H. Spencer-Oatey (ed.) *Culturally Speaking. Managing Rapport through Talk across Cultures* 11–46. London: Continuum.

Spencer-Oatey, H. (2005) (Im)politeness, face and perceptions of rapport: unpackaging their bases and interrelationships. *Journal of Politeness Research* 1: 95–120.

Spencer-Oatey, H. (2007) Theories of identity and the analysis of face. *Journal of Pragmatics* 39: 639–656.

Sueda, K. (1995) Differences in the perception of face: Chinese *mien-tzu* and Japanese *mentsu*. *World Communication* 24: 23–31.

Tanaka, S. and Kekidze, T. (2005) *Kao to lico* – Kao gainen no nichi-ro taishô kenkyû [*Kao* and *lico*: Japanese-Russian contrastive study of the concept of 'face']. *Seikai no Nihongo Kyôiku [Japanese-Language Education around the Globe]* 15: 103–116.

Terkourafi, M. (2005) Beyond the micro-level in politeness research. *Journal of Politeness Research* 1: 237–262.

Terkourafi, M. (2007) Toward a universal notion of face for a universal notion of cooperation. In I. Kecskes and L. Horn (eds.) *Explorations in Pragmatics: Linguistic, Cognitive and Intercultural Aspects* 313–344. Berlin: Mouton de Gruyter.

Terkourafi, M. (2008) Toward a unified theory of politeness, impoliteness, and rudeness. In D. Bousfield and M. Locher (eds.) *Impoliteness in Language* 54–89. Berlin: Mouton de Gruyter.

Ting-Toomey, S. (1988) Intercultural conflict styles. A face-negotiation theory. In Y. Kim and W. Gudykunst (eds.) *Theories in Intercultural Communication* 213–238. Newbury Park, CA: Sage.

Ting-Toomey, S. and Kurogi, A. (1998) Face work competence in intercultural conflict: an updated face-negotiation theory. *International Journal of Intercultural Relations* 22: 187–225.

Ting-Toomey, S. (2005) The matrix of face: An updated face-negotiation theory. In W. Gudykunst (ed.) *Theorizing about Intercultural Communication* 71–92. Thousand Oaks, CA: Sage.

Ukosakul, M. (2003) Conceptual metaphors underlying the use of Thai 'face'. In E. Casad and G. Palmer (eds.) *Cognitive Linguistics and Non-Indo-European Languages* 275–303. Berlin: Mouton de Gruyter.

Ukosakul, M. (2005) The significance of 'face' and politeness in social interaction as revealed through Thai 'face' idioms. In R. Lakoff and S. Ide (eds.) *Broadening the Horizons of Linguistic Politeness* 117–125. Amsterdam: John Benjamins.

Usami, M. (ed.) (2005) *BTS ni yoru Tagengo Hanshikotoba Koopasu* [Conversation Corpus of Various Languages Using the Basic Transcription System]. Tokyo: Tokyo University of Foreign Studies.

Watts, R. (2003) *Politeness*. Cambridge: Cambridge University Press.

Watts, R., Ide, S. and Ehlich K. (1992) Introduction. In R. Watts, S. Ide and K. Ehlich (eds.) *Politeness in Language* 1–17. Berlin: Mouton de Gruyter.

Wilson, T. (1991) Social structure and the sequential organisation of interaction. In D. Boden and D. Zimmerman (eds.) *Talk and Social Structure* 22–43. Oxford: Polity Press.

Yabuuchi, A. (2004) Face in Chinese, Japanese and U.S. American cultures. *Journal of Asian Pacific Communication* 14: 263–299.

Part I

Face in interaction

2
Face as emergent in interpersonal communication: an alternative to Goffman[1]

Robert B. Arundale

In the early 1950s, Erving Goffman began examining an aspect of the human experience that had received only passing attention in the social sciences: 'the countless patterns and natural sequences of behaviour occurring whenever persons come into one another's immediate presence' (1967: 2). His approach was broadly ethnographic in that he participated in and observed others engaged in face-to-face encounters in Canada, the UK, and the USA, and then stepped back both to create rich, sensitive descriptions of what he had experienced and observed, and to create conceptual frameworks for understanding these phenomena. Goffman noticed in human encounters what other scholars had not noticed, and in describing and interpreting these noticings both established the study of face-to-face interaction as a domain worthy of investigation and provided a range of resources for examining and understanding it (Schegloff, 1988).

More than 50 years after its publication in 1955, Goffman's framework for understanding what he identified as 'face' and 'facework' in human encounters remains the standard approach to these phenomena, particularly in research on linguistic politeness. Since the millennium, however, conceptualisations of linguistic politeness have come under intense scrutiny (e.g. Eelen, 2001), especially Brown and Levinson's (1987) politeness theory. Bargiela-Chiappini (2003) argues that careful reappraisal of Goffman's approach to face can provide productive alternatives to Brown and Levinson's individualistic and cognitively oriented conceptualisation of face and politeness. This paper demurs in arguing that despite its widespread use in studying politeness phenomena, Goffman's conceptualisation of face and facework is sufficiently problematic to warrant developing alternative explanations. Examining Goffman's account and assumptions carefully not only makes these problematic issues evident but also points to one alternative account of face and facework that addresses them. Using both Goffman's account and the alternative in examining a short segment of interaction illustrates the differences between them.

2.1. Goffman's conceptualisations of face and facework

Face

In quite broad terms, one of the many foci of Goffman's observing of face-to-face encounters was the participants' continual 'positioning' of themselves with respect to others in the contingent flow of their particular local, social environment. In 1955 he introduced the concept of 'face' as a way to understand this positioning, and added new concepts throughout his career, as in his 1959 metaphor of an actor's performance in a play as a means of understanding a person's presentation of self to others. Goffman's dramaturgic perspective was apparent four years earlier in his observation that 'Every person...tends to act out what is sometimes called a *line* – that is, a pattern of verbal and non-verbal acts by which he expresses his view of the situation and through this his evaluation of the participants, especially himself' (1967: 5). Using the concept of 'line,' Goffman defined 'face' as 'the positive social value a person effectively claims for himself by the line others assume he has taken during a particular contact'. Note that it is other persons who observe and assess the 'line' an actor has taken, so that while 'face is an image of self', it is specifically an 'impression they have possibly formed of him', rather than the actor's own impression of himself or herself. In other terms, 'face' is the image a social actor believes is attributed to him or her by the others who comprise the local social environment, rather than the image the actor has constructed of his or her own person. Face is one's 'my your me' rather than one's 'my me'.

As Goffman framed it, face is a subjective, psychological phenomenon, but it is also actively social in that face is experienced as the person carries out a line of actions in the immediate presence of specific others in a situated encounter. He noted that a person's 'social face can be his most personal possession and the center of his security and pleasure', which has been taken to indicate that 'face' has the same enduring characteristics as 'identity' (see Arundale, 2006: 202), but added immediately that face 'is only on loan to him from society; it will be withdrawn unless he conducts himself in a way that is worthy of it' (1967: 10). To pursue the metaphor, it is evident that Goffman saw the loan of face not as a long-term mortgage, but as a very temporary loan to be redeemed in the immediate encounter by one's consideration of the faces of the present others to whom one is in debt (1967: 10-11). Albeit a rather temporary possession, face is clearly an individual possession. Goffman did note at one early point that 'the person's face clearly is something that is not lodged in or on his body, but rather something that is diffusely located in the flow of events in the encounter' (1967: 7), but he did not sustain that interpretation, and most who have followed him have treated face as the personal possession of each of the individuals in an encounter.

Facework

Goffman (1967: 9) noted that on entering

> a situation in which he is given a face to maintain, a person takes on the responsibility of standing guard over the flow of events as they pass before him. He must ensure that a particular *expressive order* is sustained – an order which regulates the flow of events, large or small, so that anything that appears to be expressed by them will be consistent with his face.

For Goffman, this 'expressive order' involved 'acts through whose symbolic component the actor shows how worthy he is of respect or how worthy others are of it' with the consequence that '[o]ne's face ... is a sacred thing, and the expressive order required to sustain it is therefore a ritual one' (1967: 19). Should anything in the flow of events in an encounter be interpretable as inconsistent with or as threatening the face of one of the participants, a state of 'ritual disequilibrium' is created and 'an attempt must be made to establish a satisfactory ritual state for them'. For Goffman, then, 'facework' comprised 'the actions taken by a person to make whatever he is doing consistent with face' (1967: 12), these actions encompassing both avoidance processes by which an actor seeks to prevent threats to face, and corrective processes employed to restore a state of ritual equilibrium or to 'save face' when face is threatened.

Drawing on early work on interchanges in talk, Goffman (1967) specified the nature of face-saving facework more precisely:

> The sequence of acts set in motion by a threat to face, and
> terminating in the re-establishment of ritual equilibrium, I shall call
> an *interchange*. Defining a message or move as everything
> conveyed by an actor during a turn at taking action, one can say
> that an interchange will involve two or more moves and two or
> more participants. (1967: 19-20)

An interchange is a 'naturally bounded unit' in which the flow of messages is guided by the 'practices, conventions, and procedural rules'
the actors bring into play (1967: 33-34). Though he acknowledged certain 'system' requirements governing spoken interaction, the key factor
in Goffman's explanation of the genesis and maintenance of these practices was the 'functional relationship between the structure of the self
and the structure of spoken interaction' (1967: 36), the heart of that
relationship being the ritual order for expressing respect for self and for
others (1967: 38, fn.29).

Goffman (1967: 13) argued that '[w]hether or not the full consequences
of face-saving actions are known to the person who employs them,
they often become habitual and standardized', adding that '[e]ach person, subculture, and society seems to have its own characteristic repertoire of face-saving practices' comprising a 'ritual code' governing
interchange units. Goffman saw the ritual code of facework as one of
'the elements of behaviour which must be built into the person if practical use is to be made of him as an interactant', the person being 'built
up not from inner psychic propensities but from moral rules that are
impressed upon him from without' (1967: 45). As a 'self-regulating participant in social encounters' (1967: 45), however, a 'person's performance of face-work, extended by his tacit agreement to help others
perform theirs, represents his willingness to abide by the ground rules
of social interaction. Here is the hallmark of his socialization as an
interactant' (1967: 33).

Although Goffman argued that the ritually ordered interchange unit
is the 'basic concrete unit of social activity and provides one natural
empirical way to study interaction of all kinds' (1967: 20), he only specified the moves in the ritual interchange for corrective facework, not for
avoidance facework. The first move following an offending or threatening action was the 'challenge' or calling of attention by self or by others
to that action, the second move was the 'offering' or opening by the
offender or others 'to correct for the offense and re-establish the expressive order' (1967: 20), the third was the 'acceptance' of the offering as
satisfactory in restoring the order, and the fourth move was 'thanks' by
the offending actor. The ritually ordered interchange unit remained central

in Goffman's 1971 extension of his treatment of facework. In place of the more specific corrective interchange, he argued for a more general 'remedial interchange' in which the first move following the actual or virtual offence was the providing of a 'remedy' in the form of an account, apology, or request, the second was a response by the offended party that provided 'relief' and restored the ritual equilibrium, followed by a third move showing 'appreciation', and a possible fourth move involving 'minimization' of the event. The first three moves in the interchange unit for remedial work are coterminous with the last three moves of the unit for facework. Goffman (e.g. 1971: 164) argued that the ritual order of the remedial interchange provided the underlying structure for much of ordinary face-to-face interaction, but in explaining how participants accomplished remedial work he ceased using the concepts of face and of facework.

2.2. Problems in Goffman's explanation

Goffman observed, described, interpreted, and explained the dynamics of face-to-face encounters in ways others before him had not done, and perhaps could not have done. His legacy of observation, description, and interpretation is an impressive, innovative, and insightful achievement that will remain influential across the social and human sciences. Goffman's explanation of the phenomena he examined does not have the same durability, however. Because he drew upon the theoretical resources of his day, and because such resources have continued to evolve, scholars who draw upon Goffman's account of face and facework today need to critically examine his explanatory framework and the assumptions on which it rests. Failure to do so invites inconsistency in theoretical formulations, and the consequent restriction on acuity in analysing, interpreting, and explaining empirical observations.

Goffman's studies of face-to-face encounters are evidence that he was implicitly aware of what today would be explained as the social construction of persons and of the social order. But Goffman was not a social constructionist, for the underlying epistemology had yet to be clearly articulated (Crotty, 1998), and there were no social constructionist theories of interaction in the mid-1950s (Pearce, 1995). To explain what he had observed, Goffman (1967: 19, fn.14) turned to then innovative research in social psychology that had clear objectivist and positivist commitments. His explanation of face and facework is social psychological in that it takes the individual as its unit of analysis, and explains how that individual is influenced by or influences his or her social environment (Arundale, 2006: 200). Such explanations are epistemologically and theoretically distinct from interactional achievement accounts that take the dyad as their unit of analysis, and explain both persons and the social order as emergent, systemic, or non-summative outcomes of interaction. This paper contrasts Goffman's social psychological account of face and facework with an alternative, interactional achievement explanation based in research in interpersonal communication.

Face

In view of subsequent theory and research, Goffman's definition of 'face' as 'my your me' appears problematic, though there is wide agreement that however it is defined, face is a phenomenon associated with actions carried out in the immediate presence of others in a situated encounter. Face for Goffman was a personal, individual possession, although he avoided the theoretical and methodological problems that accrue from reifying face, or from treating it as a pre-existing entity or force capable of causing individual action (Bavelas, 1991). But, in framing it as one's view of the image of oneself that others form given one's actions, Goffman psychologised face in a way that limits the cultural generality of the concept. Bargiela-Chiappini (2003: 1463) reflects the stance of other researchers in observing that 'Goffman's ideal social actor is based on a Western model of [the] interactant, almost obsessively concerned with his own self-image and self-preservation'. Goffman's treatment of face is problematic, for example, even in examining the Chinese face practices that he acknowledged as one influence on his conceptualisation (1967: 5-6). Theorists and researchers employing Goffman's definition need to consider not only the cultural specificity Bargiela-Chiappini identifies, but also whether or not a social psychological conceptualisation is a productive basis for a culture-general definition, in view of an alternative definition in which face is not an individual possession.

Facework

Goffman's explanation of facework is likewise problematic in view of contemporary research and theoretical resources. In defining 'interaction' as 'the reciprocal influence of individuals upon one another's actions when in one another's immediate physical presence', Goffman (1959: 15) limited accounts of facework to 'rule-following' explanations, 'reciprocal influence' in this context being one actor's producing of an action in a 'pre-established pattern of action' (1959: 16) as a cue for another actor to produce theirs. The underlying metaphor is again that of the actor, guided by a script that specifies a particular sequence of actions by individual players. Provided that each actor has internalised his or her role in the scene, enacting the script meshes each individual's actions into the pre-established pattern. Rule-following explanations provide reasonable accounts for interaction that proceeds according to the script, each actor's contribution being explained as prescribed by the rule, or in Goffman's version the interchange unit, he or she has internalised apart from and prior to the encounter (see Hutchby and Wooffitt, 1998: 50-51). But rule-following accounts prove quite problematic in explaining how participants address the multiple and varied contingencies arising in ordinary talk, requiring additional rules for handling various departures (as in Goffman, 1971: 149-166), and/or an explicit caveat that actors may somehow improvise variations on the established rules (1971: 166-170).

Rule-following explanations are strictly additive or summative, precisely analogous to the meshing of one gear with another to transfer power (Arundale, 2006: 196). They are formally incapable of explaining the emergent and specifically non-summative effects arising in the sequencing of participants' contributions (Krippendorff, 1970), as for example how a current contribution confirms or alters the on-going interpreting of prior contributions so as to afford and constrain the interpreting of future contributions (Arundale, 1999). Schegloff (1988: 100) argues that in seeking to explain interaction in terms of ritual, largely apart from its system aspects, Goffman was unable to explain 'how the participants together shape the trajectory of the interaction'. Goffman's rule-following explanation also assumed that the ritual code governing facework interchanges was 'built into' or 'impressed upon' each individual during socialisation. As Eelen (2001) argues is also the case for theories of politeness, Goffman's conceptualisation of the place of the individual vis-à-vis society is distinctly Parsonian (Arundale, 2006: 198). Though they develop different arguments, Eelen (2001) and Garfinkel (1967) concur that framing individuals as passively following rules or scripts imposed on them by society is not a productive conceptualisation.

In developing his conceptualisation of interchange units, Goffman also limited research on facework to the common method in objectivist social psychology of 'observer coding' of interaction: a coding system is established in advance on the basis of theory or research, and the observer decides which code applies to each utterance or behaviour without regard to evidence of the interactants' understanding of their acts. Goffman determined whether an actor's move was a face-threatening 'challenge', or a face-saving 'offering', and Brown and Levinson (1987) adopt the same stance in categorising face threats and redress strategies. But there are principled arguments, both with regard to studying face in particular (MacMartin, Wood and Kroger, 2001) and the interpretation of action in general (Wilson, 1970), that observers need to provide warrants that their understandings of the acts they examine are consistent with the participants' interpretings of those acts in the moment of interaction.

2.3. An alternative explanation of face and facework

Goffman's account of face and facework was an innovative application of the theoretical resources available in the 1950s. Subsequent developments in research and theory make apparent that his explanation is no longer viable and alternative frameworks are needed for studying the phenomena to which he called attention. As one starting point, consider that Goffman's observations, descriptions and interpretations of face and facework involve complex interconnections between individual level phenomena and social level phenomena, even though his social psychological and rule-following account explained social phenomena principally in terms of individual phenomena. What alternative framing might one employ that avoids the problematic aspects of Goffman's account of face and facework, and that also avoids privileging either individual or social phenomena?

From an epistemological (Krippendorff, 1984) perspective, consider first that, in the realm of the human, identifying an event as a social phenomenon rests on identifying two or more individuals linked in some relational state. From an ontological (Krippendorff, 1996; Stewart, 1978, 1995) perspective, consider second that at no point in the developmental span from procreation onward do individuals exist as human agents apart from the agency of other humans. In the human experience, then, not only are individuals qua individuals dependent upon the nexus that is the social, but also the social qua social is dependent on individuals in nexus. What is individual in nature and what is social in nature are fully interdependent, while at the same time, individual phenomena and social phenomena are distinct and functionally contra-dictory poles of human experience.

This entwining of the individual with the social can be productively framed as a dialectic, in the sense of Yin and Yang rather than in the sense of a Hegelian dialectic of thesis and antithesis leading to synthesis. Following Baxter and Montgomery (1996: 8), a dialectic differs from a dualism in that it involves two distinct phenomena 'that function in incompatible ways such that each negates the other', but that are nevertheless unified because they function interdependently in an on-going, dynamic, and interactive manner. In human activity, social functioning is distinct from individual functioning in that what is a fully social activity (marrying someone) cannot be accomplished solely through individual activity, just as a fully individual process (perceiving a tree) cannot be carried out as a social process. Yet the individual and the social are also unified, definitionally because what is individual presupposes what is social, just as the opposite is true, and dynamically because individuals in interaction with one another constitute the social, just as social interaction is constitutive of individuals (Arundale, 1999: 128).

Framing the individual and the social as a dialectic privileges neither pole of the dialectic as the basis for explaining phenomena involving the other pole. As a consequence, the dialectic has potential as an alternative, albeit quite abstract, framework for conceptualising the individual and the social phenomena involved in face and facework, and for doing so in ways that avoid the problems of Goffman's social psychological and rule-following account. Theory and research in interpersonal communication since the 1960s provide the basis for an alternative conceptualisation of face that is consistent with the individual/social dialectic. Research on the interactional achievement of talk over the same time span provides the basis for an alternative conceptualisation of facework in which face is emergent in the interaction that constitutes both the individual and the social.

Face

On the basis of a critical overview of more than three decades of theory and research in interpersonal communication, Baxter and Montgomery (1996) argue, in formulating their Relational Dialectics Theory, that as persons engage in the back and forth of everyday communication, they form and sustain relationships that can be described using three dialectics. Relationships are characterised by *openness* or sharing with, as

well as by *closedness* from one's partner, by *certainty* about the relationship, as well as by *uncertainty* about it, and by *connectedness* with
the other, as well as by *separateness* from them. These three pairs of
oppositional terms do not identify individual needs, but rather characteristics, conditions, or states evinced in the interpersonal relationship
that persons form and reform as they communicate over time. Baxter
and Montgomery provide evidence for all three dialectics, in quite
different types of relationships, but it is the dialectic of connectedness
and separateness that is of primary interest in seeking a new
conceptualisation of face.

In Baxter and Montgomery's (1996: 9) terms, connectedness and separateness form 'a functional opposition in that the total autonomy of
parties precludes their relational connection, just as total connection
between parties precludes their individual autonomy'. Any interpreting
of separateness in a relationship is framed in view of the current understanding of connectedness and has implications for it, and vice versa,
because each state involves and defines the other. Initiating interpersonal communication with an unknown other initiates the dialectical
interplay of connectedness and separateness and initiates the relationship. In established relationships, the interplay between connection
and separation is always present, so that the relational partners are
continually poised 'between unity and differentiation' (1996: 79), that
is, between being a social entity and being individual entities. The ten-
sional interplay of connectedness and separateness is dynamic, it is not
resolvable, it cannot be eliminated short of ceasing all communication,
and relationships are neither driven by nor oriented toward maintaining balance between the contradictory poles. Connectedness and separateness are fundamental to relationships in that no relationship exists
except as two separate or differentiated individuals achieve some form
of social connection or unity. The connectedness/separateness dialectic is integral with the individual/social dialectic in that connectedness
generates what is social, while separateness generates what is individual. However, unlike the highly abstract individual/social dialectic,
the connectedness/separateness dialectic is conceptualised within the
framework of a comprehensive, empirically grounded, social constructionist theory of interpersonal communication.

Arundale (2006) uses this dialectic in developing Face Constituting
Theory, defining 'face' as 'connectedness and separateness in human
relationships'. This alternative conceptualisation captures Goffman's
insight that face involves complex interconnections between the individual and the social, but obviates the individualistic commitments of

his social psychological account. In this alternative framing, face is not an individual phenomenon, but rather a *relational* phenomenon in that face arises in the dialectic interplay between what is individual and what is social. Note that the term 'relational' is used here and in Face Constituting Theory in a sense entirely distinct from uses of the term in other theories of face and facework (2006: 202-203). Importantly, this marked departure in defining face provides the basis for addressing the Western cultural specificity of Goffman's account, and for framing an alternative account of facework.

Relational Dialectics Theory (Baxter and Montgomery, 1996) antici-pates that connectedness and separateness will be understood differ-ently at different times, in different relationships, and in different cultures. 'Connectedness' in relationships indexes a complex of meanings and actions that may be apparent as unity, interdependence, solidarity, association, congruence, and more, between the relational partners. Because of the dialectical opposition, 'connectedness' is always linked reflexively with 'separateness', which indexes meanings and actions that may be voiced as differentiation, independence, autonomy, disso-ciation, divergence, and so on. These alternative understandings of connectedness and separateness are relatively culture-general in that the dialectics derive from a conceptual framework that explains human relationships as constituted within the matrix of communication that comprises any culture, and that anticipates and accounts for diverse types of relationships within, as well as across cultural groups. These alternate voicings of connectedness and separateness are more culture-general, as well, in that one finds among them abstract expressions of the varied construals of 'face' apparent across different cultures. Before commencing research on face within a given cultural group, then, one must undertake or employ ethnographically grounded research that establishes how persons in that group understand the dialectic of con-nectedness and separateness. In doing so, one re-specifies the culture-general conceptualisation of face in terms of a culture-specific construal of connection face and separation face. Arundale (2006) provides sev-eral examples of such construals, and argues that because of the radi-cally different conceptualisation, connection face and separation face cannot be substituted for Brown and Levinson's (1987) positive face and negative face without engendering fundamental theoretical incon-sistencies.

Facework

Framing face in view of the individual/social dialectic also entails adopting an alternative framework for conceptualising facework, one that avoids the problems of Goffman's rule-following, Parsonian account. Because interaction among individuals constitutes what is social, and because social interaction is constitutive of individuals, face is a phenomenon constituted or 'interactionally achieved' by persons in conversation. Note that, whereas Goffman's definition of 'interaction' as 'reciprocal influence' was consistent with the ordinary use of the term to index simply 'a situation in which people converse', the term 'interaction' is employed here and in Face Constituting Theory in a special, technical sense to index 'the conjoint, non-summative outcome of two or more factors', as in statistical interaction (see Arundale, 2006: 196-197).

Arundale (1999), Clark (1996), and Sanders (1987) all provide models capable of explaining the interactional achievement of meaning and action, though only Arundale (1999, 2006) provides an account of facework. Interactional achievement models conceptualise meaning and action as the dynamically evolving, emergent outcomes of two or more individual's producing and interpreting of utterances and behaviours in sequence (the use of the gerund indexing the dynamic nature of production and interpretation). Such models explain the emergence of meaning and action in conversation not as the summative meshing of gears, but as a non-summative process, akin to the interaction among musicians through which jazz is created in the moment, rather than played following a score. That is, whereas social psychological models explain conversation as the output of one individual or system serving in turn as the input to a separate, independent system, interactional achievement models treat the dyad as an integral unit and explain conversation as the conjoint outcome of a single two-person system (Krippendorff, 1984).

Following Arundale's (1999) more extended treatment, a first speaker's utterance affords some range of interpretings, but does not determine which one of these interpretings will be operative in the conversation. The adjacent utterance of the second speaker affords another range of interpretings. Both speakers now assess the consistency between the two ranges, and in doing so retroactively constrain their interpretings of the first utterance. More concretely, assume a first speaker utters 'That's a nice jumper'. If the second utters 'You can't borrow it', the two interactively achieve operative interpretings of the first utterance as a request. If the second speaker were instead to say 'Thanks', the two would interactionally achieve operative interpretings of the first utterance as a compliment. All conversational action, topic managing, and turn-taking is achieved interactionally, whether the result is an unanticipated outcome, as in the first case above, or more commonly the recreating of a familiar pattern, as in the second case. Very often the interpretings constituted by each of the participants are similar, though interactional achievement models explain how participants can and do constitute both complementary and divergent interpretings.

Goffman's rule-following explanation of facework is fully consistent with the broader social psychological (and Parsonian) account of persons and the social order he adopted, but entirely inconsistent with an interactional achievement (and social constructional) account of persons and sociality. An interactional achievement account entails instead what is termed here a 'norm-orienting' explanation of conversation in general (cf. Hutchby and Wooffitt, 1998: 50-51), and of facework in particular. Whereas rule-following explanations presume participants enact parts in whatever pre-established script or schema they identify as applying to the current situation, norm-orienting explanations presume participants design and interpret each contribution in the given moment, employing practices from an array of normative practices for all forms of talk, the applicability of any given practice being contingent on what has transpired before and what is likely to follow the current utterance in the evolving sequence. In interpreting their and other's contributions, and in designing and producing their contributions, participants continually display to and hence update one another on, not only their current interpretings, but also their instantiations of and hence their orientations to the particular practices they are currently employing.

Norm-orienting explanations therefore conceptualise the sequencing of contributions in a conversation as fully responsive to contingencies, the trajectory of those contributions being locally and jointly constituted by the participants, rather than being determined by a pre-established, internalised ritual interchange unit (Schegloff, 2007). Instead of reproducing common sequences following a script, norm-orienting accounts reveal participants to be newly constituting sequences like those they have constituted in the past (Garfinkel, 1967; Wilson, 1970), as in the compliment example above. In the on-going process of instantiating and displaying their orientations to practices, the participants reflexively sustain those practices as normative in their own conversations, and hence regular interaction among participants within networks ranging in size from dyads up to societies socially constructs and reflexively sustains such practices as normative within those networks (cf. Arundale, 1999: 140-142). Conversations exhibit non-summativity or emergence in that each participant's interpretings and contributions afford and constrain the other's contributions and interpretings, both backward and forward in time, in ways neither participant can fully anticipate or control. Lastly, because participants display to one another both their interpretings of the emergent sequence, and their orientations to particular norms, those interpretings and orientations are available in part to the analyst in warranting his or her understanding of the participants' interpretings in the moment.

An explanation of facework framed within this more general interactional achievement and norm-orienting account of conversation would clearly address the problems apparent in the rule-following explanation that Goffman developed within his social psychological account of persons. Face Constituting Theory (Arundale, 1999, 2006) integrates the norm-orienting explanation of conversation with the new conceptualisation of face to create an explanation of facework that is a distinct alternative to Goffman's because it frames face as emergent in interpersonal communication. Key to this integration is recognising that connectedness with and separateness from others are interpretings that are interactionally achieved in conversation in exactly the same manner as all other interpretings. More specifically, 'face' is a dynamic, evolving interpreting that participants form regarding 'our persons as both connected to and separate from one another'. Although it is one among other interpretings of the current relationship, and one among other interpretings arising in the conversation, face is central because the interactional achieving of connectedness and separateness generates the relationship within which the conversation takes form. 'Face' is thus an *interactional* phenomenon, in addition to being a relational phenomenon, and 'facework' is the norm-orienting, interactional achievement of conversational practices in which interpretings of connectedness and separateness emerge, and in which they are both changed and maintained.

2.4. Two contrasting explanations of facework

Two brief and necessarily incomplete analyses of a single, short encounter serve to illustrate the differences between a Goffmanian explanation of facework and the explanation provided by Face Constituting

Theory (FCT). Sifianou (2001: 409) provides the following translation of an exchange between two young Greek women friends, originally transcribed as a field observation (with additions provided in personal communication, February 2007).

1   C: This scarf is very nice.
2   R: Do you want it? Have it. ((while removing and giving scarf))
3   C: I didn't say it so that you would give it to me.
4   R: I know. I'm giving it to you as a present.

A Goffmanian account

Had Goffman himself provided an extended analysis of the remedial work or the facework in an actual instance of interaction, his unique ethnographic approach would certainly have involved a level of description and interpretation well beyond what follows. With that caveat, this analysis is framed principally in terms of remedial work, and interpreted in terms of facework, given that the respective interchange units largely overlap, and that Goffman's explanation of remedial work is both more compelling than, and an extension of his facework explanation.

C's utterance 1 would be classified by a Goffmanian analyst as a compliment, given its canonical form, and as the first move in a remedial interchange unit, the compliment being C's remedy for or offering of face in response to a virtual offence or face threat. The analyst would locate the virtual offence in C's understanding that without the compliment, R might view C as disregarding her as a friend, thereby threatening R's face (Goffman, 1971: 158). C's complement requires R to provide a next move of relief for the remedy or of acceptance of the face offering in order to restore ritual equilibrium. The two moves in R's utterance 2 are a question followed by an imperative. The question does not qualify as remedy, but could be categorised either as a 'priming' move (1971: 154-157) by R to elicit a remedy for, or as a challenge calling attention to, a second virtual offence, which the analyst would find in noting that R's question informs C by implication that R has taken C's compliment as a request for R's scarf and hence as a threat to her face. The priming move/challenge requires C to provide a remedy or offering in her next move. R's imperative and her giving of the scarf would be seen as the relief required of R in response to C's compliment remedy for the first virtual offence, and hence as R's acceptance of C's offer of face, restoring the ritual balance and leading to C's appreciation or acceptance in her next move. Yet R's giving of her scarf to C seems to be far greater restitution than required for the virtual offence of C's being seen to disregard R as a friend, that imbalance creating a new actual offence to C by embarrassing her or obligating her to repay the gift.

A Goffmanian analyst would classify C's utterance 3 as an account, accounts being the paradigm for remedies (Goffman, 1971: 108-113). In denying that utterance 1 was a request for the scarf, C provides the remedy required for her second virtual threat to R's face of having been taken as requesting the scarf. R is thus required to provide relief or acceptance in her next move. At the same time, C's account would be seen as a priming move or challenge, calling R's attention to the offence to C's face created by R's overgenerous gift. The two moves in R's utterance 4 would be classified as assertions, the first one indicating to C that R knows C was not requesting the scarf. In making that assertion, R would be seen both as implying she knew C's utterance 1 was a compliment, thus absolving C of the second virtual offence. The assertion would thus be classified as R's relief/acceptance for C's remedy in utterance 3 for her second virtual offence, which requires C's subsequent appreciation or thanks. R's second assertion in utterance 4 is another account, clarifying her intention to present the scarf as an outright gift. A Goffmanian analyst would identify this assertion as R's remedy/offering of face in response to her actual offence to C in giving the scarf, thereby re-establishing ritual equilibrium. R's remedy requires that C provide relief/acceptance in her next move, perhaps together with her appreciation/thanks for R's relief for the second offence, and with her overdue thanks for R's relief for first offence. Minimisation by R would then be in order to close the remedial interchange unit.

Clearly other explanations of the facework in this encounter are possible, depending on how the analyst classifies the utterances, and the offences or face threats. However, the concern here is not to provide a definitive Goffmanian analysis of the facework in this encounter, but rather to illustrate what such an explanation entails. The analyst overlays the previously established ritual pattern on the talk, locating and classifying each of the required moves, and creating an interpretation of the participants' utterances in terms of the concepts that define the interchange unit. Providing an explanation of how remedial work or facework is accomplished is therefore a matter of demonstrating how the participants' actions conform to the ritual pattern. Face is treated entirely as a personal possession: each woman is seen as concerned with the image the other woman holds of her, her 'my your me', and as formulating contributions that position her with regard to the other woman in ways she wants to be seen. Face is not only a social psycho-logical phenomenon, but also a very Western one (Bargiela-Chiappini 2003).

An account using Face Constituting Theory

Analyses of facework using FCT are informed by the methodology of conversation analysis, though they lie outside the scope of its core re-search program. The analytic commitments of conversation analysis re-quire that a thorough study of an encounter be done by a native speaker in the original language, based on an audio or video recording. Hirschon (2001) argues that the cultural context of Greek politeness is characterised by a contradiction between freedom or personal autonomy, and soli-darity or engagement with others, the tension between these poles aris-ing in the obligations attendant on engaging with other persons. Although she does not use the concept, Hirschon addresses all the features that define dialectics, suggesting that solidarity and autonomy are the Greek construals of face seen as relational connectedness and separateness.

   In designing utterance 1 based on her provisional projecting of R's subsequent interpreting, C displays an orientation toward practices for complimenting, which likely include her projecting that, following the norm, R's next utterance will be some form of compliment response that would retroactively confirm utterance 1 as a complimenting action. C displays her orientation to the normative practices in that the design of utterance 1 affords being heard as complimenting, even though interactionally achieving that action depends entirely on R's providing uptake consistent with the normative expectation. Sifianou (2001) ar-gues that compliments in Greece are effectively gifts, suggesting that C may provisionally interpret her utterance as part of an action that could enhance solidarity or connectedness in her relationship with R. Yet at the other pole of the dialectic, if R's uptake were to confirm the complimenting action, there is the potential that R could interpret the normative obligation to produce a compliment response as limiting her autonomy and hence engendering separateness.

   In designing the first turn constructional unit (TCU) of utterance 2 for C to interpret, R displays both a provisional interpretation of utterance 1 as an indirect request for the scarf, as well as an orientation toward practices for questioning, provisionally projecting a yes or no in C's next utterance. Dialectically, when seen against the background of the women's solidarity as friends, C's requesting the scarf could be taken as restricting R's autonomy. R continues with a second TCU as she gives the scarf to C, the design of which both affords interpreting in terms of practices for commanding or insisting, and projects uptake by C displaying accepting or rejecting. Actions of insisting can be taken as restricting another's autonomy, which may engender separateness between the friends, yet dialectically, in the concurrent action of giving the scarf to C, R may also enhance their solidarity. Sifianou (2001) notes that spontaneous gift giving is not unusual among Greek friends, and argues that in cases where a gift is given as uptake in complimenting, the giver does not do so as obligatory repayment for the compliment gift, but as a personal, autonomous decision to share something with the other, thereby enhancing solidarity.

In the visible uptake of accepting the scarf, C displays her interpreting of R's second TCU, confirming that it has been understood as insisting. Within this Greek friendship, C's accepting could be taken dialectically not only as C's acknowledging of R's decision to share, therein confirming their personal connectedness, but also as C's accepting of R's insisting, thereby acknowledging relational separateness. In designing utterance 3 in view of practices for repairing, C displays her provisional interpreting of R's first TCU in utterance 2 as displaying R's provisional uptake of C's utterance 1 as an indirect request. That is, in constructing an utterance that affords hearing as denying that she was requesting the scarf, C displays that rather than her initial, provisional interpreting that she was complimenting R, the interpreting of utterance 1 she now takes as operative in this encounter is that she was requesting. In proffering a repair designed in view of practices for denying, C likely provisionally projects a next utterance by R accepting or rejecting that denial. If R were to accept C's denial, R would obviate the grounds for questioning C about wanting the scarf in the first TCU of utterance 2, and in doing so both release C from responding to that question, and cancel the limiting of R's autonomy entailed in C's having been taken as requesting it.

In constructing the first TCU of utterance 4 to be hearable as accepting C's denial, R displays not only her orientation to practices for repairing and for denying, but also that her initial, provisional interpreting of C's utterance 1 was indeed as a complimenting action, despite her utterance 2 uptake. R thus provides C with grounds for confirming that her provisional projecting of the meaning and action to be formulated for her utterance 3 are now operative interpretings for both of them. C and R have interactionally achieved the doing of C's complimenting R, and in a manner consistent with Sifianou's (2001: 409) finding that 'compliments are not normally interpreted as indirect requests in Greek'. They have also interactionally achieved the doing of spontaneous, mutual gift giving, the compliment to R and the scarf to C mutually enhancing their solidarity as friends. Yet dialectically, and in a manner consistent with both Sifianou and Hirschon (2001), R designs the second TCU of utterance 4 to afford interpreting as asserting her decision to offer the scarf as a gift, the focal stress on the first person singular being hearable as forwarding her personal autonomy in making that decision.

Other cultural construals of connectedness and separateness, or different emic practices for complimenting, would result in a different explanations of the facework in this encounter. This analysis omits consideration of C's and R's evaluations of face threat, maintenance, stasis, or support (Arundale, 1999), but again, rather than providing a definitive analysis using FCT, the concern is to illustrate what such an explanation entails. Analyses that explain talk as an interactional achievement assume participants have access to and mutually sustain a broad set of normative practices for talking. The analyst seeks to understand a given instance of talk-in-interaction by examining the particular orientations to practices and the specific interpretings of utterances that the participants themselves display to one another as they design their contributions to the evolving sequence, the key warrant for the analyst's understanding being each participant's uptake of the other's contributions. Providing an explanation of how facework is achieved is thus a matter of showing how the participants use particular resources to respond in real time to the contingencies arising from one another's particular contributions, conjointly affording and constraining, shaping and reshaping one another's interpretings of their utterances in general, and of face in particular. Face is treated entirely as a relational phenomenon: a culturally specific interpreting that participants achieve interactionally regarding their persons as dialectically connected to and separated from one another. Face is central to being human in that connecting creates the social out of the individual, while dialectically, separating creates the individual out of the social.

On Goffman on face

From the vantage point of some fifty years, Goffman's observations, descriptions, and interpretations of the human scene remain an influential legacy, even if his explanation of the phenomena he studied now appears problematic. Goffman framed his conceptualisation of face and facework within the positivist social psychology of the day, using a Parsonian view of the individual. Face for Goffman was an individual's 'my your me', and his explanation of facework as the maintenance of a ritual equilibrium employed a summative, rule-following model. Developments in social constructionism, in ethnomethodology, and in understanding human interaction are among the bases both for recognising limitations in Goffman's explanation, and for constructing alternatives to it. One alternative, Face Constituting Theory, rests jointly on a norm-orienting, interactional achievement model of communication, and on a theory of interpersonal relationships as the dialectical attainment of separateness and connectedness. Face is an emergent, non-summative achievement in interpersonal communication, and facework evolves as each person evokes contingencies and responds to those arising with the other's actions in the particular, local social environment they co-create by those actions. Framing face as a relational phenomenon makes evident how it is 'diffusely located in the flow of events in the encounter' (Goffman, 1967: 7), and is a marked departure from other framings that reify face, that treat it as an individual want that drives human action, or that conceptualise it as a personal possession, following Goffman.

Endnotes

1. Parts of this paper were presented at the Third International Politeness Symposium, University of Leeds, Leeds, UK, July 2007. Dr. Maria Sifianou provided key insights regarding facework in Greece, though all misconstruals are the author's responsibility.

References

Arundale, R. B. (1999) An alternative model and ideology of communication for an alternative to politeness theory. *Pragmatics* 9: 119-153.

Arundale, R. B. (2006) Face as relational and interactional: A communication framework for research on face, facework, and politeness, *Journal of Politeness Research* 2: 193-216.

Bargiela-Chiappini, F. (2003) Face and politeness: New (insights) for old (concepts). *Journal of Pragmatics* 35: 1453-1469.

Bavelas, J. B. (1991) Some problems with linking goals to discourse. In K. Tracy (ed.) *Understanding Face-to-face Interaction: Issues Linking Goals and Discourse* 119-130. Hillsdale, NJ: Lawrence Erlbaum.

Baxter, L. A., and Montgomery, B. M. (1996) *Relating: Dialogues and Dialectics.* New York: Guilford.

Brown, P. and Levinson, S. C. (1987) *Politeness: Some Universals in Language Usage.* Cambridge: Cambridge University Press.

Clark, H. H. (1996) *Using Language.* Cambridge: Cambridge University Press.

Crotty, M. (1998) *The Foundations of Social Research.* London: Sage.

Eelen, G. (2001) *A Critique of Politeness Theories.* Manchester: St. Jerome.

Garfinkel, H. (1967) *Studies in Ethnomethodology.* Englewood Cliffs, NJ: Prentice-Hall.

Goffman, E. (1955) On face-work: An analysis of ritual elements in social interaction. *Psychiatry* 18: 213-231.

Goffman, E. (1959) *The Presentation of Self in Everyday Life.* New York: Doubleday Anchor.

Goffman, E. (1967) *Interaction Ritual: Essays in Face-to-Face Behaviour.* Chicago: Aldine.

Goffman, E. (1971) *Relations in Public,* New York: Basic Books.

Heritage, J. (1984) *Garfinkel and Ethnomethodolgy.* Cambridge: Polity Press.

Hirschon, R. (2001) Freedom, solidarity and obligation: The sociocultural context of Greek politeness. In A. Bayraktaroğlu and M. Sifianou (eds.) *Linguistic Politeness Across Boundaries* 19–42. Amsterdam: John Benjamins.

Hutchby, I, and Wooffitt, R. (1998) *Conversation Analysis.* Cambridge: Polity Press.

Krippendorff, K. (1970) On generating data in communication research. *Journal of Communication* 20: 241-269.

Krippendorff, K. (1984) An epistemological foundation for communication. *Journal of Communication* 34: 31-36.

Krippendorff, K. (1996) A second cybernetics of otherness. *Systems Research* 13: 311-328.

MacMartin, C., Wood, L. A, and Kroger, R. O. (2001) Facework. In W. P. Robinson and H. Giles (eds.) *The New Handbook of Language and Social Psychology* 221–237. New York: Wiley.

Pearce, W. B. (1995) A sailing guide for social constructionists. In W. Leeds-Hurwitz (ed.) *Social Approaches to Communication* 88–113. New York: Guilford.

Sanders, R. E. (1987) *Cognitive Foundations of Calculated speech.* Albany, NY: State University of New York Press.

Schegloff, E. A. (1988) Goffman and the analysis of conversation. In P. Drew and A. Wootton (eds.) *Erving Goffman: Exploring the Interaction Order* 89–135. Boston: Northeastern University Press.

Schegloff, E. A. (2007) *Sequence Organization in Interaction: A Primer in Conversation Analysis, Vol. 1.* Cambridge: Cambridge University Press.

Sifianou, M. (2001) Oh! How appropriate: Compliments and politeness. In A. Bayraktaroðlu and M. Sifianou (eds.) *Linguistic Politeness Across Boundaries* 390–430. Amsterdam: John Benjamins.

Stewart, J. R. (1978) Foundations of dialogic communication. *Quarterly Journal of Speech* 64: 183–201.

Stewart, J. R. (1995) Philosophical features of social approaches to interpersonal communication. In W. Leeds-Hurwitz (ed.) *Social Approaches to Communication* 23–45. New York: Guilford.

Wilson, T. P. (1970) Conceptions of interaction and forms of sociological explanation. *American Sociological Review* 35: 697–710.

3
How to get rid of a telemarketing agent? Facework strategies in an intercultural service call

Rosina Márquez Reiter

3.1. Introduction

In this chapter, I examine how face is manifested in an intercultural service call between a Uruguayan telemarketing agent and a prospective Argentinean client. By doing so, I aim to contribute to the extensive body of research that has examined face in interaction and to research that has investigated aspects of the interactional behaviour of Spanish speakers in mediated service encounters (Codó Olsina, 2002; Márquez Reiter, 2005, 2006) and thus add to our knowledge of institutional talk in Spanish, a language which until now has received very little attention when compared, for example, to English (Drew and Heritage, 1992; Holmes and Stubbe, 2003), French (Boutet, 2005; Pène, Borzeix and Fraenkel, 2001), Italian (Aston, 1998; Bargiela-Chiappini and Harris, 1997) or German (Müller, 2003), to mention but a few.

The interaction I analyse here is a service call in which an institutional representative, from a multi-national company, telephones a client for the purpose of having the client's membership renewed as it had lapsed for a relatively long period of time. The conversational participants' contributions are oriented toward the achievement of a task; namely, the institutional representative wants to obtain a sale and, the client wants to obviate any possible avenues for the former to attain her goal.

Nowadays most human beings spend a considerable amount of time both requesting and being offered services over the 'phone. The modern pervasive nature of negotiating services over faceless interactions, either via the telephone or the internet, is commonplace in both developed and developing capitalist economies. This is evidenced, amongst other things, by the relatively late trend in developed economies to outsource their call centres to developing economies, and also by the late tendency of public utilities in some developed and developing economies to deal with their customers via a call centre. Therefore, mediated service encounters operated from call centres play a key role in modern consumer behaviour as far as the exchange of goods and services is concerned. Given the ubiquity and routine nature of this kind of mediated service encounter, it provides us with a suitable context in which to examine face. Moreover, given that face is as a primary concern of individuals in interaction (Goffman, 1967) and that the conversation examined is an unsolicited transactional call where the participants have opposite conversational goals, manifestations of face can be expected, if only, at the level of politeness, in the participants' efforts to achieve their conversational goal without causing offence.

The literature on Spanish service calls is rather scant and mainly based on intracultural studies in one variety of Spanish (Márquez Reiter, 2005, 2006; Orlando, 2006 Uruguayan Spanish). At the same time, studies of intercultural communication in Spanish have principally examined Spanish in contact with other languages (see, for example, Schrader-Kniffi, 2004; Zimmerman and de Granda, 2004; Roca and Jensen, 1996); rather than contact between native speakers of Spanish from different linguistic and cultural backgrounds. The call analysed is intercultural, namely between a Bonaerense (Argentinean) client and a Montevidean (Uruguayan) service provider and represents a primary occasion for contact between members of different cultural groups, albeit closely related ones.

Montevidean and Bonaerense Spanish share a number of linguistic similarities although there are some (perceived) cultural differences between them. The variety spoken in Montevideo has a great deal in common with that spoken in Buenos Aires, to the extent that some experts claim that is not always possible for native speakers of these varieties to distinguish a Bonaerense from a Montevidean (Lipski, 1994).[1] The speech similarities between Montevideans and Bonaerenses may be one of the reasons why the interaction analysed does not show any cases of misunderstanding, a common topic in intercultural communication, but a tacit understanding between the interlocutors of the pragmatic force of each other's utterances.

After a brief orientation to the concepts of face, facework and politeness, I discuss the background and methodology of the study. Then I analyse how face is manifested in the different conversational sequences with special attention to the opening, where most face concerns are verbalised. Finally I present the conclusions of the study.

3.2. The notions of face and facework

Since the publication of Brown and Levinson's (1987) *Politeness: Some Universals in Language Use* there has been a proliferation of studies on politeness, mainly, though not exclusively, from a facework perspective. Despite the increasing interest in politeness, as reflected by the extraordinarily large numbers of articles, monographs and the creation of politeness forums (www.lboro.ac.uk/departments/ea/politeness/, *Estudios del Discurso de la Cortesía en Español* (EDICE)), things are far from being settled. Most of the studies which have been carried out have (in)directly dealt with the face-saving view and, in so doing, provided (further) support for (aspects of) the theory, proposed revisions to it and some have even rejected (aspects of) it. The face-saving view has not only triggered a wealth of politeness studies in a great variety of languages and cultures but has also played an important role in alternate approaches to (im)politeness phenomena (Arundale, 2006; Bravo, 1999; Culpeper, 1996; Spencer-Oatey, 2000, 2005).

Given the existence of theoretical re-examinations of the concepts of face and facework (see, for example, Bargiela-Chiappini, 2003) and the other essays contained in this volume, my primary purpose is not to present an elaborate literature review of face. Rather, my efforts in this section are directed at:

1. providing a brief orientation to and updating some of the limitations related to the Brown and Levinson face dichotomy,

2. assessing the degree to which recent research has been successful in overcoming the limitations associated with earlier studies of face, and, based on this assessment,

3. demonstrating that future studies need to show greater consideration for the importance of levels of analysis in understanding face.

Central to Brown and Levinson's theory and to some of the approaches which have recently emerged is the concept of 'face' with its two universal basic desires for face: negative and positive face, broadly speaking, the desire for dissociation and association, respectively. One of the most important criticisms levelled against Brown and Levinson's understanding of face voiced by proponents of new and earlier models and made by primarily Asian (Matsumoto, 1988; Ide, 1989) and African (Nwoye, 1989; Strecker, 1993) scholars, is its Western orientation as evidenced by the emphasis on the individual and his or her territory. Matsumoto (1988), Ide (1989), Nwyoe (1989), Gu (1990) and Kong (1998), among others, see Brown and Levinson's face, and in particular their negative face, as inapplicable to societies where group membership is more prominent. Reconceptualisations of positive and negative face have been proposed to account for the inapplicability of Brown and Levinson's face dichotomy in some cultures and for the cultural variability observed. Ide (1989) suggests that discernment rather than face is what motivates Japanese politeness, while Nwyoe (1989) and Strecker (1993) argue that group face rather than Brown and Levinson's individualistic face is what underlies Igbo and Hamar politeness respectively. Matsumoto argues that the constituents of face are culture-dependent, a view echoed in Spanish by Bravo (1999), Hernández Flores (1999) and others who maintain that affiliation and autonomy rather than negative and positive politeness respectively explain polite behaviour in Spanish. On the other hand, Fukushima (2000) claims that Brown and Levinson's negative face accurately describes modern Japanese politeness patterns and a vast array of Hispanists have found the distinction useful in explaining politeness in the cultures examined (Márquez Reiter and Placencia, 2005).

The picture that emerges is contradictory, with some scholars arguing that Brown and Levinson's face is inapplicable to some cultures and suggesting that the components of face are culture-specific, and other investigators indicating that Brown and Levinson's face dichotomy is indeed applicable to those very same cultures. Besides the inconsistency of the research findings, it would be fair to argue that if Brown and Levinson's scheme of face is not valid in some cultures, then it is also likely to be unhelpful in the study of face of several other cultures (O'Driscoll, 1996; Márquez Reiter, 2000). Put differently, a comprehensive cross-cultural comparison may never be achieved and therefore the cultural relativity of Brown and Levinson's face may never be completely (dis)proved. As observed by Holtgraves (2002), scholars who have been unable to apply (aspects of) Brown and Levinson's notion of face have explained its irrelevance by arguing that face is manifested differently in particular cultures. Holtgraves rightly notes that 'specification of the manifestations of face within a culture needs to be undertaken before the theory can be tested within that culture' (2002: 59).

Additionally, conceptualising face from within the system as com-posed by culture-specific norms, which may or may not be shared by other cultures, would make cross-cultural research untenable due to the non-comparability of the interpretations of face. From a reductionist perspective, one could claim that some of these culture-specificities are recoverable by Brown and Levinson's negative and positive face. Spe-cifically, and as I pointed out in earlier work, echoing O'Driscoll (1996), neither positive nor negative face are primary concepts but compounds derived from a combination of 'wants dualism'. The essence of being 'unimpeded in one's actions' is the desire to be free from ties of contact and those needs which involve contact, to a greater or lesser extent, are 'positive' wants. It then follows that the needs of this universal face are inherent in the human condition though its constituents are culturally variable (Márquez Reiter, 2000). A similar view has been voiced by Gudykunst and Ting-Toomey (1988) who maintain that Brown and Levinson's positive face refers to the need for association or interde-pendence and their negative face to the need for dissociation or inde-pendence, two non-mutually exclusive psychological universals which cut across cultural boundaries (Triandis, 1980).

Shimanoff (1994:159-60) explains that '[F]acework may be defined as behaviors which establish, enhance, threaten, or diminish the images/identities of communicators. The images/identities of communicators have been linked to the basic needs of approval and autonomy (Brown and Levinson, 1978)'. Politeness, on the other hand, may be defined as the facework 'strategies involved in friction-free² communication' (Márquez Reiter, 2000: 5), that is, the facework strategies employed by interlocutors to protect and/or enhance each other's need for associa-tion or interdependence and dissociation or independence. Shimanoff (1994) further notes that 'facework includes politeness, but politeness does not incorporate all types of facework' (p.60). She explains that acts which threaten or diminish another's needs for approval and au-tonomy may be regarded as facework but not as politeness and, whereas facework may be directed toward oneself or another, politeness can only be directed toward another.

In the case of the call examined here, the client strategically aims at diminishing the professional face or institutional identity of the telemarketing agent in an effort to prevent the latter from attaining her conversational goal. This is evidenced by his conversational behaviour which runs contrary to the role expectations of a business transaction with an agent with whom there is no familiarity. Rather than express his disinterest in the call by simply alleging task-based reasons in keeping with his expected role as potential buyer and the expected role of the institutional representative as seller, he undermines the latter's professional face. He does so by swapping the business status-bound roles of seller/buyer, hence putting the agent in the fictitious position of buyer and himself in the position of seller. In doing so, the client foregrounds the personal face of the institutional representative as a fellow consumer who in a different situational context may assume the role of buyer.

Having briefly explained my understanding of face and politeness and assessed the (lack of) success in overcoming some of the limitations identified in the literature, I will now briefly dwell on the levels of analysis that are necessary to better understand face in interaction.

Arundale (2006) has recently proposed an understanding of face to account for both its relational and interactional manifestations. While it would be fair to say that the relational aspect of face has been sufficiently theorised and accounted for (i.e. orientation towards interdependence/association/positive politeness or independence/dissociation/negative politeness), the interactional aspect has been, relatively speaking, somewhat under-examined. This is partly the result of the methodological tools that have been deployed to examine facework and politeness phenomena in general. Most of the analyses that have been carried out, including some of my earlier work, have employed coding schemes that are mainly based on speech act theory.[3] Arundale's (2006) proposal could thus be said to be partly methodological in that it calls for a microanalysis of the unfolding of politeness in interaction and, therefore, of how face emerges in interaction rather than simply being an individually rooted construct.

While the inclusion of units of analysis from neighbouring disciplines such as ethnomethodological conversation analysis within a socio-pragmatic framework is a view I concur with and a methodological stance I have taken in recent work (Marquez Reiter, 2005, 2006), it could be argued that due to differing ontologies (i.e. constructivism versus critical realism) and claims about the results obtained (i.e. recurrent versus generalisable patterns), some scholars, may find the integration of approaches incompatible (Márquez Reiter, 2006: 13-4). Given the current conflicting reports of research into politeness and face, I will not advocate the general superiority of any theoretical and/or methodological perspective over another. Rather, I see theoretical and methodological value in embracing an integrative approach as both socio-pragmatics and conversation analysis make potentially unique contributions to an overall understanding of face in interaction.

3.3. Methods and background

For this study I gathered several kinds of data over a one-month period in 2006. The main source of data for this study is a recorded call between an institutional representative, the caller, and a potential client, in this case the called. The call forms part of a 200-hour service call database from a call centre. Recorded informal interviews with institutional representatives from the call centre,[4] including a post-performance interview with the agent who participated in the call, and field notes from (non)participant observation will also form part of the analysis. The analysis also draws upon the call centre's training manual for outbound calls, that is, calls made by agents to (potential) clients.

The call centre where the data comes from is the Latin American operation of a multinational company. It has more than 200 agents all of whom are native speakers of Spanish. The agents have completed secondary school and more than a third of them have university degrees or similar.[5] The vast majority of the clients are also native speakers of Spanish and come from a variety of Latin American countries and belong to the (upper) middle-class in their respective countries.

Call centre agents are required to attend a two-week training course before they start their work in the call centre. During the training period, they are given information about the company's product and operations across the world and, in particular, about the Latin American operation. They are also given training in managing calls. Specifically, they are told to follow a script for placing outbound calls:

(1)   In-house rules for the opening
   a)   Greet the (potential) client and provide organisational identification and a brief description of the company business
         Buen día, mi nombre es (Nombre y Apellido), y le estoy llamando de X Latinoamérica.
         'Good morning, my name is (first name and surname) and I am calling you[U] from X Latin America, your holiday exchange company'
   b)   Explain the reason for the call
         Le estoy llamando porque tenemos una promoción especialmente para usted...
         'I am calling you[U] because we have a promotion especially for you[U]'

The recommended opening sequences are similar to those observed in English institutional calls and are in line with the company's global image, though adapted to the Latin American market. This is evidenced by the prescribed precedence of non-essential relational elements (greetings, self-identification) over transactionally essential ones (organisational identification) and a deferential attitude (the inclusion of titles, first names and surnames) aimed at addressing a general Latin American interpersonal orientation (Daskal Albert, 1996) where the expression of *simpatía*[6] and respect are emphasised. This form of respect does not so much address considerations of space but the given social power differences between the participants as reflected by expressions of deference (i.e. title + first name + surname).

Both agents and clients are aware of the fact that their calls may be monitored for quality control procedures. Call centre employees were told that a researcher would be collecting data *in situ* for the purposes of examining communication in Spanish and permission was obtained from the company to use the data.

3.4. Analysis

The call selected for this study is illustrative of the lack of stylistic formality preliminarily observed in a vast number of the company calls with Bonaerense clients, as reflected by the presence of humorous comments and its generally non-formulaic nature. This 'informality' coincides with that reported in studies of intra and cross-cultural non-mediated service encounters in River Plate Spanish (Márquez Reiter and Placencia, 2004; Márquez Reiter and Stewart, in press/2006 for Montevidean Spanish v. Ecuadorian Spanish (Quito) and Montevidean Spanish v. English (Edinburgh) and Sánchez Lanza, 2003 for Argentinean Spanish (Rosario)) and, with some of the comments made by agents during interviews:

(2)   From an interview with a Montevidean male agent, 35 years old

> *Con los porteños hay que ir con pie de plomo porque te toman el pelo de lo lindo y en un minuto de descuido te reputean por nada para mostrarte que ellos son más porque tiene plata y vos no, y todo para controlar la conversación y conseguir lo que quieren, como por ejemplo semanas de arriba, conocen el sistema como la palma de su mano y siempre tratan de garronear algo.*

> 'With the 'porteños' one has to tread carefully because they really pull your leg and in a moment of carelessness they really insult you for nothing to show you that they are more than you because they have money and you don't, and it's all aimed at controlling the conversation and getting what they want, like for example free weeks, they know the system like the palms of their hands and always try to get freebies.'

(3)   From an interview with a Montevidean female agent, 25 years old

> *Yo estoy acostumbrada a lidiar con ellos y pese a que se toman todo*
> *para la joda y muchas veces te mal tratan, hablándote de 'pendeja de*
> *mierda lo que vos ganás en un mes yo lo saco por día, no me hinchés las*
> *pelotas', los ignoro porque son buenos compradores y así hablan ellos.*
> *Yo igual les revendo. Seguramente porque soy judía: lo que se hereda*
> *no se roba, che! Simplemente hay que saber cómo llevarlos.*

> 'I'm used to dealing with them and although they don't take anything
> seriously and often treat you badly, calling you "fucking bitch what you
> earn monthly is what I make in a day, don't break my balls", I ignore
> them because they're good customers and that's how they speak. I still
> get them to buy a lot. Surely because I'm Jewish: hey, it seems to run in
> the family. You simply have to know how to deal with them.'

It is interesting to note from the above extracts that the alleged curt
behaviour is attributed to the clients only and hence suspiciously one-
sided. As we will see, the telemarketing agent deviates from the prescribed in-house rules showing a certain orientation toward informality
and considerable tenacity in trying to achieve a sale despite the client's
overt lack of interest. Also of interest are the meta comments made by
the agents with respect to the profile of Bonaerense clients, particularly
the strategies deployed by the clients in order to obtain further benefits
and/or get rid of the agent, and those employed by the latter to pursue
their conversational goal (tread carefully, ignore curt behaviour).
Bonaerense clients are thus depicted as powerful consumers by virtue
of their spending power, their institutional acculturation, their demand-
ing nature and pro-activeness in trying to control the conversational
outcomes.

   In what follows, I present an analysis of how face is manifested in
the conversation with particular attention to the opening, where concerns for face are mostly observed. The analysis takes account of the
conversational sequences that precede and follow the expression of
face in order to give an overall picture of the place within the conversation where considerations of face are manifested.

   Openings are one of the many points at which people may initiate
their social interactions, thus constituting a prime opportunity for participants to (re-)establish their relationships for that occasion (Schegloff,
1986). During openings, participants' identification and how they relate
to one another other through talk become primary issues.[7] Structurally,
the task of establishing who the participants are at the initial stages of
the opening, following the summons-answer sequence and preceding
an explanation of the reason for the call, is procedurally essential for

the type of telephone conversation – an institutional call where the participants do not know each other – to continue (Baker, Emmison and Firth, 2001; Cheepen, 2000; Tracy and Anderson, 1999; Zimmerman, 1992). Equally important are the verbal elements chosen to formulate these sequences as they also help to (re)establish who the participants are in respect to one another as evidenced by the roles they assume, how they frame the interaction and the stylistic preference expressed (e.g. degree of (in) formality (i.e. T/V–U distinction), deference, etc.). It is not surprising, therefore, that face concerns are mainly verbalised at this stage of the conversation.

The opening of this call may sound rather different to that experienced by consumers who live in an English-speaking culture in that transactional details are not provided until line 9, when they are explicitly requested by the call-taker. As observed in several other outbound calls and as emerged in some of the interviews, the agent's reluctance to provide essential transactional information at the initial stages of the call appears to underlie her need to ensure that she is talking to the right person. The agent's interactional behaviour is primarily self-oriented as it focuses on her conversational needs, backgrounding those of the call-taker and deviating from expected norms, both institutionally (see section 3) and interactionally (delay in providing organisational identification and the reason for the call). This, together with the lack of verbal elements showing consideration for the call's possible inconvenience, makes the opening reminiscent of that of an everyday call where identification may be established through (other) recognition (Márquez Reiter, 2006) (NB. the names below are pseudonyms).

(4) The call

T = telemarketing agent
C = called- the account holder
C2 = call-taker- the wife of the account holder

1	C2:	*Hola↑*
		'hello'
2	T:	*Hola [con el señor↓]*
		'hello with Mr'
3	C2:	*[Ho:lá↑]*
		'hello'
4	T:	*Ho:la↓ con el señor Roberto Pérez↓*
		'hello with Mr Roberto Pérez'
5	C2:	*Sí::↑ (.) sí::↑*
		'Yes Yes'

6	T:	*Holá↓ si me escucha bie:n↑*
		'hello yes can you[U] hear me well'
7	C2:	*Sí sí sí↓ (.) pero [él está ocupado↓] de dónde está habla:ndo↑* =
		'Yes yes yes but he is busy where are you[U] calling from'
8	T:	*[Podría hablar-↑]*
		'Could I speak to'
9	T:	*=De X Latinoamérica Leticia Matos le habla:↓*
		'From X Latin America Leticia Matos speaking'
10	C2:	*A:h↑ sí:↓ qué pasa querida↑*
		'Um yes what's up love'
11	T:	*E:::h [m:: usted se encar-]*
		'Um are you[U] in char-'
12	C2:	*[Holá↓]=*
		'hello'
13	T:	*=Sí↑ hola↓ usted se encarga de::::: de resolver todo lo que tiene que ver con la cuenta de X Latinoamérica↑*
		'yes hello are you in charge of resolving everything to do with the account with X Latin America'
14		(0.2)
15	C2:	*E::h e:h mi esposo↑ es↓*
		'Um it's my husband is'
16	T:	*Bie:n↓* =
		'OK'
17	C2:	*=Querés hablar con él directame:nte↑*
		'Do you[V] want to speak to him directly'
18	T:	*Bue:no↓ mejo:r↑*
		'OK better'
19	C2:	*Buém? =vení Robér↓ ((por fuera del micrófono))*
		'OK Roberto come here' ((not into the receiver))

As can be seen in the opening, the call starts with an exchange of hellos followed by a switchboard request to speak to the account holder. Although *Hola* ('hello') is one of the possible ways in which participants may informally greet each other at the onset of a call, it is conditionally relevant to its first pair part, in this case to the answer to the summons, realised in this variety of Spanish by *Hola* rather than *Diga* ('tell me') or *Bueno* ('well'), to mention a few. In uttering *Hola* ('Hello') with rising intonation at the beginning of the call, both participants try to establish if/that the channel of communication is open (see overlap at lines 2 and 3). This is followed by a switchboard request, *con el señor Roberto Pérez* ('can you put me through to Mr Roberto Pérez') at the first available opportunity, when the agent realises that the call-taker cannot be the client by virtue of her gender. Although the elliptical request also deviates from the interactional behaviour prescribed to agents, it is faithful to the standard level of deference that agents should convey, namely it comprises title, first name and surname.

The call-taker confirms at line 5 that the caller has reached the right number and implicitly requests that the agent identify herself, as illustrated by the micropause and subsequent repetition of the lengthened affirmative particle, hence implying that something else is expected from the caller. The agent, however, does not take this up until the call-taker explicitly requests so at line 7. The call-taker's request is preceded by a disarmer should the target of the call not wish to take it (*pero él está ocupado de dónde está habla:ndo* 'but he is busy where are you[U] calling from'). It thus functions as a strategy to protect the call-taker's own face and her husband's possible need for privacy (i.e. the imposition of a receiving a marketing call at home rather than at the client's office[8]), in the event that she may deem the call to be unsuited or inopportune and wants to end it quickly rather than pass it to her husband. The agent responds at line 9 with a shorter version of the prescribed organisational identification as shown by the absence of a brief description of the company's business. This is followed by a direct request for the agent to give the reason for the call. The directness of the call-taker's request shows what she understands to be her rights, the caller's institutional obligations, and assumed expectations of how a call of the kind should proceed. The request is, however, mitigated by the presence of an explanation (see disarmer at line 7), thus showing concern for the agent's personal need for independence, that is, her negative face, in what might otherwise be interpreted as a command. Consideration for the agent's personal face is further reinforced by the call-taker's inclusion of the endearment term *querida* ('love') which serves to soften the direct request for the agent to specify the reason for the call and is oriented towards interdependence.

Given that it had been ascertained that the call-taker is probably the wife of the client (see lines 4-7) rather than a domestic employee or a dependent, by virtue of her voice,[9] and confirmed by the call-taker's request for the reason of the call at line 10, rather than provide the reason for the call, the caller asks a filler question to check the call-taker's authority over the account. The question is initiated at line 11, prefaced by the lengthened hesitation marker *E:::h* ('Um') and completed at line 13. It is a dispreferred indirect switchboard request that underlies the agent's cultural assumptions of the role that (upper) middle-class Bonaerense wives have in the family. Essentially, (upper) middle-class Bonaerense wives are believed to have a casting vote over the choice and type of family holidays and, sometimes are also responsible for the household finances, thus in some cases, they could be the right person to talk to.[10] As the request is non-conventionally formulated, it tactfully addresses the possibility that call-taker might be the right person to talk to after all. Consideration for the call-taker's negative face is further expressed at line 18 where the agent accepts the offer to speak to the call-taker's husband with *mejor* ('better') preceded by the discourse marker *bueno* ('OK') in initial position. The presence of *bueno* ('OK') before *mejor* ('better') signals the agent's distancing from the position previously expressed (Carranza, 1997) at line 13, where she checked the call-taker's authority over the account. In uttering *bueno mejor* ('OK better') she also shows concern for the call-taker's positive face that is, her need for approval as competent human being who is not only capable of dealing with the account but also likely to decide the holiday fortunes of the family. The choice of *mejor* (better) rather than an explicit form such as 'yes' further reinforces her distancing from her contribution at line 13 in that it implies that it would not be out of the question to discuss the matter with her, but that it would be preferable to do so with the account holder himself given that call-taker herself had offered to pass the call to her husband at line 17.

As shown below, the conversation with the account holder starts with an exchange of hellos at lines 21 and 22 followed by an elliptical request for identification by the agent. The request for identification, in line with her preceding contributions, deviates from that prescribed by the company in terms of its sequential occurrence (i.e. after a neutral/formal greeting and before organisational identification) and the lesser degree of deference (i.e. omission of the client's surname). The client confirms his identity at line 24 with *sí* ('Yes') with descending intonation and the agent proceeds to greet him and to provide self and organisational identification. The greeting offered, *cómo le va* 'how are you[U]?' is the first pair part of a 'how are you' exchange. Although an exchange of 'how are you' is not part of the house rules, it was present in the vast majority of the calls observed. Its occurrence in this call precedes the proffering of identification and thus indicates its routine politeness function in that a response is not structurally essential for the type of call to continue. The observed presence of 'how are you' elements in this and other calls within the database represents a case of synthetic personalisation (Fairclough, 1989, 1993) by which the agent attempts to appear *simpática* (Márquez Reiter, 2005, 2006; Márquez Reiter, Rainey and Fulcher, 2005), and as a result, convey a likeable image of herself and thus enhance her chances of keeping the client on the line for longer while minimising the imposition of an unsolicited call.

Once recognition is effected, the agent reiterates the 'how are you', albeit in a slightly more formal way as evidenced by the inclusion of *usted*,[11] at line 31. It is at this point that the client responds to the greeting. The response is dispreferred in accordance with his preceding contributions. Rather than respond to the 'how are you' with an expected second pair part, that is, a routine politeness formula, the client responds ironically with *Y hasta ahora bien* ('and until now well') at line 32. The client's response is a metapragmatic act. According to Thomas (1985) through these acts 'dominant participants make explicit reference to the intended pragmatic force of their own or their subordinate's utterances' (p.767). In the case of this call, the client, who is the dominant party in as much as it is up to him to renew his membership or not, markedly conveys that he is aware of the possible reason for the call and that he does not welcome it. In doing so, he attempts to effectively remove any possibility of negotiating the interactional outcome (Thomas, 1985). This is immediately responded to by the agent, as observed by the latching of lines 32-33, with a routine formula followed by contained laughter. The laughter, unlike the routine verbal element of the turn, is also metapragmatic in that it reflects the agent's interpretation of the client's second pair part as unforeseeable according to what routine dictates in these cases (Caffi, 1998).

The client reacts to the agent's laughter with yet another metapragmatic act at line 34. Due to the pragmatic ambivalence of *Qué le pasa?* ('What's up with you[U]?'), the client communicates a mocking and a dissociative attitude to the interaction while implicitly requesting that the agent specify the reason for the call. The client's metapragmatic comments foreground the caller's personal rather than her professional face, and produce, if only momentarily, a change in the style and register of the conversation. After a brief moment of realignment, as evidenced by the lengthened hesitations markers initialling the reason for the call (*E:::h m::* 'Um m') at line 35, the agent starts to explain the reason for the call and the 'negotiation of the business exchange' (Bailey, 1997) commences.

In line with her previous conversational contributions, the agent does not provide the full reason for the call until much later in the call, at line 66 (not reproduced here due to space constraints). Nonetheless, the reason for the call is perfectly clear to the client as evidenced by some of his metapragmatic contributions that reflect both institutional acculturation and a desire not to have the membership renewed (see line 32). The client explicitly expresses his disinterest in the call by means of a grounder (*está en venta* 'it's for sale' line 39), an explanation intended to leave no doubt as to his conversational intentions and thus help to politely bring the conversation to a close. The grounder is followed by an offer to sell the property to the agent instead, as illustrated at line 39. The offer functions as metapragmatic act by which the client reverts the conversational roles, assuming that of seller and putting the agent in the ironic position of prospective client, thus showing his lack of seriousness and undermining the agent's professional face. The agent responds at line 40 by sharing the joke in her capacity as a fellow human being who is unable to afford such luxuries. This shared metapragmatic awareness reflects similarities in the underlying 'cultural presuppositions of the participants as well as the different kinds of the unsaid' (Caffi, 1998:585).

3.5. Discussion

The call examined is illustrative of the lack of formality and personalisation exhibited in other calls between Montevidean agents and Bonaerense clients within the database and is in line with the level of relative informality reported in related studies of service encounters. Although the same tasks as those identified in English institutional calls are achieved (Márquez Reiter, 2006), they occur in different places in the conversations analysed, for example, the proffering of organisational identification. Further, the omission of full address terms (i.e. title + first name + surname), the occurrence of humorous metapragmatic acts, and the length of the call itself (over 140 turns) make this conversation reminiscent of an everyday call between friends. The length of the call and the delay in providing expected transactional information, reflect a different understanding of time. Time seems to have a lower value than that generally assigned to in the West; it seems to be low cost, a free good (Goffman, 1967). Therefore, a request for one's time may be difficult to refuse without incurring offence and being impolite. Unlike cultural contexts, where time and politeness appear to be in conflict in the sense that time concerns often override politeness ones, time is readily available in this call and in other calls within the database. Thus, an unsolicited and protracted service call may not be seen as an imposition.

The conversational features observed in this call show an orientation toward what Fitch (1991) terms connectedness in the context of her ethnographic work in Colombia, although she suggests that this orientation may also be present in other Latin American cultures. Fitch (1991) explains that Colombians pay significant attention to the development of relationships with service providers, particularly with those with whom they deal regularly as service relationships where a set of bonds (*vínculos*) are created are preferred over service encounters. A similar perspective is offered by Daskal Albert (1996) who in line with the work of other scholars focusing on Latin America (Díaz-Guerrero, 1967) posits a general 'interpersonal orientation' as an emic characteristic of Latin Americans. The components of this interpersonal orientation comprise the expression of *simpatía* and respect, amongst others.

Interpersonal connectedness is illustrated in the call analysed above by the humorous comments made, the length of the call and the fact that it does not seem to be seen as imposing despite the social distance between the participants. The client devotes time and energy in forming a connection in order to get rid of her. The expression of respect, however, is mainly shown by the agent in the inclusion of titles marking the social power asymmetry between the participants and in the agent's formulation of her contributions, which reflect an orientation to negative politeness (e.g. indirectness) despite her low deferential attitude (i.e. omission of full address terms).

Face concerns were found underlying the expression of politeness and in response to marked conversational behaviour. Considerations of face, in particular of negative face, were observed in a rather ritualistic conversational sequence – the opening – in that it was generally performed according to 'appropriate patterned behavior' (Rothenbuhler, 1998: 27). In the case of a transactional call of the kind examined here, routine politeness is not only expected by the company but is socioculturally essential. Face was also manifested during the unfolding of metapragmatic acts. They were initiated by the client to leave the agent in no doubt as to his conversational intentions. They occurred in the initial phases of the call, in the 'how are you' exchange and in the response to the reason for the call. These two sequences were humorously realised reflecting the relative connectedness expressed by the interlocutors in a primarily task-based conversation. The fact that they were produced in a relatively routine sequence adds comical effect in that they are not expected behaviour.

These metapragmatic acts, however, were produced to undermine the legitimacy of the call and, by default, diminish the caller's professional face. As a result of which the agent re-aligns herself and tries to re-establish her conversational identity in an attempt to proceed to the reason for the call, shift conversational direction and attain her conversational goal.

Face therefore was manifested as part of the conversational politeness norms for the occasion and grew out of the ongoing interaction upon marked interactional behaviour. It was contextually given or motivated as shown by the negative politeness orientations of some of the routine phrases employed and dynamically constructed when one of the participants deemed that some of his or her utterances might be potentially threatening to the negative face of the other. Face also emerged as the participants tried to re-establish their conversational identities in the light of a conversational shift.

3.6. Conclusion

The aim of this paper has been to examine how face and facework are manifested in an intercultural service call. To this end, the opening sequence of a conversation between a Montevidean telemarketing agent and an Argentinean client was chosen. The manifestations of face observed here are said to apply to this call only. Other calls within the database may or may not present similar manifestations but this remains to be seen. What the analysis has shown is that considerations of face and facework emerged as contingent upon the interaction and were called upon by contextual factors. In both cases face was dynamically co-constructed.

Owing to the nature of the interaction examined, namely a mediated service encounter, possible manifestations of face as signalled by extralinguistic elements that would provide further insight could not be considered. Nevertheless, the analysis presented in this chapter is novel. It focuses on intercultural communication in Spanishes where there are no apparent breakdowns of communication as far as face and facework considerations are concerned. It also examines communication in a contemporary institutional context that reflects modern capitalist societal service practices. Furthermore, it does so by means of a multi-angled data collection procedure in order to minimise the possible sources of bias of each data collection method; namely a recorded service call, recorded informal interviews with telemarketing agents from the call centre (including a post-performance interview with the agent involved in the call analysed) and field notes from (non)participant observation. Added to this, the analytical framework employed is integrative. It offers both a context external (i.e. cultural factors which influence the conversational behaviour of the participants towards pursuing one set of facework strategies more than another) and context internal (i.e. how face unfolds in the call as the participants negotiate their involvement) explanation of how face is interactionally achieved through an intercultural telephone conversation in a business context. It is thus hoped that it will provide us with a better understanding of face in intercultural encounters and advance our understanding of its interactional aspects.

Grammatical gloss

T/V indicates the use of the familiar second person singular *tú* and/ or *vos*

U indicates the use of the unfamiliar second person singular *usted*

Endnotes

1. River Plate Spanish is the Spanish variety mainly spoken in the areas in and around the River Plate basin, in Argentina and Uruguay. It is mainly spoken in the cities of Buenos Aires, Montevideo and Rosario. Linguistic differences are found at the morphological, lexical, phonological and pragmatic level. Morphologically speaking, although both Bonaerenses and Montevideans use *voseo* (the usage of the pronoun for the second person singular informal corresponding to *tú* in Peninsular Spanish), the latter also use *tuteo* (*tú*), albeit generally employing the verb conjugation which corresponds to *voseo*. Lexically, there are a few marked preferences for certain lexical items over others (e.g. *pibe*- Buenos Aires v. *gurí* ('bloke') in Montevideo, etc.). Phonologically, both varieties are characterised by a descending melodic curve at the end of utterances, reminiscent of the undisputed Italian influence in the region. As a native speaker of one of these varieties and as a linguist, I would claim that one of the features that can help us distinguish a Montevidean speaker from a Bonaerense is precisely this melodic curve. Impressionistically speaking, Bonaerenses exhibit a sharper contour. Pragmatically, Montevideans are recognised by their River Plate counterparts by the uttering of the discourse marker *tá* ('OK') and by lay stereotypical comments which describe them as *amables* ('polite') in relation to Bonaerenses.

2. The term friction seems to have been interpreted according to Brown and Levinson's generally 'paranoid' view of social interaction (Kasper, 1990), in particular as evidenced by the operalisation of their face-saving strategies. However, friction may arise not only when the need for independence or dissociation is threatened but also when the need for interdependence or association is not acknowledged in a given interaction where it is socially expected (i.e. compliment).

3. This is not a criticism of earlier politeness research which sought, amongst other things, to identify the pragmalinguistic conventions behind the realisation of speech acts in several languages based on research instruments aimed at collecting large enough instances of the speech acts under examination.
4. Informal interviews with institutional representatives (i.e. telemarketing agents) were conducted during their breaks and in the call centre's van that collects/takes employees to/from their homes. Ten hours of recorded informal interviews were collected.
5. This information was gathered from the Human Resource Department.
6. A permanent and desirable quality by which an individual is regarded as likeable and even co-operative (Triandis, *et al.* 1984).
7. Schegloff (1986) describes this process as a 'gatekeeping job'.
8. The client's records indicate his preference to be contacted at his office rather than home number.
9. This information was gathered from the telemarketing agent in an interview conducted after the call had taken place. In the agent's experience, the domestic employees of their Bonaerense clients do not tend to come from Buenos Aires, and when they do they tend to come from working-class neighbourhoods as reflected by a sharper melodic curve, addition of 's' in the second person singular indicative and a slightly more formal attitude (i.e. use of *usted* rather than *vos*).
10. This information was gathered from interviews with agents and observations of other calls to and from Bonaerense clients.
11. With Spanish being a pro-drop language, the inclusion of *usted* is syntactically unnecessary. Unlike other varieties of Spanish (e.g. Caribbean varieties), in River Plate Spanish redundant subject pronouns are uncommon.

References

Arundale, R. B. (2006) Face as relational and interactional: A communication framework for research on face, facework, and politeness. *Journal of Politeness Research* 2: 193–216.

Aston, G. (ed.) (1988) *Negotiating Service: Studies in the Discourse of Bookshop Encounters*. Bologna: Cooperativa Libraria Universitaria Editrice.

Bailey, B. (1997) Communication of respect in interethnic service encounters. *Language in Society* 26: 327–356.

Baker, C., Emmison, M. and Firth, A. (2001) Discovering order in opening sequences: Calls to a software helpline. In A. McHoul and M. Rapley (eds.) *How to Analyse Talk in Institutional Settings: A Casebook of Methods* 41–56. London: Continuum.

Bargiela-Chiappini, F. (2003) Face and impoliteness: new (insights) for (old) concepts. *Journal of Pragmatics* 35: 1453–1469.

Bargiela-Chiappini, F. and S. Harris (1997) *Managing Language. The Discourse of Corporate Meetings.* Amsterdam: John Benjamins.

Bravo, D. (1999) '¿Imagen 'positiva' vs imagen 'negativa'?: Pragmática sociocultural y componentes de *face'. Oralia* 2: 155–184.

Brown, P. and Levinson, S. (1987) *Politeness: Some Universals in Language Use.* Cambridge: Cambridge University Press.

Boutet, J.(ed.) (2005) *Paroles au Travail.* Paris: L'Harmattan.

Caffi, C. (1998) Metapragmatics. In J. Mey and R. Asher (eds.) *Concise Encyclopeadia of Pragmatics* 581–586. Oxford: Elsevier.

Carranza, I. (1997) *Conversación y Deixis de Discurso.* Córdoba, Argentina: Universidad Nacional de Córdoba.

Cheepen, C. (2000) Small talk in service dialogues: the conversational aspects of transactional telephone talk. In J. Coupland (ed.) *Small Talk* 288–311. Essex: Pearson.

Cheng, W. (2003) *Intercultural Conversation.* Amsterdam: John Benjamins.

Codó Olsina, E. (2002) 'Managing understanding in intercultural talk: An empirical approach to miscommunication.' *ATLANTIS* 24: 1–21.

Culpeper, J. (1996) Towards an anatomy of impoliteness. *Journal of Pragmatics* 25: 349–367.

Culpeper, J. (2005) Impoliteness and entertainment in the television quiz show: *The Weakest Link. Journal of Politeness Research* 1: 35–72.

Daskal Albert, R. (1996) A Framework and model for understanding Latin American and Latino/Hispanic Cultural Patterns. In D. Landis and R. Bhagat (eds.) *Handbook of Intercultural Training* (2nd edition) 327–348. Thousand Oaks, CA: Sage.

Díaz-Guerrero, R. (1967) *Psychology of the Mexican: Culture and Personality.* Austin, TX: University of Texas Press.

Drew, P. and J. Heritage (1992) *Talk at Work: Interaction in Institutional Settings.* Cambridge: Cambridge University Press.

Fairclough, N. (1989) *Language and Power.* London: Longman.

Fairclough, N. (1993) Critical discourse analysis and the marketization of public discourse: The universities. *Discourse and Society* 4: 133–168.

Fitch, C. (1991) A Ritual for attempting leave-taking in Colombia. *Research on Language and Social Interaction* 24: 209–224.

Fukushima, S. (2000) *Requests and Culture. Politeness in British English and Japanese.* Bern: Peter Lang.

Goffman, E. (1967) *Interaction Ritual.* Harmondsworth: Penguin.

Gu, Y. (1990) Politeness in modern Chinese. *Journal of Pragmatics* 14: 237–257.

Gudykunst, W. (1998) *Bridging Difference: Effective Intergroup Communication.* Thousand Oaks, CA: Sage.

Gudykunst, W. and Ting-Toomey, S. (1988) *Culture and Interpersonal Communication.* Newbury Park, CA: Sage.

Gumperz, J. (1982) *Discourse Strategies.* Cambridge: Cambridge University Press.

Hernández Flores, N. (1999) Politeness ideology in Spanish colloquial conversations: The case of advice. *Pragmatics* 9: 37–49.

Holmes, J. and Stubbe, M. (2003) *Power and Politeness in the Workplace. A Sociolinguistic Analysis of Talk at Work.* London: Longman.

Holtgraves, T. (2002) *Language as Social Action: Social Psychology and Language Use.* Mahwah, NJ: Lawrence Erlbaum.

Ide, S. (1989) Formal forms and discernment: two neglected aspects of universals of linguistic politeness. *Multilingua* 12: 7–11.

Kasper, G. (1990) Linguistic politeness: Current research issues. *Journal of Pragmatics* 14: 193–218.

Kong, K. (1998) Politeness of service encounters in Hong Kong. *Pragmatics* 18: 555–575.

Kuiper, K. and Tan Gek Lin, D. (1989) Cultural congruence and conflict in the acquisition of formulae in a second language. In O. García and R. Otheguy (eds.) *English across Cultures* 281–304. Berlin: Mouton de Gruyter.

Lipski, J. (1994) *Latin American Spanish.* London: Longman.

Mao, L. (1994) Beyond politeness theory: 'face' revisited and renewed. *Journal of Pragmatics* 21: 451–486.

Márquez Reiter, R. (2000) *Linguistic Politeness in Britain and Uruguay. A contrastive study of requests and apologies.* Amsterdam: John Benjamins.

Márquez Reiter, R. (2005) Complaint calls to a caregiver service company: the case of desahogo. *Intercultural Pragmatics* 2: 481–513.

Márquez Reiter, R. (2006) Interactional closeness in service calls to Montevidean carer service company. *Research on Language and Social Interaction* 39: 7–39.

Márquez Reiter, R. and Placencia, M. E. (2004) Displaying closeness and respectful distance in Montevidean and Quiteño service encounters. In R. Márquez Reiter and M. E. Placencia (eds.) *Current Trends in the Pragmatics of Spanish* 121–155. Amsterdam: John Benjamins.

Márquez Reiter, R. and Placencia, M. E. (2005) *Spanish Pragmatics.* Basingstoke: Palgrave MacMillan.

Márquez Reiter, R., Rainey, I. and Fulcher, G. (2005) A comparative study of certainty and conventional indirectness: Evidence from British English and Peninsular Spanish. *Applied Linguistics* 26:1–31.

Márquez Reiter, R. and M. Stewart (in press) Interactions en site commercial à Montevideo (Uruguay) et à Edimbourg (Royaume Uni): «engagement» (*involvement*) et «considérationenvers les autres » (*considerateness*). In C. Kerbrat-Orecchioni and V. Traverso (éds.) *Les Interactions en Site Commercial: Invariants et Variations.* Paris: Editions du CNRS.

Matsumoto, Y. (1988) Reexamination of the universality of face: Politeness phenomena in Japanese. *Journal of Pragmatics* 12: 403–426.

McLaren, M. (1998) *Interpeting Cultural Differences: The Challenge of Intercultural Communication.* Deheram: Peter Francis.

Müller, A. (2003) Some preliminaries for analysing genres in organizational talk. In F. Ramallo (ed.) *Papers from the Second International Conference on Discourse, Communication and Enterprise.* Munich: Lincom Europe.

Nyowe, O. (1989) Linguistic politeness in Igbo. *Multilingua* 8: 259–275.

Orlando, V. (2006) Mecanismos conversacionales en el espanol del Uruguay. Universidad de la Republica: Fondo Clemente Estable.

O'Driscoll, J. (1996) About face: A defence and elaboration of universal dualism. *Journal of Pragmatics* 25: 1–32.

Pène, S., Borzeix, A. and Fraenkel, B. (eds.) (2001) *Le Langage Dans les Organisations. Une Nouvelle Donne.* Paris: L'Harmattan.

Roca, A. and Jensen, J. (eds.) (1996) *Spanish in Contact. Issues in Bilingualism.* Somerville: Cascadilla.

Rothenbuhler, E. (1998) *Ritual Communication: From Everyday Conversation to Mediated Ceremony.* Thousand Oaks, CA: Sage.

Sánchez Lanza, C. (2003) El discurso de la cortesía en puestos de atención al público en la Argentina (instituciones de salud pública y bienestar social). In D. Bravo (ed.) *Actas del Primer Coloquio del Programa EDICE. La perspectiva no etnocentrista de la cortesía: Identidad sociocultural de las comunidades hispanohablantes.* Stockholm: Stockholm University (CD Rom).

Schegloff, E. (1986) The routine as achievement *Human Studies* 9: 111–151.

Schrader-Kniffi, M. (2004) Speaking Spanish with Zapotec meaning. Requests and promises in intercultural communication in Oaxaca, Mexico. In R. Márquez Reiter and M. E. Placencia (eds.) *Current Trends in the Pragmatics of Spanish* 157–174. Amsterdam: John Benjamins.

Shimanoff, S. (1994) Gender perspectives on facework: Simplistic stereotypes vs. complex realities. In S.Ting-Toomey (ed.) *The Challenge of Facework. Cross–Cultural and Interpersonal Issues* 159–208. Albany, NY: State University of New York Press.

Spencer-Oatey, H. (ed) (2000) *Culturally Speaking.* London: Continuum.

Spencer-Oatey, H. (2005) (Im)politeness, face and perceptions of rapport: unpackaging their bases and interrelationships. *Journal of Politeness Research* 1: 95–120.

Strecker, I. (1993) Cultural variations in the notion of face. *Multilingua* 12: 119–141.

Thomas, J. (1985) The language of power. *Journal of Pragmatics* 9: 765–783.

Tracy, K. and Anderson, D. (1999) Relational positioning strategies in police calls: A dilemma. *Discourse Studies* 1: 201–225.

Triandis, H. (ed.) (1980) *Handbook of Cross-Cultural Psychology.* Boston, MA: Allyn and Bacon.

Triandis, H., Marín, G., Lisansky, J. and Betancourt, H. (1984) *Simpatía* as a cultural script of Hispanics. *Journal of Personality and Social Psychology* 47: 1363–1375.

Zimmerman, D. (1992) Achieving context: Openings in emergency calls. In G. Watson and R. Seiler (eds.) *Text in context: Contributions to Ethnomethodology* 35–51. Newbury Park, CA: Sage.

Zimmerman, K. and de Granda, G. (eds.) (2004) I. Sección temática: El español con otras lenguas. *Revista Internacional de Lingüística Iberoamericana* 2: 9–145.

4
Analysing Japanese 'face-in-interaction': insights from intercultural business meetings

Michael Haugh and Yasuhisa Watanabe

4.1. Introduction

Face has been the subject of a vast amount of research since the publication of Goffman's (1967) seminal work on facework in social interaction. Yet while facework research has been expanding rapidly over the past thirty years it has also been dogged by accusations of an inherent analytical bias towards the claims or wants of individual agents. Brown and Levinson's (1987: 62) conceptualisation of face as encompassing, in part, the desire that one's actions be unimpeded by others (negative face), for example, has been criticised as being rooted in an individualistic or monadic self-concept that is incongruous with social interactions in 'non-Western' societies (Koutlaki, 2002; Lim, 2004; Mao, 1994; Matsumoto, 1988; Nwoye, 1992; Strecker, 1993; Ukosakul, 2003). While generally regarded as somewhat less reified within the individual than Brown and Levinson's notion, Goffman's (1967: 5) conceptualisation of face as 'the positive social value a person effectively claims for himself by the line others assume he has taken during a particular contact' has also been criticised as being rooted in a view of interactants as independent, monadic actors (Arundale, 2006: 197-200; this volume, Chapter 2; Bargiela-Chiappini, 2003: 1463). This has led to a call for a closer examination of interactional aspects of face, namely, how face is discursively co-constituted through interaction (Arundale, 2006: 208-210). This, in turn, entails a closer analysis of how face emerges through interaction as a conjoint understanding of participants.

In this chapter, we undertake an analysis of how face arises in the interactional flow of an intercultural business meeting involving

Japanese and non-Japanese members of a Japanese firm based in Australia. While this meeting involved a mixture of English and Japanese, we argue that the overall tenor of the interaction is firmly oriented towards Japanese norms of interaction, which are both constitutive of, and enacted through, interaction in the course of this meeting. It is thus suggested that through this analysis we can gain insight into how face in (Modern Standard) Japanese is interactionally achieved, in the conversation analytic sense of the 'conjoint, non-summative outcome' of two or more persons (Arundale, 2006: 196). However, it is also acknowledged that projectings or interpretings of face in interaction are not always interactionally achieved. The term 'face-in-interaction' is thus proposed to encompass projectings and interpretings, as well as interactional achievings, of face through interaction. The chapter begins with an overview of our understanding of face building upon previous work, before briefly discussing the methodological background of this study. An analysis of four key incidents involving face from our data is then undertaken, before drawing together some implications of this study for theories of face and facework.

4.2. Face in Japanese

Face has been analysed thus far as either a first-order concept that we can talk about, namely a sense of honour or prestige, or variations thereupon, or less commonly, as something that arises through social interaction as an interactional achievement. In relation to Japanese, 'first order face' has received considerable attention in various studies of the emic or folk notion of *kao* (encompassing *menboku, taimen, mentsu* and related terms) (Ervin-Tripp, Nakamura and Guo, 1995; Haugh, 2005b; Morisaki and Gudykunst, 1994; Sueda, 1995; Tanaka and Kekidze, 2005; Yabuuchi, 2004).[1] Building upon Matsumoto's (1988: 405) initial claim that 'what is of paramount importance to a Japanese is not his/her territory, but the position in relation to others in the group and his/her acceptance by others', it has been argued that the notion of 'place' is critical to an understanding of face in Japanese (Haugh, 2005b, 2007a; Morisaki and Gudykunst, 1994: 76; Tanaka and Kekidze, 2005: 110). The notion of place can be broadly defined as 'one's contextually contingent and discursively enacted social role and position' (Haugh, 2007a: 660; cf. Haugh, 2005a: 47-48), which encompasses both the 'place one belongs' (*uchi*), or group-based relationships of belonging, and the 'place one stands' (*tachiba*) or one's public persona or social standing as distinct from others. The notion of 'place' can thus be contrasted with Ide's (1989) notion of *wakimae* ('discernment') in that there is no claim made here that interactants are socio-pragmatically obligated to speak in certain ways according to the various places of each interactant.

For example, one can 'give face' (*kao o tateru*) by accepting and following advice from one's senior in front of others, thereby showing one respects that senior's *tachiba*. Alternatively, one may cause one's senior to 'lose face' (*kao o tsubusu*) by not following that person's advice, particularly when this will be apparent to other people, since this shows one does not think highly of nor accept his position, and thus one does not respect his *tachiba*.[2] The first-order notion of face (*kao*) is grounded in the discursively enacted place of those in superior roles or positions in business and other institutional contexts, and thus is dependent on the enactment of these superior-subordinate relationships, since a superior can only have face (*kao*) in this sense by virtue of having subordinates whose conduct – as well as that of the superior him/herself – either supports or threatens it. Crucial to the first-order notion of face in Japanese is also the concomitant notion of *seken*, the wider 'imagined community' that has the constant potential to judge a person's conduct as being (in)appropriate (Abe, 1995; Hasada, 2006: 191-192; Inoue, 1977; Shiba, 1999: 52). First-order face in (Modern Standard) Japanese, then, is socially constructed and perpetuated as a shared socio-cultural understanding of (in)appropriate conduct relative to a superior's place by the superior or his/her subordinates, often through talk about *kao* in conversation and other social interactions.

Yet while these studies of face in Japanese as a social construct have given us considerable insight into relational aspects of face, the interactional achievement of face in Japanese has been relatively neglected in the literature thus far. In particular, there have been few studies dealing with the ways in which face emerges through the unfolding of interaction, apart from earlier work by Chen (1990/91), Lerner (1996) and Piirainen-Marsh (1995, 1996) on face in Chinese, (American) English, and intercultural English interactions respectively. However, although conversation analytic tools provide considerable traction in the analysis of 'face-in-interaction', such an analysis requires recourse to understandings that go beyond those locally occasioned through interaction. In other words, we argue that analyses of participant understandings must be grounded in a broader theoretical viewpoint that draws from ethnographic and broader sociological perspectives if one is to successfully tease out the ways in which face arises through interaction.[3]

Face Constituting Theory proposed by Arundale (1999, 2006) provides a potentially fruitful framework in which to undertake such an
analysis of face-in-interaction. A key claim underlying Face Constituting Theory is that face is both a relational and interactional phenomenon (Arundale, 2006: 201). Face is relational in the sense that it emerges
through the dialectic of connection and separation in relationships with
other social selves (*ibid.*: 201), which in the case of Japanese, is realised
through the discursive enactment of the place one belongs (*uchi*) and
the place one stands (*tachiba*) respectively (Haugh, 2005a, 2005b, 2007a).
On the other hand, face is interactional in that 'a participant's face interpreting for any particular utterance is afforded and constrained by both
participants' interpretings of the specific utterances that precede and
follow it' and thus 'the particular interpretings of face that become operative for one participant's utterance are evident to both participants
only in the other's uptake of that utterance' (Arundale, 2006: 208). It is
in this sense that an interactional approach proves critical in grounding
the analyst's interpretation in such a way that it is consonant (although
not necessarily synonymous) with the understandings displayed by
participants in the flow of the interaction, thereby establishing the procedural consequentiality of the analysis (Arundale, forthcoming; Haugh,
2007b: 310-311). Drawing from these theoretical claims, then, the following analysis focuses on the emergence of face through interaction
apparent from the uptake of preceding and following utterances by
participants when viewed through a wider ethnographically-grounded
lens. As becomes evident in the later discussion, the use of audio-vi-
sual data proves crucial to this line of analysis.

4.3. Methodology

The data used in this chapter to illustrate how face in Japanese emerges
through interaction was collected over a 10 month period in 2004, as
part of a larger ongoing study of rapport management in intercultural
business interactions in a Japanese firm based in Australia.[4] A video
camera and a number of microphones were placed to record, without
the researcher's presence, one 'normal' working day in the office together with two meetings involving different participants. This audio-
visual data was supplemented by interviews with key members of the
firm, as well as field notes gathered in the course of observing and
talking with participants after the recordings. The focus of this present

analysis, however, is on just one of the meetings held in the firm where both Japanese and non-Japanese members of staff were present.

The firm itself employed ten people at the time of collecting the data, two of whom were non-native speakers of Japanese. The key Japanese participants involved in this particular meeting were Takashi (the president of the firm), Naoko (the general manager, and second-in-charge), and Ken (the production manager, and direct supervisor of the two non-Japanese members of staff).[5] The two non-Japanese staff members were Matthew (an Australian speaker of English who had spent a number of years studying and working in Japan), and his subordinate Carl (an Indonesian who spoke English as a second language, and had acquired Japanese informally through interactions in the company). While the Japanese interactants showed a certain degree of accommodation towards the language competence of the non-Japanese interactants, particularly that of Carl who had no formal training in Japanese language, the overall tenor of the meeting was oriented towards Japanese norms of interaction.[6] This was especially apparent in the discussion that followed Carl's presentation, which although conducted in a mixture of English and Japanese, was ultimately dominated by conversational exchanges in Japanese.

The main objective of the meeting was for Carl to seek the approval of Takashi in regards to his initial research about a new fruit juice product, and to pass on that work to Matthew for marketing purposes. The meeting also helped other participants consolidate their understanding of the development of the new product. Carl's presentation itself lasted for nearly twenty minutes, whilst the subsequent discussion about Carl's presentation, in which Takashi, Naoko, Ken and Matthew as well as Carl himself were the main participants, continued for around forty minutes. In the following section, four incidents critical to the emergence of face taken from that discussion are examined. The transcripts of these four incidents follow the standard conversational analytic transcription conventions as outlined in Fitch and Sanders (2005: xi-xiii), but also include, in double brackets, extra commentary on salient gestures and other visual cues. Code-switching into Japanese is indicated through italics, while an English translation in quotation marks follows those turns where Japanese is used by participants.

4.4. Finding face in intercultural business meetings

The first key incident involving the interactional achievement of face, more specifically saving face, begins at the point where Carl has nearly finished his presentation. When Carl assumes the ETD (estimated date of departure) for the product should be January in time for the special sales (*tokuhan*) that occur in February, Naoko takes the opportunity to frame a correction of this assumption as a clarification. In doing so, Naoko reduces the threat to Carl's face as a competent member of the team.

(1)   Carl is finishing up his presentation about the new fruit juice when
         Naoko interrupts to ask for clarification

182 C: ((reading from his notes)) And then the first *tokuhan*, it mentioned
            on ((looks at audience)) February, so the ETD will be on (2.0)
            ((looks up towards the ceiling, thinking to himself))
            'And then the first sales, it mentioned on February, so the ETD will
            be on'

183   January (3.0) ((flicks notes)) *desu.* (1.0) January, oh, ye[ah
            'In January, January oh, yeah'

184 N: [Humm? How- how- how long does it take?

185 C: It takes like about 1 month. ((swishes right arm))

186 N: Transit time

187 C: Transit times

188 N: *Dakedo ni gatsu ge-, tokuhan desho?*
            but   February   special sales probably
            'But the sales are in February, right?'

189 C: ((stunned face, mouth opened))
            A:: soo desu ne (2.0) [ah maybe ((swishes right hand))
                                          [December,

190 N: Shi- [shipment may be
                                          [December or end of November=

191 C: =*ah soo desu ne,* yep (1.0) a: December or=
            'Ah, that's right, yep ah December or'

192 N: =End of November

193 C: Yeah, OK. ((flicks paper, checks note)) *A:: soo desu ne* ((looks up
            at N))
            'Yeah, OK. Ah that's right'

194 N: (   ) Or beginning of December.

195 C: Hm, yeah, ((looks down at notes, takes notes)) un. Ok. ((looks at
            screen)) Basically like that the, ahem ((clears throat)) rough idea,
            ((looks down to table)) the situation about the prune juice, ((looks
            back to screen)) at the moment, ((looks down, touches com-
            puter))

Up until this point in the course of his presentation Carl has been attempting to project face in relation to the place he stands as a competent member of the company. When he assumes that the ETD for the new product will be in January (turns 182-183), Naoko responds by seeking clarification in turn 184 as to how long it would take for the product to be delivered to Japan. Carl responds confidently at first that it should take about one month (turn 185), but when confronted with Naoko's claim that the special sales begin in February and thus an ETD in January would be too late, his previous confidence is replaced by apparent discomfort at his mistake. The way in which Naoko is projecting a threat to Carl's face through this seeking of clarification is evident in turn 189 where Carl appears somewhat stunned and lost for words. This discomfort is also apparent in his hesitant responses and the way in which he cuts off his line of gaze with the audience in turn 195. Through this uptake, then, Carl's interpreting of a threat to his face becomes apparent, and this threat continues on through turns 191 to 195 where he acknowledges it should actually be December. However, upon examining the incident as a whole, it is nevertheless apparent that the way in which Naoko initially frames her correction as a clarification also projects concern for Carl's face, since they jointly construct the correction, thereby 'sharing' the mistake across the place they belong. By showing concern for the place he belongs, Naoko thereby mitigates the force of this face threat, thus leading to the interactional achievement of both a threat towards and concern for Carl's face in this incident.

The way in which Naoko enacts face saving in this first example stands in stark contrast to the direct threatening of Carl's face projected by Takashi in the next example. While Carl becomes rather animated in his response to a question from Ken about the difference between the proposed new product and other French products already sold in the Japanese market, having recovered apparently from the potentially face-threatening incident described above. Takashi becomes visibly agitated at this point in the discussion.

(2)   Carl is responding to a question from Ken about whether French prune juice is well received in the Japanese market. He then goes on to point out the manufacturer's claim that it is 100% juice is actually incorrect

218   C: In here ((right hand swishing pencil downwards)) I will mention that it is (0.5) wrong? cos like you can't get 100% straight juice,

219   out of the prunes, like you have to add waters, ((looks around, straight posture, hand swished numerous times for emphasis. T puts down his pen, and sits back on his chair))

220   because, prune itself is very thick ((holding right hand up in front, looks around at the audience and swishes hands numerous times)), its only contains 20 percent of moisture.

221   And I did asked them, to the manufacture ((right hand points up)), to the ((Company)) V ((puts his hand on the bottle)), like whether do you know

222   ((Product)) E, what about the <u>manu</u>facturing process chart, and everything,

223   and they said no, they are all the same ((C starts to smile a little, T starts to nod)), and they can't claim the straight juice=

224   T: =Any other point

225   C: ((look at T, stunned)) A:::::m, other point from that ((looks up, hands movement become bigger)), they are using the hybrid (.) prunes, so they have

226   selected the prunes. No- no- Not any other, not any prunes.

227   T: ((looks at C, tilts head)) (2.0) You missed the point. (1.2) You have to compare the (.) fibre ((lifts his right hand to left side))

228   C: Um hm?=

229   T: =and fib[re, ((moves right hand from left to right))

230   C: [un ummm

231   T: And(.) the sodium, s[odium ((left to right))

232   C: [ah ok

233   T: they are the nutritions. ((puts hand down))

234   C: ah, ok.= ((puts bottle down, picks up notes))

235   T: =Did you?=   [did you do that?

236   C: =ah [no, no I didn't.
                   [I-

237   T: [*Sore* important point *daro Caaru.*
        'That is an important point, Carl'

238   C: ah, ((looks down)) *soo des-,* ye=
        'Ah righ-, ye-'

239   T: =U::::n
                           'Yeah'

Carl appears to be projecting a claim here for not just face, but *kao*, as a competent member of staff by confidently 'showing off' his knowledge of the product to everyone present, a claim which is apparent from his enthusiastic demeanour in the course of turns 218 to 223. However, this claim for *kao* is blocked by Takashi in turn 224 when he impatiently asks Carl whether he has any other points to make. Takashi also thereby implies that what Carl has been outlining in turns 218–223 is already known to the participants, and thus that Carl cannot make any such claim to *kao* (i.e. status as someone knowledgeable). The interaction between Carl and Takashi from turns 224 through to 239 then leads to an interpreting of a loss of face for Carl, apparent from Carl's stunned facial expression (turn 225), concomitant body language, and hesitant responses to Takashi's line of questioning. Takashi reinforces this loss of face on Carl's part in repeating that Carl has 'missed the point' in turn 227, before going on to jointly establish with Carl the fact that he did not find out sufficient information about the nutritional content of the prune juice (turns 227–237). This loss of face in terms of the place Carl stands is thus interactionally achieved, in contrast to Carl's projected claim for *kao*, which is not interactionally achieved since neither Takashi nor anyone else ratifies Carl's projected claim.

Takashi, moreover, projects his own *kao*, namely his status as the head of the company, through this incident. In making these direct criticisms of Carl's work he thereby enacts his place as encompassing the role of someone who is expected to provide 'training' for a junior member of staff, and consequently has a level of authority which allows him to make such criticisms. The projection of *kao* by Takashi is particularly apparent in turn 237 when he adopts a fairly paternalistic tone when chastising Carl, as such a move is only consistent with someone who has enacted a place of sufficient status to adopt such a tone. This projected *kao* is tacitly endorsed by the other participants, who maintain absolute silence during Takashi's 'educational' interchange with Carl, and thus is arguably also interactionally achieved.

The loss of face on Carl's part also has implications for Ken who has been supervising Carl, since Carl's presentation reflects badly on Ken's ability to mentor Carl appropriately. The interdependent character of *kao* is therefore apparent from this interaction, since Carl's failure to make an acceptable presentation about the product has implications for his direct superior (through the place they belong). However, while Carl's loss of face may be interpreted as also being a threat to Ken's *kao* (namely, his status as someone able to mentor his subordinates appropriately, which is an expected part of the role of a supervisor in this company), this interpreted loss of *kao* cannot be said to be interactionally achieved despite Ken's presence at the meeting. Ken may indeed think the other participants think less highly of the place he stands as a result of Takashi's evaluation of Carl's performance, but there is little evidence of uptake on the part of Ken or others of such an interpreted loss of *kao* at this point in the interaction. However, in an interaction that later follows, Ken asks Carl why he did not put up the list of nutritional values of the juice that they had prepared together before the meeting. This line of questioning, through which Ken implies criticism of Carl's performance, is indicative of Ken's unhappiness with Carl, and is evidence therefore of Ken's interpreting of the above interaction where Carl loses face as also potentially threatening to his own *kao*.

This incident is followed in succession by another incident where Carl once again loses face. In this excerpt, Takashi reframes Carl's suggestion of getting a list of nutritional ingredients by pretending to be a customer as farcical due to Carl's (insufficient) proficiency in Japanese.

(3)   Carl is responding to Takashi's directive that he find out further information about the nutritional content of the prune juice

240 C: I'll- ((flips pages, takes notes)) I'll contact ((Company)) M

241 T: *Sore o yaru:- kontakuto* ((Company)) *M?* Nutrition *dete nai no?*
kore
'You'll do it – contact (Company) M? Are the nutritional (ingredients) not listed on this?'

242 C: *De,te nai n desu ne* (0.5) ((picks up and shows the bottle)) *kore dake shika nai desu ne*
'They're not listed. There's only this'

243 T: (0.7) ((T takes the bottle from C and looks at the label on it. C takes a step back, stands up straight. M starts taking notes))
((Company)) *M ni kite oshiete kureru?* ((faster, looking at C))
'Do you think (Company) M will tell us if we ask?'

244 C: *A: ja boku wa okyakusan de:* (0.8) ((swishes his hand twice)) I bought the product from you
'Okay, I'll [ask] as a customer, "I bought the product from you"'

245 T: psss ((laughter)) ((Matthew shakes head, hand on his forehead))
chotto mate yo: ((laughter)) *Caaru wa okyakusan ja ne: yo:=*
'Just a moment. You're not a customer'

246 C: ((moves his hands up and down, sounds a bit upset))
=*iya demo↑sore yarikata↓wa minna ano::=*
'Nah, but that way, everyone uhm'

247 T: =*Iya II kedo Manabu ga yaru nara ii kedo* ((looks at others)) *Caaru ga yatte tara sa:=*
'No, that's okay but it's better if Manabu does it. If you do it then'

248   ((everyone laughs)) ((Matthew right hand on chin, looks at T, and shakes his head))

249 T: =*doko no kuni no hito nanoka=*
'What nationality is this person?'

250 C: *↑SOO ↓desu yo ne* ((laughing, rocks his body back and forward)),
↑soo ↓desu yo ne, ja: Manabu san ni ano:
'That's right, that's right, okay to Manabu, uhm'

251 T: *A↑yashi↓i daro::?*
'It's a bit suspicious'

252 C: *↑Soo ↓desu ne* ((looks down, shakes his head left to right))
'That's right'

Carl starts by announcing in turn 240 that he will contact the other company to find out the nutritional contents of the prune juice. Takashi responds by first asking whether or not these details are already listed on the bottle in turns 241–243. Upon finding out they are not, he goes on to ask Carl whether he can find out further information by contacting the company directly. Carl then suggests that he can pretend to be a customer when asking that company for the details in turn 244, in response to which while the others burst out laughing, Takashi (jokingly) points out in turn 245 that it would be obvious Carl is not their customer. While the others are amused by Takashi's reframing of Carl's suggestion as somewhat silly, Carl himself initially protests, claiming that his suggestion was made in all seriousness in turn 246. Takashi, however, goes on to point out in turns 247, 249 and 251 that while it might be okay for Manabu (another Japanese member of the firm) to use such a strategy, if Carl tried then that (Japanese) company might become suspicious about the identity of the caller (since Carl's accent would clearly mark him as non-Japanese), which is greeted with further laughter from the others. Carl finally joins in on the joke (on himself) in turn 250, when he starts laughing and accepting that it might be strange for him to do such a thing.

Yet while Carl eventually laughs at the situation, it is also clear that he has lost face through this incident, as his (serious) suggestion is treated as a joke by the other participants. The others' laughter at Carl's expense, as well as Matthew's obvious exasperation with Carl (apparent from Matthew shaking his head in turns 245 and 248) indicates that the other participants do not think the place Carl stands in the company is necessarily one which is to be respected and taken seriously. Carl's loss of face is also apparent from Carl's interpreting of Takashi making a joke of his suggestion in turn 246 as face-threatening, where he becomes defensive and mildly agitated. Although Carl later joins in on the joke, his discomfort is still apparent in turn 252, when he once again cuts his line of gaze with the others by looking down towards the floor. It is apparent, then, that a loss of face has been projected by Takashi (and the others), and interpreted by Carl (and the others, especially Matthew), and thus is interactionally achieved through this incident.

While the content of Carl's presentation (and thus his face) remained the primary focus of the ensuing discussion, Matthew's face became foregrounded in an incident that occurred around 15 minutes later in the discussion. In the following excerpt, Takashi suggests that it would be better for Hanako to translate information for their Japanese customers about the juice from Carl's presentation rather than Matthew. In doing so, Takashi is projecting a potential threat to Matthew's face, as it impugns his ability to translate from English into Japanese. It also threatens Matthew's *kao* (arising from his discursively enacted place in the company as Carl's superior), as his Japanese-language competence is not normally questioned, at least not in front of Carl.

(4)   Takashi is discussing the translation into Japanese of a PR sheet containing information from Carl's presentation

584 T: *De Maseyu ga toransureeshon suru yori mo* (.) ((looks at M)) *ano Hanako san* ((touches nose)) *ga toransureeshon shita hoo ga,* ((C & M nod many times)) *ii*
'Then, rather than Matthew doing the translation, uhm, it would be better if Hanako did the translation'

585 C: *Soo desu ne* (0.3) *hai, wakarimashita* ((takes notes. M with right hand on his chin looks at T))
'That's right. Yes, I understand'

586 T: ((to M)) *Soo suru to Maseyu ga dono kotoba tsukaeba iikatte wakaru kara ne=*
'If we do that then you will know which words to use'

587 M: *=Desu ne=* ((softly, nods))
'Yes'

588 T: *=Dooshitemo yappari Maseyu mo toransureeshon dekiru kedo::*
'No matter what, actually Matthew can also do the translation but'

589 C: *Un*
'Yeah'

590 T: *Nihonjin [ga* ((M starts nodding)) *nihon no sono tsukatteru kotoba no kankaku de erabu no to ne?=* ((to C))
'Japanese [can] choose with Japanese, that kind of sense in picking words'

591 C: [Hmm,   =hmm

592 T: (1.0) ((breath in)) but, *Maseyu ga* (.) *ji- jisho de?* dictionary *de hiku no to, yappari chigau ka[ra:*
'But Matthew with a dic- dictionary? [he] picks using a dictionary so it's still different'

593 M: ((looks at C, and nods to T))   ((softly))*[Chigaimasu ne*
'It's different, huh'

594 C: ((looks at T))   [U:n
'Yeah'

595 T: *datte* ((softer tone)) dictionary *hiitatte* three four words *atte sa* choose *shinakya ikenai*
'Because you must choose from the three or four words you find in a dictionary'

596   *wake desho* ((softer tone))
'so'

597 M: *Hai* ((nods))

'Yes'
598 T: *Soshitara kono baai dore wo tsukaeba iika tte ittara Hanako san no*
           ga wakaru mon
           'So Hanako will know which words are best to use in this case'
599 C: *Un*
           'Yes'
600 T: *Soo sureba Maseyu ga sore ni,* follow *shite ikeba ii dake na wake*
           dakara= ((M looks at C, then at T))
           'If we do that then Matthew can just follow that so'
601 C: =*Un*
           'Yes'
602 T: SOKO *made, Caaru no toko de yatte hoshii wake yo=* ((points at
           C))
           'At that point, I want you [Carl] to do your bit'
603 C: =*Wakarimashita*
           'I understand'

Takashi begins by initially suggesting in turn 584 that while anyone (in the firm) could translate the information from Carl's presentation into Japanese, Hanako would probably be better than Matthew in this situation. In doing so, Takashi is implicitly reminding Matthew to keep to his assumed responsibilities in regards to checking but not necessarily making translations from English into Japanese. Carl immediately agrees with this point in turn 585, while Matthew remains silent, which perhaps prompts Takashi to go on in turn 586 to explain that in this way Matthew will have a better idea of which words in Japanese would be most appropriate in developing promotional information for customers. From Matthew's response in turn 587 to Takashi's explanation, where he only softly voices his affirmation, it is apparent that Matthew is interpreting his face (namely, the 'place he stands' as a linguistically competent member of staff) as being somewhat threatened by this line of reasoning. Takashi quickly responds to the display of this interpreting by Matthew of a potential face threat by first endorsing Matthew's ability to make appropriate translations in turn 588, before going on to explain in turns 592, 595–596 and 598 that Hanako has a 'native speaker's sense' with which to pick words rather than being reliant on the dictionary as Matthew is more likely to be. Matthew only quietly accepts this point in turn 593, which indicates that Matthew is still interpreting Takashi's assertion as projecting a threat towards his face. Takashi then appears to make an effort to lessen this threat by further softening the tone of his voice in giving the explanation for his decision in turns 595 to 596. In this way Takashi tries to avoid Matthew losing face (or *kao o tsubusanai*). The potential threat to Matthew's face is not only evident from Takashi's efforts to soften the tone of his explanation, and Matthew's discomfort with Takashi's line of reasoning, but also from Carl's apparent satisfaction with the situation (seen in his somewhat less serious countenance in comparison to that of Matthew). In this way, then, the potential threat to Matthew's face is interactionally achieved through the interpreting of a face threat apparent from Matthew's markedly subdued response to Takashi's suggestion, and the way in which Takashi responds to this interpreting by modifying his tone of voice when it becomes evident that Matthew is not entirely comfortable with talk focusing on his ability (or lack thereof) to translate from English into Japanese.

This incident thus involves a threat to Matthew's face in that it impugns his ability to translate into Japanese. However, it also threatens his *kao* in that while everyone in the company respects Matthew's ability to communicate in Japanese (which contributes to his ongoing status within the company), this line of reasoning brings into focus Matthew's ultimately non-native status as a speaker of Japanese in front of Carl. While Carl came into the company through personal connections with Takashi, and thus is treated in some respects less formally, Matthew entered the company through a formal interview, and is normally afforded more respect because of that. In this sense, then, while Matthew has *kao* within the company, Carl is yet to establish *kao* for himself (as seen in example 2). This incident also illustrates that maintaining a clear distinction between face-in-interaction in the sense outlined in Face Constituting Theory and first-order face, which in the case of Japanese encompasses the emic notion of *kao* (and related terms), is not necessarily always possible.[7] In the final section, then, the implications of this interactional analysis for the further development of a theory of face and facework are considered.

4.5. Implications

While research on face has generally diverged in its treatment of face as either a first-order socio-cultural concept that can be talked about, for example *kao* (and related terms) in Japanese, and the interactional achievement of a theoretically-defined notion of face, the analysis in this chapter has indicated that theoretical or second-order analyses should not neglect first-order socio-cultural constructs when attempting to explicate face-in-interaction. It is only through an understanding of first-order notions of face, or the emic perspective, that we can gain an understanding of the assumptions and expectations constitutive of and enacted through interaction which underlie the interactional achievement of face. However, it is also apparent that such first-order notions should not, and indeed cannot be elevated to the status of theories of facework (or second-order notions of face). In the current analysis, while *kao* did indeed appear to become salient at times, particularly when the face of more senior participants was foregrounded through the interaction, it also became clear that these emic notions do not have sufficient analytic power to fully explicate Japanese face-in-interaction. We argue that one major implication of this finding is that we need to further develop an approach that grounds the analysis of face in a theoretical framework which can encompass such emic notions, yet nevertheless goes beyond them. In other words, analyses of the relational dimensions of face should not ignore the findings of analyses of first-order face. Yet, the fact that face is *constituted in* interaction means that while a theory of face and facework may be informed by such perspectives it need not be necessarily constrained by them.

The focus in this chapter has primarily been on the interactional dimension of face in Japanese. We have argued that an approach which draws from both interactional and ethnographic perspectives is well-placed to explicate the interactional achievement of face, as well as projectings and interpretings of face that can arise in interaction. In this way, the analysis of face and facework can be grounded in an approach that draws upon participant understandings as a resource, but where the analyst is not unduly constrained by such understandings. As this particular analysis focused on incidents arising in one interactional context, namely an intercultural business meeting, there is still much to be gained from a study of the wider interactional context, as well as focusing on stimulated participant reflections on the interaction. Nevertheless, we suggest that the current analysis illustrates that a close analysis of the interactional aspects of face in Japanese is indeed possible, and thus that ongoing theorising about face and facework might benefit from the insights garnered from such analyses.

Acknowledgements

We would like to thank the two anonymous reviewers as well as Hiromasa Tanaka for their invaluable feedback on earlier versions of this chapter.

Endnotes

1. In discussing *kao* as a first-order notion, however, we are not making any claim that this conceptualisation is in any way unique to Japanese, as any such a claim would require detailed contrastive studies of emic conceptualisations of face across different socio-cultural groups.
2. For instance, one informant reported 'losing *kao*' when he promised another teacher that one of his students would attend a special training session, but the student did not turn up on the day. The loss of face arose because the breaking of the teacher's promise by the student showed up that teacher's inability to properly organise his students.
3. While some argue that conversation analytic and ethnographic methodologies could mutually benefit from greater interaction (Moerman, 1988, 1993; see also Pomerantz, 2005), others argue that such a 'mix' is not viable (Sanders, 1999). In this chapter, we assume ethnographic and conversation analytic methodologies can be regarded as ultimately complementary (see also Bargiela-Chiappini, this volume Chapter 16 and Haugh, this volume Chapter 1).
4. This larger study forms part of Watanabe's forthcoming PhD dissertation on the communicative performance of non-native speakers of Japanese in an intercultural business setting.
5. Pseudonyms are used for all the participants, as well as for the names of other firms and products mentioned in the course of the meeting.
6. Thus, although Matthew and Carl may have perceived the interaction in ways that diverged at times from the perceptions of the Japanese participants due to their Australian and Indonesian cultural backgrounds respectively, it became apparent in the course of the interaction that the interpretings of face which became salient in the interaction were oriented towards the discursive accomplishment of place, and thus Japanese interactional norms.
7. This finding also has implications for Spencer-Oatey's (2005: 102-103) related distinction between 'respectability face' and 'identity face'.

References

Abe, K. (1995) *Seken towa nanika* [What is *seken*?]. Tokyo: Kôdansha.

Arundale, R. B. (1999) An alternative model and ideology of communication for an alternative to politeness theory. *Pragmatics* 9: 119–154.

Arundale, R. B. (2006) Face as relational and interactional: a communication framework for research on face, facework, and politeness. *Journal of Politeness Research* 2: 193–216.

Arundale, R. B. (forthcoming) Relating. In M. Locher and S. Lambert Graham (eds.) Interpersonal Pragmatics. Berlin: Mouton de Gruyter.

Arundale, R. B. (this volume) Face as emergent in interpersonal communication: an alternative to Goffman.

Bargiela-Chiappini, F. (2003) Face and politeness: new (insights) for (old) concepts. *Journal of Pragmatics* 35: 1453–1469.

Bargiela-Chiappini, F. (this volume) Facing the future: some reflections.

Brown, P., and Levinson, S. C. (1987) *Politeness. Some Universals in Language Usage.* Cambridge: Cambridge University Press.

Chen, V. (1990/1991) *Mien tze* at the Chinese dinner table: A study of the interactional accomplishment of face. *Research on Language and Social Interaction* 24: 109–140.

Ervin-Tripp, S., Nakamura, K., and Guo, J. (1995) Shifting face from Asia to Europe. In M. Shibatani and S. Thompson (eds.), *Essays in Semantics and Pragmatics* 43–71. Amsterdam: John Benjamins.

Fitch, K. and Sanders, R. (eds.) (2005) *Handbook of Language and Social Interaction.* Mahwah, NJ: Lawrence Erlbaum.

Goffman, E. (1967) *Interaction Ritual: Essays on Face-to-Face Behavior.* New York: Pantheon Books.

Hasada, R. (2006) Cultural scripts: glimpses into the Japanese emotion world. In C. Goddard (ed.), *Ethnopragmatics. Understanding Discourse in Cultural Context* 171–198. Berlin: Mouton de Gruyter.

Haugh, M. (2005a) The importance of 'place' in Japanese politeness: implications for cross-cultural and intercultural analyses. *Intercultural Pragmatics* 2: 41–68.

Haugh, M. (2005b) What does 'face' mean to the Japanese? Understanding the import of face in Japanese business interaction. In F. Bargiela-Chiappini and M. Gotti (eds.), *Asian Business Discourse* 211–239. Berlin: Peter Lang.

Haugh, M. (2007a) Emic conceptualisations of (im)politeness and face in Japanese: implications for the discursive negotiation of second language learner identities. *Journal of Pragmatics* 39: 657–680.

Haugh, M. (2007b) The discursive challenge to politeness theory: an interactional alternative. *Journal of Politeness Research* 3: 295–317.

Haugh, M. (this volume) Face and interaction.

Ide, S. (1989) Formal forms and discernment: two neglected aspects of universals of linguistic politeness. *Multilingua* 8: 223–248.

Inoue, T. (1977) *Sekentei no kôzô* [The structure of *sekentei*]. Tokyo: NHK.

Koutlaki, S. (2002) Offers and expressions of thanks as face enhancing acts: *tae'arof* in Persian. *Journal of Pragmatics* 34: 1733–1756.

Lerner, G. (1996) Finding 'face' in the preference structures of talk-in-interaction. *Social Psychology Quarterly* 59: 303–321.

Lim, T. S. (2004) Towards an Asian model of face: the dimensionality of face in Korea. *Human Communication* 7: 53–66.

Mao, L. (1994) Beyond politeness theory: face revisited and renewed. *Journal of Pragmatics* 21: 451–486.

Matsumoto, Y. (1988) Reexamination of the universality of face: politeness phenomena in Japanese. *Journal of Pragmatics* 12: 403–426.

Moerman, M. (1988) *Talking Culture. Ethnography and Conversation Analysis.* Philadelphia: University of Pennsylvania Press.

Moerman, M. (1993) Adriane's thread and Indra's net: reflections on ethnography, identity, culture, and interaction. *Research on Language and Social Interaction,* 26: 85–98.

Morisaki, S., and Gudykunst, W. (1994) Face in Japan and the United States. In S. Ting-Toomey (ed.), *The Challenge of Facework: Cross-cultural and Interpersonal Issues* 47–93. Albany, New York: State University of New York Press.

Nwoye, O. (1992) Linguistic politeness and socio-cultural variations of the notion of face. *Journal of Pragmatics* 18: 309–328.

Piirainen-Marsh, A. (1995) *Face in Second Language Conversation.* Jyväskylä: University of Jyväskylä.

Piirainen-Marsh, Arja. 1996. Face and the organization of intercultural interaction. In T. Hakukioja, M. Helasvuo and E. Kärkkäinen (eds.), *SKY 1996 Yearbook of the Linguistic Association of Finland* 93–133. Jyväskylä: University of Jyväskylä.

Pomerantz, A. (2005) Using participants' video stimulated comments to complement analyses of interactional practices. In H. te Molder and J. Potter (eds.), *Conversation and Cognition* 93–113. Cambridge: Cambridge University Press.

Sanders, R. (1999) The impossibility of culturally contexted conversation analysis: on simultaneous, distinct types of pragmatic meaning. *Research on Language and Social Interaction* 32: 129–140.

Shiba, R. (1999) Seken ni tsuite [On *seken*]. *Shuukan Asahi,* 50–55.

Spencer-Oatey, H. (2005) (Im)politeness, face and perceptions of rapport: unpacking their bases and interrelationships. *Journal of Politeness Research* 1: 95–119.

Strecker, I. (1993) Cultural variations in the concept of 'face'. *Multilingua* 12: 119–141.

Sueda, K. (1995) Differences in the perception of face: Chinese *mientzu* and Japanese *mentsu. World Communication* 24: 23–31.

Tanaka, S., and Kekidze, T. (2005) 'Kao' to 'лицо' – 'Kao' gainen no Nichi-Ro taishoo kenkyuu ['Kao' and 'лицо': Japanese-Russian contrastive study of the 'face' conception]. *Seikai no Nihongo Kyooiku [Japanese-Language Education around the Globe]* 15: 103–116.

Ukosakul, M. (2003) Conceptual metaphors underlying the use of Thai face. In E. Casad and G. Palmer (eds.), *Cognitive Linguistics and Non-Indo-European Languages* 275–303. Berlin: Mouton de Gruyter.

Yabuuchi, A. (2004) Face in Chinese, Japanese and U.S. American cultures. *Journal of Asian Pacific Communication* 14: 263–299.

5
"That's a myth": Linguistic avoidance as a political face-saving strategy in broadcast interviews

Eric A. Anchimbe

> Politicians have been riddled with riddles: What do politicians and
> diapers have in common? They should both be changed regularly
> for the same reasons...They have even been skewered by a
> fanciful etymology for the word *politics*: poly...means many – and
> tics, well, tics are blood-sucking parasites! (Lederer, 2000: 4)

5.1. Introduction

The notions of face (Goffman, 1967; Brown and Levinson, 1987; Chilton, 1990) and linguistic avoidance (Caffi and Janney, 1994; Janney, 1999) are not at all new in the literature on public discourse or conversational analysis. This paper follows on the heels of many others to reiterate that face within face-to-face communication, contrary to Brown and Levinson's (1987) premise that social relations are some sort of a natural state of affairs to which interlocutors respond (Chilton, 1990: 201), is not constructed according to fixed socio-cultural or natural states of static relations but is constructed and re-constructed in a dynamic and spontaneous way determined by the type of social interaction interlocutors are involved in. The paper tries to show that face-saving, as explained by Brown and Levinson (1987) and their followers, and *political face-saving* are different phenomena. Brown and Levinson (1987: 61) depict face as a sort of natural human social 'right': 'all competent adult members of a society have (and know each other to have) 'face', the [positive] public self-image that every member wants to claim for himself'. They further refer to one's right to a 'positive public self-image' and state that 'people co-operate (and assume each other's co-operation) in maintaining face in interaction'. As they further assume in their theory, interlocutors always *want* to co-operate with each other in protecting each other's faces by using 'politeness strategies'.

In politics in general, and political interviews especially, this clearly is not assumed by the interlocutors. Quite the contrary. In political interviews, the interviewer's job is to ask questions that systematically threaten the candidate's *political face* (i.e. a *public political image* which is more laden than the ordinary public self-image). The political face embodies the candidate's individual self-image, the one drawn from in times of election campaigns; his or her political career; the political ideology of his or her party; and the ideology of *other* (international) alliances his or her party or country may be member to. The interviewee's job is to demonstrate how cleverly s/he can deal with the threats posed by the interviewer's questions. In short, the political interview is a highly ritualised, mediated, *public* game of politically face-threatening thrusts by the interviewer and parries by the interviewee. It is like the children's game 'dodge-ball', where one player throws a ball at the other and, if the other can successfully dodge it (i.e., avoid it), s/he wins. The interviewee in is hence *not* assumed to have a natural right to political face by the interviewer. In fact, ironically, it is the other way around: the interviewer is assumed to have a right – a responsibility, even – to threaten the interviewee's political face and the interviewee is expected to allow this to happen without attacking the interviewer back.[1] Interestingly, we can speak in this context of a bizarre form of co-operation between interviewer and interviewee in which, 'politicians have to act, to pretend, or to put it more harshly (though not unfairly) to 'live a lie'. But individual leaders can respond to those circumstances in various ways – by trying to be more accomplished at pretending than others' (Fairclough, 2000: 8).

The above stance is linked up with patterns of linguistic avoidance in political interviews that are clearly directed at (political) face-saving. Linguistic avoidance refers to interlocutors' ability to avoid topics and concepts they deem harmful to their face. In avoidance, 'parts of speech, grammatical categories, and patterns of syntactic choice can be modified and manipulated in utterances to allow speakers to figuratively 'withdraw' or 'escape' from threatening concepts in linguistic space' (Janney, 1999: 261). The aim of bringing together these two notions, i.e. face-saving and linguistic avoidance, is to come up with an analytical framework for the evaluation of mediated political discourse in this time of the war on terror, when both a physical threat of violence and a linguistic threat of diplomatic or interpersonal relation breakdown exist. This framework is supported by the premise that political statements (on the international platform) in broadcast political interviews (especially in times of war) have fourfold effects: on the political aspirations and political positive face of the politician making them; on the political party s/he represents; on his or her country; and on the alliance or coalition his country is member to. It therefore makes sense to refer to politicians on the international platform as being four-faced and not three-faced as proposed by Bull, Elliott, Palmer and Walker (1996) in national politics. Bull *et al.*'s (1996) model is concerned with national issues like elections but the four-face model referred to here includes international diplomatic issues, and so increases the diverse, exigencies of the audience(s). Given that the interviews analysed here were also directed at an international audience, it could be said that Chirac and Blair are preserving their four-faces from the threats intimated in the interviewers' questions.

Since this collection concerns *face*, it makes sense to say here that *face*, from the large amount of literature generated on it within psychology, sociology, and linguistics, is of crucial importance in political interviews. During interviews politicians, Bavelas, Black, Bryson and Mullett (1988) propose, are often placed in an avoidance-avoidance conflict situation, in which all replies to a question have implicitly negative consequences. Because they must give a reply (no matter how evasive), such a reply is determined by the communicative exigencies of the social situation. These could be controversial issues that, if addressed, may repel voters or supporters, topics unfamiliar to the politician; or issues that need more time to explain than that accorded by the interview(er). In all these, Bull *et al.* (1996) add, the politician keeps his faces in mind and therefore works hard not to put any of them in *danger*. The avoidance-avoidance conflict perspective is based on equivocation alone but linguistic avoidance involves more than just equivocation (see section 5).

5.2. The data

Data for this paper were collected from transcripts[2] of interviews given by French President Jacques Chirac and British Prime Minister Tony Blair. Chirac was interviewed on 16th March 2003 by Christiane Amampour for American television channels CBS and CNN.[3] Blair was interviewed on BBC's 'Newsnight' by Jeremy Paxman on 6th February 2003.[4] The transcripts were not transcribed by me but downloaded from the websites of these media organisations. Chirac's transcripts were translated by CNN. I did not consult the French original transcripts for risk of transforming the paper into a comparative or contrastive work. Variation could be expected but this should not distort the findings. I chose interviews because they give the speaker the chance to 'save' himself from supposed media distortion, political accusation, falsehood, and above all to defend his position.

The period during which these interviews were given is also important: the build-up to the invasion of Iraq (February–March 2003); and the two interviewees could be said to belong to two opposing camps: one for the war (Blair) and the other against the war (Chirac). The invasion of Iraq looked imminent given that the Americans had plotted Iraq, alongside Iran and North Korea on an 'axis of evil', responsible directly and indirectly for terrorism. Tony Blair was under pressure at home for 'tagging along on Mr. Bush's shirt-tails all the time'. Chirac was opposed to unilateral action and the use of force. He felt pressed by the need to maintain the old Franco-American cross-Atlantic relationship built over several centuries. The world is full of Saddam-like tyrants, he argued, and if they all had to be removed from power, the world would be turned into a battlefield. Under these pressures, both leaders adopt avoidance strategies to push forth their positions but at the same time protecting their public political images against the negative impressions associated with supporting the war or with opposing it. Presenting interviews from people opposed to one another suggests that in political interviews, interviewees use similar strategies to achieve different goals. It should not therefore be surprising to find both Chirac and Blair using the valence strategy but each to support his own position.

5.3. The 'double-face' of the media

The media have become increasingly decisive in the success or failure of political ideologies and strategies. Media coverage of political events and reporters' perspectives on these have a strong impact on politicians, public opinion, and political agendas. The role of the media, as Lauerbach (2006: 197) remarks, has changed tremendously within the liberal horizons of democracy from that of an honest mediator or watchdog to almost that of a political institution, attached in several differing ways to the political, belligerent ideologies or parties. This could affect the division of labour in the interviews and distort the 'dodge ball' game style of this discourse type. It is therefore not surprising that American newspapers in election times endorse presidential candidates and then become news-friendly with them. This in a way transforms political discourse into some sort of social order (Fairclough, 2000), the major concerns of which are not what the politicians and their respective institutions actually do but what they say they (would) do, what they say of others, and what they say of burning social issues. So as Janney (2002) rightly says of Information Warfare (I-War) or Cyber-war in perception management, it is becoming increasingly difficult to know 'what is real' from media coverage of events around the world. What this all boils down to is that the more the public political image of the opponent is threatened, the more one's own is maintained. So beyond the bizarre 'dodge-ball' co-operation in political interviews, political opponents benefit from this double-face of the media to save their faces.

5.4. Approaches to political interviews and face-saving

Presently there is a considerable literature on political interviews on the one hand, and on face-saving on the other, but these up to now have not yet been integrated in a manner that helps us explain the special interactional dynamics of political face-saving strategies in political interviews. This section reviews some of the approaches so far and situates the framework used here within existing research. Over the past three decades, there have been a number of prominent analytic approaches to political interviews and news interviews. Diverse as they have been and divergent as the contexts and persons of their study have also been, these frameworks have basically been complementary and supplementary (see Fetzer, 2006). These interdisciplinary perspectives show that (mediated) political interviews, interactive as they are in nature, could be studied from various angles: question framing (Bull, 1994), interviewer neutrality (Clayman, 1992), equivocation (Obeng, 1997), role performance or division of labour (Blum-Kulka, 1983), evasiveness (Harris, 1991), etc.

Focusing on news interviews, conversational analysis approaches have paid attention to the 'interactional organisation and reconstruction of the communicative event, on its context-sensitive employment of the turn-taking system and on the interactional organisation of neutralism' (Fetzer, 2006: 181). Their subject has therefore been the microscopic level of the communicative event. Beyond this level, critical discourse analysis approaches have taken up the more macroscopic issues of language production and language reception in political interviews (Chilton, 1990), covering among other things, ideological stances and conversationalisation. Social-psychological approaches (Bull and Mayer, 1993; Bull *et al.*, 1996; Obeng, 1997) have investigated strategies employed by interlocutors for face-saving, equivocation and evasiveness. This latter framework is partially adopted in this paper and is complemented by the multimodal communicative approach to linguistic avoidance proposed by Caffi and Janney (1994) and Janney (1999).

Context-based approaches to political interviews have investigated hedging and evasiveness (Jucker, 1986; Harris, 1991), misunderstanding, and misrepresentation – generally treating them as indirect speech strategies. They show that participants are somehow involved in a hidden game of not falling into the trap. As Fairclough (1989: 49) summarises, this is perhaps because, in mass-media discourse 'the nature of the power relations...is often not clear, and there are reasons for seeing it as involving hidden relations of power'. A further approach has focused on the roles of the interviewer and the interviewee – division of labour (Blum-Kulka, 1983) – emphasising 'the genre's constitutive speech acts, their felicity conditions, the participants' roles and their complementary rights and obligations' (Fetzer, 2006: 181).

Since the appearance of Brown and Levinson's (1987) (universal) politeness theory, research on face has taken several divergent dimensions. From works that support the hypothesis through works that expand it to similar contexts (Chilton, 1990) to those that reject it within specific socio-cultural contexts (Matsumoto, 1988; de Kadt, 1998; Terkourafi, 1999), the main line of thinking has been that face is far more than the individual's need but one that places the individual within the broader spectrum of the society. It is true that 'face is something that is emotionally invested, and that can be lost, maintained, or enhanced, and must be constantly attended to in interaction' (Brown and Levinson, 1987: 61), but the manner in which particular societies and cultures, and individuals in given interactional situations, respond to it causes it to be constructed and re-constructed dynamically and in different ways. What this paper will not do is reapply Brown and Levinson's face theory, but rather it will show how face, beyond the limits they put on it, is a general co-occurent social consciousness that is motivated by, or benefits from, several patterns in discursive interaction, among them linguistic avoidance.

5.5. Linguistic avoidance and related concepts

The aim of this essay is to identify the link between linguistic avoidance and face-saving, or put differently, to illustrate how politicians avoid *threatening* concepts or topics in interviews as a means of saving their (four-fold) public political faces. Janney (1999) illustrates that just as there are prototypical ways of physically avoiding harmful objects in the physical world, languages also have equivalents that make humans move away from *threatening* concepts in speech. I intend to use some of the dimensions defined by him to show that avoidance is not only moving away from threatening topics but also at the same time preserving one's face and shifting the responsibility to the *other* who might either be involved in the exchange or be the main element of reference. Janney's avoidance strategies are based on courtroom evidence meant to influence the partner's perception and interpretation; the strategies incorporated from his work are used here for face-saving. I adopt here his definition of linguistic avoidance as follows:

> a complex, systematic, pragmatic skill involving choices in
> different linguistic systems (pronoun, determiner, person, aspect,
> modality, number, tense, voice, degree, negation etc.) that modify
> meanings at different levels of linguistic organisation (word,
> phrase, clause, sentence, discourse). (Janney, 1999: 260)

The pragmatic skill of avoidance in speech uses both metaphor (non-linguistic inference) and iconicity (linguistic elements: uses of words, grammatical features and syntactic patterns) as 'figurative representations of speakers' orientations to concepts in speech' (Janney 1999: 260). This indicates that physical avoidance patterns such as: closing boundaries to the threatening object, becoming non-committal to the object, increasing distance to the object, and yielding to the object, could be realised in speech: 'talking away', 'talking around' the negative concept, re-contextualising, and redefining the concept. In the following example (Janney 1999: 265), the respondent, O.J. Simpson during his civil case hearing, (positively) redefines a 'lie' as 'moral dishonesty' in order to avert the threat of being treated as a liar in court, which has the physical threat of conviction.

(1)   Simpson
      Q: *That was a lie*, wasn't it?
      A: I think *it was morally dishonest* of me. Yes. I don't know if I would
           call that a lie.

Several pragmatic concepts exist whose overall focus is avoidance; but as the following perspectives show, there has been little consistency in the terminology. Brown and Levinson's (1987) notion of hedging is perhaps the closest. Many other notions exist, among them, vague language (Channell 1994:20 – especially if 'it is "purposely and unabashedly" vague'); (non)involvement (Tannen 1989); (non)commitment to the message (Schiffrin 1987); equivocation (Bull *et al.* 1996); evasion (Harris 1991); voicing and ventriloquising (Lauerbach 2006); and avoidance-avoidance conflict (Bavelas *et al.* 1988). They all involve avoidance of some sort in different situations.

5.6. Linguistic avoidance as political face-saving strategy

As said earlier, in national politics, Bull *et al.* (1996) propose that politicians are three-faced, and are involved in saving these three faces: 'their own personal face, the face of the party which they represent and face in relation to supporting or not supporting significant others' (Bull *et al.*, 1996: 267). On the international front, the politician is four-faced: his own face, the party face, the country face, and the international alliance face. The need for international support for the war on terror has made the international alliance face very important (e.g. 'The Alliance of the Willing'). Since 'what is primarily at issue in news interviews', as Jucker (1986: 71) says, 'is the interviewee's positive face', the desire to maintain it – and that of the others linked to him or her – becomes a conscious effort realised through several strategies. This is a complex situation because, although the interview itself may take place only between the interviewer and the interviewee (in the presence of the radio or television crew), the overall audience is millions of listeners spread across different and often conflicting perspectives, countries or alliances.

The politician therefore has these listeners in mind each time s/he interprets a question as *threatening* and hence decides to avoid it. Jucker identifies 13 ways in which the politician's face may be threatened during an interview; Bull *et al.* (1996) illustrate 19 subcategories regrouped into 3 superordinate categories of face that politicians must defend. Previous research shows that politicians adopt several ways to maintain their positive face: by not replying to questions (Bull and Mayer, 1993), or by evading or equivocating them. The present study reports another such level politicians use to maintain their faces in political interviews, and this is linguistic avoidance. It identifies six linguistic avoidance strategies used by politicians for public political face-saving. Politicians are involved in carefully choosing words, phrases, syntactic structures, and discourse patterns that talk around, redefine, distance and remake concepts and topics that are potentially threatening to them. The six avoidance strategies illustrated here are: valence strategy, generalisation strategy, specificity strategy (Janney 1999), correction strategy, non-committal strategy, and evidentiality strategy.

Valence strategy: from negative to less negative or positive connotation

Even though interviewers, just like the media discussed earlier, are supposed to be neutral arbitrators, it is difficult to maintain such neutrality at all times. Interviewers too get swayed or repelled by the responses or non-responses they receive. That aside, questions, generally 'do more than simply request information:...they encode points of view, opinions and attitudes' (Bull *et al.*, 1996: 268). Christiane Amanpour and Jeremy Paxman, besides trying to get the most out of these world politicians, have strong opinions of the issues they handle in their interviews. It is therefore expected that their questions will not be positively, or to put it differently, neutrally framed.

One way to avoid the negative connotations or face-threatening concepts within a question is to choose words that transform the negative concept into a less negative, neutral, or positive one. In (2) (see italicised areas) Chirac breaks up the expression 'psychodrama of divorce' and prefers responding to 'psychodrama' and not 'divorce'. By avoiding 'divorce', which in its basic sense is negative, he makes us believe the Franco-America relationship is still intact. He prefers to move 'psychodrama' from the real world to situate it in theatre, which in essence is simply make-believe, and as he adds 'very superficial' and not 'deep-rooted'.

(2)   Chirac
    Q: Mr. President, you talk about friendship. You talk about relationship almost based on love. Yet some of your commentators here are saying that this story has entered the realm of *psychodrama of divorce.*
    A: As you have rightly pointed out in citing other sources, *it indeed [is] a psychodrama.* And psychodrama is all about *drama and theatre.* It is *very superficial.* It isn't *deep-rooted.*

(3)   Chirac

> Q: The fact is, Mr. President, that in America many people think it's
> just because *you are a friend, a pal of Saddam Hussein.*
>
> A: (laughter) That is *a myth.*

(4)   Blair

> Q (Davies in the crowd): But does that mean that we'll be tagging along
> on Mr. Bush's shirt-tails all the time?
>
> A: No, but it means...
>
> Q (Davies): Well that's what it's looking like at the moment.
>
> A: No, we've *got to do what's right for us.* OK, and what I'm saying to
> you is I believe this is a threat that concerns us.

At a time when Saddam Hussein is being painted as the most destructive force on earth, any claim to previous direct contacts with him implicitly makes one a co-member of his destructive enterprise. Chirac
and Amanpour are aware of this, and while Amanpour tries hard to clip
Chirac to Saddam, Chirac does his best to normalise his past relationship with Saddam. In (3) he takes the threatening concept – being a pal
of Saddam (3Q) – away from the normal world to the world of mythology. Myths are often not true. He definitely avoids answering the question but reacts to it. In (4) Blair prefers not to react to the threatening
assessment, 'tagging along on Mr. Bush's shirt-tails' but to transform the
concept into a positive one: 'we've got to do what is right for us'. He
uses the inclusive plural pronoun 'us' which shows his actions are meant
for the good of the nation, including the person who posed the question. This is not directed at saving only his individual face but especially that of his government, the nation, and other members of the
international alliance for the invasion of Iraq.

Generalisation strategy: from clear concept or reference to vague ones

The more generalised ideas are the less personal they become. So transforming a clearly stated issue into a general and vague one through the
use of indefinite adjectives, distances the politician from the negative
consequences of being directly linked to the issue. This gives him or
her the chance to maintain a positive face, since the issue becomes
general and therefore likely to happen to any normal person or country
(6); or is not worth getting into in greater detail (5). In (5) Chirac's turn
starts with laughter and an assessment, both hearable as discrediting
the allegation intimated in the interviewer's question. He however avoids

reacting to the specific issue raised, namely, Saddam Hussein sponsoring his campaigns, but prefers to generalise the reference to himself and the overtly threatening issue. He refers to himself and the accusation more generally by using the indefinite pronouns 'anyone' and 'anything', thereby making himself look like the common guy on the street and the accusation like any gossip around the corner. This protects his public political face, which otherwise would be threatened by the rather personal accusation in the expression 'your electoral campaign'. It also preserves France's face by not linking her to Saddam Hussein – as hinted at in (3).

(5)   Chirac
    Q: There have also been persistent allegations that Saddam Hussein put money into *one of your electoral campaigns.* How do you respond to that?
    A: (laughter) That's preposterous. *Anything* can be said about *anyone* of course. As we say in French, 'The more exaggerated it is, the more likely people will believe it'. I think that is the level of that sort of statement.

(6)   Chirac
    Q: Can I ask you again about the nuclear reactor at Osirak? You know in those days many people called it 'Os-Chirac' [...]
    A: ...in those days *all of the major democracies, all of them, each and everyone of them,* had contacts and trade exchanges with Iraq, including on weapons. Even weapons of mass destruction sometimes, including bacteriological, biological weapons.
    Q: *Which countries* are you *specifically* talking about?
    A: *All of the major democracies. Each and every one* of them.

The focus in (6) is not on Chirac's answer to the implicit accusation that the (French-built) nuclear reactor at Osiraq helped Saddam Hussein develop nuclear capability, but on the fact that his (France's) actions were simply 'business as usual' at the time the reactor was built. He includes France as a co-member in the category 'all of the major democracies' and elaborates what kinds of collaborations with Iraq this group of countries engaged in. He however avoids naming names. He prefers to remain generalised and vague, of course, while responding to the question, since everyone must know the 'major democracies' that had trade contacts with Hussein at the time. When asked to name names, he refuses by repeating the relevant segment from his previous answer, i.e. here he indeed avoids answering the question (meaning, he responds to it but does not answer it). In bringing in 'all of the major democracies' Chirac protects his (France's) international face and, remaining vague on names, protects the faces of 'friends' or threatens the faces of current 'enemies' who then were friends.

Specificity strategy: from a general concept to a specific one

Within a very general concept may be found a particular concept that more than the general one gives the politician more credibility. In this case s/he sifts through the larger set (of unfavourable but related concepts) to pick up the one that helps him or her to maintain a positive face. The botched pre-Iraq war American intelligence generated distrust for all American intelligence. So when Paxman asks Blair if he believes American intelligence (7), the only way to avoid being linked to the inaccuracies of the past, Blair believes, is to be specific, i.e. contextualise his response as much as possible and to refer to 'this' rather than 'all' American intelligence. Similarly, he moves from the more general, indefinite pronoun, 'anything' (8) to what is still an indefinite reference, but one which is less general, though undisclosed – 'things' (undisclosed, perhaps because it is classified information). When pressed further that no 'mass weapons' were being picked up, he tries to make the point clearer but still uses vague and less specific words: 'movement of material'.[5]

(7)   Blair
      Q: And you believe *American intelligence?*
      A: Well I do actually believe *this intelligence.*

(8)   Blair
      Q (Male 1, speaker from crowd): So how come America has got spy satellites and they can't seem to *pick anything* up.
      A: Well they are of course *picking things* up.
      Q (Male 1): They don't seem to be picking *any mass weapons* up or anything other.
      A: Well they're *picking up certainly movement of material* and one of the things that Colin Powell was talking about yesterday was the movement of material shortly before an inspection took place. So, you know, you've got to put it all together and make a judgement.

Correction strategy: from an earlier (misunderstood) position to a new (intended) one

A common aspect of public life is to withdraw, redress or reassess earlier statements on grounds that they were misunderstood, taken out of context, over-applied to incompatible situations, or analysed with bias. Political statements generally take shape according to the social context of the communicative exercise. What may make a strong positive impact in times of war may turn out to be a negative trademark in times of peace. Saving the positive multi-layer face that politicians have therefore implies staying away from those earlier-held positions that are potentially negative at the current moment. This is done by avoiding emphasis on them and, if this cannot be done, rather than refusing them, instead 'correcting' them and/or reanalysing them in ways favourable to the current social context. In (9) Blair refuses the claim made by Paxman but then reanalyses the situation incorporating some of the issues Paxman raises, namely, that the sanctions contained Saddam. To show consistency in his position, he adds the sanctions contained Saddam only to a certain point and no more. This saves him from the looming threats of being linked to the inaccurate American intelligence mentioned above and to the *illegality* of the war.

(9) Blair

Q: Well *you said* of those UN resolutions and the sanctions which followed them in the year 2000, you said that they had contained him. What's happened since?

A: I didn't actually, I *said they'd* contained him up to a point and the fact is –

Q: I'm sorry Prime Minister – We believe that the sanctions regime has effectively contained Saddam Hussein in the last ten years, you said that in November 2000.

A: Well I can assure you *I've said* every time I'm asked about this, they have contained him up to a point and the fact is the sanctions regime *was beginning to crumble*, it's why it's subsequent in fact to that quote *we had* a whole series of negotiations about tightening the sanctions regime but the truth is the inspectors were put out of Iraq so –

To situate the issue in the past, Blair avoids the question 'What's happened since' (which would have taken him into the present), and insists on what he said in the past, adopting the past tense 'I said they'd…' He continues with this tense in his second turn: 'I've said', 'was beginning…', 'we had', which effectively create a discourse distance to a near past, hence emphasising his current position – the one he wants to be accepted.

Non-committal strategy: avoiding making binding commitments

Another linguistic face-saving strategy is to maintain a position that is deemed positive at the time and from which one could retreat or, as the case may be, emphasise on in future. This is generally done by avoiding words that commit or bind one to a future action. Blair does this (10) by not responding to the request to 'give an undertaking' but by rather supporting the second part of the request, which concerns the UN's authorisation of the use of force. By not strictly submitting himself to the request of the speaker, there is no binding point if he decides to change his position in the future. He begins his response by referring to the past 'we've said', meaning whatever he says now does not take priority over what had been said or decided on before.

(10) Blair

    Q: OK, so they report back next week. Will you give *an undertaking to this audience*, and indeed to the British people that before any military action you will seek another UN Resolution, specifically authorising the use of force.

    A: We've said that *that's what we want to do.*

(11) Chirac

    Q: So you are saying you would be prepared *to accept a 30-day or a 60-day deadline?*

    A: I think *whatever the inspectors propose and suggest* in that respect must be accepted. We have given the inspectors a mission, and we have a moral and political obligation *to follow their advice* or else to explain why we are not following it.

In (11), Chirac does not commit himself to any deadline, but prefers to accept 'whatever' (indefinite and vague) proposal the inspectors make. Besides not committing himself, he also shifts responsibility to a third party, the inspectors – to avoid being held to account if it happens to fail (see also following section).

Evidentiality strategy: shifting authorship to a third party

The linguistic avoidance strategy of making concepts less evidential takes place in two ways: using different classes of modal verbs (e.g. *I would say yes*), and shifting authorship of sensitive information to a third party. It is the second that is illustrated here. By shifting authorship, the politician also shifts any consequences for inaccuracies, falsehood, and controversies to that third party. Thus by avoiding taking responsibility for the facts, s/he also avoids losing the positive face s/he wants to maintain. Blair refrains from declaring the use of veto by 'one of those countries' as 'unreasonable' (12). He prefers to shift it to the judgement of the inspectors or one based on their feedback. Chirac shifts authorship of the fact that Saddam Hussein has no weapons of mass destruction to 'ElBaradei and his expert team' (13). He avoids saying what he 'believes', which in fact is what the question requires.

(12) Blair
   A: Because supposing one of those countries – I'm not saying this will happen, I don't believe it will incidentally. But supposing in circumstances where there plainly was a breach of Resolution 1441 and everyone else wished to take action, one of them put down a veto. In those circumstances it would be *unreasonable*.
   Q: And who are we to say it's 'unreasonable' as you put it?
   A: You say that, if in circumstances where *the inspectors – not us –* have come back to the UN and said we can't do our job.

(13) Chirac
   Q: Do you *believe* that Saddam Hussein has weapons of mass destruction, for instance, chemical or biological weapons?
   A: I don't know. I have no *evidence* to support that. But what we can say today, *listening to what ElBaradei is saying and his expert team, it seems* that there are no nuclear weapons or no nuclear programs that would lead to the construction of nuclear weapons.

The above strategies show that framing in discourse determines what meaning the audience is allowed to have. This is not only to evade, persuade, misinform, distort, etc. as previous research has clearly illustrated, but also, as shown here, to save face. Avoiding talking about something, redirecting attention to some other less threatening issue, and not committing oneself to certain demands enable the politician to portray an acceptable positive image, which, though it might not be upright or ideal, nevertheless shows s/he is doing the right thing, for the nation, party, or international alliance.

5.7. Conclusion

Political face-saving in broadcast interviews goes beyond the face-to-face demands of individual face needs (Brown and Levinson, 1987), even though such needs are submerged in it as well. It rather takes into account the four-fold faces politicians respond to (especially at the international) level and is shaped by expectations of the audiences and the interactional context (the interviewer's questions). This is why face-saving as proposed by Brown and Levinson and political face-saving are considered different in this paper. The difference lies in the fact that, whereas interlocutors in Brown and Levinson's (1987: 61) face-saving theory co-operate on basis of 'mutual vulnerability of face', the interlocutors in political face-saving discussed here do not. Their relationship does not permit them to cater for each other's face. The interviewer poses the questions – thus on the offensive and authoritative side, and the interviewee answers them – thus defensive. The interviewer in political face-saving is not bound to co-operate and does not normally do so. Besides trying to show neutrality, it is the interviewer's preoccupation to get the most (negatively) explosive information from the interviewee. The interviewer is therefore not included in the mutual vulnerability mentioned above because s/he asks the questions. S/he frames the questions according to the impact s/he expects and most often this is in disregard of the positive public image of the politician. Amampour's and Paxman's questions are framed in ways that threaten the positive public political images of Chirac and Blair. In an attempt to avoid losing their faces, the interviewees engage in the bizarre 'dodge-ball' co-operation in which they withdraw from, talk around, avoid, or redefine topics they judge as threatening.

By studying linguistic avoidance as a means of political face-saving, this paper has explained some of the interactional dynamics in broadcast political interviews. The framework applied here, I think, can be further applied to other interactive discourses than those on the 'war on terror'. It could as well be applied not only to other contexts in which the interviewer is out to get information to be able to help the interviewee (e.g. doctor-patient exchanges, police-assault victim interviews, etc.) but also to those where the aim is actually to implicate him in one way or the other (courtroom testimonies, presidential debates, police-suspect grilling, etc.). What this essay did not take into account, which should be investigated in further research, is the place of bodily movements and prosodic signals in political face-saving. It would be important to investigate how political face-saving through avoidance is facilitated by: facial expressions, voice tones, postures and gazes, vocal stress and intonation, and (hand) gestures. If this is done, it could be possible to say if the speaker is *redundant* in passing on the message, *contradictory* – facial expression vs. utterance, *inconsistent* in bodily movements, *superficial* in message content or simply *uncooperative* – e.g. insisting every topic is classified. It may also be important to study the absentee role of the audience and the impact it has on the politician. Political interviews expose politicians not only to the often *aggressive* questions of the interviewer but also to the critical eyes of the different audiences – who may not be present at the recording or in the studio, but are present in their minds and out there. Their public political images, if they have to survive the next elections, must be preserved in the eyes of these audiences.

Endnotes

1. It has to be mentioned here that the interviewer does not adopt this *threatening* position in all political interviews. The political atmosphere at any given period impacts the ways the roles in an interview are handled. Interviewers too have limitations in attacking the interviewee's face, for instance, if the interviewer continually interrupts the interviewee or repeats too often a hostile question, this is often considered by the audience as deliberate 'rudeness' and can cause the interviewer to lose 'face'.

2. I decided not to do a linguistic transcription of the interviews because I wasn't going to analyse the inference-rich nonverbal social conduct that interview participants demonstrably orient to, such as inter- and intra-turn pauses, overlaps, and prosodic formats. The strategies seem clear enough, at least at this level of analysis. This explains why the transcripts were simply downloaded from CNN and BBC websites.

3. Interview available at http://edition.cnn.com/2003/WORLD/europe/03/16/sprj.irq.amanpour.chirac/. (viewed 3/11/04).

4. Interview available at http://news.bbc.co.uk/2/hi/programmes/newsnight/2732979.stm. (viewed 10/08/06).

5. I consider this less specific and not outright general because 'movement of material' could be clearly understood from the development of the events at the time, especially Colin Powell's presentation to the UN Security Council on Iraq's supposed use of mobile WMD laboratories and hiding of banned weapons from UN inspectors by constantly moving them from one location to another.

References

Bavelas, J. B., Black A., Bryson L. and Mullett, J. (1988) Political equivocation: A situational explanation. *Journal of Language and Social Psychology* 7: 137–145.

Blum-Kulka, S. (1983) The dynamics of political interviews. *Text* 3: 131–153.

Brown, P. and Levinson, S. C. (1987) *Politeness. Some Universals in Language Usage.* Cambridge: Cambridge University Press.

Bull, P. (1994) On identifying questions, replies, and non-replies in political interviews. *Journal of Language and Social Psychology* 13: 115–131.

Bull, P., Elliott, J., Palmer, D., and Walker, L. (1996) Why politicians are three-faced: the face model of political interviews. *British Journal of Social Psychology* 35: 267–284.

Bull, P. and Mayer, K. (1993) How not to answer questions in political interviews. *Political Psychology* 4: 651–666.

Caffi, C. and Janney, R. (1994) Toward a pragmatics of emotive communication. *Journal of Pragmatics* 22: 325–373.

Channell, J. (1993) *Vague Language.* Oxford: Oxford University Press.

Chilton, P. (1990) Politeness, politics, and diplomacy. *Discourse and Society* 1: 201–224.

Clayman, S. (1992) Footing in the achievement of neutrality: the case of news interview discourse. In P. Drew and J. Heritage (eds.) *Talk at Work* 163–198. Cambridge: Cambridge University Press.

de Kadt, E. (1998) The concept of face and its applicability to the Zulu Language. *Journal of Pragmatics* 29: 173–191.

Fairclough, N. (1989) *Language and Power.* London: Longman.

Fairclough, N. (2000) *New Labour, New Language?* London: Routledge.

Fetzer, A. (2006) Minister, we will see how the public judges you. Media references in political interviews. *Journal of Pragmatics* 38: 180–195:

Goffman, E. (1967) *Interaction Ritual. Essays on Face-to-face Behaviour.* New York: Pantheon Books.

Harris, S. (1991) Evasive action: How politicians respond to questions in political interviews. In P. Scannel (ed.) *Broadcast Talk* 76–99. London: Sage.

Heritage, J. and Roth, A. (1995) Grammar and institution: questions and questioning in the broadcast news interview. *Research on Language and Social Interaction* 28: 1–60.

Janney, R. W. (1999) Linguistic avoidance in the O. J. Simpson transcripts. In W. Falkner and H-G. Schmid (eds.) *Words, Lexemes, Concepts – Approaches to the Lexicon* 259–272. Tubingen: Gunter Narr Verlag Tubingen.

Janney, R. W. (2002) Co-text, contextualisation, and the Israeli–Palestinian conflict in the internet. In E. Mengel, H-J. Schmid and M. Steppat (eds.) *Anglistentag 2002 Proceedings.* Trier: Wissenschaftlicher Verlag Trier.

Jucker, A. (1986) *News Interviews: A Pragmalinguistic Analysis.* Amsterdam: Benjamins.

Lauerbach, G. (2006) Discourse representation in political interviews: The construction of identities and relations through voicing and ventriloquizing. *Journal of Pragmatics* 38: 196–215.

Lederer, R. (2000) Politicians incorrect. *The Vocabula Review* 2: 1–7.

Matsumoto, Y. (1988) Reexamination of the universality of face: Politeness phenomena in Japanese. *Journal of Pragmatics* 12: 403–426.

Obeng, S. G. (1997) Language and politics: verbal indirection in political discourse. *Discourse and Society* 8: 49–83.

Schriffin, D. (1987) *Discourse Markers.* Cambridge: Cambridge University Press.

Tannen, D. (1989) *Talking Voices. Repetition, Dialogue, and Imagery in Conversational Discourse.* Cambridge: Cambridge University Press.

Terkourafi, M. (1999) Frames for politeness: a case study. *Pragmatics* 9: 97–118.

van Dijk, T. (1988) *News as Discourse.* Hillsdale, NJ: Erlbaum.

6
Two sides of the same coin: how the notion of 'face' is encoded in Persian communication

Sofia A. Koutlaki

6.1. Introduction[1]

The starting point of this enquiry has been Brown and Levinson's seminal politeness theory (1978, 1987) and the underpinning notion of face, consisting of two sides, negative and positive face. I set out to discover whether, and to what extent, Brown and Levinson's description of a universal concept of 'face' applied to Persian communication and social reality and to arrive at an emic description of Persian face.[2]

Following the ethnographic tradition, spontaneous conversations among acquaintances were tape-recorded and transcribed. These conversations took place in London and Tehran in 1993-1994 during social encounters: in London among the members of mutually acquainted families of professional personnel of an Iranian company, male and female in the mid-thirties to mid-forties age range; in Tehran, participants belonged to a wider range of educational and professional backgrounds and ages. Thus, all settings involved family or acquaintances in situations where the face of the participants needs to be negotiated and upheld. Based on this extensive body of data, the analysis was supplemented by post-event comments which, although subjective, proved enlightening and useful (Spencer-Oatey, 2007: 654).

In the course of data analysis, a complex picture of Iranian politeness and face emerged, in which certain aspects of Brown and Levinson's construct appeared to have little relevance in Iranian communication. At the same time, the analysis led to the formulation of an account of Persian face comprising two interrelated aspects, *šæxsiæt*[3] and *ehteram* (also known as *aberu*), the first being mainly rooted in the individual's unalterable characteristics and the second being more dynamic but both being actuated into full realisation in interaction.

This chapter makes brief reference to Goffman's and to Brown and Levinson's ideas by way of locating the present work within previous theories. It then provides an account of the Persian concept of face and an analysis of folk terms and expressions. A brief exposition of the three Persian politeness principles through analysis of conversational extracts demonstrates how Persian 'face' is constituted in interaction and how considerations for both aspects and both interlocutors come into play in Persian communication and behaviour. In conclusion, it looks at the implications of this research for Goffman's views and Brown and Levinson's theory.

6.2. The concept of face in the literature

An important basis of my description of face in Persian is Goffman's (1972) concept of face, described as an individual's 'most personal possession and the center of his security and pleasure'. Although face belongs to the individual, it 'is only on loan to him from society'; it will be taken away from him if he, through inappropriate behaviour, shows he is unworthy of it (Goffman, 1972: 322).

An individual's position in society places certain limitations on behaviour: in order to maintain face, a person is expected to live up to their self-image, to show self-respect and not to carry out actions or take part in activities that are out of keeping with that self-image (Goffman, 1967: 7). Such limitations in behaviour stem from pride ('from duty to himself' Goffman, 1967: 9) or honour and, in effect, render the individual his own 'jailer', albeit in a cell of his liking (Goffman, 1967: 9-10). In the same way that an individual is concerned with his or her own face, s/he is also expected to show consideration for others' faces and to work towards upholding their faces because s/he identifies emotionally with them and their feelings (Goffman, 1967: 9-10).

Brown and Levinson's (1978, 1987) seminal politeness theory, harking back to Goffman's ideas, is predicated on a central notion of face, defined as 'the public self-image that every member wants to claim for himself'. According to this purported universal theory, face consists of two aspects, negative and positive face, defined respectively as a model person's 'want to have his freedom of action unhindered and his attention unimpeded,' (Brown and Levinson, 1987:129) and '[his] perennial desire that his wants (or the actions/acquisitions/values resulting from them) should be thought of as desirable' (Brown and Levinson, 1987:101). In polite communication, every act that potentially threatens face is usually accompanied by strategies directed at redressing an interlocutor's negative or positive face.

After numerous criticisms levelled at the notion of negative face mainly by researchers of different cultures (de Kadt 1998; Hill *et al.*, 1986; Ide, 1989; Koutlaki, 1997, 2002; Mao, 1994; Matsumoto, 1988; 1989; Nwoye, 1992), current thought favours the re-visit and re-interpretation of Goffman's concept of face (Bargiela-Chiappini, 2003), which, being dependent on others, 'is only realized in social interaction' (Watts, 2003: 107) and is therefore mutually constructed (de Kadt, 1998: 176) or co-constituted (Arundale, 2006: 196) rather than being rooted in the individual, as Brown and Levinson postulate.

6.3. Face in Iranian culture[4]

My earlier work (1997, 2002) points to the centrality of face considerations in the expression of politeness in Persian. After three years in Iran as participant observer (1997–2000) and many more conversations with Persian native speakers since, I now discern face considerations in mundane and diverse behaviours, such as the size of fruit on offer to guests and petrol-station etiquette which are closely linked to face needs.

Iranians see themselves and others as both individuals and members of social groups, primarily of their family but also of their age, gender, status and professional networks. By adhering to the established behavioural conventions within each network, every member affirms his allegiance to the group, upholds the group's collective face and stakes his claim to his own face.

In parallel with Goffman's pride and honour, Persian face consists of two sides: *šæxsiæt* ('personality', 'character', 'self-respect', 'social standing'), which is understood as the outcome of various parameters such as education and the upbringing a person has received and *ehteram* ('respect', 'esteem', 'dignity'), demonstrated through conformity to the conventions of ritual (*tæ`arof*) politeness and to other behavioural norms in interaction with others. Although the former is more static and the latter more dynamic, their manifestations are closely related. A speaker demonstrates his *šæxsiæt* through his behaviour, including conformity to societal norms and paying the appropriate amount of *ehteram* to an interlocutor (cf. Spencer-Oatey's distinction (2005: 102) between *respectability* (or pan-situational) face and *identity* (or situation-specific) face).

The main difference between *šæxsiæt* and Brown and Levinson's notion of positive face is that the latter refers to an individual's want to be desired, respected and liked, and his wants shared by others; in other words, it is rooted in the individual. Conversely, the Iranian concept does not exist independently of the group and acquires its meaning in connection with it: a person's *šæxsiæt* reflects positively on that person's familial or other identity network. Its impairment affects not only the individual but also the members of the network and its loss is more serious.

The preservation of all interactants' face is paramount. So, for example, requests are refused or suggestions dismissed in ways that do not damage the face of either interlocutor and that of their wider group. One such example involves a speaker M1 (male, early thirties), who would like to borrow a car from M2, his brother-in-law (early forties).

(1)

1   M1:   *færda mašineto lazem dari? con-*
            tomorrow car-of-you-SING need you-SING-have? because-
            mixastæm dustæmo bebæræm frudgah
            I-wanted friend-of-me to-take airport
            'Do you need your car tomorrow? I wanted to drive my friend to
            the airport'

2   M2:   *næ, lazem nædaræm, væli dændæš xærabe*
            no, need I-not-have, but gear-of-it broken-down-is
            mitærsæm ke væsæte rah bezærætet
            I-am-afraid that middle-of road leave-you-SING
            væ bærat moškel ijæd kone, væellah mæsalei næbud
            and for-you-SING difficulty makes, otherwise difficulty not-was
            'No, I don't need it, but there is something wrong with the gear
            box. I'm worried it breaks down on the way, and it creates a
            greater difficulty for you, otherwise it would be no problem'

Familial obligations demand that members must provide any assistance possible to other members. M2 performs an indirect refusal of M1's direct request by presenting the loan of the car as impossible due to circumstances beyond his control. In doing so, M2 also shows conformity to the established norms of family loyalty, gives *ehteram* to M1 and at the same time preserves his own *šæxsiæt*, ensuring that the relationship continues with the same warmth. As M1 explained in a post-event comment, he appreciated the *ehteram* he was given through the way

M2's refusal was formulated. According to M1, M2's effort to preserve M1's face counted more than the outcome of the interaction. At the same time, since M1's sister is M2's wife, her face preservation directly depends on the facework the two interlocutors are engaged in. The delicate balance struck in this interaction points to the loss of face the sister/wife would sustain together with either interlocutor's face damage or loss.

Criticism is another potentially face-threatening situation. The following extract features criticism of a third party, which takes place off-record because in religious terms it is considered backbiting and is heavily proscribed. In the extract below M3 (male, early thirties) and M4 (male, early forties) talk about a common family friend, referred to as *haj aqa* ('pilgrim-sir'– a term of respect), who is also a colleague of M4's and who was supposed to bring a parcel from M3's parents in Tehran to M3 in London. *Haj aqa* failed to turn up to pick the parcel up and eventually M4 and F1, his wife, who also happened to be in Tehran at the time, brought it to its destination. M3 is obviously displeased with *haj aqa*'s negligence. When M4 describes how much trouble M3's father went through to travel across Tehran in order to hand the parcel over to him the conversation continues:

(2)

1   M3:   *are næ næ be qole mæ'ruf ædæm... nemidunæm...hm hm*
                 yes no no to saying famous someone..I-not-know...hm hm
                 'Yes...no no as they say, people..I don't know... hm hm'

2   M4:   *are haj aqa-*
                 yes pilgrim-sir
                 'Yes, the pilgrim-sir...'

3   M3:   *bæle...bæziha ye formi...*
                 yes indeed...some people...one way...
                 'It's true, some people [behave] this way...

4   F1:   *dæstešun dærd nækone, khoda hefzešun kone*
                 their hands not be tired, God protect them
                 'That was very kind of them, may God always be with them [M3's parents]'

M3 avoids saying anything specific about *haj aqa*'s behaviour, but M4 clearly understands M3's displeasure. At the same time, M4 also hesitates to join in with a direct criticism. Haugh (2007: 101) writes that 'a politeness implicature is not co-constituted unless both the speaker and the hearer understand an implicature to have arisen'. In the above example, not only do both interlocutors co-constitute an (im)politeness implicature, but bystander F1, M2's wife, also understands such an implicature to have been created. She enters the conversation with good wishes for M3's parents and the embarrassing moment is over. Here, avoidance of criticism has a *šæxsiæt*-preserving function: M3 avoids overt criticism so as not to damage his *šæxsiæt* and *haj aqa*'s social position and thus create an adverse impression of *haj aqa* and himself on M4, who also acts as he does from the same motives. With her interruption, F1 stems the implicature and its negative effects on both males' faces, and by extension, enhances her own face.

6.4. The principles of Persian politeness

In practice, the two aspects of Persian face are attended to in verbal communication through adherence to three politeness principles: Deference, Humility and Cordiality.[5]

1. Deference Principle: show deference to other; raise other in respect to self.

2. Humility Principle: show respect to other; lower self in respect to other.

3. Cordiality Principle: show interest in other's affairs, concern for other's needs, comfort and welfare; express your agreement, sympathy with and friendliness towards other.

Although these principles are presented separately for the purposes of analysis, they often co-exist in interaction, as it will become clear below. An overview of each principle and the analysis a brief extract demonstrates the interplay between the two aspects of Persian face in practice.

The Deference Principle

In Persian, deference often works reciprocally among equals, thus expressing solidarity, involvement and cordiality. Deference attends to the other's *šæxsiæt* by directly or indirectly acknowledging other as superior, or better than self, even if only nominally so, by paying him *ehteram*. At the same time, self is shown as knowledgeable in the ways of behaviour in society, and therefore self's *šæxsiæt* is satisfied too. This maxim includes a common strategy of praising one's interlocutor in terms of accomplishments, abilities, knowledge or possessions. This means that the Deference and the Humility Principles often mirror each other in practice: speakers who elevate an addressee will often humble themselves.

Scollon and Scollon (1995:44) maintain that a deference politeness system is one in which participants are seen as equals or near equals but treat each other at a distance, for example among professional colleagues who do not know each other well. In equating deference with distance and independence, Scollon and Scollon follow Brown and Levinson, who argue that deference is a negative politeness strategy. The following analysis shows that in Persian deference strategies are directed at enhancing both interlocutors' *šæxsiæt*, which bears some similarity to Brown and Levinson's positive face, in that both relate to a person's good attributes being recognised by others.

In interaction, deference is encoded through a wide array of verbal elements: other-raising and other-praising formulaic polite forms of verbs, such as '*tæšrif avordan*' (lit.'to bring honour' for 'to come'); formulaic phrases and sentences in invitations, apologies, gift offers, food offers, expressions of thanks and compliments; the use of polite pronouns (second person plural for a singular addressee and third person plural for a singular referent - see Extract 4) and other-raising terms of address and reference like *jenab-e-ali* ('your excellency' – used for adult males) and *særkar xanum* (for adult females) (Keshavarz, 1988: 569).

By way of illustration, I look at how compliments in Iranian society often serve a dual function: through the application of the Deference Principle, a speaker elevates an interlocutor's *šæxsiæt* by giving *ehteram*; at the same time, a speaker also lowers the self, adhering to the Humility Principle and showing his own *šæxsiæt*. In a recorded conversation, the hostess has laid the dinner cloth and invites the guests to 'tuck in'. She says to another female guest: *befærma`id; ælbætte be qæzahaye šoma nemirese.* ('Please start; of course this is not as good as the food you cook'). Her utterance functions both as a compliment and a ritual (*tæ`arof*) apology: she presents the guest's cooking as superior to hers and indirectly apologises for the inferior quality of her own. The guest subsequently reverses the situation saying that she does not know how to cook at all. The motive behind this utterance is to elevate the guest in deference and to exhibit her humility, with the effect of enhancing both interlocutors' face. The guest's response mirrors that of the host in content and function.

A female informant expressed the view that a hostess who apologises for or degrades the food she has cooked feels very confident about her dishes and is actually 'fishing for compliments'. In reality, however, even though someone may be proud of her accomplishments and achievements and not consider that those of her interlocutor are remotely similar, she has to present the self as lower and praise the other, in order to attend to her own and the other's *šæxsiæt*.

An other-raising compliment functioning as an expression of thanks was recorded on tape. F2 visited F3's house for the first time and brought her a present (*cešm roshani* – lit. 'eye-brightening'). F3 thanked her with *šoma ke umædin xunæmuno rošæn kærdin* ('you brightened our house with your arrival').[6]

The following example demonstrated the strongly formulaic nature of compliments and compliment responses in Persian. Extract 3 is taken from the same interaction and features a *faux pas* which shows how deeply ingrained compliment and compliment response formulae are in the speakers' minds.

(3)   F2, a female in her late thirties, admires F3's pendant, the latter also
       being female but in her twenties

1   F2:   *ce qædr qæšænge!*
            how much beautiful is
            'What a beautiful pendant!'

2   F3:   *piškeš.*
            You can have it.

3   F2:   *qabeli nædare.*
            worth not-has
            'It's not worthy [of you]'
            ((F2 laughs in embarrassment))

4   *mæno bebin ce hærfai mizænæm!*
            me you-SING-look what talk I-do)
            'What did I say, silly me!'

In utterance 3, F2 uses a functional equivalent of 2, which is used as a compliment response, minimising the value of the object and nominally offering it to the compliment initiator. The customary succession of compliment and compliment response is so strong in speaker F2 that she gets 'carried away' by it and commits a *faux pas* by denigrating the object of her compliment, hence her embarrassment in utterance 4.

In Persian, even though a speaker humbles the self while elevating an interlocutor's status he hardly expects him to agree with the force of the compliment. The expected response would be a 'mirroring' of the speaker's behaviour: the interlocutor will humble self and elevate the speaker. A possible response to a compliment is *extiar darid, maro šærmænde mikonid* ('you are free to say anything you like, but what you say embarrasses me') (Rafiee, 1992:85-86). Rafiee adds that some Iranians will characterise a speaker as immodest or arrogant if he responds with an expression of thanks as acceptance of a compliment. The recipient cannot express outright acceptance because of the operation of the Humility Maxim. In the body of my data several responses to compliments took the shape of one or more expressions of gratitude, of which Persian abounds. Native speakers explain that an expression of thanks in such cases does not mean an acceptance of the compliment, but an acknowledgement of a speaker's intention to give *ehteram*. By using an expression of gratitude one is simply acknowledging the intention behind the compliment and thanks the initiator for it, but one does not accept the compliment. It is all part of the make-up of Persian communication and the importance of attending to the *šæxsiæt* of self and the other in interaction.

The Humility Principle

Similarly to deference, humility is expressed through the use of various strategies: self-lowering forms of verbs; first person plural pronoun *ma* ('we') to indicate one speaker (the opposite of the 'royal plural' in English); formulaic expressions in invitations, apologies, gift offers, food offers, expressions of thanks and compliments; formulaic expressions in response to them; 'low' forms of verbs, such as *xedmat residæn* (lit. 'to arrive at your service' for 'to come'); and self-lowering formulaic reference terms, e.g. *bænde* (male slave), *hæqir* (humble), *moxles* (sincere), *caker* (devoted servant), all used by males (Keshavarz 1988:567).

The following extract was recorded at a university in Tehran. During my visit to a fellow sociolinguist (M5, male, mid forties), he offered to ask his senior colleague (M6, male, late fifties) to come to his office to meet me and talk about politeness and face. This was the first time they saw each other after the Iranian New Year holiday (21 March) and according to the custom, M5 should have called first on M6, his senior in years, to offer his New Year wishes. When M6 came in, M5 said to him:

(4)

1   M5:   *behærhal bayæd orzxahiye maro bepæzirin ke zudtær*
          anyway must apologies of-us you-PL-accept that earlier
          xedmætetun næresidim. væzifeye ma bud ke-

to-service of-you-PL we-not-arrived. duty of-us was
xedmætetun beresim.
to service of you-PL we-arrive.
'Please accept my [lit. 'our'] apologies for not coming to see you
earlier. It was my [lit. 'our'] duty to pay our respects [first]'
((Shortly afterwards, after introducing me, he explained how I
came to be there))

2   M5:   *išun ye mæqale næqabeli maro xundæn...*
         they one article worthless of-us they-read...
         'she [lit. 'they'] happened to read an unworthy article of mine [lit.
         'us']'

3   M6 : *xaheš mikonæm...*
         request I-do
         'Please [i.e. don't say that]'

Here, the combined effect of the use of *ma* (we) instead of 'I', the choice
of *xedmæt residæn* ('to come to somebody's service'), instead of *amædæn*
('to come'), together with M5's apology for neglecting his 'duty' to visit
M6 first and his reference to his article as 'unworthy', create a strong
overall impression of humility, simultaneously conveying deference to
M6. Through his utterances, M5 pays *ehteram* to M6 and enhances his
own and M6's *šæxsiæt*. M5 humbles himself thus elevating his *šæxsiæt*
through the use of the phrase 'unworthy article' (cf. Chen 1993: 68 who
reports that Chinese academics often refer to their work as 'my humble
work'). It seems that he did not want to appear as showing off in the
presence of his senior colleague, especially as the article was written in
English. M6's response indicates that he is aware of what M5 is trying to
do and is in effect telling him that he does not need to, at the same time
also enhancing his own and M5's face.

After talking with M6 for more than half an hour, I thanked him for
his time. His formulaic response *bebæxšid væqte šomara gereftim* ('sorry
we [lit. 'I'] took your time') underscored the deeply ingrained nature of
the Humility Principle: he cast himself as the 'intruder' and offered an
apology, shoring up his *šæxsiæt* and giving me the prompt to do the
same by remonstrating and offering profuse thanks and apologies.

The Cordiality Principle

Behaviour conforming to this maxim asserts and strengthens relationships through the demonstration of interest in others' affairs, appreciation of their efforts, helpfulness and concern for their welfare and comfort.

Such behaviour can take the shape of: health and other enquiries; repeated offers of refreshments; repeated genuine or ritual (*tæ'arof*) offers of help and refusals thereof (Koutlaki 2002); ostensible and on-the-spot invitations; apologies functioning as thanking expressions and other expressions of thanks; and extended closings of interactions.

The following extract is an extended closing featuring ostensible invitations, apologies as thanking expressions and other expressions of thanks. It takes place at the end of a dinner party. M7 (male, early thirties), M8 (male, early forties), F4 (M8's wife, mid-thirties) and F5 (M7's wife, late twenties) have had dinner at the house of M8's boss, M9 (male, early forties). F6, the hostess, is M9's wife, in her mid-thirties. The guests are making their way to the front door. (As becomes clear from the utterance numbering, some utterances have been omitted here to avoid repetitiveness.)

(5)

4   M8:   *zæhmæt dadim.*
               trouble we-gave
               'Sorry for the trouble we gave you'

5   F4:   *zæhmæt dadim, jæmoruræm nækærdim.*
               trouble we-gave, tidy-up-too not did
               'Sorry for the trouble – I didn't even help you tidy up'
               ((section omitted))

8   F6:   *bebæxšin dige.*
               you-PL forgive more
               'Sorry [you've had a bad time]'
               ((section omitted))

10   M7:   *æz un ruz ta hala ma xedmæt næresidim*
               from that day until now we service not-arrived
               šoma eftexar bedino dær xedmæt bašim ma enšallah.
               you-PL honour give-and at service we-be God willing
               'Since that day we haven't had the chance to be at your service [for dinner] – to do us the honour to be at your service, God willing'

11   M9:   *enšallah enšallah enšallah.*
               God-willing God-willing God-willing
               'Hopefully we will'

12   F6:   *bebæxšin bæd gozæšt.*
               you-PL-forgive bad passed
               'I'm sorry you've had a bad time'
               ((to F5))

13   F6:   *æz kadoye...qæšængetun xeili mæmnun.*
             from present nice-of-you-PL very obliged
             'Thank you for your lovely present'

14   F5:   *xaheš mikonæm in qabeli nædare– xaheš mikonæm.*
             request I-do this worth not-has request I-do
             'You're welcome, it was nothing really, you're welcome'

15   F6:   *zæhmæt kešidin.*
             trouble you-PL took
             'Thank you for coming'

16   F5:   *zæhmæt dadim.*
             trouble we-gave
             'Sorry for the trouble'
             ((The guests proceed to the front door while the hosts accompany
             them))

17   M6:   *xob dige xoda hafez.*
             well God protector
             'Good night then'

18   F6:   *tæšrif biarin bazæm aqaye...M7.*
             honour you-PL-bring again Mr M7
             'Do come again, Mr M7'

19   F5:   *šomam hæm intor ælan dige nobæte šomast.*
             you-PL too this-way now you-PL-is
             'You too. Now it's your turn'

20   M7:   *xaheš mikonæm–*
             request I-do
             'Please'
             ((section omitted))

22   F4:   *šomam tæšrif biarin.*
             you-PL too honour bring
             'You must come too'

23   M7:   *cæšm, cæšm, ætmæn...šoma fe'læn–*
             alright, alright, definitely...you-PL now
             'We will, definitely, but you should-'

24   F6:   *dige yad gereftin dige.*
             now memory you-PL-took
             'You know the way now'
             ((section omitted))

27   M7:   *enšallah ke...xedmæt miresim šoma tæšrif biarin.*
God-willing that...service we-arrive you-PL anyway honour you-PL
bring
'Hopefully we will come but you will also come'

28   F6:   *baše.*
let-it-be
'Okay'

29   M9:   *enšallah.*
God willing
'Hopefully'

30   F4:   *aqaye M9 zæhmæt dadim, bebæxšin.*
Mr M9, trouble we-gave, you-PL forgive
'Sorry for the trouble, Mr M9.'

31   M9:   *xaheš mikonæm.*
request I-do
'Don't mention it'
((section omitted))

49   F6:   *xeili xošhal šodim, zæhmæt kešidin.*
very happy we-became, trouble you-PL-took
'It's been nice having you here, thank you for taking the trouble to
come'

50   F5:   *xaheš mikonæm, zæhmæt dadim.*
request I-do, trouble we-gave
'The pleasure was all ours, sorry for the trouble'

51   M7:   *xaheš mikonæm.*
request I-do
'The pleasure was all ours'
((The guests come out to the street, the hosts following. Everyone
says *'xoda hafez'* ('goodbye') to everyone else. After a final round
of *'xoda hafez'*, the guests get in their cars and drive off.))

The numerous apologies by the host and the guests in utterances 4, 5, 8, 12, 16, 30 and 50 orchestrate an elaborate facework sequence: guests nominally apologise for their visit and the trouble they have given the hosts, whereas the hosts also nominally apologise for the 'bad' time the guests have had with them. The net effect of this complex interaction is that all participants pay face to an interlocutor at the same time enhancing their own and their family's face.

Coulmas, writing about Japanese, points out that thanks and apologies are both appropriate in certain contexts, where '[t]he link between the object of gratitude and the object of regret is the concept of

indebtedness' (1981: 79). His account of Japanese apologies shows strik-
ing similarities with Persian, in that the use of apologies conveys the
speaker's conformity to social rules; in fact, very often this seems to be
their only purpose. Because a benefactor has taken trouble on another's
behalf, the one who benefited holds herself responsible and feels that
an apology is called for (ibid. 84).

Ostensible invitations, featured in the above extract in utterances 10,
18, 19, 22, 24 and 27, are par excellence face-enhancing expressions of
cordiality. Beeman, in his extensive account of Persian communication
writes (1986: 185–186):

> an offhand invitation [SAK: ostensible] will be interpreted as
> something else – most often a move to break the interaction
> event, or a proper closing. A common example of this occurs
> when one person accompanies or conveys another to his or her
> home. The invitation at the door to come inside for tea or for
> dinner is a *sincere expression – of thanks or regard –* but it is rarely
> a sincere invitation, even though issued as a petition...Such
> situations give the guest (he/she who was accompanied or
> conveyed) a final opportunity to turn the tables and place himself
> in a subordinate position. The conventional use of these petition-
> invitations is so widespread for purposes of closing off interactions
> that everyone (except foreigners) knows not to accept them. If an
> invitation is sincere, it will be repeated up to three times after the
> first denial. Even then it is rarely wise to accept unless one is
> willing and ready to begin the gradual move toward intimate
> equality. (Beeman 1986: 185–186, my emphasis)

In my experience, such expressions of thanks or regard (according to
Beeman) or cordiality and warmth in my own terms are very common
and only very close relatives or friends have acceptance as a real op-
tion. This fieldwork example shows this convention in action. Recorded
in my field notes were three lunch invitations, two of which were refused and one that was taken up. During the first days after the Iranian
New Year in Iran (21 March), it is customary for all members of the
extended family to visit each other, starting with younger members visiting the older ones. As all visits must usually be completed within the
first twelve days of the New Year, visitors come at any time of the day,
as people try to visit everyone who lives in the same area on the same
day, in order to save time.

On that day, it was near lunchtime when the hostess's niece and her
husband came to visit. When they indicated their intention to go, F7
said *tæšrif dašte bašin bæraye nahar* ('honour you-PL have for lunch'

i.e. 'honour us by staying for lunch'), but they excused themselves saying that they had another engagement. F7 did not insist more.

Later, another niece, her husband and children came to visit and the same invitation with the same results ensued. Still later, F7's brother in-law, his wife and daughters came and the same invitation was repeated. At first he refused very strongly, saying that they had had lunch, but then he added *diruz* ('yesterday'), which, according to F7, indicated that they would not mind staying as they had not had lunch. After some more insistence and refusal they decided to stay, having realised that there was enough food and that it would cause the hosts no inconvenience.

When I asked F7 why the outcome of the last invitation was different from the other two, she replied that there were several reasons: whenever her family visits these last guests, they are usually offered lunch or dinner, so such invitations are not unusual between them. Apart from that, she knew that they had not had lunch and that they were planning to visit some more relatives in the same area, so they would not be returning home until much later.

Ostensible invitations are often issued as a matter of course when guests come to one's house near a mealtime. Informants explained that such invitations show hospitality and good manners and that one would expect to be invited as a sign of respect even if it is known and expected that one would refuse. The absence of an invitation is likely to be interpreted as lack of manners and proper regard and therefore will be perceived as lack of *ehteram* on the part of the host towards the guest, but will also reflect badly on the host's *šæxsiæt*. It was said that such invitations are a social duty and routine, like saying *sælam* ('peace' – the Islamic greeting) first.

An informant explained that when a guest is already in one's house, if an invitation to the guest to stay for a meal is meant genuinely, it will be issued early on during the visit and will possibly be followed by bringing house-clothes for him or her to change into. If the host does not really want the guest to stay for a meal, he does not mention the meal during the visit. However, it is a social convention to issue at least one *tæ'arof* invitation, often more, usually when the guest is ready to go, perhaps when putting on his shoes/overcoat, which is perceived as the signal of definite departure. At that point the host may say '*mimundin hala*' ('you could have stayed, you know'). This timing makes it clear that the invitation was not meant to be taken up but is nevertheless an expression of hospitality, good manners and *ehteram* towards the guest.

6.5. Conclusion

The present work demonstrates two important characteristics of Persian facework, the collectivist nature of face and the dual function of Persian speech acts in enhancing both interlocutors' and their family's/group's face. It also highlights some similarities with and some important differences from previous theories.

In common with Brown and Levinson, Persian face is realised and negotiated through specific verbal behaviours, which have a direct impact on speakers' and addressees' face. However, unlike Brown and Levinson, whose construct of face is *firmly rooted in an individual's wants*, Persian face is *collectivist*. Since face considerations underpin all communication among speakers who have a social relationship, Persian face (*šæxsiæt*) does not only consist of one's individual positive or negative face wants; it also includes group face wants, enhanced through adherence to social conventions. Such a concept of collective face is in line with the closely-knit ties that exist among members of nuclear and extended family, and the circles of friends and acquaintances. Verbal behaviour, such as ritual (*tæ'arof*) politeness, formality and the speech acts examined in this chapter, as well as non-verbal behaviour, such as sitting upright and not stretching one's legs in the presence of seniors, all attend to a speaker's face, and by extension to his family/group's face, but also, very importantly, to an addressee's and his family/group's face simultaneously. Similarly, unacceptable behaviour reflects badly not only on the initiator but also on his family or group.

I have shown that, in Persian at least, some speech acts, characterised as Face Threatening Acts (FTAs) by Brown and Levinson but functioning as Face Enhancing Acts in Persian,[7] tend to the maintenance of both interactants' and their extended group's face (*šæxsiæt*) through the demonstration of *ehteram*.

Another important difference between the present description of Persian face and Brown and Levinson's schema relates to the function of specific FTAs. According to Brown and Levinson, acts such as offers and compliments threaten the addressee's negative face, expressions of thanks and unwilling offers threaten the speaker's negative face, while apologies damage the speaker's positive face. Such views, apart from a passing reference (1987: 67) to the possibility of an act threatening both negative and positive face, have two implications: firstly, that individual speech acts can have only *one function* and secondly, that individual speech acts have only *threatening effects*. Literature has documented the possibility, or rather the certainty, of the co-existence of self-respect and considerateness during an encounter and has recognised that discourse can, and often does, have multiple goals (see e.g. Tracy and Coupland 1990; Penman 1990).

This discussion of Iranian face therefore comes full circle back to Goffman's views: firstly that an individual operates with consideration towards both his and others' face simultaneously (Goffman 1967:11), as I have shown in the analysis, and secondly, that a person's face is on loan to him from society. In Iranian society, as in other collectivist societies, an individual is expected both to adhere to social norms and to avoid socially reprehensible behaviours in order to hold on to his face and to uphold that of others.

Endnotes

1. I would like to thank the anonymous reviewers of this chapter whose constructive comments have improved it greatly. Errors, omissions and inaccuracies remain my own responsibility.
2. An emic account of data employs terms and categories that are meaningful to the speakers under study; an etic account employs terms and categories that have been agreed *a priori* (Saville-Troike, 1989).
3. The English letters I have used in the transliteration of Persian text have approximately the same values as in English, apart from the following (descriptions based on Lambton 1961): **x**: voiceless velar uvular with scrape, approximating to **ch** in the Scottish word *loch*; **š** : voiceless post-alveolar fricative, corresponding to **sh** in *show*; **q**: voiced or voiceless uvular plosive, according to phonetic context; **æ** as in English *hat*; **a** as in English *bath*.
4. The terms 'Persian' and 'Iranian' are often used interchangeably in the literature, because Persian (Farsi) is the official language of The Islamic Republic of Iran and the Persians the most numerous ethnic group. The term 'Iranian' includes Persians, Azeri Turks, Kurds, Arabs and other ethnic groups living within the political borders of the country and speaking different languages. Since my research examined communication in the Persian language, I have opted for the use of 'Persian' to refer to the language, face and communication; I have used 'Iranian' to refer to the society, the people, the culture and the New Year holiday. I accept that this decision may be seen as arbitrary and that I have not always applied it consistently.
5. My formulation of these principles owes a debt to Leech's (1983, 15–151) Maxims of Politeness. For a fuller discussion, see Koutlaki (1997, ch.6; 2002).
6. A similarly formulaic compliment with the function of thanks for a visit is quoted by Rafiee (1992: 156) as *kolbe xærabeye maro monævvær kærdid* ('you have brought light to our dilapidated hovel').

7. This statement should not be taken to mean that there are no FTAs in Persian; criticism, backbiting, 'real' apologies and being 'shown up' are some such. For a more detailed exposition see Koutlaki (1997, ch. 5).

References

Arundale, R. B. (2006) Face as relational and interactional: a communication framework for research on face, facework, and politeness. *Journal of Politeness Research* 2: 193–216.

Bargiela-Chiappini, F. (2003) Face and politeness: new (insights) for old (concepts). *Journal of Pragmatics* 35: 1453–1469.

Beeman, W. O. (1986) *Language, Status and Power in Iran.* Bloomington, IN: Indiana University Press.

Brown, P. and Levinson, S. C. (1978) Universals in language usage: politeness phenomena. In E. N. Goody (ed.) *Questions and Politeness. Strategies in Social Interaction* 56–310. Cambridge: Cambridge University Press. (Reissued 1987 with corrections, new introduction and new bibliography)

Chen, R. (1993) Responding to compliments: A contrastive study of politeness strategies between American English and Chinese speakers. *Journal of Pragmatics* 20: 49–75.

Coulmas, F. (1981) 'Poison to your soul': thanks and apologies contrastively viewed. In F. Coulmas (ed.) *Converational Routine* 69–91. The Hague: Mouton.

de Kadt, E. (1998) The concept of face and its applicability to the Zulu language. *Journal of Pragmatics* 29: 173–191.

Goffman, E. (1967) *Interaction ritual: Essays on face-to-face behavior.* New York: Doubleday.

Goffman, E. (1972) On facework: an analysis of ritual elements in social interaction. In J. Laver and S. Hutcheson (eds.) *Communication in Face-to-face Interaction. Selected Readings* 319–346. Harmondsworth: Penguin.

Haugh, M. (2007) The co-constitution of politeness implicature in conversation. *Journal of Pragmatics* 39: 84–110.

Hill, B., Ide, S., Ikuta, S., Kawasaki, A. and Ogino, T. (1986) Universals of Linguistic Politeness. Quantitative evidence from Japanese and American English. *Journal of Pragmatics* 10: 347–371.

Ide, S. (1989) Formal forms and discernment: two neglected aspects of linguistic politeness. *Multilingua* 8: 223–248.

Keshavarz, M. H. (1988) Forms of address in post-revolutionary Iranian Persian: a sociolinguistic analysis. *Language in Society* 17: 565–575.

Koutlaki, S. A. (1997) *The Persian System of Politeness and the Persian Folk Concept of Face, with Some Reference to EFL Teaching to Iranian Native Speakers.* Unpublished PhD thesis, University of Wales College of Cardiff.

Koutlaki, S. A. (2002) Offers and expressions of thanks as face enhancing acts: tae'arof in Persian. *Journal of Pragmatics* 34: 1733–1756.

Lambton, A. K. S. (1961) *Persian Grammar.* Cambridge: Cambridge University Press.

Leech, G. (1983) *Principles of Pragmatics.* London: Longman.

Mao, L R. (1994) Beyond politeness theory: 'face' revisited and renewed. *Journal of Pragmatics* 21: 451–486.

Matsumoto, Y. (1988) Reexamination of the universality of face: politeness phenomena in Japanese. *Journal of Pragmatics* 12: 403–426.

Matsumoto, Y. (1989) Politeness and conversational universals – observations from Japanese. *Multilingua* 8: 207–221.

Nwoye, O. G. (1992) Linguistic politeness and sociocultural variations of the notion of face. *Journal of Pragmatics* 18: 309–328.

Penman, R. (1990) Facework and Politeness: Multiple goals in courtroom discourse. *Journal of Language and Social Psychology* 9: 15–38.

Rafiee, A. (1992) *Variables of Communicative Incompetence in the Performance of Iranian Learners of English and English Learners of Persian.* Unpublished PhD thesis, University of London.

Saville-Troike, M. (1989) *The Ethnography of Communication: An Introduction.* Oxford: Basil Blackwell.

Scollon, R. and Scollon, S. (1995) *Intercultural Communication.* Oxford: Basil Blackwell.

Spencer-Oatey, H. (2005) (Im)politeness, face and perceptions of rapport: Unpackaging their bases and interrelationships. *Journal of Politeness Research* 1: 95–119.

Spencer-Oatey, H. (2007) Theories of identity and the analysis of face. *Journal of Pragmatics* 39: 639–656.

Tracy, K. and Coupland, N. (1990) Multiple goals in discourse: An overview of issues. In K. Tracy and N. Coupland (eds.) *Multiple Goals in Discourse* 1–13. Clevedon: Multilingual Matters.

Watts, R. J. (2003) *Politeness.* Cambridge: Cambridge University Press.

Part II

Face, identity and self

7
Face, identity and interactional goals

Helen Spencer-Oatey

7.1. Introduction

The aim of this chapter is to demonstrate that the effective study of face needs to take an identity perspective that is action-oriented. This is important because it will help us understand the face concerns that emerge dynamically in interaction as significant to the interlocutors. Much work in face and politeness theory takes an *a priori* approach to face sensitivity. Brown and Levinson (1987), for example, argue that certain speech acts are intrinsically face-threatening to either the speaker or the hearer, and Leech (2005) maintains that some types of illocutionary goals, such as requests or criticism of a hearer, compete or are at odds with the social goal of maintaining good communicative relations. In this chapter, I argue that such an *a priori* approach ignores the dynamic aspect of people's face sensitivities. Furthermore, much work in face and politeness theory has focused on the face concerns of the hearer and has paid less attention to those of the speaker. In this chapter, I argue that a speaker's own face concerns may emerge as crucially important in authentic interaction, and that a speaker's self-presentational concerns thus need to be incorporated into the study of face and given equal weighting to those of the hearer.

   A number of years ago, Tracy and Baratz (1994: 290) argued, rightly in my view, that the goal of face theory should be to help us understand 'what is going on interactionally'. In order to achieve this, we need to take an action-oriented approach to the study of face – one that analyses the communicative activity as a whole, not just face issues. This means broadening our focus of study in two main ways. Firstly, we need to give fuller consideration to all of the interactional goals that each of the participants may hold (i.e. not just their face concerns), and secondly it may mean extending our unit of analysis from a single communicative activity, such as a meeting, to a more complex series of activities, such as a delegation visit, which comprises a series of meetings, social events and so on.

I start the chapter with a brief review of two approaches to the study of identity that are particularly relevant to the analysis of face. I then apply insights from these approaches to the analysis of some authentic interactional data, and I conclude the chapter with a brief discussion of the research implications of such an approach.

7.2. Theories of identity

There are many different theoretical approaches to the study of identity. Here I focus on two that are particularly relevant to the study of face: self-aspect/attribute approaches to identity (e.g. Simon, 2004; Jones and McEwen, 2000) and self-presentation (e.g. Leary, 1996; Schlenker and Pontari, 2000). First, though, I would like to clarify my interpretation of the concept of identity. Simon (2004) starts his book by warning that identity may be an analytic fiction and that the search for its essence as a 'thing' may be a misleading endeavour that diverts our efforts from a more promising process-oriented course. Nevertheless, he maintains that if it is taken as a shorthand expression or placeholder for social psychological processes revolving around self-definition or self-interpretation, including the variable but systematic instantiations of this, the notion of identity will serve as a powerful conceptual tool. Campbell, Assanand and Di Paula (2000: 67) offer a useful definition of the self, compatible with this, which can be paraphrased as follows:

> The self-concept is a multi-faceted, dynamic construal that contains beliefs about one's attributes as well as episodic and semantic memories about the self.

Self-aspect/attribute approaches to identity

Simon's (2004) 'Self-Aspect Model of Identity' proposes that a person's self-concept comprises beliefs about his/her own attributes or self-characteristics. These can be huge in number, and typically include elements such as:

- Personality traits (e.g. shy)

- Abilities (e.g. poor dancer)

- Physical features (e.g. curly hair, slim)
- Behavioural characteristics (e.g. usually gets up early)
- Religious beliefs (e.g. Christian, atheist)
- Social roles (e.g. project manager)
- Language affiliation(s) (e.g. English, Chinese)
- Group memberships (e.g. female, academic, Christian)

People may differ in the degree to which they differentiate their various attributes (i.e. the number of different facets that an individual spontaneously uses in thinking about the self) and the degree to which they are integrated (i.e. the extent to which the various facets are interrelated). Nevertheless, people (consciously or unconsciously) perceive and evaluate their self-aspects in a number of different ways, as shown in Table 7.1.

Table 7.1: Ways in which self-aspects can be perceived and evaluated

Criteria	Evaluative Judgements		
Valence	Negative ←→ Neutral ←→ Positive		
Actuality	Actual ←——→ Ideal		
Currency	Past ←→ Present ←→ Future		
	Context 1 ←→ Context 2 ←→ Context 3		
Centrality	Core ←——→ Peripheral		

Valence refers to the degree of attraction or aversion that an individual feels towards a given self-aspect. For all of us, we evaluate certain aspects of ourselves positively, we dislike other aspects, and we are neutral about yet other aspects. Actuality refers to the distinction between ideal and actual characteristics. Some attributes reflect what we are like in reality; others reflect what we are striving to be like or what we think we ought to be like. Currency refers to time and contextual judgements regarding self-aspects. In terms of time, we judge some attributes as applying to what we used to be like; we judge others as reflecting what we are currently like, and we anticipate that yet other attributes will apply to us in the future. In terms of context, we judge some attributes as applying to us in certain contexts, and other attributes as applying to us in other contexts. Centrality refers to the extent to which a given self-aspect is crucial to, or defining of, our sense of who we are; some elements are core while others are more peripheral.

Superficially it may seem as though this conception of identity is rather static and fixed, but in reality it is quite the opposite. People can construe their identity attributes in very dynamic ways. Jones and McEwen (2000), for example, are particularly interested in the dynamic multiplicity of identity, and have used in-depth, open-ended interviews to explore this issue. They report the following findings:

- People have a core sense of self that is not externally visible and that incorporates 'valued personal attributes and characteristics'. The interviewees frequently described this core as their 'inner identity' or 'inside self'.

- Surrounding the core, and at times integrally connected with it, are more externally defined attributes, such as gender, race and religion, which themselves are often interconnected (e.g. interviewees talked of themselves as a black woman or Christian man).

- The relative salience (or centrality) of different identity attributes varies across individuals, across contexts, and across time (e.g. race was very salient for the black women in the study but was rarely salient for the white women).

- Contexts (which in the study were interpreted as socio-cultural conditions, family background, career decisions and life planning, current experiences, etc.) have a major impact on the ways in which people construct and experience their identities.

Impression management and self-presentation

Schlenker and Pontari (2000) define impression management and self-presentation as follows:

> We define *impression management* as the goal-directed activity of controlling information about some person, object, idea, or event to audiences. People try to control information about themselves, friends or associates, enemies, ideas (e.g. their political ideologies and opinions), organizations (e.g. their companies, political parties), and events (e.g. activities in which they were engaged). *Self-presentation* is a more specific term that refers to the control of information about self. (Schlenker and Pontari, 2000: 201)

Schlenker and Pontari (2000) start with the assumption that people pursue multiple goals in their daily life, and that these vary in importance and in the amount of cognitive attention required. They argue that self-presentation concerns are relevant to all social interactions, not just to highly evaluative situations such as first dates and job interviews. The concerns can operate in foreground or background modes, but are never absent. Like computer anti-virus programs, they may run unobtrusively for much of the time, but the moment a problem arises, they capture the user's attention. This is a useful analogy for considering face.

Schlenker and Pontari (2000) acknowledge that to some people, self-presentation is inherently pretentious and duplicitous in that if information is controlled to have a desired impact, it cannot be genuine or sincere. However, they strongly refute this viewpoint, explaining that all effective communication requires appropriate modification for the audience, and that the truthfulness or duplicity of the speaker is another issue altogether.

Tracy (1990: 215) argued many years ago that face theorists could benefit from paying more attention to self-presentation theories, especially in terms of the wider range of identity claims recognised in self-presentation studies compared with studies of face. However, since then there has been little uptake of her recommendation. This chapter aims to help rectify this situation.

Face and identity

What then, is the interconnection between face and identity? To what extent do the concepts overlap? I suggest that cognitively the two are similar in that both relate to the notion of 'self'-image (including individual, relational and collective construals of self; see Spencer-Oatey, 2007) and both comprise multiple self-aspects or attributes. However, face is only associated with attributes that are affectively sensitive to the claimant. It is associated with positively-evaluated attributes that the claimant wants others to acknowledge (explicitly or implicitly), and with negatively-evaluated attributes that the claimant wants others NOT to ascribe to him/her.

Furthermore, I maintain that in the course of an interaction, people only feel a threat/loss/gain in face when they perceive that an attribute they are claiming is not ascribed to them by others (or vice versa, in the case of negatively-evaluated traits). For example, if someone wants to be regarded as fashionable and is told that s/he is 'old fashioned', this will be more face-threatening to him/her than to someone who cares less about fashion. Moreover, people may attach varying importance to different attributes in different contexts; for instance, a working mother may claim the attribute 'efficient' more strongly at work than at home. So frameworks that make *a priori* assumptions about face sensitivities will inevitably be inaccurate; they can provide a useful starting point, but interactants always need to be on the look out for personal and contextual variations. (See Spencer-Oatey, 2007 for further discussion of the interrelationship between the concepts of face and identity.)

7.3. Research procedure

The data used in this chapter to illustrate the value of an action-oriented identity approach to the study of face were collected in the summer of 1997, as part of a study of rapport management in Chinese–British business interactions. That study took place at the University of Bedfordshire from 1996 to 2000, and the data were collected jointly by Jianyu Xing and me. The research design for the study was emergent rather than pre-specified.

The business background

The Chinese–British business interactions took place in England at the headquarters of a British engineering company. This British company designs, manufactures and sells an engineering product that is used in industrial plants throughout the world. In every contract signed in China, they agree to host a delegation of up to six people who are involved in some way in the deal. The cost of the delegation visit is added to the contract price, and there is an unofficial understanding that any balance remaining at the end of the visit is given to the visitors as 'pocket money'.

The British company handles all the administration associated with the visit, and prepares a programme of events which includes a welcome meeting, training sessions, local business visits, sightseeing, shopping and social activities, and ends with a close-out meeting. The visit normally lasts about 10 days, and the official purpose is to inspect the products purchased, to receive technical training, and to have an enjoyable time sightseeing. In the case of this particular visit, however, the products had already been shipped and installed, so the visitors were unable to inspect the goods.

The data and data collection

Three types of data were collected for analysis during the 10-day visit: (1) video recordings of all the official meetings between the British and Chinese business people; (2) field notes of supplementary aspects of the visits; and (3) interview and playback comments made by the participants. The British and Chinese participants were interviewed separately.

Prior to the visitors' arrival, the British company prepared the following programme for them:

Day 1: Arrival

Day 2: Welcome Meeting and Tour of the Factory (morning)
Manufacturing Review followed by shopping (afternoon)

Day 3: Engineering Review (morning)
Quality Review (afternoon)

Days 4–9: Sightseeing

Day 10: Close-out Meeting

However, the Chinese visitors cancelled all the training sessions before the start of the Welcome Meeting, and so the only formal meetings that took place were the Welcome Meeting, which took place on Day 2 and lasted just over 23 minutes, an 'Emergency' Meeting, which took place on Day 9 and lasted just over 37 minutes, and the Close-out Meeting, which took place on Day 10 and lasted just over 3 hours and 52 minutes.

Owing to the practical constraints of the participants' schedule, the interview and playback session with the Chinese had to be conducted at the end of Day 6, although field notes were collected throughout the visit. The interviews and playback sessions with the British participants were conducted shortly after the visitors had left. Prior to each of the playbacks, participants were told that they should ask for the tape to be stopped whenever they wanted to make some comments, at moments when they felt (un)comfortable, or when they felt there was some kind of miscommunication or misunderstanding. We had told them earlier that we were researching intercultural communication, but they did not know the exact focus of the study.

In all aspects of the data collection, Xing and I endeavoured to maximise the validity and reliability of the data. Over the previous few years, we had developed very good relations with staff at the host company, and during the visit, Xing spent as much time as possible socially with the Chinese visitors (e.g. accompanying them on sightseeing trips) in order to develop a good rapport with them and build up their trust. We did this deliberately, so that both British and Chinese partici-pants would have confidence in us, so that they would not feel too uneasy about the recording, and so that they would be honest and open with us in the interviews and playback sessions. We were very satisfied with the ways in which they seemed to 'conduct their business as normal' and with their co-operation during the follow-up sessions, but we recognise of course that our presence may still have affected the proceedings. (For more details on the research procedure, see Xing, 2002.)

The participants

The Chinese delegation comprised six men (all names have been changed): Sun, the delegation leader, who was accompanied by Xu, Ma, Shen, Chen, and Lin. Four of them were engineers by training and the other two were economists; nearly all of them were managers in Chinese companies that were associated in some way with the busi-ness deal.

The key British staff involved in the visit were Jack (chair of the Welcome Meeting), Sajid (in charge of the programme arrangements, and chair of the Close-out Meeting), Tim (sales manager for China, and chair of the Emergency Meeting), Lynn (administrator), and Steve (engineer).

The British company hired as interpreter a Chinese PhD student who was researching engineering at a local university. They had previously used very successfully someone in a similar role, but they had never met this particular person before. Xing was also present to operate the video camera and to observe.

7.4. An action-oriented identity approach to the analysis of face

In analysing the data from a face perspective, three key issues emerged: participants' self-presentational concerns, the identity attributes that they became face-sensitive to, and their interactional goals. I deal with each of these issues in turn, and for each one I first consider how it has been handled by other theorists and researchers of face and (im)politeness.

Face and self-presentation

Brown and Levinson (1987), in their classic model of face and politeness, discuss the face needs of both speakers and hearers. However, they give greater emphasis to the hearer, in that they argue that face is maintained by each person upholding the face wants of the other. Moreover, in line with this, their description of facework strategies focuses much more strongly on the face needs of the hearer than on those of the speaker. Similarly, Leech (2005: 13), in his reformulation of his maxims of politeness (1983), maintains that: 'It is important to note that the hearer-oriented constraints are generally more powerful than the speaker-oriented ones.' (See also Leech, 2007: 181.)

However, a number of researchers (e.g. Koutlaki, 2002; Ruhi, 2007) have recently drawn attention to the importance of fully incorporating a 'self' perspective on face. For example, Koutlaki analyses offers and expressions of thanks in Persian, and argues that rituals such as repeated offers and refusals fulfil a dual function – they enhance the face of both of the interlocutors simultaneously, not just the face of the hearer. In other words, a speaker not only maintains or enhances the face of the addressee when, for example, performing 'polite rituals' such as repeated offers; s/he also maintains or enhances his/her own face by demonstrating through this behaviour that s/he is a respect-worthy person. Similarly, Ruhi (2007) analyses compliment responses, and reports that many examples in her corpus demonstrate self-presentation concerns. She argues that self-presentation is an integral part of relational work, including the management of face, and that it should therefore be given greater weight in theoretical frameworks.

In this case study, I also found self-presentation to be an important issue. For example, in the Welcome Meeting for the Chinese visitors, the Chairman gave them a brief introduction to his company which included the following comments:

(1)

> Jack: [name of company] is quite an old established company. It started in about 1814 or 1815 and it's been a manufacturing company ever since. It's a well established company and it has um a long experience of engineering and manufacturing....We have approximately two and a half thousand of [name of one of company's

products] installed around the world, so so we are obviously very experienced um in the design and the manufacture of these products...

Here, in giving the welcome speech, the Chairman is representing his company, and in speech act terms, he is complimenting his own company, even though he is a member of it. Membership of the company forms part of his collective identity (Spencer-Oatey, 2007), and any positive evaluation of the company can be construed as positive evaluation of the speaker's (collective) self. Brown and Levinson (1987) treat 'boasting' as face-threatening for the hearer, and in Leech's (2005, 2007) framework, it counts as a breach of the principle of modesty. In other words, both frameworks treat self-complimenting as detrimental or unhelpful for the smooth management of relations. However, in the follow-up interview, the Chinese participants did not feel it was in any way inappropriate. This is demonstrated by the following discussion, which took place immediately after they were played back the video recording of this section of the meeting.[1]

(2)

Sun: *This bit, of course this bit would be like this. He had to boast a little, that's understandable, that's understandable.*

Researcher: *He said it again, that they are very experienced in manufacturing and design.*

Sun: *This this this is understandable. It's all absolutely understandable, because*

Shen: *Their products are operating very well in China at the moment...* [section omitted]

Sun: *There are also defects...*

Shen: *It doesn't matter whether there are problems or not, even if there are some problems, you still need to boast a bit about yourself.*

Sun: *This is not at all strange.*

Chen: *We allow him to boast a bit on this sort of occasion.*

Clearly, the Chairman's presentation of the strengths of his company was regarded as completely acceptable. His (collective) self-complimenting was not perceived by the visitors as in any way face-threatening, and it had no negative impact on their relations.[2] This illustrates the inaccuracy of deciding *a priori* which speech acts will necessarily be face-threatening or face-enhancing.

However, in their discussion of the Chairman's welcome speech, others in the group honed in on elements that the Chairman had NOT said – they felt he had not conveyed sufficient gratitude for their order. The visitors had heard on the Chinese grapevine that the British company was in serious financial difficulties, and they believed it was the Chinese contracts that had saved it from bankruptcy. (This was denied by the British company.) So a few of the delegation members felt that the British Chairman should have expressed more heartfelt thanks, and that by failing to do so he had made a big mistake:

(3)

> Xu: *What is the use of only boasting about your own products? There is no market elsewhere for their products, the only market is us in China, and in China only we at [name of company] are helping them to get orders for their products....So at that moment, I felt saying words like this* [i.e. praising his own company and its products], *in saying words like this, he was making a big mistake. He should have said ' you have made a lot of effort to sell our product and I hope you will continue'. He should have said more in this respect.*

This omission fits in with Leech's (2005) constraint that a speaker should place a high value on the other party's qualities. However, as far as the British company was concerned, their sales were going well and they did not want to present themselves as indebted to the Chinese visitors. The British Chairman wanted to portray the company in a good light, and if he had acknowledged that they were highly dependent on the Chinese visitors' help in procuring sales that would have been very face-threatening for him and the company. He had his own self-presentation concerns in relation to the company, and this was his overriding concern when he gave his welcome speech.

From these extracts, therefore, we can see clearly that self-presentation is an important interactional concern that interrelates with issues of face. On the one hand, positive self-presentation is not always face-threatening to others, and conversely, even if it is (either explicitly or through failure to mention certain things), speakers may feel it is justifiable in a given context for the sake of upholding their own face. This suggests that a hearer-dominated approach to face needs to be complemented by a speaker-oriented approach, and that the relative balance of focus may vary from situation to situation and from person to person.

Face and identity attributes

Brown and Levinson (1987) identify two types of face concern: positive face (a person's desire to be appreciated and approved of by selected others in terms of personality, desires, behaviour, values and so on) and negative face (a person's want to be unimpeded by others, not to be imposed upon, and to be free to act as s/he chooses). However, Tracy and Baratz (1994) argue that this twofold distinction is too general and that it cannot capture the dynamic face concerns that people have in different contexts.

> This same woman in an interaction with her daughter's teacher may want to be seen as a good mother, while at her league basketball game she may want to be seen as a good athlete. To say that in both these situations, this woman wanted to be seen as competent glosses over the important differences between what it means to be seen as a good mother and what is involved in being seen as a good athlete.
>
> Thus, Brown and Levinson's model...is built around preconceived categories of face-concerns which are presumed to be universally-relevant. This premise detracts from the potential value of the theory because it forces researchers to ignore what may be the central face-concerns for the individuals in the interactions. (Tracy and Baratz, 1994: 290–291)

The importance of analysing the various identity attributes that people may claim in specific interactions is also illustrated in the Chinese-British business data, and emerged clearly, for example, during the close-out meeting of the visit. In this meeting, the British company gave each of the visitors an envelope containing 'pocket money', which was the cash left over after the costs of the visit had been deducted from the figure in the contract allocated to the visit (see section 3.1 above). The visitors opened their envelopes, counted the money, and then claimed that the amount was too little. They insisted that the contract be brought in for them all to study, and that the British provide a detailed list of all their expenses so that they could see clearly how the cash balance (i.e. the pocket money) had been calculated. During the discussions, the Chinese visitors argued that none of the formal dinners (at which British staff were present) should have been counted as an expense, because that would mean that they were paying for the British to enjoy themselves. They also disagreed that the costs of the interpreter should be included as an expense, arguing that the British were responsible for paying for that service. The conflict continued for two hours and twenty-nine minutes, and during this time, some delegation members became extremely angry. However, one of them was concerned about the impression they were conveying, and commented in Chinese to his colleagues as follows:

(4)

>Chen: *One thing is that we should not let people say we are stingy;*
>*secondly, we should not give the impression of being too weak;*
>*thirdly, we should negotiate in a friendly manner.*

This comment (which functioned as an aside during the ongoing discussion because it was in Chinese and directed at the Chinese delegation only) shows, on the one hand, the importance of people's self-presentational concerns (as discussed in the previous section) and the explicitness with which they may refer to them; on the other, it shows how people may be face-sensitive to specific identity attributes that emerge in the unfolding interaction and how these may need to be balanced appropriately. In Brown and Levinson's (1987) terms, Chen was simply concerned about the delegation's positive face; however, such an analysis is far too general to capture the specifics of the interaction. It is much more illuminating to go a step further and explain that Chen was claiming three identity attributes that became face-sensitive to him as the arguments with the British hosts developed: generosity/lack of stinginess, power, and friendliness. Interestingly, he is hinting that the delegation needs to maintain an appropriate balance between these various attributes. If they ignore their own financial concerns, the British might regard them as easy to take advantage of; on the other hand, if they are too insistent in challenging every small item of expense, the British might regard them as stingy, and if they are too harsh in their style of negotiation, they might be regarded as unfriendly. A detailed, identity attribute approach to face, that explores the dynamically unfolding face concerns of the interlocutors can reveal this interactionally meaningful complexity in a way that a twofold distinction between positive and negative face is unable to achieve. This is especially important when the various attributes are potentially in competition with each other.

Face and interactional goals

In a recent article (Spencer-Oatey, 2005), I argue that there are three key elements that underlie the management of rapport: people's face sensitivities, their perceived sociality rights and obligations (along with the behavioural expectations associated with them), and their interactional goals. In that framework, I focus on the factors that influence the (lack of) rapport that people perceive in interaction, and I treat interactional goals as one of the factors that can impact on such perceptions.

However, the role of interactional goals can also be analysed in a complementary way, in terms of how they interact with relational goals. Even though it is fully accepted that language has a transactional (task-focused) function as well as an interpersonal (relationship-focused) function, much analysis of face and (im)politeness has focused almost exclusively on the relational aspects of the interaction: the strategies available for managing them, the pragmatic choices that people make, and how such choices are evaluated. Yet the ways in which people balance the tensions that may emerge between their various interactional goals can be of crucial concern in real-life encounters, as the Chinese–British business data illustrates.

Towards the end of their visit, the Chinese delegation decided that they would like to stay in London for the last night of their trip. They mentioned it over the weekend to their British hosts, but no arrangements were made. Then, on the day before their departure, they simply checked out of their local hotel and took all their luggage with them to the British company. An Emergency Meeting was arranged, and was chaired by Tim, the sales manager for China. During this meeting, the following interaction took place.

(5)

Tim: but you have to remember, we we have to pay this hotel ((gestures with one hand)). and we also have to pay this hotel ((gestures with other hand)) so we have two hotels to pay now. ((Chinese visitors explain that they have already checked out of their hotel))

Tim: yes yes, but this but this hotel, because we have cancelled now, we also have to pay for tomorrow. So it's a double expense, two expenses, yeah?
((Chinese visitors ask why the local hotel needs to make this charge and the British administrator, Sajid, explains that it is because of the late cancellation. The Chinese visitors comment that they had mentioned earlier that they wanted to stay in London on the last night.))

Tim: anyway it doesn't matter. we we will take you to London, today, and we will arrange a hotel in London for you.

Xu: *so that will mean an extra night's charge, won't it? could we pay the extra night's charge for the local hotel and they pay for our hotel in London?*

Sun: *we don't want to pay twice, that's the point.*

Tim: uhhuh. well it's up to them. when Sajid will give them some spending money, ok, and all our arrangement is for us to provide them some spending money. ok we will give them some

> spending money, but because we have to pay two hotels; the
> amount will have to be reduced, be a small adjustment. ((gestures
> with fingers))
>
> Sun: *that counts as us paying, so in that case we won't go.*
> Xu: *we simply won't go.*

The Chinese visitors were clearly very annoyed about this, and if Tim
had wanted to avoid these bad feelings he could probably have found
ways of doing so. For example, he could have been less explicit about
the impact this would have on the amount of money the visitors would
receive in pocket money, or he could perhaps have found ways of ab-
sorbing, averting or reducing the extra charge to them. This would no
doubt have kept the relations smoother but as Tim explains in a follow-
up interview (Extract 6), this would have had a negative impact on
other interactional goals that were important to him.

(6)

> Tim: well, I had some advance warning um of their demands, yes, I
>   wasn't unhappy, but I felt, um, there were two concerns for me,
>   one I wanted to make sure that they, when they left England, they
>   had a good impression of our company, so that was important. But
>   secondly, it was also important to us, to our company that we
>   didn't get involved in any additional expenditure, that which we'd
>   already agreed, for two reasons, A we can't afford the additional
>   expenditure, but whatever we agreed with this party that informa-
>   tion could get passed on to the next delegation, and if you weren't
>   careful, then the cost of these delegations would escalate, and
>   with each visit, there would be additional demands and additional
>   demands, and it gets tougher and tougher.

As can be seen from these comments, Tim wanted to balance two goals:
a relational one associated with leaving a positive impression of his
company, and a transactional one of ensuring that no additional costs
were incurred. On this occasion, he gave priority to the latter, while
still not ignoring the former.

Tim's comments also illustrate the importance of people's longer-
term goals. He needed to consider not only his goals for the current
interaction, but also his company's longer-term business goals. In other
words, he needed to take into account how his current balancing of the
desires of the British and Chinese participants might impact not only on
the British staff's rapport with the current visitors but also on the
company's future business, including their dealings with a range of
people, not just the present participants. An action-oriented approach
to the study of face, which has an extended timeline that includes the

longer-term objectives of the interlocutors as well as their current and previous concerns and objectives, is thus needed for analysing the dynamic construction and management of face in authentic interactions. (See also Ruhi, 2007, for similar findings in relation to compliment responses.)

7.5. Research implications

What, then, are the research implications of an action-oriented identity approach to the study of face? Firstly, it impacts on the type of research data that need to be collected. As has been illustrated throughout this chapter, I regard face sensitivity as a subjective evaluation that cannot always be judged from the discourse data alone. Supplementary data, in the form of post-event interview comments, which if possible include playback comments, are needed in order to gain insights into people's rapport-related concerns and reactions, as well as into their interactional goals. If this type of data is used in combination with the discourse data, together they can provide rich insights into the ways in which face concerns emerge and are managed in authentic interaction. Of course, this is not meant to imply that the reflective data represent the 'true' picture of people's evaluations. I believe people frequently reinterpret and reconstruct their evaluations of significant interactions, and as the extracts in this chapter have hinted at, different participants may have different opinions. The aim is thus not to establish a single 'truth', but rather to build up a rich, in-depth picture of the range of concerns and evaluations, both positive and negative, that interlocutors may hold and (re-)construct.

Secondly, it suggests that a more longitudinal approach to the study of face could be useful when ongoing relationships are involved. This is something that is rarely undertaken in this area, but has the potential to yield some interesting insights. Perhaps Lazarus's (2006) recent call to psychologists for a narrative approach to the study of emotions is something that researchers of face and (im)politeness could usefully consider incorporating.

7.6. Concluding comments

The focus of this chapter has been on the 'self' – self as speaker and/or self as hearer – since it is the notion of self that links face and identity.

This is not to deny the importance of 'other' in the conceptualisation and analysis of face. Clearly, concern for the face of others is crucial for the effective management of rapport; however, this chapter is trying to redress an imbalance in much of the politeness literature whereby the face needs of others are stressed more than the face needs of self. The chapter has aimed to demonstrate how an identity perspective on face, which acknowledges concerns about self-presentation, incorporates the notion of self-attributes, and takes an action-oriented approach to the study of face, can offer a very useful complementary perspective to an 'other' analysis of face.

Endnotes

1. An English translation of utterances originally spoken in Chinese are printed in italics in the following extracts.
2. It could be argued that the speaker is complimenting others and that this does not count as (collective) self-praise. However, Extract 3 shows that the hearers treated it as (collective) self-boasting, and so that is how I treat it in the analysis.

References

Brown, P. and Levinson, S. C. (1987) *Politeness. Some Universals in Language Usage.* Cambridge: Cambridge University Press. Originally published as Universals in language usage: politeness phenomenon. In: E. Goody (ed.) (1978) *Questions and Politeness: strategies in Social Interaction* 56–311. New York: Cambridge University Press.

Campbell, J. D., Assanand, S. and Di Paula, A. (2000) Structural features of the self-concept and adjustment. In A. Tesser, R. B. Felson & J. M. Suls (eds.) *Psychological Perspectives on Self and Identity,* 67–87. Washington, D.C.: American Psychological Association.

Jones, S. R. and McEwen, M. K. (2000) A conceptual model of multiple dimensions of identity. *Journal of College Student Development* 41: 405–414.

Koutlaki, S. A. (2002) Offers and expressions of thanks as face enhancing acts: tæ'rof in Persian. *Journal of Pragmatics* 34: 1733–1756.

Lazarus, R.S. (2006) Emotions and interpersonal relationships: toward a person-centered conceptualization of emotions and coping. *Journal of Personality* 74: 9–46.

Leary, M. R. (1996) *Self-Presentation. Impression Management and Interpersonal Behaviour.* Boulder: Westview Press.

Leech, G. N. (1983) *Principles of Pragmatics.* London: Longman.

Leech, G.N. (2005) Politeness: Is there an East-West divide? *Journal of Foreign Languages*, 6. Viewed 15/02/07 at http://www.ling.lancs.ac.uk/staff/geoff/leech2006politeness.pdf.

Leech, G.N. (2007) Politeness: Is there an East-West divide? *Journal of Politeness Research* 3: 167–206.

Ruhi, Ş. (2007) Higher-order intentions and self-politeness in evaluations of (im)politeness: the relevance of compliment responses. *Australian Journal of Linguistics* 27: 107–145.

Schlenker, B.R. and Pontari, B.A. (2000) The strategic control of information: impression management and self-presentation in daily life. In: A. Tesser, R. B. Felson and J. M. Suls (eds.) *Psychological Perspectives on Self and Identity* 199–232. Washington DC: American Psychological Association.

Simon, B. (2004). *Identity in Modern Society. A Social Psychological Perspective*. Oxford: Blackwell.

Spencer-Oatey, H. (2005) (Im)Politeness, face and perceptions of rapport: unpacking their bases and interrelationships. *Journal of Politeness Research* 1: 95–119.

Spencer-Oatey, H. (2007) Theories of identity and the analysis of face. *Journal of Pragmatics* 39 (4): 639–656.

Tracy, K. (1990). The many faces of facework. In H. Giles and W. P. Robinson (eds.) *Handbook of Language and Social Psychology* 209–226. Chichester: John Wiley and Sons.

Tracy, K. and Baratz, S. (1994) The case for case studies of facework. In: S. Ting-Toomey (ed.) *The Challenge of Facework* 287–305. Albany: State University of New York.

Xing, J. (2002) *Relational Management in British–Chinese Business Interactions*. Unpublished PhD Thesis, University of Bedfordshire.

8
Evoking face in self and other-presentation in Turkish

Şükriye Ruhi

8.1. Introduction

Face is a useful yet elusive theoretical construct that affords further scrutiny in the various disciplines contributing to the study of interpersonal communication. While some scholars link the concept to socio-psychological values such as respect, honour, status, reputation, credibility, competence, relational indebtedness, and concern for self's and other's well-being (e.g. Kansu-Yetkiner, 2006; Ting-Toomey and Kurogi, 1998; Strecker, 1993), others have underscored the inter-relationship between face and identity claims (e.g. Tracy and Baratz, 1993; Ting-Toomey, 2005; Spencer-Oatey, 2007, this volume, Chapter 7).

With insights to be gained from the literature on self-presentation theory (see also, Spencer-Oatey, this volume, Chapter 7), this chapter explores the inter-relationship between face and self-presentation in naturally occurring spoken discourse in Turkish. The study looks into aspects of interaction that trigger the use of idioms derived from the lexical concept face and describes the role these expressions have in the management of self-presentation. Building on Goffman's (1974) notion of 'social frame', the study shows that evoking face in discourse via 'face' idioms is a 'front-stage' (Goffman, 1959: 22), goal-oriented (linguistic) act that constructs an interpretive frame for representing self and other. The analysis of the data shows that face does not intrinsically incorporate any particular, stable social value or self-aspect that may be attributed and/or claimed by interlocutors across interactions. The analysis further reveals that, contrary to the focus in Goffman (1959, 1967/1982) on the individual's face claims and the response to these claims, face is an interactively achieved social accomplishment, where interactants may actively project (desirable) face attributes to others.

In the following sections, I first briefly review conceptualisations of face and self-presentation and point to the limitations of identifying face with specific symbolic, social values and affective concepts. I then describe the data employed in the study and delineate the analytic framework for investigating the discursive construction of face with reference to the self-presentation categories in Schütz (1998). The data are analysed for illustrations of the management of self and other-presentation with 'face' idioms in Turkish and for the presence of emotive responses. In the conclusion, I touch upon areas of inquiry that may further our understanding of the inter-relationship between face and self-presentation and suggest that the locus for investigating face is the affective dimension of interpersonal communication.

8.2. Face as 'social frame' and self-presentation

Pinning down face[1]

Goffman defines face as 'as the positive social value a person effectively claims for himself by the line others assume he has taken during a particular contact' (1967/1982: 5) and states that it resides in 'the flow of events in the encounter' (p. 7). In this sense, while the individual/group may have certain face claims, face is ultimately accorded by others.

While Goffman did not restrict the content of face to specific social values, varying interpretations regarding the constitution of face exist in emic and conceptual studies. A number of emic studies focus either on emotion-laden concepts as honour and shame (e.g., Kansu-Yetkiner, 2006; Ukosakul, 2003) or link the concept to specific self-aspects such as one's place in a social network or one's well-being (e.g., Haugh, 2007; Strecker, 1993). A significant number of studies equate face with situation-specific identity or self-aspect claims (e.g., Tracy and Baratz, 1993; Ting-Toomey and Kurogi, 1998; Ting-Toomey, 2005; Holtgraves, 1992). Spencer-Oatey (2007, this volume), on the other hand, delimits face to those aspects of identity toward which interactants show affective sensitivity.

While it is clear that the content of face is strongly linked to self-image claims and identity issues in several cultural contexts, it is not so clear whether face as public self-image is universally the single or the main mediating factor in relational management. A number of studies argue that attending to the well-being of others, building solidarity, and creating an ethos of genuine concern for others are fundamental to upholding people's self-images and maintaining rapport (see, for example, Strecker (1993) on Hamar, Terkourafi, cited in Bargiela-Chiappini (2003: 1462) on Greek, and Ruhi and Işık-Güler (2007) on Turkish).

A further problem in defining emic face is that its description may not correspond to the way the concept 'face' occurs in idioms in naturally occurring discourse. Kansu-Yetkiner, for instance, defines face in Turkish culture 'as the equivalent of honor' and maintains that it 'refers to a person's social reputation, prestige, esteem, intrinsic worth, and moral integrity' (2006: 26). With this definition of face in Turkish, Kansu-Yetkiner is actually referring to an enduring face value, which Spencer-Oatey refers to as 'respectability face' (2005: 102). Spencer-Oatey defines respectability face as 'the prestige, honor or 'good name' that a person or social group holds and claims within a (broader) community' (2005: 102), based on the 'pan-situational' understanding of Chinese face, *mianzi* and *lian* in Ho (1976, 1994) versus Goffman's (1967/1982: 5) situation-specific face claims such as the social values and attributes toward which people show sensitivity in interaction, that is, 'identity face' (Spencer-Oatey, 2005: 103).

I would certainly agree that being in 'good face' or having a 'good name' involves the attributes that Kansu-Yetkiner provides in her description. However, as I demonstrate below, the lexical concept 'face' is of a different category compared to 'content' words such as 'honour', 'reputation' and 'integrity'. It allows for the construction of a broader spectrum of meanings than can be encapsulated through the terms above. The lexical concept 'face', I will argue, functions in a manner that is parallel to social indexical pronouns: it indicates that self is being represented in the discourse with regard to its (preferred) social image. Just as there may be several representations of an entity if photographed from different angles and under different lights, so too for representations of self via the 'face' concept.

The following extract, from a dialogue in a popular TV romantic comedy series, *Yabancı Damat* 'The Foreign Son-in-Law', is illustrative of the multi-dimensional nature of the concept and shows how 'face' can refer to self, represented in terms of its relations with others.[2]

(1)

    Kahraman: *yüzüne bakmadım*
        Face-AGR-DAT look-NEG-PAST-AGR
        'I paid no attention to her'
        Koca evi dar ettim ona
        Huge house-ACC narrow
        make-PAST-AGR 3.PER.PRO.SING-DAT

'I made it miserable for her to live in [this] huge house'
(Yabancı Damat, Part 55)

Up to this point in the dialogue, Kahraman has been telling a close friend how deeply he regrets the way he has recently been behaving toward one of his daughters, Nazlı. Nazlı had moved back into his house owing to a quarrel with her husband some days ago. During this stay, Kahraman thinks mistakenly that Nazlı is seeing a man, after the local newspaper prints her photograph with a male friend, drinking coffee, under the caption 'Is this the real cause of the separation?'. Kahraman learns that this is all paparazzi news only too late because Nazlı, hurt and indignant owing to her father's attitude, has left the house without any word of her whereabouts. In this extract, we observe that Kahraman describes his previously disaffiliative behaviour toward his daughter (i.e., sulking, refusing to talk, and showing how deeply offended he is) with the idiom *yüzüne bakma-* (literally, 'not to look at someone's face'; 'not to pay attention to; to be cross with'). In other words, Kahraman presents his disaffiliative behaviour as a 'relational face' issue, which 'concerns the quality of interpersonal attention directed to a person/group' (Ruhi and Işık-Güler 2007: 693).

Face idioms such as used in extract (1) show that face is a shorthand interpretive conceptual 'social frame', which organises experience and 'provide[s] background understanding for events that incorporate *the will, aim, and controlling effort of an intelligence, a live agency*' (Goffman 1974: 22, emphasis added). While attention to face is an ubiquitous phenomenon in interaction, evoking face via formulaic face idioms explicitly embeds self and/or others in an evaluative frame in terms of self-aspects that are perceived as significant for the interlocutors' interactional goals. In other words, evoking face either through figurative expressions derived from the lexical concept face or through other (non-)verbal behavioural forms pertaining to self's image marks locations of 'disturbance' in the unfolding discourse, where interlocutors negotiate perceptions of self and others. Thus investigating face through the use of formulaic expressions in discourse allows us to independently locate points where face sensitivities and associated self-presentational acts surface in social interaction. Such an investigation can further our understanding of the cultural interpretive schemas activated in relation to face issues.

According to Goffman's understanding of self-presentation, conveying perceptions of self's and/or other's face value (e.g. 'lose face') is a 'front-stage' linguistic phenomenon that forms part of 'the expressive equipment of a standard kind intentionally or unwittingly employed by the individual during his performance (Goffman 1959: 22). As has been mentioned above, self's and/or other's verbal or non-verbal behaviour can be evaluated and responded to through several means. For instance, wearing a blouse presented as a gift by a friend on the very next occasion that the recipient will meet her friend is symbolic of appreciation in Turkish culture. However, the discursive use of idioms or expressions related to 'face' indicate that self-image issues are cognitively foreground phenomena for the speaker(s) in the unfolding discourse. Thus placing the investigation of face as self-image within the broader perspective of impression management and self-presentation (as, indeed, is the case in Goffman's (1967) descriptions of the rituals of social interaction) can open the way to refining our understanding of the relationship between face and self in the dynamics of interaction.

In the following section I briefly review approaches to the study of self-presentation in social psychology and introduce the analytic scheme employed in the investigation of the data.

Self-presentation

The major tenet in self-presentation theory is that 'much human behaviour can be understood as being the result of the individual's attempts to *communicate* information rather than to seek it' (Baumeister, 1982: 22, italics in the original). Schlenker and Pontari (2000) and Schlenker (2003) further develop the theoretical framework for investigating the way people manage the packaging of relevant information about self and/or others by studying self-presentation under the broader category of impression management. Schlenker (2003: 492) defines such behaviour as 'the goal-directed activity of controlling information' that tries 'to shape an audience's impression of persons, groups, objects, ideas, and events' (see the quotation from Schlenker and Pontari (2000) in Spencer-Oatey, this volume (Chapter 7, section 2.2), on the distinction between impression management and self-presentation).

Schlenker views the study of self-presentation as including both the management of relevant information about self by self and the way people, 'as targets, respond to the self-presentation of other' (2003: 492). He also underscores that self-presentation is not necessarily self-serving and that any successful impression management – including 'truthful' presentations of self and the supportive presentation of others – involves as much skill as duplicitous self-presentation (pp. 510–512). The role attributed to self-presentation by Schlenker (Schlenker, 2003;

Schlenker and Pontari, 2000) is significant for the study of face in several respects. It underscores the idea that self-presentation may be a
projection of one's 'true' self. It implies that people's self-presentational
concerns are embedded in their respective agendas, which Schlenker
defines as 'goals and associated scripts or plans for goal achievement.'
It thus supports the idea that speaker concerns – whether these relate
to face issues or the relational and/or the transactional aspects of interpersonal communication – are dimensions that deserve better theoretical representation in the study of face (Ruhi, 2007; Spencer-Oatey, this
volume).

Schütz (1998: 612, *passim*) takes the perspective of the addressor in
describing self-presentation and distinguishes four styles on the basis
of two intentions: the intention to achieve positive impressions or the
intention to avoid negative impressions. Schütz describes the four styles
as follows:

1. The assertive style involve strategies to achieve as a positive self-
   projection (e.g. ingratiation, helping others, gaining admiration
   for integrity)

2. The offensive style sets to achieve a positive self-projection by
   being aggressive (e.g. by making others look bad)

3. The protective style avoids damage/opportunities to enhance self-
   image (e.g. self-depreciation; modesty; minimising interaction)

4. The defensive style incorporates compensatory acts to repair self-
   images that have been threatened or damaged (e.g. apologising
   for a misconduct)

These categories can be usefully employed in describing the presentation of others in interaction, too. For example, appreciating the food
served by the host can achieve a positive self-projection as it provides
evidence of awareness of social norms. From the perspective of the
host, it can boost their self-image as a competent cook. In the same
manner, sympathising with another's failure by providing excuses can
achieve the protection of his/her self-image. Thus, the various self-
presentational styles impact on both self and other presentation. In this
sense, I side with Schlenker in attributing both a self-serving and a
supportive goal to impression management and self-presentation. In
the following, I describe the nature of the data and focus on self and
other presentation as evinced by the use of face idioms, employing
Schütz' categorisation.

8.3. Data collection and 'face' idioms in Turkish

The data for this study are part of an ongoing project on the compilation of face and (im)politeness expressions in written and spoken Turkish discourse (cf. Ruhi and Işık-Güler (2007) for a study of 'face' idioms in written discourse). The spoken data comprise field notes on 'face' idioms occurring in authentic spoken discourse over a period of five weeks, recordings of two highly popular weekly drama series and a 19-hour audio-/video-recording of authentic conversation in focus-group academic meetings and family settings in which I was a participant. I have long-standing relations with the interlocutors in the academic meetings and, while the participants in both settings are familiar with my research on Turkish, they were unaware of the specific focus of the recordings. To maintain consistency in data, I will refer only to the samples of 'face' idioms occurring in authentic interaction.[3]

To give some background on the range of 'face' idioms in Turkish, in Tables 8.1 and 8.2 below I list those that occur in written discourse (the

Table 8.1. 'Face' idioms implying a positive impact on face

Lexical realisation and morphological gloss	Paraphrases
yüz akı (face white-COMP)	not having anything to be ashamed of, someone's reputation, honour, or credit, someone or something that brings honour to the person
yüzüne bakabil- (face-AGR-DAT look-ABIL)	to be able to look someone in the face
yüz bul- (face find)	to be considered worthy of interaction, to be emboldened, to become presumptuous, to be spoiled by kind treatment
yüzünü dön- (face-AGR-ACC turn)	to turn one's face (toward something or somebody); to aspire; to try to be like
yüzü ol- (face-AGR be)	having the face to do or say something
yüzü tut- (face-AGR hold)	having the face to do or say something
yüz ver- (face give)	to show interest in someone, to be indulgent, to give encouragement

Table 8.2. 'Face' idioms implying a negative impact on face

Lexical realisation and morphological gloss	Paraphrases
yüzlü (face-with)	brazen, unabashed (dialectal)
yüzsüz (face-without)	shameless, brazen, unabashed
yüz karası (face black-COMP)	someone or something that brings disgrace or shame
yüzüne bakama- (face-AGR-DAT look-ABIL.NEG)	not being able to look someone in the face
yüzü kızar- (face-AGR redden)	to blush; to be embarrassed
yüz kızartıcı (face redden-CAUS-NOM)	embarrassing, shameful
yüzü olma- (face-AGR be-NEG) AND *yüzü yok* (face-AGR EXIS.NEG)	not having the face to do or say something (either because one does not want to harm the relationship or because one has not be haved in accordance with expectations)
yüzü tutma- (face hold-NEG)	not having the face to do or say something; to avoid doing something that would hurt someone else
yüz ver-	to show interest in someone, to be indulgent, to give encouragement
yüzüne vur- (face-AGR-DAT hit)	to cast something in someone's face

lists have been compiled from Ruhi and Işık-Güler, 2007). As previously observed in Ruhi and Işık-Güler (2007: 696), 'face' idioms are used sparingly in authentic spoken discourse and a fuller description of usage of the 'face' idioms in Turkish would require a large-scale corpus, which is unavailable for the language at the moment.

Of the idioms listed above, *yüz ver-* and its negative form, *yüz verme-* occur the most frequently in authentic spoken interaction. In Table 8.3, I list the occurrences of the idioms in the field notes and the recordings.

Table 8.3. 'Face' idioms in the authentic data – number of occurrences

Idiom Positive impact	No.	Idiom Negative impact	No.
yüz akı (face white-COMP)	2	*yüz karası* (face black-COMP)	5
yüzüne bakabil- (face-AGR-DAT look-ABIL)	1	*yüzsüz* (face-without)	5
yüz bul- (face find)	3	*yüzüne bakama-* (face-AGR-DAT look-ABIL.NEG)	3
yüzü ol- (face-AGR be)	2	*yüzü kızar-* (face-AGR redden)	3
yüz ver- (face give)	3	*yüzü yok* (face-AGR EXIS.NEG)	4
		yüzü tutma- (face-AGR hold-NEG)	3
		yüz verme- (face give-NEG)	7

The idioms listed in Table 8.3 occurred mostly within family settings and during daily interaction at a workplace. It is likely that the task-oriented nature of the academic meetings, which appear to have proceeded smoothly, did not trigger the use of the idioms. As is evident in the list, there is a significant bias toward the use of idioms encoding a negative impact. I will comment on this negativity in the discussion.

8.4. Self-presentation and other-presentation

In the following sections, I will first focus on the self-presentational acts of speakers and then illustrate instances of other-presentation.

'Face' idioms in self-presentation

In section 2.2, we had noted that Schütz identifies four styles in self-presentation. The discussion of extracts from the data will reveal that 'face' idioms emerge in the data mainly for defensive and protective self-presentations.

In extract (2), Canan and Işık are co-workers in the photocopying room of a workplace where there is a temporary shortage of photo-copying paper. Canan runs out of paper while doing her photocopying and Işık gives some of her own and tells Canan that she need not return any. A short while later, Canan comes to Işık's office with some paper.

(2)   Upon seeing the paper

1   I: *A şimdi kızıcam*
            Oh now get-angry-AGR
            Ben demiştim bende çok var diye
            I say-PERF-PAST-AGR I-LOC plenty exist POST
            'Oh, now I'm going to get angry! I had told you that I have plenty'

2   C: *Olur mu*
            Be-AOR Q
            Şimdi böyle vereyim de bi daha istemeye **yüzüm olsun**
            Now like.this give-OPT-AGR ADD one again ask-NOM-DAT face-
            POSS be-OPT
            'How can that be! Let me give [them] now so that I have the face
            to ask [for paper] another time too'
            (field notes)

In this dialogue, Canan employs the idiom *yüzü ol-* 'to have the face to do or say something' as both a defensive and a protective self-presenta-tional strategy. By having accepted Işık's offer of paper, she has placed herself in debt and may have threatened her self-face. The use of the idiom implies that her self-image might be threatened if she relies too much on the good will of others (turn 2). She thus achieves a positive self-presentation by suggesting that she would not want to exploit Işik's generosity. In this manner, her act of replacing the paper creates the impression that she is considerate towards other people's needs, which, in turn, would allow her to be treated with consideration too in further interaction.

Extract (3) illustrates a case of attack on self's face for the purpose of forestalling a negative evaluation. Emre is visiting his parents for the weekend and is unpacking during the dialogue with his mother:

*(3)

1   E: *Ya anne çamaşır çok azdı*
            Well mother washing very little-PAST
            ben de yıkamadım (.)
            I ADD wash-NEG-PAST-AGR

> **yüzsüz yüzsüz** *getirdim burda yikariz diye[4]*
> faceless faceless bring-PAST-AGR here-LOC wash-AOR so.that
> 'Well mother there was very little laundry so I didn't do my
> laundry. So I brought [it] shamelessly so that we could do it here'

2   Ayşe *Tamam oğlum (.) iyi etmişsin*
        Fine son-POSS (.) good do-PERF-AGR
        'That's fine my son, you did well [to do that]'

Emre usually does his own washing but at the time this dialogue was
recorded there was a severe shortage of water in the town where Emre
lives and people were using water sparingly. Given these circumstances,
his not having done his laundry is quite reasonable. In spite of this,
Emre presents his behaviour as a shameless act (cf. *yüzsüz yüzsüz*). By
attacking his self-face, Emre is presenting his behaviour as creating a
burden on his mother. This unpresumptuous and apologetic self-
presentation prevents any possible resentment that the mother might
have felt if he had not provided any explanation. His self-face attack
thus achieves a positive self-presentation by indicating an awareness of
his own responsibilities.

   In extract (4), I turn to a case of assertive self-presentation. The utterance, which occurs during a seminar given to pre-service teachers by
the young principal of a school on job opportunities, illustrates such
assertive/protective self-presentations. Previous to the utterance, the
principal was talking about how teaching can also entail administrative
duties. She describes how she had been 'pushed into' an administrative
role by the general director of the school:

(4)

> *Ben de* **yüzümün akıyla** *bu işi yapmaya çalıştım*
> I ADD face-POSS-GEN white-COMP-COM this job-ACC do-NOM-
> DAT try-PAST-AGR
> 'And I've been trying to accomplish this work with the whiteness
> of my face
> [i.e. And I've been trying to accomplish this work without a
> blemish on my face/without losing face]'
> (field notes)

While the principal employs what appears to be an assertive self-
presentation style in this utterance, the use of the idiom *yüz akı* 'not
having anything to be ashamed of, someone's good reputation, honour,
or credit; someone or something that brings honour to the person' actually implies an avoidance of face damage rather than face enhancement
by performing according to internally or externally imposed behavioural

expectations. The idiom thus has an element of modesty in self-presentation, which makes the self-presentational style protective rather than truly assertive (cf. Ruhi and Işık-Güler (2007: 691–692) for further illustrations of the idiom).

As has been mentioned in the previous section, the majority of face idioms occurring in the data are those that imply a negative impact on face. This suggests that face maintenance (not face enhancement) is a basic cultural schema in Turkish interaction. This negative bias indicates that face idioms occur mostly to protect self-face from (possible) threats. The bias is to a certain extent to be expected as face sensitivities are likely to emerge not when interaction is running smoothly but when people feel (emerging) discrepancies between what they wish to project and what appears to be emerging within the interaction. To use Jing-Schmidt's words, the negativity bias might be a reflection of 'vigilance towards threats' (2007: 435). In this respect, the evoking of face through the face idioms provides frames mainly for defensive and protective acts in the context of the behavioural norms and expectations that underlie the ongoing interaction (e.g., sharing of resources, as in extract 2; performance of household chores, as in extract 3).

Thus far I have concentrated on evoking face in self-presentation. In section 4.2, I will illustrate cases of other-presentation.

'Face' idioms in other-presentation

Extract (1) in section 2.1 above, which is drawn from a TV series, opens another window on impression management and shows that face is actively constituted not only through self's presentational acts but through what others project of self in interaction. In the extract, while Kahraman expresses heart-felt regret about his behaviour toward his daughter in that episode, his self-criticism follows a series of offensive other-presentations (his sulking, his avoiding interaction with his daughter, etc.). Through this behaviour, the father communicates the idea that Nazlı has gone against proper conduct and is, therefore, unworthy of social interaction. Positive and negative other-presentations are performed via face idioms in authentic interaction too and show that appropriate self-presentation is often suggested – if not dictated – to self by others.

Extract (5) illustrates a case where a fellow student, Ayhan, damages Erhan's face. Erhan had lent his camera to his classmates and gives unsolicited advice on how to operate it. Ayhan criticizes him saying,

(5)

> *Ha başladı yine.* **Yüz buldu** *ya*
> Hah start-PAST again. Face find-PAST after.all
> 'Well there he goes again. He has found face after all!'
> [i.e. He has become presumptuous again]
> (field notes)

Although *yüz bul-* 'to find face' encodes a positive impact in that the person receives attention from others in interaction, the use of the expression is not complimentary as it implies that the speaker views the attention received by someone as unwarranted or mismanaged.

The active role that others have in constituting one's face is also evident in extract (6). In this interaction, a five-year-old child is at a neighbour's house, playing with the adult members of the family, who are very fond of him. The child has been misbehaving during play (e.g. using taboo words and gestures). After a few warnings to the child about his behaviour, one of the adults, Aylin, tells the others who frequently play with him not to 'give face' to him after the child has left the house.

(6)

1   Aylin: ((to family members, irritated tone))
>   *Olmuyor böyle (.)*
>   Be-NEG-PROG like.this (.)
>   *Siz de* **yüz vermeyin** *bir iki gün*
>   You.PLU ADD face give-NEG-IMP one two day
>   'This isn't right. You, too, don't pay attention to him for a few days'

2   Aysun: *Tabii tabii*
>   'Of course, of course'

3   Orhan: *Zaten vermiyoruz*
>   As.it.is give-NEG-PROG-AGR
>   'As it is, we don't'
>   (i.e. We don't when he behaves like [that])

What Aylin means by 'not giving face' in this context are things like not playing with the child and not responding to his appeals for attention. In the following days, the family members reported that they responded to the child's greetings minimally and that Orhan explicitly requested that the child apologise for his misbehaviour.

Monitoring other's self-presentation is not performed only in an offensive style. It can be effected with a protective style too. Extract (7) is one illustration, which occurs during a conversation among family members about workplace matters. The daughter in the family, Aynur, has recently taken up her first job in a firm. The topic of the conversation had shifted to confidentiality at work:

(7)

1	Mother:	((to Aynur))
		Orda konuşulanlar orda kalır
		there-LOC talk-PASS-PLU there-LOC stay-AOR
		'Whatever is spoken there stays there'

| 2 | Father: | *Aman Aynur* |
| | | Be careful Aynur! |

3	Grandfather:	*O zaman sonra* **yüzün kızarmaz**
		that time then face-POSS redden-NEG.AOR
		'That way your face would not redden [with embarrassment]'
		[i.e. That way, later, you would not lose face]

This kind of advice-giving via 'face' idioms that are meant to protect other-face by suggesting proper conduct is quite rare in friendly relations in spoken interaction. While extensive data are required to corroborate this judgement, I interpret the absence as indicative of the binding role of face in interaction such that evoking 'face', even in acts that are supportive of others' self-presentations, is an extremely sensitive topic which may result in misunderstandings among interlocutors. The negative affect that people are likely to feel toward being advised on self-presentation is not due to the cultural sensitivity on 'being advised', but being advised with reference to the 'face' frame (cf. Bayraktaroğlu (1992) on the supportive role of advice-giving in Turkish). This form of advice-giving would imply that the person is being evaluated with respect to social worth.

The discussion above may suggest that positive other-presentation does not exist in the Turkish context. We observe that positive other-presentation via 'face' idioms such as *yüz akı* 'not having anything to be ashamed of, someone's reputation, honour, or credit, someone or something that brings honour to the person' and *yüzü ağar-* 'to bring honour to someone' abounds in written discourse, especially in newspaper language. An internet search, for example, that was conducted for the compilation of 'face' idioms in written discourse yielded over fifty thousand tokens for *yüz akı*. I would suggest that since the idiom implies a positive evaluation either in comparison to what is expected of an interlocutor or in comparison to what a person aspires to achieve himself/herself with respect to behavioural expectations in role relationships, the idiom is likely to suggest a patronising attitude when used for other-presentation. In this respect, it may not communicate sincere feelings.

What we observe is that assertive other-presentation in Turkish discourse is conveyed by other supportive forms (e.g. congratulating, complimenting, praising, etc.) and idioms that appeal to self's emotions.[5] Bayraktaroğlu (1992: 334), for example, provides an interesting extract from authentic discourse on the extent to which assertive other-presentation can occur in Turkish during troubles-talk. In (8) below, a mother has been complaining about how her son has not been admitted to a university programme because he did not work enough to get good points in the university entrance exam. Her friend responds

(8)

> *Eh gene puvanı fena değil canım iyi yani*
> Well again points bad not canım good that.is
> 'Well anyway his points aren't bad *canım*. I mean, [they're] good'[6]

Since the son has not been admitted to a university, qualifying his results as good is irrelevant.

The extracts in this section and in 4.1 show that self-presentation via 'face' idioms emerge in discourse in evaluative comments concerning the projection of a self-image that people consider desirable or appropriate at points in discourse where there might be an incongruence between self's and other's perception of self. The data show that positive self-presentation is often effected by adopting a protective style (cf. extract 2). Even when a more assertive style is adopted – as in extract (4), for example – it implies that self is aspiring to avoid face loss rather than face gain.

Defensive or offensive self-presentation emerges when there is a real or possible incongruence between the social image that the person wishes to claim for self-face and the one that may emerge or be granted by others (cf. extract 3). Offensive other-presentation, on the other hand, emerges when self-presentation is contested by others (cf. extracts 5 and 6). The data show that people may take up an active role to support others in their self-presentational styles by explicitly suggesting norms of interaction. For example extract (7), which advises another on appropriate workplace behaviour, works as a protection against possible future threats to other-face.

Face, self-presentation and affect

A common thread that unites studies on face has been the observation that enhancement of and damage to self's image/face arouse specific emotional/emotive reactions such as embarrassment, shame and anger (see, for example, Ho, Fu and Ng, 2004; Kansu-Yetkiner, 2006). It is surprising then that little research on face and (im)politeness research has responded to Goffman's (1967) focus on the affective dimension of the inter-relationship between face and self-presentation, where he frequently refers to feelings of embarrassment. One notable exception, though, is the ethnomethodological study on the motivational bases of withholding compliments by Rodriguez and Ryave (1998), where the authors find that a variety of (social) emotions such as antagonism, competitiveness and fear of comparison impact the (non-)performance of a compliment. This study is significant in drawing attention to the links between face, affect and the self-presentational choices that people make to effect outcomes in relational work that are in line with their goals both during and after an interaction (Ruhi, 2007).

The extracts in the foregoing sections, too, reveal that face issues in interaction arouse emotive responses. The rising tones in extracts (6) and (7), where the interlocutors display irritation and concern for other, respectively, clearly indicate that the impact of affective responses to self/other-presentation. The explicit reference to feeling shame in extract (3), especially, illustrates further that a variety of feelings can work as undercurrents in managing self- and other-face in interaction.

The present data also suggest that display of feelings, that is, emotive discourse can be an important dimension of face in social interaction. The reference to feeling anger, for example, in extract (2), where Işik implies that she will feel offended if Canan replaces the paper, indicates that showing feelings can be used strategically to achieve interactional goals – in this case, Işik's self-presentation as a generous person. Viewed from this perspective, the explicit reference to face through the use of 'face' idioms is likely to highlight the emotions of self with respect to social value in interaction as they explicitly lay self- and/or other-presentation on the table, so to speak, for possible evaluation.

8.5. Concluding remarks

The data in this study show that where an interlocutor is referred to with 'face' idioms, self is evaluated or projected with respect to behavioural expectations and norms regarding role relationships and interactional goals. Thus aspects of self with which face is associated may incorporate a range of attributes – having feelings of indebtedness, consideration towards sharing of household chores, modesty in claiming strengths, etc. In this respect, face is linked to those aspects of self that impinge on the role relationship and the specific interactional goals.

The illustrations of self- and other-presentation suggest that self- and other-face management may be geared not only toward interactional goals in the unfolding discourse but may also concern future interaction. In this regard, the study of face needs to be conducted not only for 'particular contact[s]' (Goffman, 1967/1982: 5) but also for extended time spans so as to investigate the impact of self-presentational styles on (changing) face values. The employment of unobtrusive, qualitative research methodology such as focused diary keeping could help unravel such aspects of face management (cf. for example, Rodriguez and Ryave, 1998).

It has been observed that self-presentations effected through the use of 'face' idioms reveal a negativity bias. As suggested in section 4.1, this bias may be natural since sensitivity to incongruences that may have a negative impact on face is likely to be a foreground cognitive phenomenon in interaction (cf. Jing-Schmidt (2007) on a similar negativity bias in the use of emotive intensifiers). Whether the same bias also exists in other languages, though, remains to be explored.

As has been noted in the previous section, I suggest that more research needs to be conducted on the inter-relationship between face and emotion. I would argue that probing the affective of social interaction, especially in relation to the emotions generated by and the emotions that lie at the basis of impression management and self-presentation, is a line of research that needs to be developed to enhance our understanding of face in social interaction (cf. Spencer-Oatey, this volume, for other suggestions in the same direction). Such a focus on emotion and emotive discourse may unravel aspects that have remained in the 'backstage' in studies on the inter-relationship between face, the self and interpersonal communication.

Morphological Glossary

ABIL	abilitative
ACC	accusative
ADD	additive connective
AGR	person agreement
AOR	aorist
CAUS	causative
COM	commitative
COMP	compound marker
DAT	dative
EXIS.NEG	negative existential
FUT	future
GEN	genitive
IMP	imperative
LOC	locative
NEG	negation
NOM	nominaliser
OPT	optative
PASS	passive
PAST	past
PERS	person
PERF	perfective
PLU	plural
POSS	possessive
POST	postposition
PRO	pronoun
PROG	progressive
Q	question particle
SING	singular

Endnotes

1. In this section and the subsequent ones, I use single quotes for face when referring to the occurrence of the term in idioms in Turkish.
2. Idiomatic translations have been preferred where possible.
3. Permission to use the extracts from authentic conversation has been obtained and pseudonyms have been used throughout.
4. Reduplication of adjectives produces adverbs in Turkish.

5. Cf., for example, Ruhi and Işık-Güler (2007) on the concept of *gönül* 'heart, mind, desire' and related idioms that appeal to the emotive dimension of interaction.
6. *Canım* is a procedural lexical unit, whose literal meaning is 'my life/soul'. It often occurs as a mitigator both in assertive and in offensive presentational acts.

References

Bargiela-Chiappini, F. (2003) Face and politeness: new (insights) for (old) concepts. *Journal of Pragmatics* 35: 1453–1469.

Baumeister, R. F. (1982) A self-presentational view of social phenomena. *Psychological Bulletin* 91: 3–26.

Bayraktaroğlu, A. (1992) Disagreement in Turkish troubles-talk. *Text* 12: 317–342.

Brown, P. and Levinson, S. C. (1987) *Politeness. Some Universals in Language Usage.* Cambridge: Cambridge University Press.

Goffman, E. (1959) *The Presentation of Self in Everyday Life.* New York: Doubleday.

Goffman, E. (1967/1982) *Interaction Ritual: Essays on Face-to-Face Behavior.* New York: Pantheon Books.

Goffman, E. (1974) *Frame Analysis: An Essay on the Organization of Experience,* New York Harper: Colophon Books.

Goffman, E. (1981) *Forms of Talk.* Oxford: Basil Blackwell.

Haugh, M. (2007) Emic conceptualisations of (im)politeness and face in Japanese: implications for the discursive negotiation of second language learner identities. Journal of Pragmatics 39: 657–580.

Haugh, M. and Hinze, C. (2003) A metalinguistic approach to deconstructing the concepts of 'face' and 'politeness' in Chinese, English and Japanese. *Journal of Pragmatics* 35: 1581–1611.

Ho, D. Y-f. (1976) On the concept of face. *American Journal of Sociology* 81: 867–884.

Ho, D. Y-f. (1994) Face dynamics: from conceptualization to measurement. In S. Ting-Toomey (ed.) *The Challenge of Facework* 269–286. New York: State University of New York Press.

Ho, D. Y-f., Fu, W. and Ng, S.M. (2004) Guilt, shame and embarrassment: revelations of face and self. *Culture & Psychology* 1: 64–84.

Holtgraves, T. (1992) The linguistic realization of face management: implications for language production and comprehension, person perception, and cross-cultural communication. *Social Psychology Quarterly* 55: 141–159.

Jing-Schmidt, Z. (2007) Negativity bias in language: A cognitive-affective model of emotive intensifiers. *Cognitive Linguistics* 18: 417–443.

Kansu-Yetkiner, N. (2006) *Blood, Shame and Fear: Self-presentation Strategies in Turkish Women's Talk about their Health and Sexuality.* Unpublished PhD Thesis, Groningen Dissertation Linguistics 58.

Rodriguez, N. and Ryave, A. L. (1998) Withholding compliments in everyday life and the covert management of disaffiliation. *Journal of Contemporary Ethnography*, 27: 323–346.

Ruhi, Ş. (2007) Higher-order intentions and self-politeness in evaluations of (im)politeness: the relevance of compliment responses. *Australian Journal of Linguistics*, 27: 107–145.

Ruhi, Ş. and Iştk-Güler, H. (2007) Conceptualizing face and relational work in (im)politeness: Revelations from politeness lexemes and idioms in Turkish. *Journal of Pragmatics* 39: 681–711.

Schlenker, B. R. (2003) Self-presentation. In M. R Leary and J. P. Tangney (eds.) *Handbook of Self and Identity* 492–518. New York: The Guilford Press.

Schlenker, B. R. and Pontari, B. A. (2000) The strategic control of information: impression management and self-presentation in daily life. In A. Tesser, R. B. Felson and J. Suls (eds.) *Psychological Perspectives on Self and Identity* 199–232. Washington, D.C.: American Psychological Press.

Schütz, A. (1998) Assertive, offensive, protective, and defensive style of self-presentation: a taxonomy. *Journal of Psychology* 132: 611–628.

Spencer-Oatey, H. (2005) (Im)Politeness, face and perceptions of rapport: unpackaging their bases and interrelationships. *Journal of Politeness Research* 1: 95–119.

Spencer-Oatey, H. (2007) Theories of identity and the analysis of face. *Journal of Pragmatics* 39: 639–656.

Strecker, I. (1993) Cultural variations in the concept of 'face'. *Multilingua* 12: 119–141.

Terkourafi, M. (2001) *Politeness in Cypriot Greek: A Frame-based Approach.* Unpublished PhD dissertation, University of Cambridge.

Ting-Toomey, S.(2005) The matrix of face: an updated face-negotiation theory. In W. B. Gudykunst (ed.) *Theorising about Intercultural Communication* 71–92. Thousand Oaks: Sage.

Ting-Toomey, S. and Kurogi, A. (1998) Facework competence in intercultural conflict: an updated face-negotiation theory. *International Journal of Intercultural Relations* 22: 187–225.

Tracy, K., and Baratz, S. (1993) Intellectual discussion in the academy as situated discourse. *Communication Monographs* 60: 300–320.

Ukosakul, M. (2003) Conceptual metaphors motivating the use of Thai 'face'. In E. H. Casad and G. B. Palmer (eds.) *Cognitive Linguistics and Non-Indo-European Languages* 275–303. Berlin: Mouton de Gruyter.

9
Face and self in Chinese communication

Ge Gao

9.1. Introduction

The concept of face is not unique to Chinese culture (e.g. Brown and Levinson, 1978; Goffman, 1955; Ho, 1976; Hu, 1944; Ting-Toomey, 1988). Face has been extensively researched over the years especially since the development of Face Negotiation Theory (Ting-Toomey, 1988). Research on Face Negotiation Theory helps us understand that people in collectivistic cultures are more other-face oriented than people in individualistic cultures. It also explains that, given their face concerns, Chinese and Taiwanese tend to adopt obliging and avoidance conflict management styles (Ting-Toomey *et al.*, 1991). More recently, face and facework were examined in relation to self-construals, power distance, a third party, relational closeness, and status to further our understanding of cross-cultural similarities and differences in face (Oetzel *et al.*, 2001). While Face Negotiation Theory provides a valuable theoretical framework for cross-cultural and cross-national comparisons and generalisations, exploratory and descriptive inquiries of the notion of face in a specific cultural context such as Chinese culture can also serve important purposes in advancing our knowledge in this area. Specifically, descriptions of indigenous concepts of face, their meanings, and situational variables can inform Face Negotiation Theory with regard to its boundary conditions and culture-specific *versus* culture-general dimensions. Descriptive accounts can also localise our understanding of face by providing appropriate cultural contexts. Context specific knowledge is especially rich and informative in understanding situated experiences and in developing skills in the application of face. This chapter represents the effort towards this goal.

Although face is a familiar concept to those who read works published in English, to Chinese speakers the closest equivalent of face can be found in two concepts: *mian zi* (面子) and *lian* (脸). In the *XinHua* (1998) dictionary, the first two entries for both *mian* and *lian* are 'face' and 'image'. In Chinese social interactions, *mian zi* and *lian* are synonymous in some contexts, but they evoke very different meanings in others. To the author's best knowledge, there has been little data-based research focusing on how *mian zi* and *lian* emerge in Chinese social interactions, differences between *mian zi* and *lian* in Chinese communication, or the relationship between *mian zi* and *lian* and the Chinese self concept. The purpose of this chapter is to hone in on the issues of face in the context of Chinese culture, to present findings from survey data collected in Chinese in China, and to examine those findings in the context of previous work on *mian zi*, *lian*, and other related concepts.

9.2. Data

The author surveyed 64 participants anonymously using an open-ended survey in Chinese. The English version of the survey is included in the Appendix. The survey approach was adopted after requests for personal interviews were denied for reasons of inconvenience. The survey questions were designed to be open-ended to solicit free responses from participants about the descriptions of indigenous concepts of *mian zi* and *lian*, their meanings, and various situational variables in the use of the terms. Teachers and administrators were then recruited to participate from a university in Shanxi province and a combined middle/high school in Beijing through two personal contacts of the author. Of the 64 participants in the study, 59.4% were males and 34.4% were females (6.3% didn't answer the question). The average age was 36 years old (with 4 no responses) and the standard deviation is 12 years and the age range is between 20-57 years. The average length of teaching was 15 years (with 15 no responses). Self identified positions included 32.8% middle school teachers, 17.2% high school teachers, 14.1% college lecturers, 6.3% administrators, and 28% did not fill in this category. The education level was as follows: 53% of four years college degrees, 34% of three years of college degrees, 5% of vocational school training, and 8% no response.

This sample of participants is unique in three aspects. First, this sample deviates from the widely surveyed college students. It surveyed mostly teachers of middle school, high school, and university in two different geographical locations. Secondly, different age groups are represented in this sample to speak to different experiences of their social interactions. Finally, this group of participants appeared to be more expressive and articulate than ordinary survey participants as evident in the current survey, thus making teachers suitable cultural informants in exploratory studies such as this.

Participants were encouraged to answer each question fully by the author's personal contacts. It appeared that participants took care in answering questions and their responses were clearly written and detailed. Multiple examples were given in their answers. The author reviewed the returned surveys many times to get a sense of the overall picture of the data. The data were then compiled and copied onto separate sheets of paper question by question, and participant by participant. Though the process was tedious, it enabled the author to become thoroughly familiar with a large spectrum of responses concerning each question. Given that the purpose of this exploratory study was to seek descriptions of indigenous concepts of *mian zi* and *lian*, their meanings, and situational variables, the data included in this study attempted to capture not only the recurring thoughts, but also the array of descriptions, attached meanings, and situations of *mian zi* and *lian*. The large spectrum of responses may not be meaningful percentage-wise; nevertheless, they represent the richness of situated experiences that can inform future studies. The data reported in the paper were translated into English and they represent both the saliency and the diversity of participants' responses.

9.3. Findings and discussion

Mian zi and the Chinese self

Participants drew close associations between *mian zi* and the Chinese self in their accounts. First, *mian zi* was defined as self respect, self-esteem, self-love, vanity, pride, and self defence. These definitions embody the Chinese self concept. Some examples of the embodiment given by participants include:

1. One who does not need *mian zi* is not a real person.

2. Self respect [*mian zi*] and life co-exist.

3. A person needs *mian zi* like a tree needs bark.

4. No one likes to harm her/his self esteem [*mian zi*].

This close connection between *mian zi* and the Chinese self concept has been touched upon in one study that is relevant to the current findings. Yu and Gu (1990) recognised that *mian zi* and self esteem are mixed together in Chinese culture.

Mian zi also represents the Chinese 'social self'. Participants defined *mian zi* as prestige, reputation, image, dignity, approval and respect from others, social position, and social status as shown in the following statements:

5. To be recognised and valued by others [*mian zi*] gives me confidence in life and work.

6. [I] Do not want to be looked down upon by others [loss of *mian zi*]. I'd like to have some dignity.

7. [I] Do not want to be disgraced in front of others [loss of *mian zi*].

8. A person lives in a mixture of personal relationships. How others perceive me [*mian zi*] is a consideration.

This notion of *mian zi* as the social self is found in several previous studies. For example, Hu (1944) conceived *mian zi* as 'the kind of prestige that is emphasized in [the United States]: A reputation achieved through getting on in life, through success and ostentation' (p.45). King and Myers (1977) used the term of social or positional face. In addition, the word 'other' figures very prominently in participants' definitions of *mian zi* as the social self. The 'other' can choose to support a person's social self by recognising and responding to his/her need for recognition and prestige in social interactions or vice versa. Two earlier studies examined the role of the 'other,' an insight pertinent to this study. Yu and Gu (1990) asserted that one's self-esteem is formed on the basis of others' remarks. If remarks are positive, one has *mian zi* and, consequently, one's self-esteem is increased. Haugh and Hinze (2003) reported that public knowledge and external evaluation are crucial even to self-proclaimed losses or gains of 'face'.

Furthermore, *mian zi* denotes the Chinese 'relational self' as revealed in participants' definitions of goodwill, affection, friendship, face honourable conduct, mutual respect, and personal relationships. The pivotal role of *mian zi* in the configuration of the relational self is explained by participants as follows:

9. It will be difficult to accomplish anything [without *mian zi*] and it will affect one's work.

10. *Mian zi* involves personal relationships too much.

11. I cherish my own *mian zi*. I also show consideration for others' *mian zi. Mian zi* is not entirely vain; sometimes it can be very real.

No previous research to date has focused on *mian zi* as the Chinese relational self. In summary, participants' responses reveal that *mian zi* defines not only the Chinese social self, but also the self concept and the relational self. We can say that *mian zi* is an integral part of the Chinese self.

Mian zi and context

Mian zi is not significant in every context in Chinese social interactions. Participants identified several contexts in which *mian zi* is most important. In public settings (*gong gong chang he* 公共场合), *mian zi* is perceived as cause for great concern as in: '*Mian zi* is very important in public. Otherwise, one loses reputation and dignity.' In dealing with critical events and matters of principle, concern for *mian zi* is paramount as one participant explained. *Mian zi* is also crucial when one's self-esteem is involved, one's reputation is harmed, and when one needs recognition from others as commented by others.

In addition, participants indicated that *mian zi* plays a critical role in certain relationships such as encountering strangers, subordinates, friends, parents, the younger generation, and those one cares for as expressed in the following two statements: '[I] don't like not having *mian zi* in front of people that I like. I want to do everything appropriately.'; 'One cannot not have *mian zi* in front of girlfriends, wives, parents, and children. Otherwise, one cannot be considered as a man.' Recognising the role of context in understanding *mian zi* is very important because it indicates that *mian zi* is not a static construct, but rather it emerges in communicative interactions with others.

Differences between mian zi and lian

The concepts of *mian zi* and *lian* can be combined as in the case of *lian mian* (脸面) or used separately and their meanings are often interchangeable except in cases such as loss of *mian zi* (丢面子) and loss of *lian* (丢脸) or *bu yao lian* (no *lian*; 不要脸). The literal translation of *lian* is 'face.' Hu (1944) defines *lian* as something which 'represents the confidence of society in the integrity of ego's moral character, the loss of which makes it impossible for him to function properly within the community' (p.45). *Lian*, he notes, 'is both a social sanction for enforcing moral standards and an internalized sanction' (p.45). Having or not having *mian zi* is externalised and conditioned by how successful one is in meeting established social rules, while *lian* tends to be internalised.

Hu's definition and explanation of the difference between *mian zi* and *lian* represents both the earliest and the most influential work on *lian*. However, little research has been conducted on the difference since then. In 1993, Zuo surveyed Chinese students on the two concepts. In 1998, Gao explored the differences between *mian zi* and *lian* in a Chinese TV series. In 2003, Haugh and Hinze cited many examples of loss of *mian zi* and *lian* from their Chinese respondents and in Chinese contemporary novels. These studies support the importance of and differences between the two concepts; yet how loss of *mian zi* and loss of *lian* differ remains unanswered.

In this study, participants provided many instances of differentiation between loss of *mian zi* and loss of *lian* that point to seven dimensions. These seven dimensions include breadth, severity, nature, morality, agency/accountability, time/space and visibility, as illustrated in Table 9.1 below.

First, loss of *mian zi* and loss of *lian* differ in breadth. Participants explain that loss of *mian zi* covers a much broader spectrum of events as compared to loss of *lian*. Loss of *mian zi* involves 'poor performance on the job, mistakes, misunderstanding, criticism, and rejection by others'. Loss of *lian*, on the other hand, is restricted to issues of significant consequences such as accidents on the job, public ridicule and humiliation, as well as immoral conduct. This finding is supported by Zuo's

Table 9.1 Differences between loss of *mian zi* and loss of *lian*

Dimensions	Loss of *mian zi*	Loss of *lian*
Breadth	broad spectrum of events	issues of significance
Intensity	low	high
Nature	trivial matters	matters of principle
Morality	absent	present
Agency	self or other provoked	self provoked
Time/Space	temporal, situational	permanent, fixed
Visibility	less	more

(1993) survey of 107 college students in Wuhan, China. When asked to evaluate among a list of 30 events that involved: (1) loss of *lian*, (2) loss of *mian zi*, (3) loss of both *lian* and *mian zi*, and (4) no loss of *lian* or *mian zi*, twenty out of 30 events were judged as loss of *mian zi* events.

Second, the level of severity differentiates the two. Loss of *mian zi* is far less severe than loss of *lian*. As one participant explained, 'when you invite a lady to dance, but get rejected, you experience loss of *mian zi*', whereas 'when your child commits a crime, you experience loss of *lian*'. This finding is compatible with two previous studies. Zuo's (1993) survey research reported that respondents not only differentiated between loss of *lian* and loss of *mian zi* events, but also judged the former as more severe. In Gao's (1998) study, when a married woman was caught seeing her ex-lover, the married woman said that she didn't have *lian* to see anyone because she was too ashamed and she wanted to die. In this example, life became unworthy of living because her loss of *lian*. A person without *lian* is no longer viewed as one with self esteem or integrity. Thus the profound effect of loss of *lian* in a person's life is by no means equivalent to that of loss of *mian zi*.

Third, the nature of an event is another dimension that sets the two apart. Participants explained that loss of *mian zi* concerns trivial matters such as not having enough money to buy a gift that the girlfriend likes, whereas loss of *lian* involves matters of principle such as imprisonment due to corruption. Zuo's (1993) study provides support for this finding. In the study, loss of *mian zi* was mostly concerned with improper manner in public or a lack of ability. Some examples of loss of *mian zi* include being drunk at a banquet, not able to keep a promise, and public embarrassment such as loosening one's belt while eating.

Fourth, loss of *mian zi* and loss of *lian* differ in morality. Participants stated that loss of *lian* is associated with morality, ethics, and lawfulness, whereas loss of *mian zi* does not denote these meanings. Three previous studies provide ample support for this dimension of difference. In Zuo's (1993) study, breaking the law and violating ethical and moral principles were perceived as loss of *lian*. An exposed extramarital affair, stealing, committing a crime, bullying the elders and the young, and exposed corruption are examples of loss of *lian*. The morality dimension of the loss of *lian* was also found in a study of a popular TV series in China (Gao, 1998). In the study, loss of *lian* was associated with situations in which one's personal integrity was in jeopardy such as when a married woman was accused of being in love with another man. The married woman was deemed to be *bu yao lian* (lit. not need *lian*; shameless). The accusatory phrase *bu yao lian* is often reserved for acts that are shameful and so open to being condemned. In another instance, a widow shouted 'You *bu yao lian*' to a man who approached her with bad intentions. There were several other similar instances in the TV series where a person who was perceived as engaging in an immoral act was denounced as *bu yao lian*. Gao (1998) noted that *bu yao lian* is a very condemning accusation because it implies loss of both integrity and dignity of being a person. In Bedford's (2004) study, Taiwanese women identify loss of *lian* as an experience of shame, and older Chinese are perceived to be more concerned about loss of *lian* compared to the young because of their greater sense of shame.

The notion of agency and accountability is the fifth dimension that separates loss of *mian zi* and loss of *lian*. Participants perceived loss of *lian* to be self provoked as a result of actions carried out by the self, while loss of *mian zi* can be either self provoked or other provoked and it can be attributed to both the self and others. Participants gave many examples. To illustrate, when people engage in an illegal act, they incite loss of *lian* and, therefore, they are responsible for their own behavior. On the other hand, when one tries to borrow a book from a friend but the friend refuses, the friend causes loss of *mian zi*. When one does not know the answer to a question, the consequent loss of *mian zi* can be attributed to the person him/herself.

Sixth, the element of time/space sets apart loss of *mian zi* and loss of *lian*. Participants perceived the former as temporal and situational, while the latter is permanent and fixed. A person who has experienced loss of *lian* will have a 'stained' identity. However, loss of *mian zi* will not have a lasting effect on a person's identity. This finding is consistent with Zuo's (1993) work indicating that loss of *lian* creates a long-term and psychological effect, while loss of *mian zi* is situational and temporary.

Lastly, visibility separates loss of *mian zi* and loss of *lian*. Loss of *lian* is more visible to others as compared to loss of *mian zi* as explained by one participant: 'Everyone knows if you have experienced loss of *lian*, but loss of *mian zi* is subtle and can be difficult to detect.'

In summary, loss of *mian zi* and loss of *lian* have significant, yet different consequences in the personal and social lives of the Chinese. Loss of *mian zi* and loss of *lian* differ along seven dimensions as shown in this study. This understanding will help us better explain and interpret the meaning and practice of *mian zi* and *lian* in Chinese social interactions.

Giving and saving/leaving mian zi

Two of the most practiced skills in Chinese social interactions involve *gei mian zi* (给面子, 'to give *mian zi*') and *liu mian zi* (留面子, 'to save *mian zi*'). Participants in this study were very articulate about their understanding and experiences of these two skills. Participants defined *gei mian zi* as attending to others' reputation and self-esteem, respecting others' rights, supporting others, giving others confidence, building others' image, understanding others, making allowances for others, tolerating others, and accommodating others. In other words, *gei mian zi* amounts to the ultimate confirmation of the important role of 'other' in Chinese social interactions. Through *gei mian zi*, others' personal and social identities are maintained, affirmed, and/or promoted. *Gei mian zi* can also be utilised strategically to accomplish personal goals in Chinese communication.

One example of a strategic use of *gei mian zi* in achieving personal goals is reported in Gao's (1998) study. She found that *gei mian zi* was used as a plea for making requests, mediating conflicts, and gaining compliance. A plea tends to be the strongest and the most persuasive when a person's public self is put forth waiting to be honoured. To illustrate, the speaker asks that the addressee attend to her self-esteem and support her by stating, 'Xiao Geng has helped me a lot for the last two years. To give me *mian zi*, would you please do him this favor?' (Gao 1998: 475) This type of *mian zi* appeal is a very powerful form of persuasion in Chinese communication. However, one caveat is that not every person's *mian zi* that is put forth is honoured. *Mian zi* is mostly likely to be honoured in established relationships. To ensure the effectiveness of persuasion, one should exercise care in selecting whose *mian zi* to put forth.

Liu mian zi is another widely practiced skill in Chinese social interactions. Participants defined *liu mian zi* (to save/leave *mian zi*) as forgiving others, treating others leniently, not making others lose *mian zi*, not hurting others' self esteem and pride, and not tarnishing others' image. Some perceived an ability to save/leave *mian zi* as a measure of one's personal quality, self cultivation, and level of tolerance. Participants believed that it is necessary to save/leave *mian zi* in public settings, in protecting others' self esteem, and in all situations that do not involve matters of principle.

Participants described multiple ways to *gei mian zi*. These multiple ways can be categorised into three major communication strategies that have important implications for understanding and practicing *mian zi* in Chinese social interactions, as seen in table 9.2 below.

Table 9.2 Communication strategies for giving *mian zi*

Communication strategies	Examples of giving *mian zi*
Intervention	changing topic of a discussion interrupting a conversation
Supportive talk	speaking up others' strengths agreeing to others' ideas speaking for others accepting others' criticism forgiving others' mistakes not revealing others' mistakes in public not criticising others not questioning others not gossiping
Indirectness	implicit language polite talk remaining silent about others' shortcomings

The first strategy involves communication intervention such as changing the topic of a discussion and interrupting a conversation when one feels the other person's *mian zi* is vulnerable. A second strategy is to engage in supportive talk such as speaking up about others' strengths, agreeing to others' ideas, speaking for others, accepting others' criticism, and forgiving others' mistakes, as well as refraining from revealing others' mistakes in public, criticising others, questioning others, or gossiping.

Previous research findings provide support for the second communication strategy of *gei mian zi*. Gao and Ting-Toomey (1998) explained that not arguing or disagreeing overtly with others in public, especially in the presence of a superior, gives others *mian zi*. Meanings in messages are not to be negotiated in public because to negotiate conceivable meanings in public is to question others' authority and to pose threat to others' *mian zi*. Conversations in public, therefore, tend to be ritualised to avoid *mian zi* being threatened. G*ei mian zi* means refraining from gossiping (*yi lun* 议论). Hellweg, Samovar and Skow (1991) found that, in business negotiations, any proposal-counter-proposal style of negotiating is avoided. Bond and Lee's (1981) research revealed that more critical comments were given about a speaker in the speaker-*uninformed* condition (i.e. the speaker will not hear the comments) than in the audience informed condition (i.e. the audience will hear the comments).

A third strategy described by participants involves indirect communication such as using implicit language, polite talk, and remaining silent in regards to others' shortcomings. In addition to indirect communication, participants identified several behaviours as acts of *gei mian zi.* They include giving others special treatment, making a concession in a conflict situation, doing things for others even though one is not expected to, and providing assistance to others. Utilisations of such approaches were found in contemporary novels (Haugh and Hinze, 2003).

Participants' descriptions of ways to *liu mian zi* can be classified into three communication strategies, as seen in Table 9.3 below.

Table 9.3 Communication strategies for saving/leaving *mian zi*

Communication strategies	Examples of saving/leaving *mian zi*
Avoidance	not investigating wrongdoing not criticising in public not exposing a lie not naming names
Indirectness	mentioning instead of discussing a problem being indirect *han xu* (implicit communication)
Tact	selecting an appropriate method of criticism making an excuse to avoid refusal smiling covering up others' embarrassment diffusing a problem remaining silent leaving leeway in one's expression

The first strategy is avoidance such as not investigating wrongdoing, not criticising in public, not exposing a lie, and not naming names. Participants characterised this strategy as the mindset of playing the fool, turning a blind eye to things, and going through the motions. Support for this approach is found in previous research. According to Gao and Ting-Toomey (1998), in Chinese culture, criticism often is perceived as affectively based and relational in nature. Young (1994) explains that: 'Chinese regard one's ideas as entangled with one's identity or sense of personal worth; an attack on one's ideas is therefore an attack on one's self, or, more specifically, one's face.' (p.125) In another study, mainland Chinese and Taiwanese report a higher degree of obliging and avoiding styles of conflict management than do their U.S. counterparts (Ting-Toomey *et al.*, 1991). Chu and Ju (1993) found that when asked what they would do if they have a quarrel with a neighbour and receive verbal abuse, over half of the Chinese respondents indicated that they would exercise verbal control in a situation like that and one third indicated that they would go to a neighbourhood committee for a settlement.

Indirect communication is the second strategy, which includes mentioning instead of discussing a problem, being indirect, and *han xu* (implicit communication). This finding is consistent with previous research. Gao and Ting-Toomey (1998) identified *han xu* as an important characteristic of Chinese communication. The practice of *han xu* indicates that Chinese rarely give definitively affirmative or negative answers equivalent to 'yes' or 'no;' rather, Chinese carefully and cautiously formulate their replies to attend to the *mian zi* needs of both the speaker and the recipient. Wierzbicka (1996) reported that Chinese perceive the response 'sorry, I can't' as 'unsubtle' and offensively 'frank'. Moreover, concern for *mian zi* allows little freedom for refusing a request. Link (1992) contends that the practice of indirect communication not only shows concern for the *mian zi* of the petitioner, but also saves oneself from losing *mian zi* in the event of rejection from the upper level. It appears that *han xu*, even at the cost of precision, accuracy, and clarity, is actively pursued in Chinese social interactions.

The third strategy of *liu mian zi* is tactful communication. Being tactful means selecting an appropriate method of criticism, making an excuse to avoid refutation, smiling, covering up others' embarrassment, diffusing a problem, remaining silent, and leaving some leeway in one's expression. This finding is consistent with previous studies. For example, being assertive reflects the ill character of an individual and threatens the harmony and cohesion of interpersonal relationships (Bodde 1953; Tseng 1973). Chinese tend to adopt an unassertive style of communication to protect *mian zi* and to preserve interpersonal harmony, as well as the cohesion of the group (Gao and Ting-Toomey 1998). Gao and Ting-Toomey continue to explain that Chinese have learnt to be strategically unassertive by articulating their intentions in a tactful manner and leaving room for negotiations in private. The ambivalence embedded in Chinese responses is congruent with the cultural belief of *liu you yu di* (留有余地, making allowances for unforeseen circumstances). To illustrate, when a 'yes' is expressed as *wen ti bu da* (问题不大, no big problem) there is room for retreat. An informant in Young's (1994) study explains aptly: 'You need to feel your way and test your boss's mood. If you suspect any negative feedback, you can retreat. Westerners can tolerate failures, but Chinese are traditionally trained in terms of saving face.' (p.163) Chu and Ju (1993) reported that more than half of the Chinese respondents would prefer means such as 'not say anything', 'ask the leader to mediate', and 'ask a third person' to a direct approach if they experience a difference of opinion with someone in the work unit.

Participants offered different opinions in regards to whom to give *mian zi* or for whom to save *mian zi*. Some felt that it is important to give everyone *mian zi* for reasons of group solidarity and co-operation. Some felt that giving *mian zi* depends on the situation. Still some felt that it is more important to give *mian zi* to *zi ji ren* (自己人, insiders) than to *wai ren* (外人, outsiders), especially when personal interests are involved. Others felt that the issue of *mian zi* does not apply to *zi ji ren* because one should be able to openly criticise and talk about *zi ji ren*. On the issue of saving *mian zi*, participants felt the nature of a relationship (*zi ji ren* versus *wai ren*) influences such an undertaking. As some participants explained, they can be forthright with *zi ji ren* and save less *mian zi* with them as compared to *wai ren*. With *wai ren*, they need to use more caution and take the outcomes more into account. This area of research is potentially rich and it warrants further exploration.

It appears that to navigate social interactions in the Chinese culture, one needs to learn not only when and how to *gei mian zi*, but when and how to *liu mian zi* when a person's self-concept is challenged. The ability to *gei* and *liu mian zi* is an essential component of a Chinese person's social competence.

9.4. Conclusion

Mian zi and *lian* are essential to the narratives of Chinese social interactions. They influence how Chinese view themselves, relate to others, and communicate with others. As Young (1994) noted, 'face goes deep to the core of a Chinese person's identity and integrity' (p.19). Yu (2003) explained that the Chinese concept of 'face' concerns the entire society and commands saliency in both daily practice and talk as compared to Brown and Levinson's (1987) face, which only pertains to a small academic community and has limited use in society. Given this context, descriptive accounts of indigenous concepts of face, their meanings, and situational variables seem pertinent in enriching our knowledge of this important concept. In this chapter, participants provided a glimpse of how *mian zi* and *lian* emerge in Chinese social interactions, differences between *mian zi* and *lian* in Chinese communication, and the relationship between *mian zi* and *lian* and the Chinese self concept. Specifically, there is a close connection between *mian zi* and the Chinese self concept. *Mian zi* also defines the social and relational self of the Chinese. There are several contexts in which *mian zi* is most important. Some of the contexts include public setting, critical events, certain relationships, and when one's self concept is involved. In addition, seven dimensions of differentiation between loss of *mian zi* and loss of *lian* emerged in participants' accounts. They include breadth, severity, nature, morality, agency/accountability, time/space and visibility. Participants also described communication intervention, supportive talk, and indirect communication as strategies of *gei mian zi* and communication avoidance, indirect communication, and tactful communication as strategies of *liu mian zi*. These findings, although limited in their generalisability and application, are fruitful outcomes of exploratory studies such as this one.

This chapter represents one of the very few data-based research studies on *mian zi* and *lian* inside China. The findings in this study pose interesting research areas for furthering our understanding and knowledge of *mian zi* and *lian*. One such area is the empirical testing of seven dimensions of differentiation between loss of *mian zi* and loss of *lian*, and the strategies of *gei mian zi* and *liu mian zi*. By engaging in vigorous testing, we will be able to assess the applicability and generalisability of these dimensions. Another area of future research involves investigations of various broad and specific 'contexts' of *mian zi* and *lian* in Chinese social interactions such as gender (men/women), relationship (*zi ji ren* and *wai ren*), social networks, and hierarchy (age, status). In this study, the relationship context of *zi ji ren* and *wai ren* was only briefly introduced. Previous research findings also invite further examination of the importance of context in the formulations and practice of *mian zi* and *lian*. For example, Zuo's (1993) study found that women attached more importance to both *lian* and *mian zi* and they showed more sensitivity to them and gave them a higher overall ranking than their male counterparts. Redding and Ng's (1982) work showed the relational context of a *zi ji ren* 'insider' and a *wai ren* 'outsider' as illustrated in their work: 'Recently, a secretary introduced her younger brother into my department. He is not the type of subordinate I want, but I took him only because I had to give face to his sister.' (p.212) Future research can also focus on strategies of communication in the application of *mian zi* and *lian* to assess their applicability and generalisability.

In summary, *mian zi* and *lian* are two pervasive concepts in the Chinese culture and they have a broad impact on many aspects of the lives of the Chinese. The findings of this exploratory study will inform many future studies of these two Chinese concepts of face.

References

Bedford, O. A. (2004) The individual experience of guilt and shame in Chinese culture. *Culture and Psychology* 10: 29–52.

Bodde, D. (1953) Harmony and conflict in Chinese philosophy. In A. F. Wright (ed.) *Studies in Chinese thought* 19–80. Chicago: University of Chicago Press.

Bond, M. and Lee, P. (1981) Face saving in Chinese culture: A discussion and experimental study of Hong Kong students. In A. Y. C. King and R. P.L. Lee (eds.), *Social life and development in Hong Kong* 289–304. Hong Kong: Chinese University Press.

Brown, P. and Levinson, S. C. (1987) *Politeness: Some Universals in Language Usage.* Cambridge: Cambridge University Press.

Chu, G. C. and Ju, Y.A. (1993) *The Great Wall in Ruins: Communication and Cultural Change in China.* Albany, NY: State University of New York Press.

Gao, G. (1998) An initial analysis of the effects of face and concern for other in Chinese interpersonal communication. *International Journal of Intercultural Relations* 22: 467–482.

Gao, G. and Ting-Toomey, S. (1998) *Communicating effectively with the Chinese.* Thousand Oaks, CA: Sage.

Goffman, E. (1955) On facework: An analysis of ritual elements in social interaction. *Psychiatry* 18: 213–231.

Haugh, M. and Hinze, C. (2003) A metalinguistic approach to deconstructing the concepts of 'face' and 'politeness' in Chinese, English and Japanese. *Journal of Pragmatics* 35: 1581–1611.

Ho, D. Y-f. (1976) On the concept of face. *American Journal of Sociology* 81: 867–884.

Hu, H. C. (1944) The Chinese concepts of 'face.' American Anthropologist 46: 45–64.

Hellweg, S.A., Samovar, L. A. and Skow, L. (1991) Cultural variations in negotiation styles. In L. A. Samovar and R. E. Porter (eds.), *Intercultural communication: A reader* (6ᵗʰ edn.) 66–78. Belmont, CA: Wadsworth.

King, A. Y. and Myers, J. T. (1977) *Shame as an Incomplete Conception of Chinese Culture: A study of Face.* Hong Kong: Social Research Centre, The Chinese University of Hong Kong.

Link, P. (1992) *Evening Chats in Beijing: Probing China's Predicament.* New York: W. W. Norton.

Oetzel, J., Ting-Toomey, S., Masumoto, T., Yokochi, Y., Pan, X. H., Takai, J. and Wilcox, R. (2001) Face and facework in conflict: A cross-cultural comparison of China, Germany, Japan, and the United States. *Communication Monographs* 68: 235–258.

Redding, S. G. and Ng, M. (1982) The role of 'face' in the organisational perception of managers. *Organisation Studies* 3: 201–219.

Ting-Toomey, S. (1988) Intercultural conflict styles: A face-negotiation theory. In Y. Y. Kim and W. B. Gudykunst (eds.), *Theories in Intercultural Communication* 213–235. Newbury Park, CA: Sage.

Ting-Toomey, S., Gao, G., Trubisky, P., Yang, Z. Z., Kim, H. S., Lin, S. L. and Nishida, T. (1991). Culture, face maintenance, and styling of handling interpersonal conflict: A study in five cultures. International Journal of Conflict Management 2: 275–296.

Tseng, W. S. (1973) The concept of personality in Confucian thought. *Psychiatry* 36: 191–202.

Wierzbicka, A. (1996) Contrastive sociolinguistics and the theory of 'cultural scripts': Chinese vs English. In M. Hellinger and U. Ammon (eds.) *Contrastive Sociolinguistics* 313–344. Berlin: Mouton de Gruyter.

Xin Hua Zi Dian [Xinhua Dictionary] (1998) Beijing: *Shang Wu* Publishing House.

Young, L. W. L. (1994) *Crosstalk and Culture in Sino-American Communication.* Cambridge: Cambridge University Press.

Yu, M.-C. (2003) On the universality of face: Evidence from Chinese compliment response behavior. *Journal of Pragmatics* 35: 1679–1710.

Yu, D. H. and Gu, B. L. (1990) Zhong guo ren de qing mian jiao lu [Chinese face concerns]. In *Zhongguoren de Xin Li: Vol. 3. Zhongguoren de Mian Ju Xing Ge: Renqing Yu Mian zi* 63–107. Taipei: Zhang Lao Shi Chu Ban She.

Zuo, B. (1993) A socio-psychological study of the recognition of the concepts of face among college students [in Chinese]. In Q. S. Li (ed.), *A Collection of Research on Chinese Social Psychology* 122–140. Hong Kong: Hong Kong Shi Dai Wen Hua Press.

Appendix: Survey of *mian zi* and *lian*

Section I:

1. What is the meaning of '*mian zi*?
2. Is '*mian zi*' important to you? Why? Please explain.
3. In what situations, do you feel, '*mian zi*' is important? Give examples.
4. Is there a difference between '*mian zi*' and '*lian*'?
   _____ yes _____ no
   If yes, please explain how they are different. Give examples.
5. Does 'losing *mian zi*' differ from 'losing *lian*'?
   _____ yes _____ no
   If yes, please explain:
   In what situations, one loses '*mian zi*'?
   In what situations, one loses '*lian*'?
6. What is the meaning of 'giving *mian zi*'?
7. What are some of the ways of 'giving *mian zi*'?
8. Is there a distinction between insiders and outsiders with regard to 'giving *mian zi*'?
   _____ yes _____ no
   If yes, please use examples to explain how 'giving *mian zi*' differs from insiders and outsiders.
9. What is the meaning of 'leaving some *mian zi*'?
10. In what situations is, 'leaving some *mian zi*' necessary?
11. What are some of the ways of 'leaving some *mian zi*'?
12. Is there a distinction between insiders and outsiders with regard to 'leaving some *mian zi*'?
    _____ yes _____ no
    If yes, please use examples to explain how 'leaving some *mian zi*' differs between insiders and outsiders.

Section II:

1. How old are you? _____ years
2. What is your sex? _____ male _____ female
3. What is your occupation? _____
4. What is your education (please select one)?
   _____ postgraduate
   _____ college
   _____ junior college
   _____ TV university
   _____ high school
   _____ junior high
   _____ other
5. In which city do you live? _____ province _____ city _____ county

10
Face, politeness and interpersonal variables: implications for language production and comprehension

Thomas Holtgraves

Face and facework are invaluable concepts for understanding interpersonal communication. Their importance derives from the fact that they provide a means of organising the effects of a variety of interpersonal influences on many different aspects of communication. In this chapter I describe some of these effects as a means of demonstrating this organising function. In doing this I will be treating face as an abstract, high-level theoretical construct, a theoretical tool that can be usefully applied to interpersonal communication. I first sketch in broad terms the various shades of meaning given to the concepts of face and facework. Then, I provide a brief overview of Brown and Levinson's (1978, 1987) politeness theory, as this has been the major vehicle for examining the role of face in interpersonal communication. I then consider the role of face management processes in language production, person perception, impression management and language comprehension. Finally, I consider cultural and individual differences in the manner in which face is manifested in conversation.

10.1. Face and facework

Following Goffman (1967), I take face to be the positive public image that each person effectively claims for him- or herself when in the presence of other people. Hence, one's face is the public display of one's identity. However, as Spencer-Oatey (2005) has argued, face is not the same as one's identity. Rather, it is a subset of one's identity, a portion of one's identity that is most relevant for the current interaction. For example, it is one's academic identity that is on display in a seminar, an identity that will not be on display in the grocery store. Relatedly, it is important to note that face does not refer to the content of an identity that one might wish to project in an interaction (e.g. friendly, witty, intelligent, etc.). Rather, face is entailed in the projection of *any* identity.

To have face is to successfully project some identity within an encounter, with success defined as the ratification of that identity by others who are present. It is in this way that Goffman viewed face as an interactional – rather than individual – construct (Arundale, 2006). It is interactional because one cannot simply claim to have face; face must be ratified by others. Face, then, is the result of a collaborative process; threats to another's face are simultaneously threats to one's own face. Hence, it is assumed that people co-operatively engage in protecting and supporting one another's face; in short, they engage in facework.

Facework is critical for understanding interpersonal communication and it refers to those communications designed to create, support, or defend a particular image. Following Durkheim (1915), Goffman argued that facework includes both avoidance rituals (Durkheim's negative rites) and presentation rituals (Durkheim's positive rites). The former refer to actions designed to avoid (either symbolically or actually) threats to an individual's face (e.g. not calling attention to another's faults, not restricting another's freedom, etc.). The latter refer to those approach-based rituals (compliments, greetings, etc.) designed to affirm and support a social relationship.

Facework for Goffman is not a trivial thing, but neither is it an objective of social interaction. Rather, it represents the ritual attention that interactants must give to one another so that they can effectively participate in a social interaction. Facework, then, is a requirement for social interaction, a mechanism that accounts for the emergence of orderly social interaction from the chaos of self-serving individuals.

10.2. Facework and linguistic politeness

The role of face in interpersonal communication was made explicit by Brown and Levinson (1978; 1987) in their well-known theory of politeness. By wedding the concepts of face and facework to the linguistic variability associated with politeness, they succeeded in providing an overarching theoretical framework for a diverse set of conversation behaviours. Now, there has been considerable debate regarding the validity of Brown and Levinson's theory of politeness (e.g. Bargiela-Chiappini, 2003; Watts, 2003), but there is no doubt that it has been an extremely generative approach.

Similar to Goffman, Brown and Levinson view face as the public display of one's identity. In contrast to Goffman, however, they argue for the existence of two, universal types of face: positive and negative face. The former refers to a universal desire for approval by others (approach-based face) and the latter a universal desire for autonomy of action (avoidance-based face). Because these desires exist independent of any particular interaction (and hence exist within the individual), this conception of face places relatively greater emphasis on its psychological (rather than interactional) properties. This need not lessen the interactional foundations of face within any particular encounter, but it does point to the relatively enduring aspects of face and in so doing allows for a consideration of individual and cultural variability (see below). Moreover, these concepts match up quite well with other social psychological theories of motivation (e.g. Bakan, 1966; McAdams, 1985). Positive face is roughly aligned with affiliation motives (need for affiliation, communion, positive regard, etc.) and negative face is roughly aligned with autonomy motives (need for power, independence, etc.).

This theory highlights a fundamental dilemma that exists for social interactants. People want to pursue various goals yet doing so can create face-threatening situations, a dilemma that is handled by engaging in facework. One of the major contributions of the Brown and Levinson model was to provide detailed and specific linguistic mechanisms for engaging in facework. In this model, facework involves deviating from maximally efficient communication (i.e. communication adhering to Grice's (1975) maxims of relation, quantity, quality and manner). There are, of course, many ways this can be accomplished and Brown and Levinson (1987) organised politeness into five super-strategies. In general, these strategies are ordered in terms of their level of indirectness, with greater indirectness (e.g. off-record forms) conveying greater face support (Brown and Levinson, 1987; see also Leech, 1983; Lakoff, 1973).

Equating indirectness with facework has proven somewhat problematic because indirectness does not always provide greater face support (Blum-Kulka, 1987; Holtgraves and Yang, 1990). This may be because very indirect remarks (e.g. off-record forms) sometimes have the appearance of manipulativeness (Lakoff, 1977) and because indirectness can occur for reasons other than facework. In fact indirectness can sometimes be face-threatening (e.g. a backhanded compliment). Moreover, Brown and Levinson's super-strategies differ in ways other than degrees of indirectness and it is probably the case that linguistic strategies that orient to a specific type of face threat will be regarded as more face-supportive than a strategy that is not so oriented (Holtgraves, 1992). For example, negatively polite strategies would be more face supportive for acts threatening the hearer's negative face and positively polite strategies would be more face supportive for acts threatening the hearer's positive face. Overall, then, deviations from maximally efficient communication *potentially* implicate some degree of facework on the part of the speaker, with the exact amount dependent on the context (see below), specific strategy used and so on.

10.3. Facework and interpersonal variables

One of the greatest strengths of the Brown and Levinson model was the linking of the fundamental dimensions of power and distance with the operation of face management. Threats to face can vary in their degree and the greater the face-threat the greater the facework (all else being equal). Degree of face-threat is not determined in isolation but rather in terms of the context (broadly defined) within which the act occurs. The degree to which an act is face-threatening is a result of the weightiness of the act and weightiness is assumed to be an additive weighting of three factors: the culturally determined degree of imposition of the act itself, the hearer's relative power, and the degree of social distance between the speaker and hearer.

   Much research has examined the impact of these variables on a speaker's level of face support – or politeness (for a review, see Holtgraves, 2001). In general, strong support has been found for the power variable, with most studies demonstrating that higher speaker power is associated with relatively lower levels of politeness (Ambady *et al.,* 1996; Blum-Kulka, Danet and Gherson, 1985; Brown and Gilman, 1989; Holtgraves and Yang, 1990; 1992). Fairly consistent support has been found for the imposition variable, with increasing imposition associated with increasing politeness (Brown and Gilman, 1989; Gonzales, *et al.,* 1990; Holtgraves and Yang, 1992; McLaughlin, Cody and O'Hair, 1983; Okamoto and Robinson, 1997). The effect of relationship distance has been the most problematic for the theory. Consistent with the theory, some researchers have reported greater politeness as a function of increasing distance (Holtgraves and Yang, 1992; Wood and Kroger, 1991), others have reported the exact opposite (Baxter, 1984; Brown and Gilman, 1989). As noted by Slugoski and Turnbull (1988) (see also Brown and Gilman, 1989) a potential problem with the distance variable is that it confounds distance (i.e. familiarity) and affect (i.e. liking). When liking is held constant, however, distance does appear to have the predicted effect on a speaker's level of politeness (i.e. increasing politeness in more distant relationships) (Holtgraves and Yang, 1992).

The specification of the effects of power and distance on face-threat is one of the greatest strengths of the face management approach to politeness. These two dimensions are clearly two (if not *the* two) major dimensions underlying social interaction (McAdams, 1985; Wish, Deutsch and Kaplan, 1976). Are there other contextual variables that will influence face-threat and hence a speaker's level of politeness? Of course. And it is possible that other dimensions may need to be included (Slugoski and Turnbull, 1988), including more situation-specific rights and obligations (Fraser, 1990; Tracy, 1990). At the same time, power, distance and imposition are high-level, abstract variables that should subsume more specific variables. Gender, class, situation formality and so on have an effect on politeness levels, but can be viewed as having their effect on politeness through their effects on power, distance and imposition. Even intrapersonal variables such as mood may have an effect on politeness via their effect on one of these three variables. For example, Forgas (1999) has demonstrated that people in a sad mood prefer to produce greater levels of politeness relative to people in a happy mood. But it is possible that people in a sad mood perceive themselves as being lower in power and it is power that influences their preference for greater politeness. In short, facework and the short list of social variables that influence it, provides an abstract, high-level framework for explaining a variety of influences on interpersonal communication.

Although the focus of empirical research on politeness has concentrated on the impact of interpersonal variables on a speaker's level of politeness, there are additional communication areas in which facework can play an important role. In the following sections I consider two such areas: person perception and language comprehension.

Person perception and impression management

Our impressions of others arise out of our social interactions with them and an important source of information in that regard is the manner in which we communicate with one another. Facework plays an important role in this process in several ways. First, perceptions of speakers on specific dimensions such as status and relationship distance can be affected. The logic is straightforward. If power and distance influence the degree of face-threat and hence the use of a particular linguistic form, it follows that the use of a particular linguistic form will be informative for observers (including the hearer) regarding the speaker's perceived power and distance. For example, if high-status speakers use less polite forms than lower-status interactants for performing the same act, then the use of less polite forms should result in perceptions of higher speaker status, other things being equal. In a cross-cultural study using participants from the United State and Korea, Holtgraves and Yang (1990) found that less polite request forms were associated with perceptions of greater speaker power. This effect was similar for Koreans and Americans and occurred with relatively minor wording changes. For example, 'Would you get the mail?' resulted in perceptions of greater speaker power than 'Could you get the mail?'. There are, of course, obvious limits to such an effect. In fact, when a high-status speaker is extremely polite to a subordinate it will often result in perceived sarcasm (Slugoski and Turnbull, 1988). Other research has demonstrated that levels of politeness/facework can influence perceptions of participants on additional dimensions such as assertiveness, credibility, attractiveness, etc. (Holtgraves, 1992).

Note that these findings should not be construed as indicating that language-based person perception is static. Although politeness levels may reflect a speaker's perceived power, interactants may actively manipulate politeness levels as a means of impression management. An important issue in this process is the fact that politeness is determined by at least three social variables: power, relationship distance and degree of imposition. Given the existence of multiple determinants of politeness, it is not clear on which dimension(s) a speaker will be perceived as a function of his politeness. If a speaker uses a very polite form, for example, will others infer relatively low status, that the act is very threatening, or that the relationship is a distant one? Sometimes information exists regarding one or two of the dimensions such that inferences will be most likely drawn on the unspecified dimension. For example, a boss (high power) making a request to an employee (high distance) with a relatively polite form may implicate, through the high level of politeness, a view that the request is somewhat imposing.

At the same time, the existence of multiple determinants allows people to strategically vary their politeness as a means of negotiating and/or altering the interpersonal context; it is, in effect, an important component of impression management. So, a higher power person (e.g. a boss)

who moves from negative politeness to positive politeness may be attempting to negotiate a closer relationship. Or, a person in an established relationship may begin to use less politeness as a means of
negotiating higher power in the relationship. Or the use of relatively
impolite forms in a relationship for which power and distance are
established might serve to convey the view that the act (e.g. a request)
is not very imposing. And so on. In this way the interpersonal underpinnings of politeness can take on a game-like quality. If one's bid for
higher status (via decreased politeness) is not challenged, the bid has,
in effect, been accepted and the speaker is now defined as the one with
higher power in the relationship.

The existence of multiple politeness determinants can also result in
interpersonal misperceptions or misunderstandings. A speaker may
assume his politeness level reflects one dimension (e.g. closeness), but
his interlocutor may assume it reflects a different dimension (e.g. status). So, John might assume he has a relatively close relationship with
Mark and accordingly feel free to use positively polite forms (e.g. 'How
'bout getting me a beer'). But positive politeness represents a relatively
low level of politeness and thus can implicate high speaker power;
Mark might view John as making a claim for higher status in their relationship.

Facework and language comprehension

The role of face and facework in language comprehension has received
much less attention than their role in language production. However,
given the co-ordination required for language use (Clark, 1996) it
seems likely that facework will play a parallel role in language
comprehension.

A fundamental task for theories of language comprehension is to
specify how recipients recover a speaker's intended meaning. This is
particularly difficult when a speaker's utterance involves indirectness
of some sort. Grice's (1975) theory of conversational implicature is frequently invoked as an explanation for this process. Hence, upon hearing a maxim violation, recipients are assumed to reject the literal meaning
of the utterance in favour of an alternative, indirect, meaning. But Grice
says nothing about which *specific* implicature (out of a very large number of possible implicatures) a person will make. It is here that facework
provides a partial solution to this problem. A major (though not exclusive) motivation for speaking indirectly is to manage face. Hence, a

hearer who encounters a maxim violation is likely to assume that the speaker is engaging in face management and this realisation should serve as a constraint on the interpretation process. Consider the following example.

(1)

> Andy: What did you think of my presentation?
> Bob: It's hard to give a good presentation.

Bob fails to directly answer Andy's question and in so doing violates the relation maxim (the reply is not completely relevant) or possibly the quantity maxim (the reply does not provide enough information). As a result Andy is likely to generate an implicature as a means of making sense of Bob's reply. But which implicature? Given an awareness that maxim violations frequently occur as a means of managing face, a likely interpretation is that Bob is indirectly conveying negative information (a poor view of Andy's presentation).

Consistent with this logic, Holtgraves (1998) found that participants are very likely to interpret replies that violate the relation maxim as conveying face-threatening information and that when face management as a reason for the violation is removed, the remarks violating the maxim become very difficult to comprehend. Other experiments have demonstrated that these indirect meanings are generated when the utterance is comprehended (rather than when queried about the meaning of the remark) and that they are a result of a Gricean inference process (Holtgraves, 1999).

If face management is recognised as the motive behind a relevance violation, then any contextual information suggesting that face management processes are operative should facilitate recognition of an indirect (face-threatening) meaning. For example, the occurrence of 'well' (a marker of a dispreferred turn) at the beginning of an utterance can be interpreted as indicating that the speaker is engaging in face management (Jucker, 1993), and hence should facilitate recognition of a face-threatening interpretation of that reply. Research suggests that it does. Specifically, in an experiment reported in Holtgraves (2000), face-threatening interpretations of indirect replies were more quickly verified when the reply contained a 'well' preface (e.g. 'Well, I think it's hard to give a good presentation') than when it did not (e.g. 'I think it's hard to give a good presentation').

Other speaker variables such as occupation (Katz and Pexman, 1997) and personality (Demeure, Bonnefon and Raufaste, 2007) can influence remark interpretation via the operation of face management. One very important variable in this regard is the speaker's relative status. People who are relatively low in status are more concerned with managing the face of their conversational partners and hence are more likely to use indirect constructions (Holtgraves and Yang, 1992). It might be expected, then, that the indirect remarks of low status speakers (because they are expected to be indirect) would tend to be interpreted relatively quickly and accurately. In general, however, research tends to suggest the opposite. Specifically, for requests, the indirect remarks of higher status speakers are more quickly and accurately recognised as directives than the same utterances of low status speakers (Holtgraves, 1994). Moreover, the remarks of the former are more likely to be remembered later as directives than the remarks of the latter (Holtgraves, Srull and Socall, 1989). Directives – regardless of their form – are face-threatening and high status speakers are more likely to issue them than are lower status speakers. Because of this, people appear to be primed to give directive interpretations to the indirect remarks of high status speakers.

Finally, Bonnefon and Villejoubert (2006) recently demonstrated another way in which facework/politeness can influence language comprehension. They argue that people have an expectation that speakers will tend to be polite when conveying face-threatening information (similar to Holtgraves, 1998). This expectation can influence the interpretation of certain terms in probability statements. Specifically, when statements describe the probability of a certain medical problem, people tend to overestimate the conveyed probability of more severe conditions (relative to less severe conditions) because they tend to interpret 'possibility' as a politeness marker rather than as a marker of uncertainty.

10.4. Individual and cultural differences

Facework is typically viewed at the level of human nature, as a social interactional process that is engaged in by everyone. This is certainly the view of Goffman and, to a lesser extent, Brown and Levinson. But such a view has proved controversial on several different grounds. One criticism has been the charge that facework and politeness (and related theories such as speech act theory (Searle, 1969) and Gricean (1975) inferencing) are not universal. Some researchers, for example, have claimed that the Brown and Levinson (1987) politeness hierarchy is actually reversed in some cultures; in Sabra culture directness is preferred to indirectness (Katriel, 1986). Others have claimed that negative face is relevant only in Western cultures, cultures where there is an emphasis on individual autonomy. Rosaldo (1982), in her analysis of Ilongot speech acts, argued that directives in that culture are not threatening and hence will tend to be performed directly (see also Matsumoto, 1988).

Clearly there is great cultural variability in terms of facework/politeness. The crucial question is whether this variability is a result of differing cultural conceptions of face, or whether these differences can be explained at a lower level of abstraction. Brown and Levinson (1987) assumed positive and negative face to be universal desires, but that cultures will vary in terms of what threatens face, who has power over whom, how much distance is typically assumed and so on. Thus, certain acts are more threatening in some cultures than in other cultures and hence greater facework will be expected for those acts in the former than in the latter. For example, directives appear to be more threatening in Western cultures than in Ilongot culture and hence are more likely to be performed politely in the former than in the latter.

When facework is viewed as a high-level construct, then cross-cultural differences in politeness can be explained as a function of perceived distance, imposition and power. This is because cultures and subcultures may systematically differ both in terms of the default values for these variables, as well as in terms of the weighting given to these variables. Regarding the former, Scollon and Scollon (1981) report that Athabaskans tend to assume greater distance when interacting with unacquainted individuals than do English speaking Americans. As a result, the former display a preference for negative politeness strategies and the latter a preference for positive politeness strategies, preferences that can result in misunderstanding when members of these groups interact.

In terms of the weighting of the variables, Holtgraves and Yang (1992) have demonstrated that South Koreans weight the power and distance variables more heavily than do US Americans (see also Ambady *et al.*, 1996). This means that South Koreans tend to vary the politeness of their remarks as a function of power and distance to a greater extent than do US Americans. This is an important finding and one that dovetails nicely with the concept of individualism-collectivism. In collectivist cultures, such as Korea, strong distinctions are drawn between in-groups and out-groups and this results in greater overall variability in social interaction (Gudykunst, Yoon and Nishida, 1987; Wheeler, Reis and Bond, 1989). Hence, the findings for politeness are consistent with the overall pattern of greater behavioural responsiveness to social situations for collectivists relative to individualists. Another possibility in this regard has been suggested by Ting-Toomey (1988; 2005) who has argued that the politeness of people in collectivist cultures focuses more on other-face and the politeness of people in individualistic cultures focuses more on self-face.

Clearly, the specific manifestations of face show great cultural and subcultural variability. But by treating face at a relatively high level of abstraction it is possible to use the construct to explain cross-cultural similarities and differences in language use. The importance of such a framework should not be underestimated. Examining cross-cultural politeness without such a framework would result in a purely descriptive enterprise, a listing of features that appear to be cross-culturally different, but which at a higher level may reflect similar underlying motivations. Of course care must be taken that such an approach remains falsifiable; specification of the manifestations of face within a culture needs to be undertaken before the theory can be tested within that culture.

A second and related, criticism is the argument that face and facework are entirely situated concepts, what some theorists (e.g., Bargiela-Chiappini, 2003; Watts, 2003) suggest is the original intent of Goffman's formulation. In this view, face – through language – is created anew in each encounter. Face is a totally situated and emergent product of the interaction of two or more people. No doubt this is the spirit of Goffman's depiction of face. On the other hand, it is unrealistic to assume that interactants start each interaction totally from scratch. Clearly, there are aspects of one's personality that transcend situations and provide some continuity to how one communicates with others. In short, there are relatively consistent individual differences in the extent to which individuals are concerned with face. One manifestation of this is the existence of individual differences in the production and comprehension of indirectness (Holtgraves, 1997). In much the same way that cultural variability may be explained via cultural differences in the perception and weighting of power, distance and imposition, so too might individual differences be explained at this level. Hence, people who use relatively greater levels of politeness/indirectness may do so because they perceive themselves as being relatively low in power or distant from their interlocutor. Note that this framework allows for the inclusion of psychologically important variables such as self-esteem. People with low self-esteem may perceive themselves as being relatively low in power and hence speak more politely/indirectly.

10.5. Conclusion

Language is nothing if not an interpersonal phenomenon; its use both reflects interpersonal processes (e.g. status) and influences those same processes. Understanding language thus requires an understanding of its interpersonal dimension. But how are these various interpersonal influences to be captured? It is here that the concepts of face and facework are extremely useful. Face, as a theoretical construct, provides an important mechanism for understanding the role of a variety of interpersonal processes in language use.

In this chapter I have focused on the role played by face and facework in the production and comprehension of language on any particular occasion of use. Language production can be viewed through the lens of politeness theory (Brown and Levinson, 1987) and the interpersonal variables in this approach – power and psychological distance – are no doubt the two major dimensions underlying social interaction in all cultures. There have now been numerous empirical investigations of the effects of these variables on face and politeness. Importantly, the relation between facework/politeness and interpersonal variables is reciprocal. Politeness not only reflects interpersonal processes, it is also a resource used by interactants for negotiating and influencing these processes.

Facework plays a parallel role in language comprehension. And of course it must; variables that influence language production must play a parallel role in language comprehension (Holtgraves, 1998, 2005). One important way in which face plays a role in comprehension is by providing a reason for why a speaker is speaking indirectly. The standard Gricean (Grice, 1975) model assumes that violations of conversational maxims will prompt recipients to search for an alternative interpretation of the speaker's remark. But what interpretation will a recipient generate? It is here that facework plays a role. Speakers frequently use indirectness/politeness as a means of performing face-threatening acts so as to minimise the threat of those acts. Recipients, in recognising that facework is being undertaken, can use that information to generate a reasonable (face-threatening) interpretation of the utterance.

A complete account of face and communication must explain individual and cultural variability in these processes. Regarding the latter, numerous theorists have criticised the concept of face for not being valid over cultures. As illustrated in many of the chapters in this volume, the specific cultural manifestations of face vary widely; what is face-threatening in one culture need not be threatening in another culture. Still, the regulatory role played by face in social interaction is probably universal. Regarding individual differences, people may vary in their perceptions of and concerns with interpersonal variables and these differences are then reflected in the manner in which their facework is linguistically realised.

Finally, just as face and facework play an important role in the use of language on a particular occasion (the focus of this chapter), so too do they play a role in the development and change of language over time. It has been argued that language evolved primarily for interpersonal reasons (Dunbar, 1996). Hence, the structure of a language at any one point in time will reflect the underlying motivations giving rise to its existence. Compare, for example, natural human languages with computer languages. The primary differences are precision (where computer languages have the edge) and interpersonal sensitivity (where human languages have the edge). Clearly, human languages are responsive to interpersonal concerns in ways that computer languages are not and need not be; their structure reflects those concerns. In short, understanding the role of face in interpersonal communication will require both a synchronic perspective (how these processes play out on any particular occasion) and a diachronic perspective (how these processes have influenced the structure of language over time).

References

Ambady N., Koo, J., Lee, F. and Rosenthal, R. (1996) More than words: Linguistic and nonlinguistic politeness in two cultures. *Journal of Personality and Social Psychology* 70: 996–1011.

Arundale, R. B. (2006) Face as relational and interactional: a communicative framework for research on face, facework and politeness. *Journal of Politeness Research* 2: 193–216.

Bakan, D. (1966) *The Duality of Human Existence.* Chicago: Rand McNally.

Bargiela-Chiappini, F. (2003) Face and politeness: new (insights) for old (concepts). *Journal of Pragmatics, 35,* 1453–1469.

Baxter, L. A. (1984) An investigation of compliance gaining as politeness. *Human Communication Research* 10: 427–456.

Blum-Kulka, S. (1987) Indirectness and politeness in requests: Same or different? *Journal of Pragmatics* 11: 131–146.

Blum-Kulka, S., Danet, B. and Gherson, R. (1985) The language of requesting in Israeli society. In J. Forgas (Ed.), *Language in Social Situations* 113–139. New York: Springer-Verlag.

Bonnefon, J. and Villejoubert, G. (2006) Tactful, or doubtful? Expectations of politeness explain the severity bias in the interpretation of probability phrases. *Psychological Science* 17: 747–751.

Brown, P. and Levinson, S. (1978) Universals in language usage: politeness phenomena. In E. Goody, (ed.) *Questions and Politeness* 56–289. Cambridge: Cambridge University Press.

Brown, P. and Levinson, S. (1987) *Politeness: Some universals in language usage.* Cambridge, UK: Cambridge University Press.

Brown, R. and Gilman, A. (1989) Politeness theory and Shakespeare's four major tragedies. *Language in Society* 18: 159–212.

Clark, H. H. (1996) *Using Language.* Cambridge: Cambridge University Press.

Clark, H. H. and Schunk, D. (1980) Polite responses to polite requests. *Cognition* 8: 111–143.

Demeure, V., Bonnefon, J. F. and Raufaste, E. (2007) Utilitarian relevance and face management in the interpretation of ambiguous question/request statements. *Memory and Cognition* 36: 873-881.

Dunbar, R. (1996) *Grooming, Gossip and the Evolution of Language.* Cambridge, MA: Harvard University Press.

Durkheim, E. (1915) *The Elementary Forms of Religious Life.* London: Allen and Unwin.

Forgas, J. P. (1999) On feeling good and being rude: Affective influences on language use and request formulations. *Journal of Personality and Social Psychology* 76: 928–939.

Fraser, B. (1990) Perspectives on politeness. *Journal of Pragmatics* 14: 219–236.

Goffman, E. (1967) *Interaction ritual: Essays on face-to-face behavior.* New York: Anchor.

Gonzales, M. H., Pederson, J., Manning, D. and Wetter, D. W. (1990) Pardon my gaffe: Effects of sex, status and consequence severity on accounts. *Journal of Personality and Social Psychology* 58: 610–621.

Grice, H. P. (1975) Logic and conversation. In P. Cole and J. Morgan (eds.), *Syntax and Semantics 3: Speech Acts* 41–58. New York: Academic Press.

Gudykunst, W., Yoon, Y. C. and Nishida, T. (1987) The influence of individualism–collectivism on perceptions of communication in in-group and out-group relations. *Communication Monographs* 54: 295–306.

Holtgraves, T. M. (1992) The linguistic realization of face management: implications for language production and comprehension, person perception and cross-cultural communication. *Social Psychology Quarterly* 55: 141–159.

Holtgraves, T. M. (1994) Communication in context: The effects of speaker status on the comprehension of indirect requests. *Journal of Experimental Psychology* 20: 1205–1218.

Holtgraves, T. M. (1997) Styles of language use: Individual and cultural variability in conversational indirectness. *Journal of Personality and Social Psychology* 73: 624–637.

Holtgraves, T.M. (1998) Interpreting indirect replies. *Cognitive Psychology* 37: 1–27.

Holtgraves, T. M. (1999) Comprehending indirect replies: When and how are their conveyed meanings activated. *Journal of Memory and Language* 41: 519–540.

Holtgraves, T. M. (2000) Preference organization and reply comprehension. *Discourse Processes, 30,* 87–106.

Holtgraves, T. M. (2001) Politeness phenomena. In H. Giles and W. P. Robinson (Eds.) *The handbook of language and social psychology* (2nd edition) London: John Wiley and Sons.

Holtgraves, T.M. (2005) Context and the comprehension of nonliteral meanings. In H.L. Colston and A.E. Katz (eds.), *Figurative Language Comprehension: Social and Cultural Influences* 73–98. Mahwah, NJ: Erlbaum.

Holtgraves, T., Srull, T. and Socall, D. (1989) Conversation memory: The effects of speaker status on memory for the assertiveness of conversation remarks. *Journal of Personality and Social Psychology* 56: 149–160.

Holtgraves, T. M. and Yang, J. N. (1990) Politeness as a universal: Cross-cultural perceptions of request strategies and inferences based on their use. *Journal of Personality and Social Psychology* 59: 719–729.

Holtgraves, T. M. and Yang, J. N. (1992) The interpersonal underpinnings of request strategies: General principles and differences due to culture and gender. *Journal of Personality and Social Psychology* 62: 246–256.

Jucker, A. H. (1993) The discourse marker *well*: A relevance–theoretical account. *Journal of Pragmatics* 19: 435–452.

Katriel, T. (1986) *Talking Straight: Durgri Speech in Israeli Sabra Culture.* Cambridge: Cambridge University Press

Katz, A. and Pexman, P. (1997) Interpreting figurative statements: speaker occupation can change metaphor to irony, *Metaphor and Symbol* 12: 19–41.

Lakoff, R. (1973) The logic of politeness: or, minding your p's and q's. *Papers from the Ninth Regional Meeting of the Chicago Linguistic Society* 292–305.

Lakoff, R. (1977) Women's language. *Language and Style* 10: 222–248.

Leech, G. (1983) *Principles of Pragmatics.* London: Longman.

Matsumoto, Y. (1988) Reexamination of the universality of face: Politeness phenomena in Japanese. *Journal of Pragmatics* 12: 403–426.

McAdams, D. P. (1985) *Power, Intimacy and the Life Story.* Homewood, IL: Dempsey.

McLaughlin, M. L., Cody, M. and O'Hair, H. D. (1983) The management of failure events: Some contextual determinants of accounting behavior. *Human Communication Research* 9: 208–224.

Okamoto, S. and Robinson, W. P. (1997) Determinants of gratitude expression in England. *Journal of Language and Social Psychology* 16: 411–433.

Rosaldo, M. Z. (1982) The things we do with words: Ilongot speech acts and speech act theory in philosophy. *Language in Society* 11: 203–237.

Scollon, R. and Scollon, S. (1981) *Narrative, Literacy and Face in Interethnic Communication.* Norwood, NJ: Ablex.

Searle, J. R. (1969) *Speech Acts.* Cambridge: Cambridge University Press.

Slugoski, B. and Turnbull, W. (1988) Cruel to be kind and kind to be cruel: Sarcasm, banter and social relations. *Journal of Language and Social Psychology* 7: 101–121.

Spencer-Oatey, H. (2005) (Im)Politeness, face and perceptions of rapport: unpackaging their bases and interrelationships. *Journal of Politeness Research* 1: 95–119.

Ting-Toomey, S. (1988) Intercultural conflict styles. In Y. Y. Kim and W. B. Gudykunst (eds.) *Theories in Intercultural Communication*. Beverly Hills, CA: Sage.

Ting-Toomey, S. (2005) The matrix of face: An updated face-negotiation theory. In W. Gudykunst (ed.), *Theorizing about Intercultural Communication* 71–92. Thousand Oaks, CA: Sage.

Tracy, K. (1990) The many faces of facework. In H. Giles and P. Robinson (eds.), *Handbook of Language and Social Psychology* 209–226. London: Wiley.

Watts, R. J. (2003) *Politeness*. Cambridge: Cambridge University Press.

Wheeler, L., Reis, H. T. and Bond, M. H. (1989) Collectivism-individualism in everyday social life: The middle kingdom and the melting pot. *Journal of Personality and Social Psychology* 54: 323–333.

Wish, M., Deutsch, M. and Kaplan, S. (1976) Perceived dimensions of interpersonal relations. *Journal of Personality and Social Psychology* 33: 409–420.

Wood, L. A. and Kroger, R. O. (1991) Politeness and forms of address. *Journal of Language and Social Psychology* 10: 145–168.

11

In the face of the other: between Goffman and Levinas

Alexander Kozin

11.1. Introduction

In sociology, the concept of face is inseparable from the name of Erving Goffman. An intrinsic component of his theory of the situated order, the elementary structure of interaction face-to-face has exerted unprecedented influence on human studies, redefining the idea of what should count as the social order as well as the social actor. Originally, Goffman defined face-to-face interaction as 'the reciprocal influence of individuals upon one another's actions when in one another's immediate physical presence' (1967: 15). Two emphases in this quote, *reciprocity* and *presence*, are crucial for appreciating the significance of Goffman's project. The view of the social order as what is already 'there' and yet 'here and now' helped refocus sociological inquiry from abstract systemic relationality to observable human relations, or 'moments and their men' (1967: 2). Approached from the latter perspective, face was defined as 'a pattern of verbal and non-verbal acts by which the person demonstrates his/her understanding of the encounter and its context in terms of the other's place in it and, more importantly, his own view of the self' (1967: 5). In sum, as an intersubjective accomplishment, by instituting the Other as the sufficient and necessary condition for all forms of sociality, Goffman debunks the egological view of individuality in favour of the interpersonal self.

At the same time, having admitted of Goffman's overall contribution to sociology does not mean to neglect fundamental shortcomings of his approach (Drew and Wootton, 1988; Psathas, 1980). As someone who is heavily dependent on the Other for the continuous and uninterrupted construction of his self, Goffman's actor appears to be but a performer, a manipulative and immoral opportunist without a stable ideology or identity, to that matter (Manning, 1992; Bauman, 1990). Goffman himself attests to this characterisation by writing: 'Any individual who displays certain social characteristics has the moral right to expect that others will value and treat him in an appropriate way.' (1967: 13) The performative self thus shows its core to be nothing more than a display of social expectations (Travers, 1994; Burns, 1992). If one needs to attend to others, it is only to dupe them by presenting oneself as the kind of a person they would accept and value.

Distressing to the contemporary view of self as authentic, the immoral actor without any ground or mass has prompted much critique from a variety of disciplines (Schudson, 1984; Smith, 2006). Goffman himself acknowledged the critique of immoralism and, in his later work, made a redemptive move by employing some insights from the phenomenological sociology of Alfred Schütz. Adapting the Schützean notion of *We-relation* to his project allowed Goffman to resituate face-to-face relationship within a community whose stress on the consequentionality of public behaviour came to stand for morality *ipso facto*. However, moving to the larger *signitive–symbolic* realm turned out to be a blessing in disguise. The immediate benefit of reaching outside the tangible was a definition of morality that did not contradict the thesis of the empty self. On the other hand, by placing morality above, as it were, face-to-face interaction compromised the concreteness and the consequentionality of the interpersonal exchange. In his later works Goffman 'solved' this apparent problem by removing face from his technical vocabulary. Finding this loss most unfortunate for theorising interaction, some sociologists suggest that face should be rescued from oblivion. Several routes have been proposed to this effect.

For example, recognising the essential role of facework for the concept of self in Goffman makes Rawls (1987) suggest that it should be revived through the ethnomethodological and conversation analytic imports from Harold Garfinkel and Harvey Sacks. Although somewhat appreciative of Garfinkel, Goffman was notoriously critical of Sacks and his method. Rawls attributes this reaction to Goffman's misunderstanding of the conversation analytic agenda when it comes to the studies of how self is constituted in talk. In the same vein, Psathas (1996) and Ostrow (1996) consider face-to-face interaction to be the most intriguing and at the same time most problematic contribution of Goffman to the sociological theory. They propose that the problems with face in Goffman originate in and thus can be still redeemed through the phenomenological sociology of Alfred Schütz. Specifically, both Psathas (1996) and Ostrow (1996) claim that Goffman was too hasty in appropriating Schütz and, as a result, employed his insights unsystematically in a patchwork fashion. A systematic account of key phenomenological concepts could have helped Goffman avoid much trouble with the notion of the morally implicated social actor. I find the above suggestion worth pursuing and therefore would like to turn to the phenomenology of Emmanuel Levinas.

The choice of Levinas as company for Goffman is both accidental and opportune. It is accidental in a sense that neither Goffman nor Levinas show any familiarity with each other's work. It is opportune because, just like Goffman in sociology, Levinas the philosopher takes credit for the discovery of face as a basic structure of sociality and the foundation for the relationship with the Other. In addition, both Goffman and Levinas developed their corresponding concepts of face at about the same time and under similar circumstances. Both 'sociology of occasions' and 'phenomenology of sociality' were nurtured on the side of their respective traditions, respecifying them at the disciplinary margins (Friedson, 1983; Williams, 1986; Peperzak, 1995; Bergo, 1999). In view of these similarities, a complementary relationship between Goffman and Levinas seemed to be simply a matter of gestation. The fact that Levinas conceived of his project in the philosophical domain only strengthened the connection. By seeking to overcome the order of totality, Levinas offered a path beyond presence, being, and the self. It is from this perspective that Levinas equates face with the overwhelming responsibility for the Other: 'Infinity presents itself as a face in the ethical resistance that paralyzes my powers and from the depths of defenceless eyes rises firm and absolute in its nudity and destitution.' (1969: 200) Following this definition, we might say that the destitute face that commands the Other complements the expressive face that performs the Self.[1]

In this chapter I would like to investigate the relationship between the two conceptualisations of face. The main objective of this study is to determine whether the concept of face is capable of sustaining both the pragmatics of self-presentation as well as the ethical imperative of the absolute. I begin by examining the grounds of those arguments that have addressed this very connection and end up favouring it in different configurations. After an imbedded critique of these configurations, I offer an alternative theory of face which attempts to bypass this critique by identifying the common conceptual ground for Goffman and Levinas. I call this theory 'traumatic face.' In order to construct this theory I borrow from the underthematised and peripheral matters that can be found in both scholarships. These borrowings allow me to situate traumatic face at the crossing of the empirical and transcendental realms and their corresponding modes of inquiry. Hence, the theory's immediate value, for in addition to prompting us to reconsider certain misconceptions about either scholar, their juxtaposition presupposes a methodological contribution: the most persistent problem of social sciences is the problem of reconciling the seemingly irreconcilable, the self-understanding consciousness and the world of the Other. I further discuss practical implications of my theorising in the conclusion of the chapter.

11.2. Saving the face

I would like to open my short exegesis with a relatively straightforward discussion by Smart (1996). In the wake of his critique of contemporary cultural analyses, Smart suggests that both the social and academic concerns should put stronger emphases on the constitutive parameters and patterns of embodiment because 'the questions of ethics and morality are articulated with the body' (1996: 68). With this focus Smart intends to move beyond the staple sociological, and that means Goffmanian, conceptualisation of facework into the discussion of the ethical body. In his critique of Goffman, Smart forwards two co-extensive claims. First, he claims that the most basic error in Goffman's theory of interaction lies in his ignoring the signifying potential of the face and thus having little appreciation of its relation to the body. Proceeding with his argument, Smart then claims that, for Goffman, facework is the same as impression-management. And since the aim of impressing an image of one's self on others is to manipulate them, naturally, Goffman's self has no other business to conduct with the Other but to deceive that other into accepting him for whom he has set himself out to be. The consequences of this reading are obvious – the 'modern subject is less concerned with being moral than with appearing to be so' (Smart 1996: 71).

Called in to save both the subject and morality, Levinas brings over the notion of subjectivity which, according to Smart:

> is constituted through a primary relationship of responsibility for the other...In this instance face is not work performed in the interest of the self, rather *it embodies the demand of the other which orders, ordains, and constitutes the subjectivity of the self.*
> (1996: 72-73, emphasis added)

In this reversal of his self-other asymmetry Smart sees a challenge to Goffman's own definition of facework: 'Facework appears to be very much a matter of care for the self with consideration for others occupying a secondary position.' (Smart 1996: 70) Although correct in his interpretation of the reverse asymmetry in the self – other relationship in Levinas, Smart ends up misplacing the relationship itself. When Levinas presents face-to-face relationship as a transcendental accomplishment of inter-subjectivity, he presents it as the accomplishment of time: 'the encroachment of the present on the future is not the feat of the subject alone, but the inter-subjective relationship.' (1987: 79)

This kind of a relationship does not belong entirely to the matter accessible to touch, smell, or vision; nor can it be placed only in the symbolic realm. A phenomenologist, Levinas rejects the self-sufficient and self-contained idea of the subject, world, or the Other as it contradicts our most immediate experience. For him, the relationship of the subject to the world and other subjects is a relationship of co-determination. The vulnerability of the subject in this relationship is beyond doubt. The vulnerable subject is an emotional subject, and, as such, accessible to us through empathy. A transcendental phenomenologist, Levinas seeks to examine the limits of this co-determinate relationship. He finds them in ethics which rejects the view that ethical responsibility for the Other can be founded on some routinised benevolence in relation to the other person, for example, care. For Levinas there are other, by far more significant, dimensions of responsibility for the Other. One such essential is love: 'Love aims at the Other; it aims at him in his frailty.' (Levinas, 1969: 256) With this thesis, Levinas extends his examination of the exteriority of face into the sphere he calls 'beyond'. Love is beyond face because it can be experienced only in *voluptuosity* and *caress*. Caress differs from touch in that it 'transcends the sensible' (Levinas, 1969: 257). It expresses love but is unable to tell it. This means that caress does not signify appearances. Nor does voluptuosity, which is a 'mysterious object foreign to expression' (Levinas, 1969: 260). Voluptuosity is nudity itself, and, just like the nudity of face, it is exterior to it. This kind of exteriority does not stop at the symbolism of the social order. Nor can it be reduced to the embodied other. Exteriority is always already outside. For Smart, however, the ability of face to include the body makes it an instrument of politics; hence, the need for body ethics, which is in fact a politics of morality: 'Politics is opposed to morality as philosophy is opposed to naïveté.' (Levinas, 1969: 21)

Raffel (2002) makes another attempt to correct Goffman's problem with the immoral self by engaging Levinas. Similarly to Smart, Raffel investigates the possibility for a synthesis of face-to-face action and face-to-face ethics. However, in contrast to Smart, Raffel chooses to develop his argument via Sartre. In this regard Raffel makes two claims. First, he is resolute about Sartre's influence on Goffman.[2] According to Raffel, this influence manifests itself in Goffman's repeated references to Sartre's *Being and Nothingness*; these references, although randomly scattered in many works, are quite explicit in attributing to Sartre this or that turn of thought. The same influence by Sartre Raffel ascribes to Levinas, who, despite never admitting of such influence, has, according to Raffel, an ongoing argument with Sartre. Specifically, Raffel presumes that in *Totality and Infinity* Levinas follows the structure of *Being and Nothingness*. The influence of Sartre on both is taken to form a sufficient ground for helping absolve Goffman from the accusations of immorality and introduce Levinas as a sociology-friendly figure, Raffel's main objective.

At the same time, the recovery of Goffman qua Sartre for Raffel does not mean returning to Sartre: 'A Sartrean person can never "be" a homosexual because the self only exists as a not, as possibility, as other than every activity, even the activity of being honest.' (2002: 183) Granted, even the social actor who has no authentic core would still be capable of self-reflection and self-evaluation. Necessary for ensuring consistency of self-presentation and repetition, self-reflection and evaluation are not, however, sufficient for producing a selfless relationship with the Other; hence, the problem of immorality. Unawares, Goffman imported this problem into his own theory, missing in the process the essential element in Sartre's theory of the self, namely, the freedom to act. Although somewhat redemptive of Sartre and his notion of the self, this idea of freedom did not appeal to Raffel nearly as much as its modification in Levinas, whose main significance in helping out Goffman therefore lies in building 'a realistic alternative version of the self' (Raffel 2002: 187). It is in this sense that Levinas follows in Sartre's intellectual footsteps by striving to 'articulate the kind of existence of being that the self has' (Raffel 2002: 187). Freedom figures in this kind of existence as a need to act morally.

I find the above interpretation of Levinas's philosophy problematic. Clearly, Levinas defines his project as a recovery of metaphysics through ethics, whilst metaphysics should be understood not as totality but as infinity, an ethical relation of transcendence. According to Peperzak (1997), the main import of Levinas's project in this text is an unprecedented critique of Western totalitarianism which 'reduces the human and the divine Other to a totality' (ibid. 5). The key solution offered by Levinas in the aftermath of that critique, therefore, is precisely the discovery of the un-realistic notion of the absolutely other as 'immediacy without contact' (Levinas, 1969: 52). The priority which is given to the absolutely other in the I–Other relation destabilises the self, makes it uncertain, and thus allows for transcendence of face: 'The way in which the other presents himself, exceeding the idea of the other in me, we here named *face.*' (Levinas, 1969: 50, emphasis added) From here it follows rather plainly that face belongs to me and, at the same time, always exceeds me. In this duality, there is no place for selective action: the absolute ethics demands absolute responsibility. A singular responsibility means a singular course of action and thus no freedom.[3]

In *Totality and Infinity*, in his only reference to Sartre, Levinas addresses this point head on:

> 'The encounter with the Other in Sartre threatens my freedom,
> and is equivalent to the fall of my freedom under the guise of
> another freedom…But to us here there rather appears the problem
> of justification of freedom: does not the presence of the Other put
> in question the naïve legitimacy of freedom? (Levinas, 1969: 303)

In other words, the idea that one can satisfy the ethical imperative by choosing to act responsibly is not sufficient for the absolute ethics. The self can either acknowledge the call of the Other, which means responding to it absolutely, to the point of self-abnegation, or choose not to hear it. The act of responding to the Other can be neither willed nor reasoned – it should rest with the individual entirely: 'The I always has one responsibility more than all the others.' (Levinas 1982: 99) In the meantime, proceeding farther down the Sartrian path makes Raffel state that the encounter with the Other elevates the self to 'a higher, less complacent level of self-consciousness' (2002: 190). Here we see the parallel that Raffel draws between Sartre's attentive self and the alleged self-conscious self of Levinas. On the basis of this connection Raffel creates a bridge between praxis and ethics, apparently linking Goffman to Levinas. When Goffman says that one's business is first to observe the Other, he implies that the Other's morality comes as an aftermath of performing the self for the Other. By seeing in this argument a productive fusion of pragmatics and ethics, Raffel in fact equates absolute ethics with the everyday moral judgement and thus dilutes Levinas to the following generalisation: 'Only interaction with others (i.e. our dealings with the social world) can make us fully human.' (Raffel, 2002: 200)

In sum, my examination of two positions that favour the Goffman–Levinas connection indicates an unfortunate pattern of misrepresenting Levinas and his concept of face in terms of their manifestations, be it facework or face-body or face-action. Even more unfortunate is the direction of reading Levinas. Both Smart and Raffel approach Levinas as an empiricist who could repair the broken model of another empiricist, rejuvenate the moral face within the frame of the face ethics. Given this approach, the detachment of the transcendental side of face, as in the Godly, the divine, and the absolute was inevitable. So was the loss of the absolute ethics, the very condition of being human for Levinas. This kind of reductive reading of Levinas was accompanied by an equally reductive interpretation of Goffman, whose empirical allegiances were too much taken for granted. Goffman's conceptual and hermeneutic confusions have been the staple critique of contemporary sociologists, turning Goffman's problems into the problem with Goffman. If at this point the critique of the empirical connection between Goffman and Levinas seems unsuitable, we should ask ourselves if we should not proceed along a different path.

While approaching this path, I suggest that we might benefit from Robert Bernasconi's essay 'Rereading *Totality and Infinity*' (2005) which shows that the majority of interpretations of Levinas fall in either the empirical or transcendental quadrant. The empirical angle creates a predisposition of taking the ego for the self, the social world for interaction, ethics for morality, and the face for overall behaviour. The transcendental reading, on the other hand, tends to take the self for transcendence, the social world for the divine order, the Other for God, and ethics for the absolute response to the Other. Without denying the significance of each separate direction of inquiry Bernasconi argues that:

> Levinas is using the language of transcendental philosophy and
> the language of empiricism not in order to draw them together
> into a transcendental empiricism, but in an effort to find a way
> between these twin options given to us by the philosophical – and
> non-philosophical – language that we have inherited. (2005: 42)

I would like to suggest then that this language is ambiguous indeed; moreover, Levinas advances ambiguity as a strategic resource and a phenomenal domain in its own right. From this perspective, Levinas's face would be a purposefully ambiguous structure of the social order.[4] As such, this structure is asymmetrical and not only because the Other was granted an ethical priority over the self, it would also be ambiguous in the transcendental sense as 'the beyond the possible' (Levinas

1969: 21). It is in this phenomenal in-between of face and not in the social dealings with face then that one could find 'hospitality' and 'welcome'.[5] With this depiction we can think of ambiguity not as the divide between the human Other and the absolutely other, but as a productive sphere that generates its own existents. In the next section I examine ambiguity as a specific feature of face, for it is in that feature that I find the strongest link between the ethics of Levinas and the pragmatics of Goffman. I also suggest that, along the way, we shall reconsider Goffman's own conceptualisations of face. I thus would like to proceed with the following question: *How shall we conceive of face as ambiguous?*

11.3. The face of ambiguity

From the critique of the one-sided approach to face, there has risen an intimation that unconfined to either its embodiment or to consciousness, face in fact features the dual mode of appearing: it is both the human face and the divine face. There is the everyday face that we project and perceive in our everyday dealings, and at the same time there is the ethical face that hovers over, so to say, without making itself visible or accessible. The everyday face is there to express its bearer. In this way it interprets his or her self. However, in order to invoke the ethics of the absolutely other and thus allow for the conception of time as a condition of responsibility for the Other, face must surpass both the hermeneutic and the ontological dimensions; hence, the ethical face. The ethical face that calls to the Other is not the face that cries or laughs; emotional states are too specific for it:

> The Other remains infinitely transcendent, infinitely foreign; his
> face in which his epiphany is produced and which appeals to me
> breaks with the world that can be common to us, whose virtualities
> are inscribed in our *nature* and developed in our existence.
> (Levinas 1969: 194)

This apparent impassion is not a lack of passion; the absolute face is before passion, it is expression before the expressed: 'face is the expression itself' (Levinas, 1969: 194). It is thus simultaneously inaccessible absolutely and, at the same time, is disclosed only in the human face as a theme. Essentially, the theme is a mediating structure of consciousness. It helps resolve the discrepancy between empirical accessibility and transcendence. It does so by uniting two kinds of temporality: as experienced and as lived. The difference between the two is the difference of access. The life-world cannot be accessible *in toto*, but only partially, through its persistent manifestations, its themes.

In sum, the encounter with the Other, the face-to-face encounter is not a neutral occurrence demanded by the social world. The Other who is present in the flesh inspires awe by his/her sheer presence; yet, the source of awe and mystery exceeds this presence. In *Time and the Other*, Levinas writes:

> The relationship with the Other, the face-to-face with the Other, the encounter with the face that at once gives and conceals the Other, is a situation in which an event happens to a subject who does not assume it, who is utterly unable in this regard, but where nonetheless in a certain way it is in front of the subject. (1987: 78–79)

The simultaneous deployment of two components, face as a specific human face and face as the relation to the social world represented by and in the Other, allows the encounter with face appear as an event. The event of disclosing the dual face as Levinas conceived of it is similar to the duality of the ritualised presentation of the self in Goffman. Below I would like to investigate this similarity. The purpose of this investigation is to identify the status of duality for each line of thinking.

Goffman describes the key objective of his study as the 'analysis of syntactical relations among the acts of different persons mutually present to one another' (1967: 2). It therefore appears as if he places his interests in examining the face-to-face encounter firmly in the horizontal realm, as an embodied encounter. However, upon a close scrutiny, one discovers two senses of ambiguity in Goffman: on the one hand, his actors are quite capable of experiencing awe before each other, and to experience awe means to suspend relationships; on the other, in order to account for aberrations and deviations in mutual presentations, the actor must allow for the possibility of a change. The former sense resembles that of Levinas, who stresses proximal relation as a relation without context. In comparison, for Goffman, when the principle of territoriality is put into question, we become at a loss, for the loss of the familiar environment means the loss of all the associated rituals. The second sense of ambiguity rises in-between the two kinds of rules: substantive and ceremonial. According to Goffman:

> A substantive rule is one which guides conduct in regards to matters felt to have significance in their own right...A ceremonial rule is a conventionalised means of communication by which

> participants express their appreciation of self and others. (1967: 53–54)

The first set of rules refers to morality, and law. The second set of rules governs interaction and is expressed in such social structures as politeness and etiquette.

Respectively, there are two kinds of faces that are governed by these rules: one is the rigid social face, the other is the flexible personal face. One does not show itself very often; the other always expresses itself. The two faces, just like the two sets of rules, are not clearly demarcated from each other but presuppose a neutral zone that allows for the creation of such mixed identities as a charming criminal or a kind torturer. In their discrepant self-presenting, these selves are mysterious, for they do not walk the straight line. According to Goffman, the line includes 'activities that are consequential, problematic, and undertaken for what is being felt as their own sake' (Goffman, 1967: 185). When the person maintains the line, his conduct presents him in the eyes of others as internally consistent with the situation. In the case of mixed identities, the line is ambiguous, its direction uncertain. The uncertainty pressures one to recognise a discrepancy in the Other; the discrepancy is situated between the image and the character. Following the earlier distinction, image belongs to what is immediately given to the other. Character on the other hand is more deeply rooted. 'Thus a paradox,' writes Goffman (1967: 238). The line that separates character and self-presentation is the source of both articulate contact and ambiguous presumption. We cannot help but conclude from here that face for Goffman is an ambiguous structure and that the behavioural line crosses this ambiguity to the point of disambiguation. Returning to Levinas, it might be helpful to ask if his notion of face does not feature an analogous structure.

According to Levinas, the space of ambiguity which is upheld by the two faces is delimited by way of transcendence. The matter that transcends this space is called trace. Its significance for face lies in the power to disclose. Trace does not point to the absent presence of something beyond itself, nor does it carry a statement. It rather lifts the veil over the mystery of the Other, and through this opening, signifies the Other. Levinas writes: 'The signifier, he who gives a sign, must present himself before every sign, by himself - present in the face.' (1969: 181–182) Qua the signifying trace face reaches beyond the relation with the present and, in the present, outside of language and communication. From this perspective, it is appropriate to accept the elaboration about the trace made by Paul Ricoeur: when experienced in the face of the Other 'the trace indicates passage and not presence' (1988: 119). While the absolute face is revealing but without revelation and the human face but expresses its theme, the trace as the thoroughfare connotes the relation between the two spheres and the two faces. Returning to the previous discussion, the trace is the condition for the appearance of the theme. The relation which is stirred up by the trace is iconic; it is predicated on likeness: the ethics of the everyday is like the absolute ethics.

Furthermore, Ricoeur (1985) shows that trace is distinguished from all other signs because it disarranges them and their order. The trace is then this disarrangement expressing itself. It is the ambiguator that generates – in and by its passing – the space for ambiguity. The trace left by a wild animal disarranges the vegetation of the forest, claims Ricoeur; compare it to Levinas – 'the relationship between signified and signification is unrightness' (Ricoeur, 1985: 59). Unrightness is the moral waywardness, a deviation from the known path. The presence that is predicated on absence comes to connote absence not as an absence but as ambiguity – 'the face expresses ambiguity' (Ricoeur, 1985: 145). Ambiguous expression differs from telling or narration as well as revelatory epiphany since it discloses (in the phenomenological sense of the word) itself as an extreme experience. It is the extreme experience then that gives us the ambiguous face. I wish to call this face the *traumatic* face. The traumatic face occurs in 'a situation in which an event happens to a subject who does not assume it, who is utterly unable in this regard, but where nonetheless in a certain way it is in front of the subject' (Levinas, 1987: 78–79). It rises on the threshold between the two ways of being, creating an outlet into the social world. There, in its testifying its trauma, face discloses ambiguity of the relationship between expression and revelation.

This view does not contradict but extends Goffman's view of the collusion between the two modes as what is achieved through the interface between the ritualistic face which 'involves the acts through whose symbolic component the actor shows how worthy he is of respect or how worthy he feels others are of it' and the sacred face sustained by an expressive order other than the ordinary – 'in the situations of dire strain, we become vulnerable, that is, unable of controlling our selves, unable to manage face' (Goffman, 1959: 19). In this kind of situation, we show face as it is detached from both our law-binding universalism and the need to present itself as someone who is unique. According to Goffman, this kind of face is a lost face. The lost face is the face of bewilderment, a flustered face that failed to keep its course uninterrupted. And it is this kind of face, the pre-ritualistic face of ambiguity that implicates us most profoundly. The above examples exemplify but minor traumatism. In comparison, the Levinasian sense of the extreme is far more penetrating and therefore concrete. It comes in correspondence with the ambiguity formed at the limit of the absolute. Below I would like to present an example of traumatic face.

11.4. Trauma's many faces

The experiences of the traumatic face that are most pertinent to our historical memory are those of World War II. They are the experiences that belong to the survivors of the War's atrocities. A survivor of the Nazi concentration camp, Levinas came face-to-face with the extreme trauma. In the trace of that experience he glimpsed the absolute Other. Neither performative, nor divine, this Other showed himself in the wake of the disarranged everydayness, habituality, and triviality. Importantly, by showing the passage of the Other, the traumatic face testified to its own, ethical identity. The encounter with the extreme is not homogenous; it undergoes various transitions and in doing so testifies to an identity that is neither empirical nor divine but, according to Levinas, 'signification without a context' (1969: 23). In his response to Levinas, Jacques Derrida (2001) proposes that absolute horror should refuse a response; no dialogue should be conducted about the unspeakable; speech is unable of expressing the experience of annihilation. Horror cannot be communicated in language, nor can it be rendered otherwise.

In his 1999 book *Remnants of Auschwitz: On Testimony and Archive* Giorgio Agamben re-examines this thesis and disagrees. Silence should not be an answer to the absolute horror, nor should the drama of death: 'After Auschwitz, it's impossible to use tragic paradigm in ethics.' (1999: 99) The extreme experiences of Auschwitz create extreme identities; those do not fit the conventional understanding of responsibility because the experience that founds them is of a different kind. For the paradigm of the extreme experience, Agamben evokes the figure of the *Muselmann*, a human being who, while under severe duress of the extermination camp, looses the human face but continues to dwell:

> This is why the prisoners have always given up speaking to the
> *Muselmann*, almost as if silence and not seeing were the only
> demeanour adequate for those who are beyond help. (Agamben,
> 1999: 63)

The *Muselmann* is someone who lost his everyday face because his experience reached beyond what separates the human and the divine. From that position, nobody could possibly articulate himself. Positioned between life and death, unable of completing/connecting the two, the *Muselmann* is a liminal figure par excellence. Unable of experiencing trauma any longer, he becomes trauma. The bearer of pure trauma has no claim to its experience and therefore expression. The latter belongs to someone else; it belongs to the witness, but not any kind of witness. Only those who reached the limit together with the *Muselmann* but never crossed it could tell about the limit. *But how would they tell?*

According to Agamben, witnesses to the impossible become impossible witnesses:

> The *Shoah* is an event without witnesses in the double sense: one cannot bear witness to it from the inside of death and from the outside since the outside is excluded from the event. (Agamben, 1999: 35)

The rejection of the inside/outside dichotomy by extreme witnessing sabotages a common measure of truth, its expression; that is why the true *Shoah* testimonials are without language. Rather, their language is impassionate, too ordinary to distinguish it from any other types of accounts, such as historical chronicles. The true testimony of the extreme leaves its trace in face. It is as if the extreme that collapses the self and the Other together suspends the dual face, freezes the passage of the divine in an iconic image and scars the human face with permanent ambiguity. Witnessing the impossible

> takes place where the speechless one makes the speaking one speak and where the one who speaks bears the impossibility of speaking in his own speech, such that the silent and the speaking, the inhuman and the human enter into a zone of indistinction in which it is impossible to establish the position of the subject. (Agamben, 1999: 120)

Nothing can tell about what happened on the way to the gas chamber but the face of the person who managed to escape it.

11.5. Conclusion

From this example, one can see how, in contrast to the absolute ethical face, the traumatic face grants partial access to the absolute Other. The degree of access corresponds to the degree of the self-other separation. Unlike the absolute face, the traumatic face describes itself; hence, the possibility of understanding the traumatic face as an expression of self at the limits of human experience. The trauma has the human face; yet, it reveals by far more than this or that face. It reveals itself as a marginal zone between the transcendental and the empirical consciousness. Levinas and Goffman help us understand this in-between by offering two different yet complementary sets of questions. Levinas poses the following questions, *How does face become traumatic? What are the conditions for the experience of trauma?* With Goffman, we can ask, *How does one perform the traumatic face? How does one present himself in this state of separation and ambiguity?* These questions can arise only in a co-determinate fashion, after the relationship between Levinas and Goffman is established as a productive fusion of two emphases: extreme morality and mediated ethics. In the above sections I attempted to show productivity of this relation by investigating the argument mounted against Goffman in favour of Levinas. My analyses of two such arguments pointed to their reductionist approach to both Goffman and Levinas. This reductionism made it appear as if Levinas could correct the mistakes made by Goffman. Instead, the theory of the traumatic face suggests the existence of an intellectual union between the sociologist and the phenomenologist.

Endnotes

1. I use the terms 'other' and 'Other' in accordance with the phenomenological convention: the former designates otherness more generally, while the latter refers to any embodied person who is not self.
2. As Smith (2006) has shown, this claim is by no means uncontestable.
3. Llewelyn (1985) argues that being-for-the-other for Levinas is not simply a contingency as it is in Sartre; rather, 'it is an unavoidable human responsibility' (ibid. 253).
4. Examining Levinas's logic, Lyotard (1986: 117) names it 'the discourse of ambiguity'.
5. The terms 'hospitality' and 'welcome' were appropriated from Levinas by Derrida (2000) who, in *Of Hospitality*, argues for the possibility of the middle ground between the ethics of action and the absolute ethics.

References

Agamben, G. (1999) *Remnants of Auschwitz: The Witness and the Archive*. Trans. D. Heller-Roazen. New York: Zone Books.

Bauman, Z. (1990) Effacing the Face: On the Social Management of Moral Proximity. *Theory, Culture, and Society* 7: 5–38.

Bergo, B. (1999) *Levinas Between Ethics and Politics. For the Beauty that Adorns the Earth*. Dordrecht: Kluwer.

Bernasconi, R. (2005) Rereading *Totality and Infinity*. In C. Katz (ed.) *Emmanuel Levinas: Critical Assessments Vol. I* 32–244. London: Routledge.

Burns, T. (1972) *Erving Goffman*. London: Routledge.

Derrida, J. (2000) *Of Hospitality*. Trans. R. Bowlby, Stanford, CA: Stanford University Press.

Derrida, J. (2001) *Cosmopolitanism and Forgiveness*, London: Routledge.

Drew, P. and Wootton, A. (eds.) (1988) *Erving Goffman. Exploring the Interaction Order*. Cambridge: Polity Press.

Friedson, E. (1983) Celebrating Erving Goffman. *Contemporary Sociology* 12: 359–362.

Goffman, E. (1959) *The Presentation of Self in Everyday Life*, New York: Doubleday Anchor.

Goffman, E. (1961) *Encounters: Two Studies in Sociology of Interaction*. Indianapolis: Bobbs-Merrill.

Goffman, E. (1966) *Behaviour in Public Places*. The Free Press: New York.

Goffman, E. (1967) *Interaction Ritual: Essays on Face-to-Face Behavior*. New York: Pantheon Books.

Levinas, E. (1969) *Totality and Infinity*, Trans. A. Lingis. Pittsburgh: Duquesne University Press.

Levinas, E. (1981) *Otherwise than Being or Beyond Essence*. Trans. A. Lingis, Pittsburgh: Duquesne University Press.

Levinas, E. (1985) *Ethics and Infinity*, Trans. A. Lingis. Pittsburgh: Duquesne University Press.

Levinas, E. (1987) *Time and the Other*. Trans. R. Cohen. Pittsburgh: Duquesne University Press.

Llewelyn, J. (1985) Levinas, Derrida, and Others vis-à-vis. In J. Llewelyn (ed.) *Beyond Metaphysics?* 185–206. Highland, NJ: Humanities Press.

Lyotard, J.-F. (1986) Levinas Logic. In R. Cohen (ed.) *Face to Face with Levinas* 117–158. Albany: State University of New York Press.

Manning, P. (1992) *Erving Goffman and Modern Sociology*. Cambridge: Polity.

Ostrow, J. (1996) Spontaneous Involvement and Social Life. *Sociological Perspectives* 39: 341–351.

Peperzak, A. (1995) *Ethics as First Philosophy. The Significance of Emmanuel Levinas for Philosophy, Literature, and Religion*. London: Routledge.

Peperzak, A. (1997) *Beyond: The Philosophy of Emmanuel Levinas*. Evanston: Northwestern University Press.

Psathas, G. (1980) Early Goffman and the Analysis of Face-to-Face Interaction. In J. Ditton (ed.) *The View from Goffman*. London: McMillan.

Psathas, G. (1996) Theoretical Perspectives on Goffman: Critique and Commentary. *Sociological Perspectives* 39: 381-393.

Raffel, S. (2002) If Goffman Had Read Levinas. *Journal of Classical Sociology* 2: 179–202.

Rawls, A. (1987) The Interaction Order Sui Generis: Goffman's Contribution to Social Theory. *Sociological Theory* 5: 136–149.

Ricoeur, P. (1985) *Time and Narrative, Vol. III*. Trans. K. Blamey and D. Pellauer. Chicago: Chicago University Press.

Sartre, J.-P. (1956) *Being and Nothingness*. Trans. H. Barnes. New York: Washington Square Press.

Schudson, M. (1984) Embarrassment and Erving Goffman's Idea of Human Nature. *Theory and Society* 13: 633–648.

Smart, B. (1996) Facing the Body: Goffman, Levinas, and the Subject of Ethics. *Body and Society* 2: 67–78.

Smith, G. (2006) Enacted Others: Specifying Goffman's Phenomenological Omissions and Sociological Accomplishments. *Human Studies* 28: 397–415.

Travers, A. (1994) The Unrequited Self. *History of the Human Sciences.* 7: 121–140.

Williams, S. (1986). Appraising Goffman. *The British Journal of Sociology* 37: 148–169.

Part III

Face, norms and society

12
Facework collision in intercultural communication

Stella Ting-Toomey

Intercultural facework collision connotes interaction frictions that happen because of escalatory intercultural misunderstandings or ignorance. It can take place when visible or invisible cultural group membership factors aggravate the already fragile miscommunication process between members of two (or more) different cultural communities. The cultural membership differences can include deep-level differences such as cultural worldviews and value orientations. Concurrently, they can also include the mismatch of applying different behavioural expectations in a particular social interaction scene.

Facework collision refers to both behavioural expectancy violations and actual communication clash issues. The clash can entail perceived incompatibility of value orientations, norms, interaction goals, facework styles, and meanings between two interdependent parties or groups. Individuals from two contrastive cultural communities may apply different meanings concerning the speech and nonverbal activities that take place in an 'activity type' such as a job interview, a feedback appraisal session, or a motivational speech (Culpeper, Bousfield and Wichmann, 2003; Culpeper, 2005). Members within a cultural community often develop a set of shared meanings and co-constitution processes of what counts as proper or improper behaviours in a given social situation (Arundale, 2006; Philipsen and Coutu, 2005; Turner, 2002).

This chapter is developed in three sections. The first section offers a synopsis of the two conceptual maps that hold promise in explaining facework collision in intercultural communication. The second section uses the core taxonomies of the two theoretical frames in analyzing a Japanese–U.S. social interaction episode. The third section provides specific recommendations on future theorising efforts concerning facework expectancies in intercultural social discourse.

12.1. Intercultural facework approaches

After half of a century of research about intercultural communication, many scholars have developed well-designed and well-tested theories to explain the differences and similarities of communication behaviours across cultures and identity groups (see Gudykunst, 2003, 2005). For the purpose of this particular chapter and because of space limitations, I have selected two intercultural perspectives that I believe have direct relevance in the study of culture, facework expectancies, and social interaction.

Conflict face-negotiation theory

Competent intercultural facework interaction depends on many factors. One of the key factors is to increase our awareness and knowledge concerning diverse facework negotiation issues in a conflict encounter. Some prominent sources of intercultural conflict may include cultural/ ethnic value clashes, communication decoding problems, and identity inattention issues. Cultural value clash issues can involve the clash of individualistic 'I-identity' value with collectivistic 'we-identity' value (Triandis, 1995, 2002) with one party emphasising 'self-face saving' tendency and the other party valuing 'relational-face compromising' interest. In connecting national cultures with face concerns, for example, research reveals that while individualists (e.g. U.S. respondents) tend to use more direct, self-face concern conflict behaviours (e.g. dominating/competing style), collectivists (e.g. Taiwan and China respondents) tend to use more indirect, other-face concern conflict behaviours (e.g. avoiding and obliging styles) (Ting-Toomey *et al.*, 1991; Cai and Fink, 2002).

Self-face concern is the protective concern for one's own identity image when one's own face is threatened in the conflict episode. *Other-face concern* is the concern for accommodating the other conflict party's identity image in the conflict situation. *Mutual-face concern* is the concern for both parties' images and the image of the relationship. Whether we choose to engage in or disengage from a conflict process often depends on our ingrained cultural conflict habits and how we negotiate various *face concerns*. 'Face' is really about identity respect and other-identity consideration issues within and beyond the actual social discourse process. It is tied to the emotional significance and estimated appraisals that we attach to our own social self-worth and the social self-worth of others (Goffman, 1967; Ting-Toomey and Kurogi, 1998; Tracy, 2005).

When our face image is being threatened in a conflict situation, we would be likely experience identity-based frustration, emotional vulnerability, shame, hurt, anger – to even vengeance. The threats to face can be on the group membership level or the individual level. Face-threatening and face-defending acts are cast as a 'process' because face-attacking and face-defending behaviours are fluid and interdependent phenomena that occur in an ongoing exchange process. In fact, Spencer-Oatey (2005: 96) proposes that the study of facework can be understood via four relational interaction categories: from a rapport-enhancement (a desire to strengthen harmonious relations between interlocutors) orientation to a rapport-challenge (a desire to challenge or impair harmonious relations) orientation.

Facework collision is part of a rapport-challenging speech event – whether it occurs intentionally or unintentionally. The conditions of an intercultural *face threatening process (FTP)* can include:

1. The more important the culturally appropriate facework rule that is violated, the more severe the perceived FTP.

2. The larger the cultural distance between the conflict parties, the more mistrust and/or misunderstanding cumulate in the FTP.

3. The more important the conflict topic or imposition of the conflict demand, as interpreted from distinctive cultural angles, the more severe the perceived FTP.

4. The more power the conflict initiator has over the conflict recipient, the more severe the perceived FTP by the recipient.

5. The more harm or hurtfulness the FTP produces, the more time and effort is needed to repair the FTP (Ting-Toomey, 2005).

Face concern becomes incrementally more salient if several of these conditions are present in a face-challenging communication situation.

For example, individuals are likely to move toward self-face saving and in-group face-saving emphasis as they perceive the escalation of the various face-threatening conditions directed at them. Cultural assumptions and values frame the underlying interpretations of what counts as a 'face-threatening' social interaction episode. In response to the heavy reliance on the individualistic Western perspective in framing various conflict and facework approaches, Ting-Toomey (1988) developed an intercultural conflict theory, namely, the conflict face-negotiation theory to include a collectivistic Asian perspective concerning cross-cultural facework. In a nutshell, Ting-Toomey's (1988; Ting-Toomey and Kurogi, 1998) theory assumes that:

1. People in all cultures try to maintain and negotiate face in all communication situations.

2. The concept of face is especially problematic in emotionally-threatening or identity vulnerable situations when the situated identities of the communicators are called into question.

3. The cultural value spectrums of individualism–collectivism and small/large power distance shape facework concerns and styles.

4. The value dimensions, *in conjunction with* individual, relational, and situational factors, influence the use of particular facework behaviours in particular cultural scenes.

5. Intercultural facework competence refers to the optimal integration of knowledge, mindfulness, and communication skills in managing vulnerable identity-based interaction situations appropriately, effectively, and adaptively.

The methodological tools in testing the theory have included case study method (Ting-Toomey and Cole, 1990), open-ended q-sort method (Oetzel, *et al.*, 2000), and, for the ease of cross-cultural comparisons, a predominant survey-recall method (Oetzel and Ting-Toomey, 2003) in testing the specific propositions in the face-negotiation theory. More specifically, for example, in a direct empirical test of the theory (Oetzel, *et al.*, 2001; Oetzel and Ting-Toomey, 2003), a questionnaire was administered to 768 participants in 4 national cultures (China, Germany, Japan, and the U.S.) in their respective languages asking them to recall and describe a recent interpersonal conflict. The major findings of the study are as follows: First, cultural individualism-collectivism had direct effects on conflict styles, as well as mediated effects through self-construal and face concerns. Second, *self-face concern* was associated positively with a dominating style and *other-face concern* was associated positively with avoiding and integrating styles. Third, German respondents reported the frequent use of direct-confrontive facework strategies and did not care much for avoidance facework tactics; Japanese reported the use of different pretending strategies to act as if the conflict situation does not exist; Chinese engaged in a variety of avoiding, obliging, and also passive aggressive facework tactics; and U.S. Americans reported the use of upfront expression of feelings and remaining calm as common conflict facework strategies. More recently, Merkin (2006) has integrated small/large power distance value dimension in explaining face-threatening response messages in multiple cultures. She found that high-status individuals from large power distance cultures (i.e., Chinese, Japanese, and Chilean respondents) tend to use both direct and indirect facework strategies to deal with face-threatening situations – depending on whether they were delivering positive or negative messages.

Corporate values' cultural grid

Ting-Toomey and Oetzel's (2001) corporate values' cultural grid may help to further explain how intercultural conflicts get entangled in different expectancy webs and facework collision issues. Indeed the most recent GLOBE ('Global Leadership and Organizational Behavior Effectiveness' - A Research Program Study of 62 Societies) research project (House, *et al.*, 2004) provided additional evidence that the foundational constructs of individualism-collectivism and small/large power distance permeate 62 countries (and with a sample size of 17,370 middle managers from three industries) at the societal, organisational, and individual levels of analysis. Basically, *individualism* refers to the broad value tendencies of a culture in emphasising the importance of the 'I' identity over the 'we' identity, individual rights over group interests, and individuated-focused emotions over social-focused emotions. In comparison, *collectivism* refers to the broad value tendencies of a culture in emphasisng the importance of the 'we' identity over the 'I' identity, in-group interests over individual wants, and other-face concerns over self-face concerns. Individualistic and collectivistic value tendencies are manifested in everyday interpersonal, family, school, and workplace social interactions.

Power distance, from the standpoint of workplace values' analysis (Hofstede, 2001), refers to the way in which a corporate culture approaches and deals with status differences and social hierarchies. People in *small power distance* corporate cultures tend to value equal power distributions, symmetrical relations, a mixture of positive and negative messages in feedback sessions, and equitable reward and cost distributions based on individual merits. People in *large power distance* corporate cultures tend to accept unequal power distributions, asymmetrical relations, authoritative feedback from the experts or high-status individuals, and rewards and sanctions based on rank, role, status, age, and perhaps even gender identity (see Emrich, Denmark and Den Hartog, 2004; Zhang, Harwood and Hummert, 2005). In combining both individualism-collectivism and small/large power distance value patterns, we can discuss four predominant corporate value dimension approaches along the two grids: impartial, status-achievement, benevolent, and communal

The *impartial approach* reflects a combination of an individualistic and small power distance value orientation; the *status-achievement approach* consists of a combination of an individualistic and large power distance value orientation; the *benevolent approach* reflects a combination of a collectivistic and large power distance value orientation; and the *communal approach* consists of a combination of collectivistic and small power distance value orientation.

Thus, managers and employees around the world have different expectations of how a workplace facework collision should be interpreted

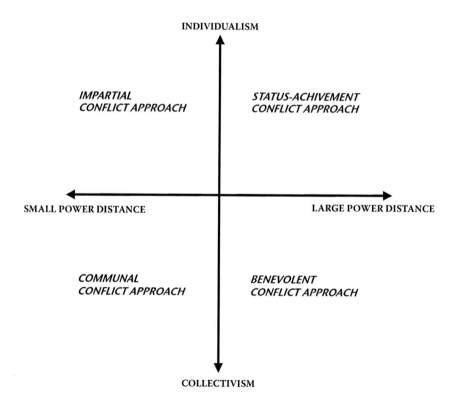

Figure 12.1. Corporate Values' Cultural Grid: Four Conflict Approaches

and resolved – depending on whether the workplace culture emphasises impartial, status-achievement, benevolent, or communal facework rituals. More specifically, in the *impartial approach* to workplace conflict, the predominant values of this approach are personal freedom and equality (Smith *et al.*,1998). From the impartial conflict approach lens, if an interpersonal conflict arises between a manager and an employee, the manager has a tendency to deal with the conflict in an upfront and direct manner. Specific feedback and concrete justifications are expected from the manager. Concurrently, an employee is also expected to articulate clearly his or her conflict viewpoints and defend his or her conflict concerns. In an equal-rank employee-employee conflict, the manager would generally play the 'impartial' third-party role and would encourage the two employees to talk things over and find their own workable solution. Both the manager and the employees would rely on the principle of objectivity or a fact-finding approach to resolve a conflict situation. Managers in large corporations in Denmark, the Netherlands, Sweden, and Norway appear to practice the impartial conflict approach (Hofstede, 2001).

Alternatively, from a *status-achievement approach* to conflict, the predominant values of this approach are personal freedom and earned inequality. For example, in France, employees often feel that they have the freedom to voice directly and complain about their managers in the workplace (Storti, 2001). At the same time, they do not expect their managers to change much because they are their bosses and, thus, by virtue of their titles hold certain rights and power resources. The managers, meanwhile, also expect conflict accommodations from their subordinates. When the conflict involves two same-rank co-workers, the use of upfront conflict tactics to aggression tactics is a hallmark of the status-achievement approach. Ting-Toomey and Oetzel (2001) also observed that U.S. management style often follows a conjoint impartial approach and a status-achievement approach because the larger U.S. culture emphasises that via individual hard work and competitiveness, status and rank can be earned and status cues can be displayed with pride and credibility.

In comparison, many managers in other parts of the globe tend to see themselves as interdependent and at a different status level than others. That is, these managers think of themselves as individuals with interlocking connections with others and as members of a hierarchical network. They practice the *benevolent approach* (a combination of collectivism and large power distance value patterns) of management style. The term 'benevolent' implies that many managers play the authoritative parental roles in approaching or motivating their employees. Two values that pervade this approach are obligation to others and asymmetrical interaction treatment. Countries that predominantly reflect the benevolent approach include most Latin and South American nations (e.g. Mexico, Venezuela, Brazil, Chile), most Asian nations (e.g. India, Japan, China, South Korea), most Arab nations (e.g. Egypt, Saudi Arabia, Jordan) and most African nations (e.g. Nigeria, Uganda) (Hofstede, 2001; Carl, Gupta and Javidan, 2004). For many of the large East Asian corporations, Confucian-driven hierarchical principles promote a parent-child relationship between the manager and the subordinate.

Under the benevolent conflict approach, while a manager can confront employees in order to motivate them to work harder, it is very rare that subordinates will directly challenge the manager's authority or face during a conflict interaction process. However, they might opt for using passive aggressive or sabotage conflict strategies to deal with the workplace tensions or frustrations. In dealing with low-premium conflicts, managers would consider the personal relationships and relational harmony in the workplace and try to 'smooth over' the conflict with subtle face-pressuring tactics. Managers would also be likely to have a direct face-talk with each conflict employee and would use strategic compliance-gaining tactics to coax each employee into compromising with the other employee. However, in dealing with high-premium conflicts, benevolent managers could act in a very directive or autocratic manner. They might also practice preferential treatment or particularistic value by treating senior employees more favorably than junior employees.

Lastly, the *communal approach* is the least common of the four conflict approaches. The values that encompass this approach are the recognition of authentic interdependent connection to others and genuine interpersonal equality. Costa Rica is the only country found to fit this approach (Hofstede, 2001). Similarly, feminist principles include holistic and integrative problem-solving, and the importance of engaging in mutual-face sensitive, collaborative dialogue (Barge, 2006). In a true communal organisation, managers and employees are considered to be co-equals and are expected to be expressive during conflict and work together to develop mutually acceptable conflict procedures and options.

With the knowledge base and conceptual tools of the conflict face-negotiation theory and the corporate values cultural grid, the next section applies some of the key ideas of both approaches in analysing a mini-case study concerning an intercultural facework clash episode.

12.2. Intercultural facework: expectancies and collisions

In any intercultural social encounter process, people hold expectations of how an interaction scene should play out and how a problematic scene should be handled or resolved. Normative expectations or anticipations are often learned via the root patterned values such as individualism-collectivism and small-large power distance. As Burgoon and Ebesu Hubbard (2005) observed:

> [E]very culture has guidelines for human conduct that carry
> associated anticipations for how others will behave. Those
> guidelines and anticipations manifest themselves in interactions
> between people. Intercultural communication, then, involves
> communicators adjusting and influencing the behaviors of each
> other, partly through the lens of expectations. (Burgoon and
> Ebesu Hubbard, 2005: 146)

Levinson (1992:69) echoes a similar point when he comments that an 'activity type' refers to 'any culturally recognized activity...whose focal members are goal-defined, socially constituted, bounded events with *constraints* on participants, setting, and so on, but above all on the kinds of allowable contributions'. The 'allowable contributions' basically refer to what should or should not take place in a culturally-grounded 'activity type' such as 'a motivational speech'.

The following brief excerpt is adapted from an organisational case study of a real-life workplace situation described by Clarke and Lipp (1998: 229–254), based on their extensive consulting experiences with U.S.-based Japanese subsidiaries. The case study method approach has been used in different contexts such as organisational communication (Keyton and Shockley-Zalabak, 2004; Schnurr, Marra, and Holmes, 2007), interpersonal communication (Braithwaite and Wood, 2000), and social discourse analysis (Tracy and Tracy, 1998; Tracy, 2005). Braithwaite and Wood (2000; see also Ellet, 2007) argue persuasively for the important use of a case study method via three functions: the direct application of relevant theories to explain specific communication situations, the promotion of deeper understanding of the layered complexities of a real-life social interaction episode, and the identification of problematic patterns of communication in the episode and the generation of practical strategies in addressing the problems.

A case study: a motivational or de-motivational speech?

A Japanese multimedia subsidiary in the United States had just completed a very successful year. All of the company goals were met or surpassed. As a result, the annual sales conference was held in Disneyland Resort Hotel in California. Many of the salespeople brought their spouses to the conference, to celebrate and enjoy a well-earned vacation. The audience at the dinner celebration consisted of mostly American salespeople and their spouses, and some Japanese technical support personnel. The Japanese president gave a brief welcome speech in halting English, but the audience appreciated his remarks.

Next, the American director of sales, William Bates, got up and introduced the Japanese vice president, Satoshi Ota-san. They had planned ahead of time to give two short motivational speeches to kick off the conference. Ota-san was about fifty years old, and he had used the last two weeks to memorize his carefully-prepared speech in English. When Ota-san stood up, his posture was rigid, his face was serious, and his tone sounded harsh. Here is what he said:

> Thank you for your hard work this fiscal year. We have broken many records, *but*...we need to be careful and not to settle down so easily. We need to keep up our fighting spirit! Our competition is working to defeat us at this very minute while we are celebrating. You have done a good job...but you must do more and aim higher. There is no time for frivolous activities. You must prepare yourselves to work twice as hard this coming year. The company has invested a lot of money in new manufacturing facilities. These facilities are producing our new product lines. It is your duty and loyalty to this company to sell these products as efficiently as possible. You must not fail! You must not let your guard down! You must not be content! I hope you will do a better job in the new fiscal year.
>
> Thank you.

The American audience sat in stunned silence during most of Satoshi Ota-san's speech. The American director of sales, William Bates, stood up quickly, physically backed away from the Japanese vice president of sales, and with an awkward smile said:

> Disregard everything he just said. We are here to celebrate your fantastic achievements this year! We have out-performed all our competitors this past year and your success is far beyond expectations. So give yourselves a big round of applause, and, let the festivities begin!

The audience applauded. William gave the signal to the hotel staff to serve the dinner. For the rest of the conference, the tension between Satoshi Ota-san and William Bates was palpable, and most of the other Americans were irritable.

What went wrong here? Why did Mr. Bates physically back away from Mr. Ota? How do you, the reader, think Mr. Ota reacted to Mr. Bates' 'Disregard everything he just said' comment? Can you identify all the facework collision bumps in the above case study? Can the facework clashes between the two key characters be reconciled?

Intercultural facework: expectancy analysis

The storyline in the aforementioned case description clearly illustrated the conditions of an intercultural *face threatening process (FTP)* in the conflict face-negotiation theory. For example, Condition 2 states that: 'The larger the cultural distance between the conflict parties, the more mistrust and/or misunderstanding cumulate in the FTP.' Clearly in this case, the Americans and the Japanese carried different cultural assumptions about the meaning of a sales conference celebration event and the meaning of a motivational speech. From the status-achievement corporate worldview, Mr. Bates and the American audience were expecting an 'individual status-recognition celebration' event. Many of them brought their spouses to mark the festivity and to enjoy a fun-filled vacation. From the benevolent corporate worldview, Mr. Ota and perhaps including some of the Japanese technical staff viewed this as another occasion to 'motivate' the sales workforce to work harder and to plan productive sales strategies in a group setting. Prescriptive expectancy concerning social discourse refers to socially normative patterns of behaviour concerning 'what should or should not happen' in a given cultural context and connotes general cultural community value-level knowledge (Burgoon, 1995). Thus, individuals hold certain socio-cognitive schemata of what should or should not happen in a public celebration conference.

Furthermore, Condition 3 in the *face threatening process* (FTP) states that: 'The more important the conflict topic or imposition of the conflict demand, as interpreted from distinctive cultural angles, the more severe the perceived FTP.' More specifically, both cultural groups encountered predictive expectancy violations concerning the particular communication context and the particular facework speech event. Mr. Ota's rigid posture and harsh tone did not create a positive initial impression on the American audience. Additionally, the content of his 'motivational speech' did not sound constructive and motivational to the American employees. The speech sounded more like a set of demands to work harder and really violated both the self-concern 'approval face' and 'autonomy face' of the American audience (Brown and Levinson, 1987; Park and Guan, 2006). In turn, Mr. Bates' awkward smile and cavalier phrase of 'disregard everything he just said' created enormous face loss for Mr. Ota and the Japanese president (as an in-group member).

Condition 4 states: 'The more power the conflict initiator has over the conflict recipient, the more severe the perceived FTP by the recipient.' Since Mr. Ota was the vice president of sales and thus had more power over many of the conference attendees, the facework violation was definitely interpreted as a major face-threatening offence in the eyes of both Mr. Bates and the American audience. From the American employees' standpoint, they came to the conference (many with their spouses) expecting to hear accolades and positive reinforcements for a very productive year in the sales division. However, what they heard was a string of negative messages of needing to work harder and needing to do a better job next year. Many of the American employees experienced severe face loss in front of their spouses (Clarke and Lipp, 1998: 237). Their professional and face identities were directly attacked. Meanwhile, Mr. Ota also experienced aggressive facework attack from Mr. Bates – since Mr. Bates directly challenged his high-status face by calling on the audience to dismiss his motivational speech entirely. Mr. Ota had tried so hard for the past two weeks to memorize his motivational speech in English. He thought for sure that the celebration occasion in Disneyland sent a strong positive signal to the employees that the company valued their hard work. He was looking forward to the speech presentation to coach and motivate his sales employees to reach for professional perfection. Indeed, face concern becomes incrementally more salient and tense as several of the face-threatening conditions are present in this particular social interaction episode

Intercultural facework: interaction collision analysis

In the assumptions of the conflict face-negotiation theory, Assumption 3 states: 'The cultural value spectrums of individualism-collectivism and small/large power distance shape facework concerns and styles.' Clearly, in analysing the 'motivational speech' case study, the corporate grid framework of the benevolent approach and the status-achievement approach provides a more complex analysis of the social interaction episode. Operating from the benevolent approach viewpoint, Mr. Ota's speech could be viewed as very motivational in the framework of a combined collectivism and large power distance values. From the collectivism frame, his speech was designed to appeal to the loyalty of the employees, their dedication to the corporation, and their duties and obligations to the workgroup. From the large power distance frame, Mr. Ota's message was to urge the employees to continue to do better and to be vigilant of their competitors. He was more concerned with paternalistic vertical facework interaction. Mr. Ota viewed workforce motivation as socially-focused and that organisational successes and failures rest with the interdependent group.

Conversely, from the status-achievement lens and interpretation, Mr. Ota's speech was interpreted as a very face-threatening and face-insulting process. From the individualism frame and expectation, Mr. Ota's speech was seriously de-moralising and de-motivating and dampened the Disneyland conference celebration theme. The American audience expected positive verbal feedback that signalled interpersonal respect and personal recognitions. While most Japanese employees did not bring their spouses as they viewed this type of occasion as formal and task-related, American sales employees 'marked' the occasion quite differently. They felt they had worked hard the entire year. It was a banner year in the corporation – thus, they were entitled to celebrate and bring their spouses with them for a fun time. They had achieved productivity in their sales and they deserved to be recognised for their unique capacities (i.e. reflecting a status-achievement value orientation). Thus, the audience's 'stunned silence' and frustrations ultimately led to Mr. Bates' emphatic outburst of 'We are here to celebrate your fantastic achievements this year!'

Mr. Bates' reactive speech was designed to 'save face' for himself and his Western audience. From his U.S.-based, status-achievement corporate experience, Mr. Bates was doing his best to retrieve a disastrous facework embarrassing situation. He was trying to connect with his audience from a horizontal facework interaction viewpoint. From this viewpoint, a motivational speech in a celebration setting should be humorous, jovial, and positively-toned. In a public social discourse setting, while negative feedback in a status-achievement corporate system is practised – it is usually mixed with enough positive reinforcement messages to appeal to the audience's mood and attention. Interestingly, from a benevolent corporate lens, using strong 'negative' motivational or criticism messages in a public-group setting actually energises the interdependent group to work harder and more cohesively. In the case of the Japanese corporate culture, their after-hours socialisation and drinking sessions reflect the 'Japanese system of aftercare [and] provides them with a way of wrapping the negative feedback in the cocoon of acceptance and Japanese-style camaraderie, Americans are however often left out' (Clarke and Lipp, 1998: 203).

In terms of different facework concerns and facework behavioural styles, while Mr. Ota (in his mindset) was practising other-face concern and corporate-face concern interests in terms of interaction support, his Western audience was interpreting his motivational speech as self-face concern and other-face threatening. Likewise, Mr. Bates' short emotional outburst was interpreted by Mr. Ota as other-face threatening and corporate-face damaging. Meanwhile, Mr. Bates' self-assessment about face could be that he actually 'saves the day' and 'saves the face of his audience' by making the quick transition between his dramatized verbal compliments of his sales force and signaling the start of the evening festivities.

In terms of specific facework behavioural styles, Mr. Ota probably thought he engaged in integrative facework strategies such as complimenting, appealing to the employees' duty and loyalty, and motivating the employees to have another successful year. While Mr. Bates would view Mr. Ota's verbal and nonverbal actions as divisive, de-motivational, and distributive in promoting self-interest over other-interest. Concurrently, Mr. Ota would interpret Mr. Bates' facework behaviours as highly inappropriate, aggressive, competitive, and an attempt to one-up him in making him look like a fool in front of the mixed U.S.-Japanese audience.

Lastly, in terms of facework violations contents, some interpersonal face threat content domains include, but are not limited to, autonomy face, approval face, status face, reliability face, competence face, and moral face (Brown and Levinson, 1987; Lim, 1994; Ting-Toomey and Takai, 2006). *Autonomy face* is concerned with our need for others to acknowledge our independence, self-sufficiency, privacy, boundaries, non-imposition, control issues, and vice versa. *Approval face* is concerned with our need for others to recognise that we are worthy companions, likeable, agreeable, pleasant, friendly and co-operative. *Status face* is concerned with our need for others to admire our tangible or intangible assets or resources such as reputation, position, status, rank, power and material worth. *Reliability face* is concerned with our need for others to realise that we are trustworthy, dependable, reliable, loyal and consistent in our words and actions. *Competence face* is concerned with our need for others to recognise our qualities or social abilities such as leadership skills, networking skills, and problem-solving skills. *Moral face* is concerned with our need for others to respect our sense of integrity, dignity, honour, propriety and moral uprightness.

In the 'motivational speech' case study description, Mr. Ota had clearly stepped over the situational boundary, interpersonal expectation boundary, and communication expectancy boundary of his Western audience. By 'chiding' them to work harder and to work twice as hard the coming year, Mr. Ota's speech had violated the autonomy face and the approval face of his American employees. Furthermore, he had not played out the appropriate and effective status face script and reliability face script in the particular social discourse setting. He had severely lost face credibility unintentionally by subscribing to his corporation's benevolent culture worldview.

While Mr. Bates might have gained some face credibility with his Western audience by 'saving the day', his discourse violation actions would be considered as an affront to Mr. Ota's autonomy face, approval face, status face and reliability face. Both characters encountered prescriptive, predictive and actual interaction facework collisions at multiple levels. Both had suffered competence facework violations and, ultimately, moral face transgressions because of the injuries and indignities they experienced in front of a large audience and in a public setting.

The boundaries between face domains are permeable and overlapped such that in negotiating status face, we also need to tend to reliability face. In dealing with autonomy face boundary issues, we also need to tend to approval face recognition issues. When the need or expectation for one face content domain is not met, there will be repercussions for other face content domains. Emotional frustrations and aggravations are prevalent in a social discourse setting when diverse *face content needs* are underserved.

In addressing the various facework clashes in the case study episode in a constructive manner, it seems that a third-party intermediary help might be needed to resolve this conflict case. A third-party professional consultant – someone or a team who understands the deep cultures and the corporate cultures of Japan and the U.S. – can help to bridge the chasm of the widening cultural divide between the two parties. They can also use appropriate facework strategies to mediate the face-sensitive issues that had erupted in this case situation. Understanding the conflict mangement preferences and approaches of both cultural parties – patience as versus immediacy for closure – would also serve as a good first step to reconcile the cultural and corporate expectancy differences.

12.3. Intercultural facework expectancies: research directions

In applying some of the core taxonomies from the two conceptual frameworks – the conflict face-negotiation theory and the corporate cultural grid, here are the key application points. First, while many previous research studies (e.g. Markus and Kitayama, 1991) have revealed that Asian cultures tend toward the use of high-context, indirect communication style, and that the mainstream U.S. culture tends toward the use of low-context, direct communication style, the analysis of this case study focused on a situational analysis of status-based facework and uncovered the positive relationship between benevolent corporate culture and direct facework style. Concurrently, a positive relationship also exists between the status-achievement corporate culture and the expectations of diplomatic or positively-toned motivational appeals in a public social setting.

Second, it is obvious that when studying facework and social discourse we need to take into account the prescriptive or culture-based expectancies concerning the social setting and the speech event topic (Brew and Cairns, 2004). Third, the concept of status-based role identities and the predictive facework expectancies need to be further conceptualised in conjunction with other relational features such as in-group/out-group audience and informal/formal interaction. Fourth, intercultural facework collision needs to be understood from the perspective of the conjoined expectancy violations and interpretive lenses of culture A and culture B. Fifth, intercultural facework discourse can best be understood as a situational package that includes the social setting, the key participants' socio-cultural and personal identities, the speech event, the language codes and nonverbal nuances, the sequential facework patterns, the identities of the eyewitness audience and their facework expectancy reactions, the time urgency, and the location conditions (see, for example, Crawshaw, *et al.*, 2007).

Furthermore, the following are some general recommendations of what more could be done by intercultural social interaction researchers to unravel the layered complexity of intercultural facework discourse.

Intercultural facework situations

The study of face-negotiation in social discourse would definitely benefit by examining the relationship between cultural value issues and situational frames. In the earlier case study analysis, one of the early prescriptive expectancy violation factors concerned how the various participants 'marked' the annual sales conference setting – whether it was a celebratory occasion or a year-end summary assessment occasion.

Furthermore, the meaning clash in what constitutes a 'motivational speech' carries a strong influence of cultural and corporate values. It seems that both Mr. Ota and Mr. Bates need to be trained to clarify meanings early on in terms of what the activity type of 'motivational speech' should entail in their respective cultural and corporate worlds. The status role identities between Mr. Ota (higher status) and Mr. Bates (lower status) and that of the mixed audience need to be further clarified in conjunction with appropriate facework code usage. The issue of whether Mr. Ota viewed his employees as in-groups or out-groups (and vice versa), and whether he perceived the employees' spouses as insiders or outsiders all converge together to influence the situated facework collision.

Future intercultural language and social interaction researchers can also pay close attention to the culturally-framed social setting and how the setting influences the identity enactment and facework assertion in the intercultural encounter scene. Status identities and cues, in-group/out-group identities, and public/private setting will have a profound effect on the facework codes that negotiators used in the social discourse process (Holtgraves, 2002; Turner, 2002).

Intercultural facework negotiation

Intercultural facework negotiators use both verbal and nonverbal messages to signal their self-face concern or other-face concern issues in a social encounter episode. Unfortunately, while discourse researchers have paid detailed attention to the verbal exchange process, the nonverbal facework data have been continually ignored (see, however, Culpeper, 2005). The big four emotions that underlie facework – pride, shame, guilt, and redemption – are all powerful emotional concepts lacking sufficient treatment in the intercultural facework discourse literature. These are complex, affective responses generated and

experienced in reaction to others and related to the cognitive appraisals of the worthiness of self-face and other-face issues. Facework emotional reactions, nonverbal emotional arousal signals, and instantaneous
cognitive appraisals also prompt subsequent facework defensive or
supportive verbal discourse moves. Imagined interaction analysis and
journal tracking may help researchers to get at some of the deeper emotions that are associated with face flush and face embarrassment episodes (McCann and Honeycutt, 2006).

Facework language researchers also need to be well-trained bilingual or multilingual researchers in order to pay close attention to the
particular relationship between identity assertions and facework codes
in different cultural scenes (Haugh, 2005, 2007). In a hybrid multicultural
world, many individuals could switch language codes strategically to
enact different face moves and face concerns. The particular language
code choice also reflects a particular line of face projection or pride or
strategy. Thus, without proper bilingual and intercultural interaction
training, many of the verbal and nonverbal intercultural facework nuances might be lost to the observers. Facework discourse scholars could
also unlock the cultural assumptions of face issues by studying the
everyday metaphors, parables, stories, family facework interactions, and
social order rituals in a particular speech community.

Intercultural facework competence

Social interaction researchers should also pay more attention to both
the discourse process negotiation dimension and the discourse reaction dimensions of competent facework co-ordination. Concepts such
as facework pre- and post-expectations, the intensity of facework violations, appropriateness/inappropriateness, effectiveness/ineffectiveness,
and interaction satisfaction/dissatisfaction can be tracked more systematically via discourse analysis, cultural pragmatics analysis, and post-
hoc facework interviews from a conjoint, co-orientation perspective.
Facework expectancy violations and collisions happen within and across
cultures. Fundamental differences in values and social organisation,
coupled with widespread ignorance about cultural differences, make
intercultural encounters prime candidates for colliding expectancies
(Burgoon and Ebesu Hubbard, 2005:154).

Although the knowledge component has been emphasised as the
most important area for intercultural facework and interpersonal conflict competence training (Ting-Toomey, 2004; Canary and Lakey, 2006),

we need more culture-sensitive and situationally-relevant qualitative and quantitative studies to test this assertion. In conjunction with culture-sensitive and situationally-attuned knowledge, intercultural facework researchers have also identified the concepts of mindfulness (Langer, 1989, 1997) and facework skills in translating cognitive facework competence into applied performance practice. According to Langer (1989), mindfulness can include the following characteristics:

(a) learning to see unfamiliar behaviour in the interaction situation as fresh or novel,

(b) learning to view a colliding situation from multiple vantage points or angles,

(c) learning to attend to the discourse context and the person-in-context with attunement, and

(d) learning to create new categories through which the novel behaviour may be understood.

Some research questions that can be potentially fruitful for social interaction researchers to ponder are: How does the concept of mindfulness get translated into the actual social discourse process? What does a mindful facework dialogue looks like as opposed to a mindless facework dialogue? What are the necessary and sufficient knowledge and situational blocks that are needed to transform a mindless facework dialogue to a mindful, productive one? At what level should we train and coach 'mindfulness' in conducting synchronised facework interaction?

Everyday facework is a well-coordinated and well-oiled social interaction process. When the communication rituals in a particular situation are socially derailed, identity repair works are interpersonally needed and socially expected. The importance of studying the relationship between situational parameters and facework tipping points in different cultures can help to shed light onto facework balance and imbalance issues, and facework competence and incompetence issues (see Andersson and Pearson, 1999).

In conclusion, all human beings like to be respected and be approved of – especially during vulnerable identity-threat social situations. How diverse individuals protect and maintain their self-face needs and, at the same time, learn to honour the face needs of the other conflict party very likely differ from one culture to the next, and differ from a particular social interaction scene to the next. The study of intercultural facework collision is a complex, multidimensional, and multi-levelled phenomenon. This chapter offers some systematic observations on how a culture-sensitive situational lens can yield some insightful learning points on intercultural status-based facework in a corporate, public setting.

Acknowledgement

I would like to thank the editors and the two anonymous reviewers for their thoughtful feedback and comments on this manuscript.

References

Andersson, L. and Pearson, C. (1999) Tit for tat? The spiraling effect of incivility in the workplace. *Academy of Management Review* 24: 452–471.

Arundale, R. B. (2006) Face as relational and interactional: A communication framework for research on face, facework, and politeness. *Journal of Politeness Research* 2: 193–216.

Barge, K. (2006) Dialogue, conflict, and community. In J. Oetzel and S. Ting-Toomey (eds.) *The Sage Handbook of Conflict Communication* 517–544. Thousand Oaks, CA: Sage.

Braithwaite, D. and Wood, J. (2000) *Case Studies in Interpersonal Communication.* Belmont, CA: Wadsworth/Thomson Learning.

Brew, F. and Cairns, D. (2004) Do culture or situational constraints determine choice of direct or indirect styles in intercultural workplace conflicts? *International Journal of Intercultural Relations* 28: 331–352.

Brown, P. and Levinson, S. (1987) *Politeness: Some Universals in Language Usage.* Cambridge: Cambridge University Press.

Burgoon, J. K. (1995) Cross-cultural and intercultural applications of expectancy violations theory. In R. Wiseman (ed.) *Intercultural Communication Theory* 194–214. Thousand Oaks, CA: Sage.

Burgoon, J. K. and Ebesu Hubbard, A. (2005) Cross-cultural and intercultural applications of expectancy violations and interaction adaptation theory. In W.B. Gudykunst (ed.) *Theorizing about Intercultural Communication* 149–171. Thousand Oaks, CA: Sage.

Cai, D. A. and Fink, E. L. (2002) Conflict style differences between individualists and collectivists. *Communication Monographs* 69: 67–87.

Canary, D. and Lakey, S.G. (2006) Managing conflict in a competent manner: A mindful look at events that matter. In J. Oetzel and S. Ting-Toomey (eds.) *The Sage Handbook of Conflict Communication* 185–210. Thousand Oaks, CA: Sage.

Carl, D., Gupta, V. and Javidan, M. (2004) Power distance. In R. House, P. Hanges, M. Javidan, P. Dorfman and V. Gupta (eds.) *Culture, leadership, and organizations: The GLOBE study of 62 societies.* Thousand Oaks, CA: Sage, pp. 513–563.

Clarke, C. and Lipp, G.D. (1998) *Danger and Opportunity: Resolving Conflict in U.S.-based Japanese Subsidiaries.* Yarmouth, Maine: Intercultural Press.

Crawshaw, R., Culpeper, J., Leech, G., Jones, B. and Harrison, J. (2007) *Pragmatics and Intercultural Communication.* Lancaster, UK: Economic and Social Research Council/Polaris House. Retrieved. 4 July 4 2007 from http://www.lancs.ac.uk/fass/projects/pic/index.htm.

Culpeper, J. (2005) Impoliteness and entertainment in the television quiz show: The Weakest Link. *Journal of Politeness Research* 1: 35–72.

Culpeper, J., Bousfield, D. and Wichman, A. (2003) Impoliteness revisited: With special reference to dynamic and prosodic aspects. *Journal of Pragmatics* 35: 1545–1579.

Ellet, W. (2007) *The Case Study Handbook.* Boston, MA: Harvard Business School Press.

Emrich, C., Denmark, F. and Den Hartog, D. (2004) Cross-cultural differences in gender egalitarianism: Implications for societies, organizations, and leaders. In R. House, P. Hanges, M. Javidan, P. Dorfman and V. Gupta (eds.) *Culture, Leadership, and Organizations: The GLOBE Study of 62 Societies* 343–394. Thousand Oaks, CA: Sage.

Goffman, E. (1967) *Interaction Ritual: Essays on Face-to-Face Behavior.* Garden City, NY: Anchor Books.

Gudykunst, W. B. (ed.) (2003) *Cross-Cultural and Intercultural Communication.* Thousand Oaks, CA: Sage.

Gudykunst, W. B. (ed.) (2005) *Theorizing about Intercultural Communication.* Thousand Oaks, CA: Sage.

Haugh, M. (2005) The importance of 'place' in Japanese politeness: Implications for cross--cultural and intercultural analyses. *Intercultural Pragmatics* 2: 41–68.

Haugh, M. (2007) Emic conceptualizations of (im)politeness and face in Japanese: Implications for the discursive negotiation of second language learner identities. *Journal of Pragmatics* 39: 657–680.

Hofstede, G. (2001) Culture's Consequences: Comparing Values, Behaviours, Institutions, and Organizations across Cultures (2nd edn.) Thousand Oaks, CA: Sage.

Holtgraves, T. (2002) Language as Social Action: Social Psychology and Language Use. Mahwah, NJ: Lawrence Erlbaum.

House, R., Hanges, P., Javidan, M., Dorfman, P. and Gupta, V. (eds.) (2004) *Culture, Leadership, and Organizations: The GLOBE Study of 62 Societies.* Thousand Oaks, CA: Sage.

Keyton, J. and Shockley-Zalabak, P. (2004) *Case Studies for Organizational Communication.* Los Angeles, CA: Roxbury.

Langer, E. (1989) *Mindfulness.* Reading, MA: Addison-Wesley.

Langer, E. (1997) *The Power of Mindful Learning.* Reading, MA: Addison-Wesley.

Levinson, S. (1992) Activity types and language. In P. Drew and J. Heritage (eds.) *Talk at Work* 66–100. Cambridge: Cambridge University Press.

Lim, T. (1994) Facework and interpersonal relationships. In S. Ting-Toomey (ed.) *The Challenge of Facework* 209–229. Albany, NY: State University of New York Press.

Markus, H. R. and Kitayama, S. (1991) Culture and self: Implication for cognition, emotion, and motivation. *Psychological Review* 98: 224–253.

McCann, R. and Honeycutt, J. (2006) A cross-cultural analysis of imagined. interactions. *Human Communication Research* 32: 274–301.

Merkin, R. (2006) Power distance and facework strategies. *Journal of Intercultural Communication Research* 35: 139–160.

Oetzel, J. G. and Ting-Toomey, S. (2003) Face concerns in interpersonal conflict: A cross-cultural empirical test of the face-negotiation theory. *Communication Research* 30: 599–624.

Oetzel, J. G., Ting-Toomey, S., Masumoto, T., Yokochi, Y., Pan, X, Takai, J. and Wilcox, R. (2001) Face behaviors in interpersonal conflicts: A cross-cultural comparison of Germany, Japan, China, and the United. States. *Communication Monographs* 68: 235–258.

Oetzel, J., Ting-Toomey, S., Yokochi, Y., Masumoto, T. and Takai, J. (2000) A typology of facework behaviors in conflicts with best friends and relative strangers. *Communication Quarterly* 48: 397–419.

Park. H.S. and Guan, X. (2006) The effects of national culture and face concerns on intention to apologize: A comparison of the USA and China. *Journal of Intercultural Communication Research* 35: 183–204.

Philipsen, G. and Coutu, L. (2005) The ethnography of speaking. In K. Fitch and R. Sanders (eds.) *Handbook of Language and Social Interaction* 355–379. Mahwah, NJ: Lawrence Erlbaum.

Schnurr, S., Marra, M. and Holmes, J. (2007) Being (im)polite in New Zealand workplaces: Maori and Pakeha leaders. *Journal of Pragmatics* 39: 712–729.

Smith, P. B., Dugan, S., Peterson, M. F. and Leung, K. (1998) Individualism, collectivism and the handling of disagreement: A 23 country study. *International Journal of Intercultural Relations* 22: 351–367.

Spencer-Oatey, H. (2002) Managing rapport in talk: Using rapport sensitive incidents to explore the motivational concerns underlying the management of relations. *Journal of Pragmatics* 34: 529–545.

Spencer-Oatey, H. (2005) (Im)politeness, face and perceptions of rapport: Unpacking their bases and interrelationships. *Journal of Politeness Research* 1: 95–119.

Storti, C. (2001) *Old World/New World.* Yarmouth, ME: Intercultural Press.

Ting-Toomey, S. (1988) Intercultural conflicts: A face-negotiation theory. In Y. Y. Kim and W. Gudykunst (eds.) *Theories in Intercultural Communication* 213–235. Newbury Park, CA: Sage.

Ting-Toomey, S. (2004) Translating conflict face-negotiation theory into practice. In D. Landis, J. Bennett and M. Bennett (eds.) *Handbook of Intercultural Training* (3rd edn.) 217–248. Thousand Oaks, CA: Sage.

Ting-Toomey, S. (2005) The matrix of face: An updated. face-negotiation theory. In W. B. Gudykunst (ed.) *Theorizing about Intercultural Communication* 71–92. Thousand Oaks, CA: Sage.

Ting-Toomey, S. and Cole, M. (1990) Intergroup diplomatic communication: A face-negotiation perspective. In F. Korzenny and S. Ting-Toomey (eds.) *Communicating for Peace: Diplomacy and Negotiation across Cultures* 77–95. Newbury Park, CA: Sage.

Ting-Toomey, S., Gao, G., Trubisky, P., Yang, Z., Kim, H. S., Lin, S. L. and Nishida, T. (1991) Culture, face maintenance, and styles of handling interpersonal conflict: A study in five cultures. *The International Journal of Conflict Management* 2: 275–296.

Ting-Toomey, S. and Kurogi, A. (1998) Facework competence in intercultural conflict. *International Journal of Intercultural Relations* 22: 187–225.

Ting-Toomey, S., and Oetzel, J. G. (2001) *Managing intercultural conflict effectively.* Thousand Oaks, CA: Sage.

Ting–Toomey, S. and Takai, J. (2006) Explaining intercultural conflict. In J. Oetzel and S. Ting-Toomey (eds.) *The Sage Handbook of Conflict Communication* 691–723. Thousand Oaks, CA: Sage.

Tracy, K. (2005) Reconstructing communicative practices: action-implicative discourse analysis. In K. Fitch and R. Sanders (eds.) *Handbook of Language and Social Interaction* 301–339. Mahwah, NJ: Lawrence Erlbaum.

Tracy, K. and Tracy, S.J. (1998) Rudeness at 911: reconceptualizing face and face-attack. *Human Communication Research* 25: 225–251.

Triandis, H. (1995) *Individualism and Collectivism.* Boulder, CO: Westview Press.

Triandis, H. (2002) Individualism and collectivism. In M. Gannon and K. Newman (eds.) *Handbook of Cross-cultural Management* 16–45. New York: Lawrence Erlbaum.

Turner, J.H. (2002) *Face to Face: Toward a Sociological Theory of Interpersonal Behaviour.* Stanford, CA: Stanford University Press.

Zhang, Y.B., Harwood, J. and Hummert, M.L. (2005) Perceptions of conflict management styles in Chinese intergenerational dyads. *Communication Monographs* 72: 71–91.

13
Face in the holistic and relativistic society

Tae-Seop Lim

13.1. Introduction

While research to date on face has advanced our understanding of politeness and interpersonal interactions, particularly in Western societies, much of it has inadvertently overshadowed elements of face that are crucial in other societies. In their self-claimed 'universal' theory of politeness, for instance, Brown and Levinson (1978, 1987) grossly reduced the rich concept of face to two simplistic elements: positive and negative face. Moreover, their Anglo-centric model, where humans are assumed to be individualistic and rational, has led many researchers to a false belief that face is an issue of two individuals who are engaged in a particular social interaction.

In Korea, face is influenced by not only the relationship between the partners but also their relative positions in broader social networks or the whole society. Thus, people of different genders, ages, and statuses have different types and degrees of face need. Furthermore, the concept of face is highly differentiated so that faces of people of different social standings are often referred to with different terms. *Che-myun* is used for grown-ups or in more formal situations; *Naht* and *Ul-gul* are used for young adults or in less formal situations; *Mo-yahng-sae* is used among people of high status in a formal situation; *Che-Mo* and *Che-Sihn* are used for older adults; and *Myun-Mohk* is used by those who failed to meet the expectations of others. All these terms, however, share the same basic meaning: the dignified public image that one has to sustain to function properly as the occupant of the particular position in the society. To understand Korean concept of face more accurately, one needs to look into the relativistic way of life in Korea, and its ideological basis, the holistic worldview.

13.2. The holistic worldview and cognitive relativity

Korea, like most other East Asian countries, is a relativist society that takes a holistic approach to the world. Lim and Giles (2007) and Lim, Allen, Burrell and Kim (2006) claim that Eastern societies are not simply collectivistic but holistic, and consequently their cultures are much more relativistic than the North American and certain European cultures. They argue that the fundamental difference between these two societies lies in their approaches to the outside world: Easterners approach the world holistically, whereas most Westerners see the world analytically.

The fact that Asians hold holistic attitudes toward the outside world was observed early on. Oliver (1971), in the discussion of the rhetorical tradition of the East, argues that ethos in ancient India does not arise from special merits of the individuals' but from their quality of representation of their family, their community, and their caste. Gudykunst and Kim (1984) also observe that the Asian attitude towards speech and rhetoric is characteristically a holistic one; the words are inseparable from the total communication context including the personal characters of the parties involved and the nature of the relationships between them. Asians, in other words, do not break down the quality of others into a set of isolated characteristics but tend to generate one global judgement based on the holistic impression (Garrett, 1993; Combs, 2004). Matsumura (1984) and Nishida (1996) observe the same tendency in Japanese and claim that Japanese believe that nature should be understood holistically. Lim *et al.* (2006) report that holism manifests itself in virtually all aspects of Koreans' lives. One of the most frequently mentioned characteristics of Asian business people is their inability to distinguish business from personal relationships. To those who are accustomed to analytic thinking, business and relationship are two different elements; but to those who are programmed to think holistically, not only business but every aspect of their lives cannot be isolated from their relationships. Collectivism observed by Hofstede (1980) is simply a manifestation of this holistic approach in the organisational setting. Holists always see their organisation as a whole and themselves as its parts, and thus put the organisation before themselves.

To understand the influence of holistic worldviews on face and face-related behaviours, one has to pay more attention to the relations among the parts constituting a whole. When systems theorists (e.g. Bertalanffy, 1969) claim that the 'whole is greater than the sum of its parts', they mean this whole to be a product of the relational forces among the parts. The relations governing parts of a whole have three distinct characteristics: prescriptive, whole-oriented, and complementary. First, the relations pre-empt and precede the parts. Relations exist even before members join the whole and one joining a whole simply means that one fills in a slot in the web of prescribed relations. Thus, members are not free to negotiate about their relations but required to take up whatever is assigned to them. Second, a relation is prescribed in line with the purpose of the whole. The relations governing two members are not about the two individuals, but about their roles to help the whole achieve its goals. Thus, relations are not interpersonal orientations but the members' co-orientations towards the whole. Finally, the relations in a whole are mostly complementary. A complementary relationship here literally refers to a relationship where parties perform different functions that complement each other to facilitate the whole to accomplish its goal.

These characteristics of the relations in the holistic society instil 'a tendency to view the world relatively vis-à-vis their members' (Lim and Giles, 2007). Holistic people perceive, think, and behave relatively. First, they perceive themselves as well as others relatively. Persons are seen not as individuals having absolute qualities, but as the occupants of relative positions that are differentiated based on the functions they serve. Thus, the perceptions of holistic people always tend to maximise differences among themselves (Goldstein and Tamura, 1975). Second, people in the holistic society think relatively. They do not believe in universal logic or absolute standards. Instead, they tend to think that as different cases are in different circumstances, they should be treated differently from each other. Similarly, holistic people believe that human lives are largely dictated by the situations and persons of different positions or in different relations are in different situations; thus, different standards and logics are to be applied to different people. Third, members of holistic societies behave relatively to the situation. Their behaviours differ noticeably dependent on whom they are interacting with and especially in terms of whether they are in- or out-group members. They also differentiate private and public situations and vary their ways of behaving accordingly.

13.3. Characteristics of face and facework in the holistic and relativistic society

The holistic approach to the world and high relativity in perception, cognition and behaviour lead Koreans as well as many of their neighbours to manifest complicated face-related behaviours. First, holism requires them to be concerned with the whole social network and their respective positions in it. Face then is not what is pertinent to the given individual or interaction but something that is configured in the context of the complicated network of relationships. Thus, face in the holistic society is pervasive, holistically assessed, public, global and long-term. Second, relativism leads people to maximise the differences between them. Thus, face is not what is endowed equally to everyone but something that is allotted relatively and complementarily.

Face is pervasive

Earlier researchers of face tend to limit the focus of face to a matter between individuals who are engaged in interaction. For example, Goffman (1967) conceptualises face as positive self-image claimed by the line others assume one has taken 'during a particular contact'. Brown and Levinson's (1987) politeness theory is about the interaction between two individuals where one performs a face threatening act. Face, however, goes far beyond social contacts and permeates virtually all aspects of living. Face influences what to buy and own, where to live, what to drive, who to associate with, what school to go to, which occupation to choose, how to adorn oneself, and how much to donate – to list just a few. Particularly in the relativistic society, these types of non-interaction-specific face are often considered more important than interaction-specific face. Face in this society even shapes people's private life and unobserved actions, for anything they do has the potential to be known to the public later.

Lim (1994, 2004) examined the complex nature of Korean face through two empirical studies. The first was to identify face-related values or 'positive social attributes' (Goffman, 1967). He interviewed 62 adults (21 young adults, 23 middle-aged, 19 elders) and asked four different questions:

- 'When would Koreans think they lost face?' (face loss situation)

- 'What do Koreans say or do to gain face?' (face gain situation)

- 'What do Koreans say or do to support the other's face?' (face support situation)

- 'What do Koreans say or do to threaten the other's face?' (face threat situation).

The study generated a total of 1509 situations, which went through three steps of collapsing processes. First, within the same situation (e.g. face loss situation) the items having the same propositional content were collapsed together. For example, 'when I don't know the answer to the questions asked by others' and 'when I can't answer to a question, because I didn't know what I was supposed to know' have the same propositional content – the situation in which one lacks the knowledge that one is supposed to have. Second, across different situations (i.e. face loss, face gain, face support and face threat) the items about the same object were combined together. For example, the items 'when I feel that my clothes look shabby' (face loss), 'wear nice clothes' (face gain), 'compliment on the other's clothes' (face support), and 'sneer at the other's clothes' (face threat) are all about the same object – clothes. Third, different objects that share the same nature of topic were collapsed together. For example, 'when I went out with the zipper of the trousers open', 'walked on the street not knowing the stockings were torn', and 'wear good shoes even though socks have holes' mention different objects but are about the same topic – appearance.

After these three-step collapsing procedures, the number of face-related items was reduced to 152, which went through a process of categorisation. The categorisation process was different from the collapsing procedures in that it was based not on the surface-level similarities but on the deeper-level commonalities. Items were categorised based on what positive social value they represented in accordance with Goffman's definition of face. Because the process inevitably involved subjective judgements, an effort was made to secure higher objectivity by employing two different raters. The first rater read through the 152 items, and sorted them by combining the items that were judged to represent the same social value. The assortment process generated 58 categories. The second rater was given the 58 categories and 152 items, and asked to assign the items to the categories. The two raters yielded 88% of agreement, Cohen's kappa being .87. The two raters resolved their disagreements by discussing the items one by one and the groupings were readjusted, but the number of categories remained the same. Then, the raters together selected the most representative item for each category. Table 1 shows 58 face-related social values and their representative items. The representative items were rephrased so that all of them would fit in with the situation of losing face.

The second study was to explore the structure of face or to investigate how the 58 items cluster together. Lim asked 356 subjects (39 teens, 170 young adults, 111 middle-aged, 36 older adults) how much face they would feel had been lost if something that could endanger each of 58 face-related social values had occurred. An exploratory factor analysis yielded thirteen initial factors that represented thirteen basic Korean elements of face: heedful, appropriate, trustworthy, discreet, reasonable, lavish, elegant, prosperous, successful, competent, autonomous, respected, and accepted. A second-level factor analysis was performed to identify higher-level components of face structure. The analysis showed that the thirteen basic elements of face could be subsumed under five broader categories of face: decency, integrity, nobility, capability, and adequacy (see Table 13.1 below).

Of the five dimensions, 'adequacy', which is concerned with the quality of one's function as the player of a certain social role, is the only one that is usually claimed through interaction with definite partners. This dimension, which comprises 'competence', 'autonomy', 'respect', and 'acceptance', is similar to what Brown and Levinson (1987) see as positive and negative face wants; other dimensions are pursued regardless of the presence of the interaction partners or third party observers.

'Decency' is concerned with the way one presents oneself in public, and comprises 'heedful' conduct and 'appropriate' behaviour. To maintain the image of a 'heedful' person one has to be prudent, neat and tidy, clean, upright, poised and mindful. Speaking to the other with food stuck in one's teeth, walking on the street with the flies open, running into others when not freshened up, being caught by police crossing the street against the traffic light, losing composure in a formal situation, or saying something that is improper for a person of one's social standing can cause loss of one's heedful face. To present self as an 'appropriate' person, one's behaviours must conform to social norms and gender roles and should not be vulgar or base. Doing something that others normally would not do (e.g. a middle-aged man working on the street without a shirt), not acting like a man or woman (e.g. a father carrying his baby on his back with the baby-carrying cloth), saying an obscenity, or reading dirty books can easily cause face loss.

'Integrity' is related to the inner states of mind that guide one's external self-presentation. In other words, it is the quality of one's character that can be inferred from one's behaviour. Persons with high integrity are expected to maintain 'trustworthy', 'discreet', and 'reasonable' behaviour. The image of being trustworthy is maintained only when one is presented to be modest, consistent, reliable, responsible, and faithful. Turning out to be a braggart by failing to do what one has talked big about, saying one thing and doing another, and betraying others' confidence all damage one's 'trustworthy' face. To be perceived

5 Second level Factors	13 Initial Factors	58 Face Wants	Representative case phrased in the face-loss situation
	Discreet	Truthful	When I turned out to be an ostentatious person.
		Practising what one preaches	When others saw me doing what I have always said is wrong.
		Not Self-opinionated	When what I insisted to be right turned out to be wrong.
	Reasonable	Reciprocating	When I was seen as a person who does not pay back to others.
		Large-hearted	When others saw me being overly fussy about trifles.
		Ethical	When others saw me act unethically.
		Courteous	When I was seen as a discourteous person.
Nobility	Lavish	Generous	When I made a smaller monetary contribution than others.
		Giving	When I realised that I was not as hospitable as I was supposed to be.
		Not meagre	When I realised that I ate voraciously while having a meal with others.
		Self-sufficient	When others paid for me because I did not have enough money.
	Elegant	Appearance being graceful	When my appearance was not as good as the appearances of others.
		Companion being Good-looking	When my companion did not look as good as the companion of the other.
		Taste being Impeccable	When I realised that the other had a better taste than I.
		Clothes being Refined	When I realised that I was wearing worse clothes than others.
	Prosperous	Well-educated	When it turned out to be that I did not have as good an educational background as the other.

5 Second level Factors	13 Initial Factors	58 Face Wants	Representative case phrased in the face-loss situation
		Family being Prosperous	When my siblings or children were not as successful as those of the other.
		Being stately	When I felt like a loser in front of a superior person.
		Affluent	When the other's house looked much better than mine.
		Helpful to others	When I could not help the other due to the lack of resources.
		Coming up to others' expectations	When I realised that I failed to live up to others' expectations.
Capability	Successful	Able	When it turned out to be that my social abilities were not as good as those of the other.
		Well-recognised	When I realised that I did not get other's recognition in my own area.
		Socially successful	When I turned out to be not as socially successful as the other.
Adequacy	Competent	Fulfilling	When others found out that I could not successfully carry out my assignments.
		Not failing	When I failed in the job others entrusted to me.
		Knowledge-able	When I did not know the answer to the question the other thought I knew about.
		Being able to defend one's rights	When others saw me not being able to stand up against a person who insulted me.
		Not being incompetent	When others saw me being reprimanded by a superior.
	Autonomous	Not being a liability to others	When my family got blamed for my own wrongdoing.

5 Second level Factors	13 Initial Factors	58 Face Wants	Representative case phrased in the face-loss situation
		Not begging for help	When I had to beg for help when the other kept giving the cold shoulder to me.
		Self-determining	When I realised that my will was controlled by the other.
		Self-governing	When others saw me under a constant supervision of another person.
		Self-reliant	When others found out that I was sponging off my parents although I was old enough to support them.
	Respected	Listened to	When others laughed at what I said.
		Not ignored	When others ignored my opinions.
		Not interfered with	When others interfered with my own business.
		Position being Acknowledged	When my authority was violated.
	Accepted	Cared for	When others did not care about me.
		Not alienated	When others left me out of their conversation in a social gathering.
		Not neglected	When others found out that I was shut out by the people around me.
		Not rejected	When the other gave me an outright denial.
		Not excluded	When others excluded me from important decision-making.

as 'discreet', one must be trustful and practise what one preaches, and should not be self-opinionated. Turning out to be an ostentatious person, doing what one has always said is wrong, or one's opinionated claim turning out to be mistaken will surely cause face loss. The wants for 'trustworthy' and 'discreet' face are what drives Asians to be extremely careful about what they say, often making them keep silence or withdraw. To keep up the image of being 'reasonable', one has to be reciprocating, large-hearted, ethical, and courteous. Those who do not pay back to others, are overly fussy about trifles, act unethically, or behave discourteously may not be able to maintain their 'reasonable' face.

'Nobility' is concerned with the relative position in the society. It is not allowed to every member of the society, but restricted to those who have a higher social and/or economic status. Naturally, nobility comprises 'lavish' behaviour, 'elegant' appearance and 'prosperous' economic conditions. To present themselves as lavish, Koreans have to demonstrate that they are generous, giving, self-sufficient, and not meagre. Thus, they always attempt to make as big a monetary contribution as did others of similar social standing, to be as hospitable as possible when treating others, not to eat too much when having meals with others, and to open up their wallets ahead of others to pay for what they ate or did together. Koreans set aside a big amount of money to sustain their 'lavish' face, which is often called 'budget for nobility maintenance'. To be 'elegant', one has to keep one's appearance graceful, partner good-looking, taste impeccable, and clothes refined. Koreans spend a lot of money adorning themselves and their family members, care very much about physical attractiveness of their dates, frequent expensive shops and restaurants, and love to wear name brand clothes. The want for 'elegant' face is what makes Koreans avid shoppers. To keep up the image of being prosperous, Koreans want to show off that they are well-educated, their family prosperous, their attitudes stately, their life affluent, their existence helpful to others and their overall accomplishment coming up to expectation. Koreans' zeal for education has a lot to do with their 'prosperous' face, which motivates parents to push their children to the limit. Koreans love to talk about their successful relatives and buy the most expensive automobiles and houses that their finances allow.

'Capability' is related to socially proven abilities rather than the actual competence one possesses. Koreans often say that he or she is a 'person of capability' to mean that the person is able, socially successful, and getting social recognition. One loses this face when it turns out that one's abilities are not as good as those of others, one is not as successful as one's siblings or friends, and one does not get the recognition of others in one's own area. To maintain this face, Koreans often exaggerate or lie about the positions they hold in their organisations.

Face is holistically assessed

Major concerns for individualists engaged in interaction are self and the other, so Brown and Levinson (1987) posit that people assess threats to face based on the relationship between themselves and their interaction partners such as the social distance and the power difference. However, holists understand that a relationship includes three parties: self, the other, and the third party or 'the seken' (Inoue, 1982), which refers to the world, the reference group, or the whole where the two parties belong together. For instance, the relationship between spouses has three parties: husband, wife, and the whole family; and in this relationship the family, not self, is the centre or anchor.

Face wants or threats in the holistic society, therefore, are calculated not simply based on the relationship between the two partners, but based on the triangular relationship between the two and their reference group, the whole. For example, the relationship between the exact same spouses will change as they grow older in the whole family network. Although the power and intimacy relationships between the two may remain the same, as they get to have children and then grandchildren, their status in the whole increases, so they need to give each other more face. Thus, Goldstein and Tamura's (1975) finding that older Japanese spouses use more formal address terms and language style towards each other is not surprising.

This holistic assessment works for virtually all relationships including the superior-subordinate relationship. Top managers cannot treat mid-range managers in the same way mid-range managers would treat their supervisees as mid-range managers hold certain degrees of status in the whole organisation. The higher the position of a subordinate is, the more respectful language the superior uses. The same phenomenon can be observed among students. As age matters a lot in Korea, students one year older (or one year ahead) take the position of a superior. Among middle or high school students, the one a year older would not care much about face of the younger, but college students would as the younger students have their own status as adults (Lim and Giles, 2007).

In dealing with their own children, parents have to be more concerned with their face as they grow older. When children are really young, parents usually address them with nicknames or terms of endearment, but as they grow older, parents tend to choose less intimate address terms. For example, when they become teens, most parent stop using nicknames and begin to use first names only. When they get married, parents go for much more formal address terms; and when the children have their own children, the elderly parents use respectful yet affective address terms that can be translated as 'kids' dad' or 'kids' mummy'. In addition to the children's age and position in the family, their position in the whole society influences parents' assessment of their face. To refer to or address a child who has a doctorate, Parents often use 'Dr. Lim,' or 'our Dr. Lim' to make it more affective. The same goes for other higher ranked relatives: uncles and aunts or older siblings would use increasingly respectful language towards their nephews and nieces or younger sibling as the latter grow older or climb up the social ladder.

Friends and equals also pay more attention to each other's face as they become older and get higher positions in the society. High school buddies will use extremely informal language towards each other until they graduate from college; but as they get married and have children, they turn to more respectful language; when they become established in their respective areas, they use very respectful language including such address terms as 'Professor Lim' and 'Executive Kim'. Equals who become acquainted as grown-ups do not use first names to address each other; instead, they use terms that show the family or social positions such as 'Jay's mother' or 'Lady Kim.'

Face is public

Although Brown and Levinson (1987) and other politeness researchers define face as a 'public' image, they tend to limit the scope of their research to the interaction between two persons. Interactions are public in the sense that they are not private, but they are not public in that they are just between two partners. Face in the holistic society is literally a public image and 'public' here refers to 'being known to a mass of people or at least to some members of the whole where they belong'. Face in Korea is often understood as something you need to face the public without shame.

Politeness in transient interaction is not regarded lightly, but is not the most crucial part of facework in the holistic society. When the other party acts presumptuously, one may feel humiliated or insulted. This will temporarily hurt one's wants to be respected, autonomous, included, or perceived competent, but will not permanently damage one's face as long as this is kept between the two concerned. A serious problem occurs when this offence occurs in presence of others or when the incident is known to others later. Then people will think one is disrespected, submissive, unwanted, and incompetent, in sum, inadequate. Breach of politeness rules that occurred privately may have more potential to damage the face of the offender than that of the offended. Holists value 'integrity' face no less than 'adequacy' face, and improperly addressing the other's 'adequacy' face results in loss of one's own 'integrity' face. One main reason for East Asians' hyper-politeness is to promote their own face by overly supporting the other's face.

East Asians are very sensitive to the existence of a potential third party when they interact with another party. When there is a possibility that what will happen between two people will be seen by or known to others, they tend to amplify the threats to face. Nevertheless, compared to Americans, Koreans are much more direct when they make requests or criticisms. Circumlocution is often regarded as a sign of dishonesty or twisted mind, and compliments are often considered flattery. In private interaction, therefore, Koreans may act less politely than Americans, particularly to those whom they feel comfortable around such as friends or inferiors. They assume that these partners would not take their action as face-significant. However, when they think the interaction may go public, they consider everything face-relevant and become extremely careful not to offend the other's face.

In the holistic society, parents do not hesitate to scold their children and superiors are not afraid of finding fault with their inferiors. The scolding and criticism can be blunt and very insulting when given privately. However, when there is a third party present, superiors usually do not perform these face-threatening acts; when they have to carry the acts out, they do so with extreme care not to demolish face of the inferiors. Inferiors in this society are accustomed to getting scolded, criticised, or bossed around by their superiors, so they would not take a harsh treatment as face-threat unless it goes public. When the same act is performed in presence of others, particularly their own inferiors or equals, it becomes a totally different story: they will take it as a great offence to their face and accuse the superior of being inconsiderate.

Because of this public nature of face, Koreans go great length to protect their face when they have people from their whole around. For instance, husbands who are usually submissive to their wives often act as if they were in charge of their relationship when they are with others. He gives orders to her in front of others just to maintain his public image of being manly, and will beg for her forgiveness when they are left alone. Taking orders or begging forgiveness from his wife in private does not threaten his face, but he will have hard time facing others if it is known to them.

To holists, not all witnesses have the same significance as a third party: total strangers are not considered a legitimate third party (Gao 1996). Those who belong to one or more wholes together with themselves are considered a third party. Koreans, therefore, act carefree in front of total strangers and do not hesitate to reveal their real selves.

Facework is global and long-term

Brown and Levinson (1987) and most North American researchers tend to centre their facework research about momentary interaction where two individuals attempt to accomplish their specific action goals. This may reflect that the Anglo-American concept of facework as somewhat transient and local. In the holistic society, face is mostly understood as a long-term relational issue. When performing a particular action, holists are less concerned with whether they accomplish the intended action goal than whether they act appropriately to the given relationship. Soldiers in war fight to win not just a battle but the war. Skilled commanders would not plan or execute a battle for its own sake but would always think of the long-term effect of the battle on the war. Face to holists is not an emotional rollercoaster they experience during a one-time contact, but a lofty tower they are building over a lifetime. Like experienced commanders in war, well-socialised holists would put any interaction in a much broader and much longer relational context and try to come up with facework that will best serve the purpose.

This does not mean that holists do not care about the efficiency of their actions. They do, but they always think also of the side effects of their actions. When the side effects are deemed to have relational significance, i.e. a potential to damage the relationship, they give up on the actions. To them, actions may fail but relationships must not be ruined. In the holistic society, showing one's concern for the relationship itself is facework for oneself: it enhances one's desirability as a co-part of the whole. In this society, giving up on an action goal often entails a gain on the relational goal.

Of the three types of facework proposed by Goffman (1967), East Asians perform more aggressive facework than avoidance or corrective facework. They build up their face not just by avoiding offending others when they want others to do something for them, but by actively presenting a desirable self to others. Goffman refers to this as gaining face 'through good deeds'.

Koreans do a variety of things to demonstrate their desirability. To show they are decent, they try to present themselves as neatly as possible and keep their houses as clean as possible; to show they are persons of integrity, they talk and act with care and behave courteously and reasonably; to show they are noble, they make hefty contributions, treat others to extravagant dinners or parties, and buy expensive automobiles, houses, clothes, and accessories; to show they are successful, they develop various job titles and hand out business cards to acquaintances just to impress. Some of these efforts may be naturally performed good deeds, but others may be artificially orchestrated feats. In either case, when Koreans say facework, they usually refer to these types of proactive facework rather than reactive strategies used to maximise the efficiency of a particular interaction.

For Japanese, facework begins with the acknowledgement of one's place in the social ladder. Japanese maintain face by 'following social conventions that keep one's role in the hierarchical order' (Nadamitsu, 2001: 21). In other words, acting appropriately to the position one is holding in the whole network of relationships is the main way of maintaining or promoting one's face. Appropriateness presupposes paying proper attention to others' face by being humble and modest, and often requires giving up on particular action goals. Japanese then also see facework as more globally-oriented than locally-oriented.

In the holistic society, facework is not a one-shot exchange, but is a process in which no definite beginning or end exists. People's face-related behaviours will be interpreted in line with the same kind of behaviors they have shown previously. For example, if people have to offer a reception which is not as lavish as the ones they used to offer before, they might feel the 'face burning' sensation. Their face can be recuperated when they prepare a better reception next time.

The impact of certain conducts on one's face does not expire. You may do a wrongdoing but feel relieved when you see nobody around you, for you think your trouble is over. However, in the event that evidence for the misconduct is found later, you may lose even more face than you would lose right after the wrongdoing. In Korea there are quite a few celebrities who lost their face greatly due to something they did when they were young and careless. There is no double jeopardy law in face punishment: one may lose face over and over again due to the same misconduct, and the later loss can be even greater.

Face is relative and complementary

Brown and Levinson (1987) and most politeness researchers assume that all fully functioning individuals have inherently the same kinds and degrees of face wants and only situational factors such as relational distance and power difference cause variations. However, East Asian researchers (e.g., Ho, 1976; Hu, 1944; Jia, 1997) have repeatedly claimed in unison that not all kinds of face are endowed to everyone in the society. Face in the holistic society is not something that is distributed freely to anyone, but is something that is rendered to those who have acquired the social positions that deserve it. Differential endowment of face, however, does not bring about inequality as, unlike power, face is not privilege but liability. It is similar to tax in that people of different positions are imposed different kinds and amounts.

Lim (1994) examined the effects of gender and age as well as relational distance and power difference on the degree of face needs. Using the 58 face-related value items developed from his face structure studies detailed in section 3.1 above, he asked subjects how much face they would feel lost in each of the 58 face loss situations, and compared their responses across two situational variables and two demographic variables. Lim reported that social distance and power difference mainly influenced the needs for 'adequacy' face, which is similar to Brown and Levinson's positive and negative faces. Age influenced 'decency' and 'nobility': in both dimensions older persons manifested more needs. Gender affected 'decency', 'integrity', and 'nobility': males had more wants for integrity while females showed higher needs for decency and nobility. Lim's (1994) research suggests that people in the holistic society are responsible for the kind and amount of face that is pertinent to their relative positions in the whole.

The countries influenced by Confucianism tend to differentiate the roles between men and women, which requires different genders to be sensitive to different kinds of face. Confucianism has emphasised the trustworthiness of its gentlemen, and elegance and prudence of its ladies, which leads men to pursue integrity and women to go after nobility and decency. Koreans are allotted more face to protect as they grow older. High school students may need to protect their adequacy face but not their integrity, decency, successful, and nobility faces. College students might want to protect some sub-dimensions of integrity and girls may begin to put up their decency face. When they go out to the society and build careers, their integrity, decency, and successful faces will become significant to their lives. When they are more or less established, they will feel required to maintain their nobility face. Nobility face, of course, is not given to all mature adults; those who knowingly belong to lower classes are excused from wasting money to protect a face they actually do not hold. Some occupations like priests and professors are highly revered, so they are granted great amounts of most face types regardless of their gender, age, or socio-economic status. Certain wrongdoings that can be considered simple mistakes in others may damage face badly if they are done by these people.

Endnotes

1.   The table is adapted from Lim (2004).

References

Bertalanffy, L. (1969) *General Systems Theory: Foundations, Development, Applications.* New York: George Braziller.

Brown, P. and Levinson, S. (1987) *Politeness. Some Universals in Language Use.* Cambridge: Cambridge University Press.

Combs, S. (2004) The useless-/usefulness of argumentation: The Dao of disputation. *Argumentation And Advocacy* 41: 58–70.

Gao, G. (1996) Self and other: A Chinese perspective on interpersonal relationships. In W. B. Gudykunst, S. Ting-Toomey and T. Nishida (ed.) *Communication in Personal Relationships Across Cultures* 81–101. Thousand Oaks, CA: Sage.

Garrett, M. (1993) Pathos reconsidered from the perspective of classical Chinese rhetorical theories. *Quarterly Journal of Speech* 19: 58–70.

Goffman, E. (1967) *Interaction Ritual: Essays on Face-to-Face Behaviour.* New York: Doubleday Anchor.

Goldstein, B. Z. and Tamura, K. (1975) *Japan and America: A Comparative Study in Language and Culture.* Rutland, VT: Charles E. Tuttle.

Gudykunst, W. B. and Kim, Y.Y. (1984) *Communicating with Strangers: An Approach to Intercultural Communication.* Reading, MA: Addison-Wesley Publishing Co.

Ho, D. Y. F. (1976) On the Concept of Face. *American Journal of Sociology* 81: 867–884.

Hofstede, G. (1980) *Cultures Consequences: International Differences in Work-Related Values.* Beverly Hills, CA: Sage.

Hu, H. C. (1944) The Chinese concept of face. *American Anthropologist* 46: 45–64.

Inoue, C. (1982) *Manazashi no Ningen Kankei [Nonverbals in Japanese Human Relations]* Tokyo: Kodansha.

Jia, W. (1997/98) Facework as a Chinese conflict-preventative mechanism: A cultural/discourse analysis. *Intercultural Communication Studies* 7: 43–61.

Lim, T. (1994) The structure of face and the determinants of face needs in Korea. *Korean Journal of Journalism and Communication Studies* 32: 207–247.

Lim, T. (2004) Towards an Asian model of face. *Human Communication (Journal of the Pacific and Asian Communication Association)* 7: 53–66.

Lim, T., Allen, M., Burrell, N. and Kim, S. (2006) The relativity and salience of identity across cultures. Paper presented at the annual convention of the National Communication Association, San Antonio, TX.

Lim, T. and Giles, H (2007) Differences in American and Korean college students evaluation of one-year age differences. *Journal of Multilingual and Multicultural Development* 28: 349–364.

Matsumura, T. (1984) Nihonteki komyunikçshon to nihon no fûdo [Japanese communication and climate]. In M. A. Tsujimura (ed.) *Komyunikeçshon no Shakai Shinrigaku [Communication in Social Psychology]* 171–189. Tokyo: Tokyo University Press.

Nadamitsu, Y. (2001) East meets East: how Chinese perceive and interpret Japanese communicative behaviour. Paper presented at the annual convention of the Japanese Communication Association, Nagoya, Japan.

Nishida, T. (1996) Communication in personal relationships in Japan. In W. B. Gudykunst, S. Ting-Toomey and T. Nishida (eds.) *Communication in Personal Relationships Across Cultures* 102–121. Thousand Oaks, CA: Sage.

Oliver, R. (1971) *Communication and Culture in Ancient India and China.* Syracuse, New York: Syracuse University Press.

14

Finding face between *Gemeinschaft* and *Gesellschaft:* Greek perceptions of the in-group

Marina Terkourafi

14.1. Introducing the players

This paper attempts to flesh out an integrated theoretical proposal about the application of the notion of face to different socio-historical settings. Following a new definition of a universalising notion of face, I look to the field of sociology, and in particular to the work of the German sociologist Tönnies about *Gemeinschaft* and *Gesellschaft*, for a principled way to link the proposed abstract, universalising notion of face with its several, seemingly diverging, local interpretations. In the last part of this essay, I explore the explanatory potential of this proposal taking contemporary Greek society as a case-study.

Face at different levels of abstraction

The term 'face' with its two aspects, positive and negative, was introduced into linguistic theorising by Brown and Levinson ([1978] 1987) as one of two pillars, alongside rationality, of their theory of linguistic politeness. Brown and Levinson (1987: 61) acknowledge two sources for their definition of face: Goffman's notion of face (1967), and the English folk notion found in expressions such as 'saving/losing face' (cf. Ervin-Tripp, Nakamura and Guo, 1995).

The intimate relationship between the scientific and the English folk notions may well lie at the root of several shortcomings noted by researchers in their efforts to apply this notion to different cultural settings (e.g. Matsumoto, 1988; Rhodes, 1989; Bayraktaroğlu, 1991; Sifianou, 1992a; Nwoye, 1992; Mao, 1994). One way of remedying these shortcomings is by integrating further distinctions (for suggestions, see Nwoye, 1992; Mao, 1994). An alternative line, inspired by a distinction between first-order and second-order politeness first proposed by Watts, Ide and Ehlich (1992), has been taken by O'Driscoll (1996). O'Driscoll suggests that '[w]hat we need is a theoretical construct, not a notion which various societies invest with varying connotations' (1996: 8); in other words, a second-order notion of face, or Face2. With this suggestion in mind, in recent work I have proposed two defining properties of a universalising notion of Face2: the biological grounding of face in the dimension of approach versus withdrawal, and the intentionality of face, i.e. its aboutness (Terkourafi, 2007a).

The biological grounding of Face2 refers to its grounding in the dimension of approach/withdrawal, a dimension that goes well beyond the realm of the human (Davidson, 1992: 259). Approach or withdrawal result when a stimulus is evaluated as friendly or hostile respectively, before it is further identified as this or that type of stimulus. Variously referred to as positive versus negative 'valence' or 'affect', this dimension has been proposed as the common substratum of all human emotions, and associated with the pre-cognitive reactive level (Ortony, Norman, and Revelle, 2005: 179–182). The literature on human emotions is interspersed with observations highlighting the phylogenetically primary, universal, and pre-conscious nature of approach/ withdrawal. These properties make approach/withdrawal a natural candidate to serve as the basis for a universalising notion of Face2 'divorc[ed] from any ties to folk notions' (O'Driscoll, 1996: 8). The biological grounding of Face2 in approach/ withdrawal thus affords us with an explanation for its universality and dualism between positive (approach) and negative (withdrawal) aspects, without for that matter introducing an unwarranted hierarchy between these two aspects.

However, the property making Face2 uniquely human is its intentionality, understood as the distinguishing property of mental (as opposed to physical) phenomena of being *about* something, i.e. directed at an object (Brentano, [1874] 1981); Husserl, [1900] 1970). Beliefs, hopes, judgements, intentions, love and hatred all exhibit intentionality, in that they presuppose that which is being believed, hoped, judged, intended, loved or hated. Similarly, Face2 is intentional in that it presupposes an Other toward whom it is directed. Awareness of the Other, in turn, presupposes an awareness of the Self, known to emerge from around nine months onwards through joint attentional behaviours with the primary caretaker (Tomasello, 1999: 57ff.; Brinck, 2001).

The intentionality of Face2 guarantees that face is irreducibly relational. Without an Other to whom they may be directed, face concerns
cannot arise: it is impossible for an individual to 'have' face in isolation. To adapt the popular adage, face is 'in the eye of the beholder'. A
consequence of this is that Self will have several faces concurrently, as
many as there are Others involved in a situation. If I am interacting with
an interlocutor in front of an audience, I am (aware of) making a bid for
face not only in the eyes of my interlocutor, but also in the eyes of each
of the members of that audience taken separately and as a group; and
mutatis mutandis for each of them. Bids for face are always bi-
directional in this way. Self and Other in this context are not monolithic
entities co-extensive with the physical body but rather socio-
psychological constructs. Thus, in the physical presence of one participant, I may be simultaneously apprehending several Others, some of
whom I may be approaching while withdrawing from others. There is
nothing preventing the same instance of behaviour counting as approach
on one level and withdrawal on another, so long as these are directed
at different Others (Terkourafi, 2007a: 324–325).

From Face2 to Face1: Gemeinschaft *and* Gesellschaft *as mediating Discourses*

The biological grounding in approach/withdrawal and the intentionality of Face2 are all that is universal about face. Its culture- and situation-
specific contents are then filled in under particular socio-historical
circumstances, yielding distinct but motivated conceptualisations of
Face1.[1] In attempting to flesh out the situated contents of Face2 in different situations and cultures, the sociological notions of *Gemeinschaft*
and *Gesellschaft* offer a useful starting point. The German words for
'community' and 'society' respectively, *Gemeinschaft* and *Gesellschaft*
were first used to contrast two types of social organisation by sociologist Ferdinand Tönnies at the end of the 19th century. Since then, the
two terms have gained currency in the social sciences, such that any
attempt to translate them is bound to fall short of conveying their richness of content.

   Writing from 1880 to 1887, in the aftermath of the industrial revolu-
tion yet before 'full knowledge of the Marxian system…was…available'
([1887] 2001: 90), Tönnies was primarily interested in the different ways
in which individuals can relate to the overarching social groupings to
which they belong. The two modes of social existence that he describes
essentially correspond to the pre-industrial/rural (*Gemeinschaft*) and

industrial/urban (*Gesellschaft*). Tönnies's approach to his topic is distinctly historical: 'Community [*Gemeinschaft*] is old, Society [*Gesellschaft*] is new, both as an entity and as a term' (2001: 19). This allows him to view the household economy of *Gemeinschaft*, where goods are mutually possessed and used in common, as an integral part of – rather than a precondition for, as in Marx's scheme – the way social relationships are structured therein. Predicated upon bonds of blood (as in a family or clan), of place (as in geographical proximity), or of spirit (as in similarity of work or opinion), a *Gemeinschaft* is characterised by a network of personal relationships, common values and ideals, and a strong sense of belonging. It is ruled by consensus based on intimate knowledge of the Other, which makes explicit arbitration superfluous: 'true understanding is by its very nature silent because its content is fathomless and cannot be comprehended in words' (Tönnies, 2001: 35). The social bond found in *Gemeinschaft* is thus attributed 'real organic life' (Tönnies, 2001: 17), uniting people 'in spite of everything that separates them' (Tönnies, 2001: 52).

By contrast, in *Gesellschaft* people 'remain separate in spite of everything that unites them' (Tönnies, 2001: 52). Relationships in *Gesellschaft* are 'purely mechanical construction[s]' (Tönnies, 2001: 17) predicated upon rationality and a high degree of role differentiation, such that '[b]y a constantly repeated process of functional division and rational choice the individual is finally reduced to starkly equal, elementary units of labour, like atoms' (Tönnies, 2001: 57). In *Gesellschaft* goods are no longer mutually possessed and enjoyed but rather exchanged, the basic relationship being that between buyer and seller. More than just goods, labour itself becomes a commodity that may be exchanged for money, this 'abstract version [that Society produces] of itself' and invests with 'value' (Tönnies, 2001: 58) in the ultimate performative act of self-affirmation. Lacking the deeper intimacy that in *Gemeinschaft* guarantees consensus, *Gesellschaft* is ruled by contract, the result of 'two divergent individual wills intersecting at one point' (Tönnies, 2001: 58) contracted for the purposes of the exchange and cotemporaneous with it. Consequently, the natural law of *Gemeinschaft* is replaced by 'a skilled judge who weighs, measures and passes an *objective* judgement. All members of the public *have* to recognise this and behave accordingly' (Tönnies, 2001: 54; original emphasis). According to Tönnies:

> In this view of Society, all basic and natural relations between
> people become replaced by abstraction. [...] The relationship of all
> to all, both before and outside convention and contract, can be
> seen as potential enmity or latent war – against which all those

willed agreements stand out like so many pacts and peace
treaties. (Tönnies, 2001: 64–65)

This last comment is strongly reminiscent of Goffman's later notion of
the 'virtual offence' (Goffman, 1971: 95–187), upon which Brown and
Levinson based their theory: 'politeness…presupposes [a] potential for
aggression as it seeks to disarm it, and makes possible communication
between potentially aggressive parties' (Brown and Levinson, 1987: 1).
Exactly a century before the revised publication of their essay, Tönnies
had been led to much the same conclusion:

> [A]ll *conventional sociability* may be understood as analogous to
> the exchange of material goods. The primary rule is politeness, an
> exchange of words and courtesies where everyone appears to be
> concerned for everyone else and to be esteeming each other as
> equals. In fact everyone is thinking of himself and trying to push
> his own importance and advantages at the expense of all the rest.
> (Tönnies, 2001: 65; original emphasis)

The above comments lead to specific predictions regarding the role of
explicit linguistic negotiation in *Gemeinschaft* as opposed to *Gesellschaft*.
In the former, explicit linguistic negotiation should be minimal, commonality of origin and purpose guaranteeing shared understandings
and serving to amplify the content of indirect modes of communication,
the perpetuation of these indirect modes in turn strengthening the sense
of common belonging. In the latter, explicit linguistic negotiation should
be necessary to bridge the gap left by the lack of deeper intimacy. Such
negotiation will itself take the form of a linguistic contract that, like
money, is only meaningful against the backdrop of the Society that in-
stitutes it (cf. Werkhofer, 1992), and that, like all exchanges between a
seller and a buyer in which 'offer and acceptance by both sides must
exactly coincide' (Tönnies, 2001: 54), is predicated upon their rationality and the differentiation of their roles. George's (1990: 89–112) analysis of the different illocutionary interpretations of the same utterance
depending on the diverging pragmatic presuppositions of speakers from
the industrial North of Italy as opposed to the rural South provides
prima facie confirmation of these predictions as well as an apt example
of the usefulness of *Gemeinschaft* and *Gesselschaft* as analytical tools
in the analysis of discourse.

Seen in this light, *Gemeinschaft* and *Gesellschaft* constitute
larger Discourses, understood as 'interlocking web[s] of practices,
ideologies and social structures … [that] prefigure which practices and
interpretations are available and how practices and structures are un-

derstood' (Kiesling, 2006: 262). As competing Discourses guiding interpretation, *Gemeinschaft* and *Gesellschaft* in their pure, unmixed form are what Tönnies called 'normal types' (*Normaltypen*), that is, abstract concepts that can explain real social action, rather than reflecting the organisation of any existing social grouping. Because *Gemeinschaft* and *Gesellschaft* structure the interactional presuppositions of social actors, in actual fact they are mixed in various proportions, and shifts from one to the other are indeed possible, if not common (see sections 2.1 and 2.2 below).

The types of social organisation for which Tönnies coined the terms *Gemeinschaft* and *Gesellschaft* exhibit interesting parallels with situations analysed in contemporary sociolinguistics by contrasting strong (cf. *Gemeinschaft*) with weak (cf. *Gesellschaft*) network ties (after L. Milroy, 1980), and solidarity (cf. *Gemeinschaft*) with power (cf. *Gesellschaft*) (after Brown and Gilman, 1960). Yet there are some advantages to adopting Tönnies's terms which should overcome any Occam-ian reluctance to 'multiply [terms] beyond necessity'. First, although network ties and solidarity/power may be considered as enabling macro-level explanations, they are constituted at the micro-level through the actions of individual speakers and hearers (cf. J. Milroy, 1993). By contrast, in *Gemeinschaft* and *Gesellschaft* the inverse is true: *Gemeinschaft* and *Gesellschaft* are the pre-existing macro-level notions from which local interpretations emerge. Second, unlike network ties and solidarity/power, *Gemeinschaft* and *Gesellschaft* are interwoven with economic aspects of social life, and in particular with specific historicised modes of production.

The prevailing modes of production in a social grouping thus provide observable and historically relevant indications for the different types of social organisation indexed by these terms. In this way, a principled link can be drawn between these modes of production and predictions about the social functioning of language. Given assumptions about the differential importance of explicit linguistic negotiation in *Gemeinschaft* versus *Gesellschaft* outlined earlier, this link is especially useful when it comes to deducing the situated contents of Face1 in specific circumstances from the functioning of particular linguistic devices therein. In the next section, I attempt to do just that, taking contemporary Greek society as a case-study and mapping the (changing) distribution of several linguistic devices (including diminutives, the T/V distinction, and responses to thanks) as a means of tracing the shifting contents of Face1 in the light of changing social circumstances.

14.2. Face and the interplay between *Gemeinschaft* and *Gesellschaft*

Tönnies envisaged the relationship between *Gemeinschaft* and *Gesellschaft* as neither mutually exclusive nor static. So much follows from the mere affirmation of their historical succession cited earlier (2001: 19). However, the continuity between *Gemeinschaft* and *Gesellschaft* is not only historical but also structural. Tönnies outlined this as follows.

> Any seller who offers the products of his own *labour* for sale can be thought of as a trader, because he is acting like one and calculating the ratio of the money he has made to his outgoings. But he will reckon the *difference* as the equivalent of his own *activity*, which in effect has produced new *value*. If the added value can be established as real and valid, he is not taking more out of the same market than he put in. If mutual exchange took place only on this kind of basis (as can be imagined in our conception of a fully developed *Gemeinschaft*), it could certainly **look like** trade of the *Gesellschaft* type in which everyone was extending his efforts into an unlimited area in order to get the highest possible price. (Tönnies, 2001: 67; italics original, bold added)

The theme of structural continuity between *Gemeinschaft* and *Gesellschaft* is taken up by Michael Herzfeld in his work on the symbolic roots of Western bureaucracy (1993). Challenging the view that 'the outward acceptance of bureaucratic and cultural "formalism" represents a radical break with the *Gemeinschaft*-oriented past' (Herzfeld, 1993: 52), he emphasises instead the persistence of pre-bureaucratic practices, a persistence which he sees in the idiom of symbolic exclusion, and the rhetoric of reciprocity and of gift-giving which are only seemingly transformed into reciprocal exchanges in feudal society and tourist encounters. In both cases, it is 'the capacity of local people to re-interpret official forms and invest them with meanings radically divergent from those of the law' (Herzfeld, 1993: 49) that mediates the passage from the literality of *Gemeinschaft* to the abstractness of *Gesellschaft*. Crucially, these 'radically divergent meanings' emerge as a result of 'the ordinary person [...] recasting [the grand images presented by the leadership] in the more familiar terms of local experience, and influencing their public evolution in turn' (Herzfeld, 1993: 49).

In this section, I explore the potential of the proposed notion of Face2 to bridge the two notions of *Gemeinschaft* and *Gesellschaft*. Given shifting definitions of Self and Other, Face2, defined as approaching/withdrawing from an Other, can motivate and explain shifting allegiances between the individual and surrounding social groupings. In this way, Face2 provides the vehicle that effectuates at the micro-level (the level of the interactional dyad) the passage from *Gemeinschaft* to *Gesellschaft* at the macro-level (the level of the larger social grouping). At the same time, *Gemeinschaft* and *Gesellschaft* generate different situated conceptualisations of Face1, which can be related to each other in a principled manner by being brought together under the single umbrella of Face2.

Gemeinschaft *and* Gesellschaft *elements in contemporary Greek society*

A *leitmotiv* of anthropological work about contemporary Greek society is the importance of the in-group and group belonging. The in-group is defined at various levels of abstraction, starting with the family/household as 'the elementary locus of "us/them" distinctions': 'secrecy is maintained within it, suspicion and even hostility without' (Hirschon, 1998: 237). Kinship is generally an important determinant of group belonging, influencing everything from interpersonal and economic exchanges to class and political allegiances (Just, 1991, 1994). At a slightly higher level of abstraction, 'community by blood...develops into...community of place' (Tönnies, 2001: 27). Bonds of geographical proximity are honoured, for instance, in the form of numerous organisations found especially in larger cities and dedicated to the preservation of the local customs of the areas of origin of their members. 'Community of place' in turn becomes 'community of spirit', in which 'sacred places or worship [of] the same deities' are shared (Tönnies, 2001: 27). In Greece:

> Participation in ritual produces a strong awareness of the worshippers' common adherence to Christianity which overrides distinctions of class and identity based on regional origin or background, a major divisive feature of Greeks' perception of one another. A sense of the widest community is [thus] achieved. (Hirschon, 1998: 225)

At the highest level of abstraction, the in-group is extended to take in the entire nation. This metaphorical interpretation of community by blood (Herzfeld, 1993: 134, 138) is tightly interwoven with the historical circumstances under which the modern Greek state came into being, and has since become an integral part of modern Greek identity (Tziovas, 1994). The first modern Greek state was founded in 1827 after a six-year war for independence from the Ottoman empire. Before that, the Greeks had been living under Ottoman rule for almost four centuries along with other Balkan people, united with them by the bonds of Orthodox Christianity that at the same time differentiated them collectively from their Muslim rulers. To motivate Greeks' struggle for independence and justify their quest for an independent state, and with religion tied up with an older dichotomy of Us (Christians) versus Them (Muslims), an alternative basis had to be sought for a uniquely Greek identity that would rally together Us (Greeks) versus Them (non-Greeks). This alternative basis was provided by language. Speaking Greek became the hallmark of belonging to the Greek nation, which was consequently geographically identified with the Greek-speaking world. During the first century of its existence, the modern Greek state – originally confined to the Peloponnese and the Southern part of Central Greece – was thus felt to be contained within the nation, justifying constant struggles to expand its territory so that it may come to encompass the nation (Tziovas, 1994: 97).

This feeling was brutally reversed in the aftermath of the Asia Minor disaster of 1922. In a mere four years, approximately 1.2 million Greeks from the Western coast of Turkey arrived as refugees to metropolitan Greece, then a country of 5 million people (Voutira, 2003: 147). Compulsory population exchanges between Greece and Turkey followed, through which the two countries sought to maximise their internal demographic homogeneity. This aim was largely achieved: 'before the arrival of refugees from Asia Minor, the population of the region of Macedonia [in Northern Greece; MT] was 42.6% Greek; by 1926, that figure had risen to 88.8%' (Pentzopoulos, 1962: 134; reported in Voutira, 2003: 147). The arrival of the refugees from Asia Minor left an indelible mark on processes of urbanisation, town planning, and working-class formation among others. Most importantly, 'now the nation had to be contained within the state' (Tziovas, 1994: 100).

Within the new perception of the state as the nation, achieving homogeneity within its bounds became of paramount importance, and the role of language was once more pivotal. While 'universal education, access to the mass media, the flight of the young to the cities, and the advent of easy mobility' (Horrocks, 1997: 301) are some reasons commonly cited for the retreat of regional varieties within Greece, their impact was probably only heightened by the ideology of linguistic homogeneity that for a long time denied or marginalised the existence of social and/or geographical variation in the country (cf. Tsitsipis, 1992; Tziovas, 1994; Moschonas, 2004). On the flipside, the distance between Greek as spoken within Greece and Greek varieties outside the national borders (e.g. in Cyprus) was implicitly emphasised (Terkourafi 2007b): as early as 1969 Cypriot was proclaimed to be 'the only living Modern Greek dialect' (Contossopoulos, 1969: 92).

The Discourse of the nation as in-group is manifested in several ways in contemporary Greek society, ranging from attitudes to immigrants (Karakasidou, 2002), which often reflect a distinction between those who speak Greek and those who do not (Voutira, 2003: 149–157); to the AIDS-epidemic-induced exclusion of foreigners and AIDS patients alike (Tsalicoglou, 1995: 90–91); to high school students' favouring '[t]he natural-organic view of the nation as an ahistorical community sharing a common origin, language, and culture' (Voulgaris, 2000: 273); to the selection of linguistic news items by the media (Moschonas, 2004: 180–189); and to Greeks' criticisms of 'the West' and Western foreign policy (Herzfeld, 1993: 135–136, 142, 148).

As a counterweight to the importance of group belonging, personal autonomy is also central to modern Greek identity. This is seen, for instance, in the ease with which Greeks disagree with each other without for that matter endangering their relationships (Tannen and Kakava, 1992), and in what Hirschon terms 'Greek adults' verbal play', meaning a loose commitment to the assertoric force of their utterances exemplified by non-serious promises and threats, and responses to insults (Hirschon, 1992, 2001).

Greeks' quest for personal autonomy combines with historical experience to produce a profound distrust of (central) authority that motivates further outward characteristics of a *Gemeinschaft* organisation. From the older example of town planning – where the massive influx of refugees after 1922 led to abandoning plans for orderly development resulting in the chaotic treeless outlook of many Greek city-centres today (Yerolympos, 2003) – to the more recent one of Value Added Tax evasion attributed to 'the low quality of public goods and services' and 'the complexities of the system' (Agapetos, 1999: 154–155), it is almost as if the state itself displayed in its dealings with citizens the same 'lack of accountability and follow-up into action' (Hirschon, 1992: 38) characterising Greeks' personal relationships.

In the whims of a state bureaucracy that appears to be as unpredictable as fate, one apprehends a *Gesellschaft* structure put together from *Gemeinschaft* materials. Rather than a manifestation of the 'sanctity of contract', as would be the case in a *Gesellschaft*, the insistence on written evidence – the hallmark of bureaucracy – is actually state officials' buffer against the arbitrariness of state decisions (Herzfeld, 1993: 142–146). Similarly, with respect to the particulars of the medicalisation of AIDS, Tsalicoglou suggests that '[b]oth the 'underdogs' and the 'modernisers' seem to agree that an efficient doctoring of society includes its policing [...] demonstrat[ing] the way in which Greece can be modern in a traditional manner, or the way in which it can remain traditional in a modern manner' (Tsalicoglou, 1995: 87). The same continuity between *Gemeinschaft* and *Gesellschaft*, according to Hirschon, characterises relationships between the sexes.

> Although the observation of external differences is important, I suggest that these are ones of style which 'do not necessarily alter the basic forms'…The expression of masculine honour and feminine worth…in the urban setting of Kokkinia as compared with the transhumant shepherds of Epirus…is undoubtedly different …None the less, in Kokkinia social life revolves around the division of the sexes and their complementary roles, while family reputation and prestige were central concerns. (Hirschon, 1998: 234–235)

The profound distrust of state bureaucracy generates a pervasive sense that one must make do on one's own resources. On the one hand, this feeds back into the importance of the in-group and of networks of friends (and friends of friends). Mutual interdependence is thus found across the board, starting from the family level, where 'adult men and women [are] not seen as individuals in their own right, apart from their families' (Hirschon, 1998: 217), to the larger societal one, where voluntarism and private initiative were already looked upon as the way forward at the time of the first modern Olympic games in 1896 (Margaritis, 1997: 91). On the other hand, the resulting initiatives and the challenge to central authority that they represent may (somewhat more optimistically) be interpreted as effectuating 'a widespread break from… dependence on the state' (Close, 1999: 341). In this way, this selfsame predication of *Gesellschaft* upon *Gemeinschaft* has the potential of setting in motion the wheels of a transition toward a full-blown *Gesellschaft*.

Some examples of Gemeinschaft *and* Gesellschaft *elements in Modern Greek*

In Section 1.2 I suggested that a *Gemeinschaft* type of social organisation minimises the need for explicitness, promoting indirectness between intimates instead. This propensity for indirect interpretation may become generalised as a tendency to 'read more' into less, aptly exemplified in the following incident recounted by Tannen (1981). During a stay in Crete, she asked her hostess if she ever prepared eggs by beating them, and why she had not seen grapes since she had arrived in Greece. Although her questions 'had not intended to hint at anything' (Tannen, 1981: 222), they were nevertheless interpreted by her hosts as hints indirectly expressing her desire for scrambled eggs at breakfast and grapes at dinner, which they subsequently sought to provide daily at their great inconvenience.

Greeks' propensity for indirectness should nevertheless not be mistaken for a desire to avoid imposition. According to Sifianou (1995), Greeks commonly use indirectness when explicitness is deemed unnecessary – as, for instance, between intimates – and even silence, that 'most indirect' of politeness strategies, can fulfill positive face needs. Following this line of thought, indirectness should be attributed to the same positive politeness orientation that has been identified in Greeks' handling of telephone conversations (Sifianou, 1989), diminutives (Sifianou, 1992b), compliments (Sifianou, 2001), expressions of praise (Makri-Tsilipakou, 2001), patterns of interruption (Tzanne, 2001), and academic writing styles (Koutsantoni, 2005), to mention but some.

If the importance of the in-group is a *leitmotiv* of anthropological studies on Greece, the importance of positive face is thus a *leitmotiv* of analyses of Modern Greek discourse. The two are in fact intimately related: a network of close personal relationships and mutual interdependence raises positive face (a tendency to approach) to a worthwhile and viable pursuit that can even take precedence over negative face (a tendency to withdraw), challenging Brown and Levinson's (1987: 73–4) assertion that negative takes priority over positive face. Nevertheless, the challenge is arguably only apparent: one has only to consider the expanded construal of the entire nation as in-group, predicated upon the metaphorical interpretation of community by blood, to explain how positive politeness may be expected across the board.

On closer inspection, however, the positive face orientation of Greek society turns out to be a matter of degree. Varieties departing from the Athenian norm are quick to remind us of this. Contrary to the extensive use of diminution[2] and V forms in Standard Greek, use of diminution and V forms in Cypriot Greek has been traditionally severely restricted. In Cypriot Greek, diminution, for instance, is not only less frequently used overall, being prototypically associated with older women addressing younger addressees, but it is furthermore morphosyntactically and semantically constrained, being primarily produced via suffixation, and

– unlike diminution in Standard Greek – unable to express 'contempt' (Terkourafi, 1999). These constraints point toward the strong endearing function of diminution in Cypriot Greek. To explain the liberal use of diminution in Standard Greek one must consequently move away from a 1:1 correspondence between diminution and attachment to positive face. Rather, it must be recognised that, at least sometimes, diminution lowers the speaker's commitment toward the performed speech act and introduces an element of fuzziness in the expected standards of precision. This enables greater flexibility in future moves and further negotiation of rights and obligations, features that are desirable in a *Gesellschaft* type of social organisation.

The above analysis is a timely reminder of the multifunctionality of linguistic expressions. Much as Brown and Levinson predicted, diminution does not function monosemously as an in-group identity marker (1987: 109) but is ambiguous between this function and that of hedging/minimising (1987: 157, 177). Moreover, the above analysis suggests that, when compared with other parts of the Greek-speaking world, the positive politeness of urbanite Greeks is increasingly mitigated by a concern for negative face and avoiding imposition. A comparison of V usage between Greece and Cyprus corroborates this point. Symmetric V usage signifying increased distance on the solidarity axis, and asymmetric V usage signifying increased power of the hearer over the speaker are now regularly encountered in urban Standard Greek. The same indexing functions are however largely replaced by T plus an appropriate choice of address term in Cypriot Greek (Terkourafi, 2005).

In light of ongoing changes in the demographic and cultural profile of Greece, not least of which are its 1981 entry into the European Economic Community (and later European Union) and becoming home to large numbers of immigrants from Africa, Asia and Eastern Europe (Karakasidou, 2002; Voutira, 2003), increasing use of diminution and V forms in Standard Greek may be associated not so much with a liberal, nation-embracing interpretation of in-group as with a *loosening* of the group of potential recipients of these forms. The fact that devices originally addressing positive face concerns, such as diminution, are now used with an ever expanding set of addressees signals a change in these devices' interactional potential that is best described as their acquiring negative politeness functions. In this way, resources already existing in the language are put to the service of new social needs, resulting in their taking on new social meanings.

An opportune example of this last point is provided by the expression *να 'σαι καλά* morphologically truncated from *να είσαι καλά*, 'may you be well', literally a wish and now generalised in Standard Greek as a response to thanks. In the following thread from an online discussion forum, several Greek native speakers (indicated as B, C, D, and E) outline this use of *να'σαι καλά* in response to a question by a non-native speaker (indicated as A):[3]

A: A friend signs a note with "na'sai kala" and I'm wondering if it means "best wishes" or "take care."[...]

B: Na 'sai kala means "be well/good". I guess it's something equivalent to "take care". It's a common way to close a conversation (sometimes we use it instead of "welcome" as an answer to "thank you") or an informal letter. Though is used more verbally and less in written. [...]

C: I would like to add that sometimes we use "Να' σαι καλά" instead of "Ευχαριστώ", to thank someone or to say "you' re welcome" instead of "Παρακαλώ", after someone has thanked us... [...]

D: Literaly means "be well" and can be used instead of "thanks" but also can have a note of irony. For example "for waiting over an hour" (if u had an apointment with someone).

A: Hmm...now I'm wondering about the difference in informality between να'σαι καλα and παρακαλω as ways to say "you're welcome." Do the Greeks have a preference for one or the other? [..]

E: I believe is more formal to say παρακαλώ for "you're welcome". I personally when I say να'σαι καλά I feel like saying "thank you for thanking me". "I don't deserve being thanked but you are very welcome"...

The distribution of *να'σαι καλά* in this new function is very wide, spanning informal and formal settings, and from spoken and written registers, including computer-mediated discourse. While a detailed study of this expression must await future research, internet searches provide a first glimpse into its popularity: *na'sai kala* (in Roman characters) returned 170,000 hits, while *να'σαι καλά* (in Greek characters) returned a whopping 353,000 hits.[4] To what does *να'σαι καλά* as a response to thanks owe its popularity? Typical responses to thanks in Greek include *παρακαλώ*, 'you're welcome', and *το Θεό*, '(you should thank) God.' The former indexes a negative politeness function in that it acknowledges the thanker's freedom from debt, while the latter indexes a positive politeness function in that, by pointing to God as the appropriate recipient of gratitude, it builds on Greeks' shared knowledge of avoidance of personal accountability and consequent attribution of both good and bad outcomes to external agencies such as God (Herzfeld, 1993: 145–147). *Να'σαι καλά* departs from this dualist scheme. On the one hand, it retains the positive-face-oriented format of a wish, grammaticalised in the use of the subjunctive mood, which has replaced the ancient optative. Yet, on the other hand, the attribution of the good outcome to God, which amplified the meaning of the response by introducing elements of a shared background, has been dropped. In other words, *να'σαι καλά* is nowadays only nominally, or *pro forma*, a positive politeness device, as is also suggested by D's reference to the possibility of using this ironically the example above.

The resulting ambiguity between a positive/approaching (well-wishing) and a negative/withdrawing (lifting of debt) function makes *να'σαι καλά* appropriate for use with a wider range of addressees than either of the responses to thanks previously available. This enables *να'σαι καλά* to bridge two different perceptions of the in-group. In its literal, well-wishing meaning *να'σαι καλά* effected approach and approval of the Other as a whole person, indexing a *Gemeinschaft*-like naturalised social bond. While still signalling approach rather than withdrawal, in its contemporary thanking/greeting function *να'σαι καλά* effects approval simply of the act of thanking rather than of the entire person of the thanker, this time indexing a *Gesellschaft*-like contractual bond. Put differently, in a *Gemeinschaft* face is given to a *person* for properties of that person as a whole, whereas in a *Gesellschaft* face is given to the situated *role* of that person, implying the fragmentation of the person to several roles, with face now being given to only some of these. Since *να'σαι καλά* approaches the Other no longer as an entire person – as it would, if it were drawing on shared background assumptions – but merely as someone in the role of thanker, it becomes appropriate for use with a wider range of addressees, who may not always necessarily share the same background assumptions. *Να'σαι καλά* is thus no longer restricted to use within the in-group. On closer inspection, the (old) terms of the *Gemeinschaft* may well be expressing (new) *Gesellschaft* meanings.

14.3. Concluding remarks

While central to the study of communication and social interaction, applications of the notion of face to empirical research are hampered by the lack of a principled way to link together manifestations of this notion in different socio-historical settings. In this paper, I have used data from contemporary Greek society to illustrate how this may be achieved, by suggesting a distinction between a universalising notion of Face2 and situated conceptualisations of Face1, and introducing the notions of *Gemeinschaft* and *Gesellschaft* from the field of sociology to mediate between these two.

Endnotes

1. As, I hope, has become evident from the previous section, the distinction between Face1 and Face2 is different from a distinction between public and private face. Face1 and Face2 lie at different levels of abstraction: Face2 corresponds to a single, universalising, abstract concept that captures what its many instantiations in different situations and cultures, the many situated Face1s, so to speak, have in common: they are all grounded in approach/ withdrawal, and are intentional, i.e. directed at an Other. Nevertheless, *what* counts as approach/withdrawal, *when* Self approaches or withdraws from Other, and *how* Self and Other are defined can only be settled in context. Because these questions are answered differently in different situations and cultures, depending on the socio-historical circumstances (the content of this section) and producing several different Face1s, our direct experience is only of these different Face1s. Face2 can never be directly experienced, since it is an abstraction – attempting to capture what the directly experienced Face1s have in common – and hence 'underspecified', i.e. not yet fixed with respect to the above questions.
2. Three types of morphological/syntactic diminution are available in Modern Greek. The first two, via suffixation and via compounding with the adjective *psilo-*, 'kind of', produce morphological diminutives, while the last one, via syntagmatic association with the hedge *liyo*, 'a bit', results in periphrastic diminution. Only the first of these is systematically exploited in Cypriot Greek (Terkourafi, 1999).
3. http://forum.wordreference.com/showthread.php?t=650940; accessed September 8, 2008; original grammar and spelling retained.
4. Figures current as of September 2008, though the existence of more than one popular song by the same title is distorting these figures somewhat.

References

Agapetos, G. (1999) VAT evasion: overview of the Greek experience. *Journal of Modern Greek Studies* 17: 151–162.

Bayraktaroğlu, A. (1991) Politeness and interactional imbalance. *International Journal of the Sociology of Language* 92: 5–34.

Brentano, F. (1981 [1874]) *Psychology from an Empirical Standpoint*. Translated by Margarete Schattle and Linda L. McAlister. London: Routledge and Kegan Paul.

Brinck, I. (2001) Attention and the evolution of intentional communication. *Pragmatics and Cognition* 9: 259–277.

Brown, P. and Levinson, S. C. (1987[1978]) *Politeness. Some Universals in Language Usage*. Cambridge: Cambridge University Press.

Brown, R. and Gilman, A. (1972[1960]) The pronouns of power and solidarity. In P.P. Giglioli (ed.) *Language and Social Context* 252–282. Harmondsworth: Penguin.

Close, D. (1999) Environmental crisis in Greece and recent challenges to centralized state authority. *Journal of Modern Greek Studies* 17: 325–351.

Contossopoulos, N. (1969) A contribution to the study of the Cypriot dialect. *Epetiris tou Kentrou Epistimonikon Erevnon* 3: 87–109. (in Greek)

Davidson, R. (1992) Prolegomenon to the structure of emotion: Gleanings from neuropsychology. *Cognition and Emotion* 6: 245–268.

Ervin-Tripp, S., Nakamura, K. and Guo, J. (1995) Shifting face from Asia to Europe. In M. Shibatani and S. Thompson (eds.) *Essays in Semantics and Pragmatics* 43–71. Amsterdam: John Benjamins.

George, S. (1990) *Getting Things Done in Naples: Action, Language and Context in Discourse Description*. Bologna: Bologna Editrice.

Goffman, E. (1967) *Interaction Ritual: Essays in Face-to-Face Behaviour*. New York: Doubleday.

Goffman, E. (1971) *Relations in Public: Microstudies of the Public Order*. London: Penguin.

Herzfeld, M. (1993) *The Social Production of Indifference: Exploring the Symbolic Roots of Western Bureaucracy*. Chicago, IL: University of Chicago Press.

Hirschon, R. (1992) Greek adults verbal play or how to train for caution. *Journal of Modern Greek Studies* 10: 35–56 .

Hirschon, R. (1998) *Heirs of the Greek Catastrophe: The Social Life of Asia Minor Refugees in Piraeus*. New York: Berghahn Books.

Hirschon, R. (2001) Freedom, solidarity and obligation: The sociocultural context of Greek politeness. In Arin Bayraktaroğlu and M. Sifianou (eds.) *Linguistic Politeness Across Boundaries: The Case of Greek and Turkish* 17–42. Amsterdam: John Benjamins.

Horrocks, G. (1997) *Greek: A History of the Language and its Speakers*. London: Longman.

Husserl, E. (1970[1900]) *Logical Investigations*. Translated by J. N. Findlay. London: Routledge and Kegan Paul.

Just, R. (1991) The limits of kinship. In P. Loizos and E. Papataxiarchis (eds.) *Contested Identities: Gender and Kinship in Modern Greece* 114–132. Princeton: Princeton University Press.

Just, R. (1994) The reformation of class. *Journal of Modern Greek Studies* 12: 37–56.

Karakasidou, A. (2002) Review essay: migrant encounters with power in Greece. *Journal of Modern Greek Studies* 20: 146–153.

Kiesling, S. (2006) Hegemonic identity-making in narrative. In D. Schiffrin, M. Bamberg and A. De Fina (eds.) *Discourse and Identity* 261–287. Cambridge: Cambridge University Press.

Koutsantoni, D. (2005) Greek cultural characteristics and academic writing. *Journal of Modern Greek Studies* 23: 97–138.

Makri-Tsilipakou, M. (2001) Congratulations and bravo! In A. Bayraktaroðlu and M. Sifianou (eds.) *Linguistic Politeness Across Boundaries: The Case of Greek and Turkish* 137–176. Amsterdam: John Benjamins.

Mao, L. R. (1994) Beyond politeness theory: face revisited and renewed. *Journal of Pragmatics* 21: 451–486.

Margaritis, G. (1997) The nation and the individual: social aspects of life and death in Greece (1896–1911). In P. Carabott (ed.) *Greek Society in the Making, 1863-1913: Realities, Symbols and Visions* 87–98. Aldershot: Ashgate.

Matsumoto, Y. (1988) Reexamination of the universality of face: politeness phenomena in Japanese. *Journal of Pragmatics* 12: 403–426.

Milroy, J. (1993) On the social origins of language change. In C. Jones (ed.) *Historical Linguistics: Problems and Perspectives* 215–236. London: Longman.

Milroy, L. (1980) *Language and Social Networks.* Oxford: Blackwell.

Moschonas, S. (2004) Relativism in language ideology: on Greece's latest language issues. *Journal of Modern Greek Studies* 22: 173–206.

Nwoye, O. G. (1992) Linguistic politeness and socio–cultural variations of the notion of face. *Journal of Pragmatics* 18: 309–328.

ODriscoll, J. (1996) About face: a defence and elaboration of universal dualism. *Journal of Pragmatics* 25: 1–32.

Ortony, A., Norman, D. and Revelle, W. (2005) Affect and proto-affect in effective functioning. In J.M. Fellous and M. Arbib (eds.) *Who Needs Emotions: The Brain Meets the Machine* 173–202. New York: Oxford University Press.

Rhodes, R. (1989) "We are going to go there": positive politeness in Ojibwa. *Multilingua* 8: 249–258.

Sifianou, M. (1989) On the telephone again! Differences in telephone behaviour: England versus Greece. *Language and Society* 18: 527–544.

Sifianou, M. (1992a) *Politeness Phenomena in England and Greece: A Cross-Cultural Perspective.* Oxford: Clarendon Press.

Sifianou, M. (1992b) The use of diminutives in expressing politeness: Modern Greek versus English. *Journal of Pragmatics* 17: 155–173.

Sifianou, M. (1995) Do we need to be silent to be extremely polite? Silence and FTAs. *International Journal of Applied Linguistics* 5: 95–110.

Sifianou, M. (2001) "Oh! How appropriate!" Compliments and politeness. In A. Bayraktaroğlu and M. Sifianou (eds.) *Linguistic Politeness Across Boundaries: The Case of Greek and Turkish* 391–430. Amsterdam: John Benjamins.

Tannen, D. (1981) Indirectness in discourse: ethnicity as conversational style. *Discourse Processes* 4: 221–238.

Tannen, D. and Kakava, C. (1992) Power and solidarity in Modern Greek conversation: disagreeing to agree. *Journal of Modern Greek Studies* 10: 11–34.

Terkourafi, M. (1999) Frames for politeness: A case study. *Pragmatics* 9: 97–117.

Terkourafi, M. (2005) Identity and semantic change: aspects of T/V usage in Cyprus. *Journal of Historical Pragmatics* 6: 283–306.

Terkourafi, M. (2007a) Toward a universal notion of face for a universal notion of co-operation. In I. Kecskes and L. Horn (eds.) *Explorations in Pragmatics: Linguistic, Cognitive and Intercultural Aspects* 313–344. Berlin: Mouton de Gruyter.

Terkourafi, M. (2007b) Perceptions of difference in the Greek sphere: the case of Cyprus. *Journal of Greek Linguistics* 8: 60-96.

Tomasello, M. (1999) *The Cultural Origins of Human Cognition.* Cambridge, MA: Harvard University Press.

Tönnies, F. (2001[1887]) *Community and Civil Society.* Translated by Jose Harris and Margaret Hollis. Cambridge: Cambridge University Press.

Tsalicoglou, F. (1995) A new disease in Greek society: AIDS and the representation of "Otherness." *Journal of Modern Greek Studies* 13: 83–97.

Tsitsipis, Lukas (1992) On some uses of poetics in the ethnographic study of speech: lessons from interaction in language shift contexts. *Journal of Modern Greek Studies* 10: 87–107.

Tzanne, A. (2001) "What you're saying sounds very nice and I'm delighted to hear it": some considerations on the functions of presenter-initiated simultaneous speech in Greek panel discussions. In A. Bayraktaroğlu and M. Sifianou (eds.) *Linguistic Politeness Across Boundaries: The Case of Greek and Turkish* 271–306. Amsterdam: John Benjamins.

Tziovas, D. (1994) Heteroglossia and the defeat of regionalism in Greece. *Kambos Cambridge Papers in Modern Greek* 2: 95–120.

Voulgaris, Y. (2000) The political attitudes of Greek students: internal tensions of an ethnocentric democratic culture. *Journal of Modern Greek Studies* 18: 269–285.

Voutira, E. (2003) When Greeks meet other Greeks: settlement policy issues in the contemporary Greek context. In R. Hischon (ed.) *Crossing the Aegean: An appraisal of the 1923 Compulsory Population Exchange between Greece and Turkey* 145–159. New York: Berghan.

Yerolympos, A. (2003) Inter-war town planning and the refugee problem in Greece: temporary solutions and long-term dysfunctions. In R. Hischon (ed.) *Crossing the Aegean: An appraisal of the 1923 Compulsory Population Exchange between Greece and Turkey* 133–143. New York: Berghan.

Watts, R. J., Ide, S. and Ehlich, K. (1992) Introduction. In R. J. Watts, S. Ide and K. Ehlich (eds.) *Politeness in Language: Studies in its History, Theory and Practice* 1–17. Berlin: Mouton de Gruyter.

Werkhofer, K. (1992) Traditional and modern views: the social constitution and the power of politeness. In R. J. Watts, S. Ide and K. Ehlich (eds.) *Politeness in Language: Studies in its History, Theory and Practice* 155–199. Berlin: Mouton de Gruyter.

15
The significance of 'face' and politeness in social interaction as revealed through Thai 'face' idioms

Margaret Ukosakul

15.1. Introduction

Foreigners living in Thailand are often told: 'You must not be too direct when dealing with the Thai. Don't make them lose face.' One does not have to live in Thailand too long in order to realise the impact of this statement on social interaction in the Thai society. To make someone 'lose face', *sǐa nâa* as they say in Thai, is a social taboo to be avoided at all costs. One learns other phrases such as *kʰǎaj nâa* 'sell face', *nâa tɛ̀ɛk* 'broken face', and *dâj nâa* 'gain face' early in one's stay in Thailand. These three terms are related to the concept of honour versus shame which will be discussed later in this chapter.

In this paper, I will first present the concept of 'face' according to Thai culture. I will then describe the relationship of 'face' to shame in the Thai context. I will then discuss how politeness involves maintaining one's 'face'. It is necessary to view politeness within a framework of social interaction. Ide (1989: 225) noted that linguistic politeness is realised through the use of intentional strategies that allow one's message to be favourably received by the addressee and also through the choice of expressions that conform to the norms of speech appropriate to the situation. Norms for social politeness, as well as the underlying value and belief systems, vary across cultures. Therefore, I will discuss some key themes and politeness strategies the Thai use in their social interaction. Finally, this paper will conclude with a discussion of the conceptual framework of shame.

The significance of the concept of face in the Thai society can be reflected in the numerous idioms based on the word *nâa* 'face'. In fact, in my research on Thai 'face' idioms (Ukosakul, 1999), I collected 171 Thai idioms which contained the word *nâa* 'face'. These idioms were sourced from dictionaries, books on Thai idioms and proverbs, radio and television programs as well as from interviews with native Thai speakers. These 'face' idioms are a part of the conventional vocabulary of the Thai language. The idioms collected were then analysed semantically using the cognitive linguistics approach, particularly, utilising Lakoff and Johnson's (1980) theory of metaphor and Lakoff's view of the embodiment of semantics (Lakoff, 1987).

Upon analysing the semantic meanings of the 'face' idioms collected, it was found that all the 'face' idioms except one describe people, whether they have to do with one's personality, values, countenance or emotions. Furthermore, a large number of these idioms were related to the notion of honour vs. shame. These honour/shame idioms express the emotion of shame or embarrassment as well as the behaviours, reactions and values associated with shame.

Why does the concept of honour vs. shame show up time and again in Thai 'face' idioms? Shame and honour are related to the concept of 'face'.

15.2. The Thai concept of 'face'

What does *nâa* 'face' mean for the Thai? In his article, an anthropological study of *nâa* 'face' in Thai, Sanit (1975) describes the significance of this word. According to his analysis of the Thai culture, the human body is divided into three parts with each part having a different level of importance which is associated with it. The most important and most meaningful part of the human body is the highest part, which is the head.

The head is at the highest position vertically and is therefore considered the most important and sacred. The Thai believe the head is exalted while the feet are base. Consequently, one must not casually touch a person's head. If one accidentally does so, it is necessary to beg the pardon of the person touched. In Thai culture, it is even considered impolite to pass objects over a person's head (Preecha, 1992). According to Sanit (1975: 496), the face, being part of the head, is considered the 'representation of the person'.

The second part of the body is from the neck down to the waist. This part has a mid level of importance. The most talked-about areas here are *t͡ɕaj* 'heart' and *tʰ?ŋ* 'stomach or abdomen'. The waist down to the feet of the human body is considered the lowest part of the body. The sole of the foot is the lowest of all and the most inferior and dirty. Thai etiquette demands that even calling attention to the foot requires one to say, 'Excuse me' (Preecha, 1992). Therefore the Thai consider it a serious insult if the sole of the foot is raised or pointed towards another person. This debasement of the feet is clearly reflected in the idiom *nâa sôn tiin* 'sole of foot face' which is an extremely demeaning insult used to rebuke someone who is utterly shameless.

Another Thai scholar, Suntaree Komin (1990) suggests that, for the Thai, 'face' is identical to 'ego'. As such, it is very sensitive and the Thai cannot tolerate any violation of the 'ego-self' (Komin, 1990: 161). This ego-orientation is the root value underlying other cultural values such as 'face-saving' or 'criticism-avoidance'. Therefore, one can say that the basic rule of all Thai interaction is preserving one another's ego or face. The well-known idiom *ráksǎa nâa* 'to preserve face' aptly describes this important social rule. Consequently, gaining face *dâj nâa* helps one feel socially accepted. Conversely, losing face and experiencing shame are particularly to be avoided. The Thai will therefore do everything they can to maintain face even when the costs of doing so are high. One idiom which expresses this notion succinctly is *kʰǎaj pʰâa ʔaw nâa rɔ̂ɔt* which literally means 'to sell one's clothes in order to save face'.

From the above, we see that the Thai use body parts metaphorically to express other meanings according to their society and culture. The semantic analysis of the Thai 'face' idioms collected in Ukosakul (1999) reveals that the word *nâa* 'face' is used metaphorically to describe four aspects of a person, namely:

1. one's personality,

2. one's countenance,

3. one's emotions – which is not surprising since we express our emotions through the face and perceive the emotions of others, primarily through their facial expressions, and

4. the concept of honour (Ukosakul, 1999).

In this sense, the Thai notion of face, similar to the Chinese, Japanese and other Asian cultures, is very often associated with the sense of dignity, self-esteem, prestige, reputation and pride.

The Thai concept of face is 'social' – it has to do with how one is perceived by others and how one wants to be perceived by others. This perceived self is reflected in several idioms which contain the word *nâa* 'face' and *ʧaj* 'heart', as in *nâa sɯ̌w ʧaj khót* 'straight face, crooked heart', *nâa nɯ̂a ʧaj sɯ̌a* 'deer face, tiger heart' and *nâa ʧʰɯ̂wn ʔòk trom* 'cheerful face, sorrowful chest'. Notice that these three idioms are made up of two distinct parts: the face represents what is external and the heart reflects what is internal and cannot be seen. However, what is internal does not agree with what is external. It is therefore not surprising that these three are used to describe hypocrisy in that a person's countenance does not reflect his or her true character or feelings.

15.3. The relationship of face to shame

Face is closely associated with the concept of shame. Ruth Benedict (1946) described the characteristics of a shame-oriented culture as opposed to a guilt-oriented one:

> True shame cultures rely on external sanctions for good behavior, not, as true guilt cultures do, on an internalized conviction of sin. Shame is a reaction to other people's criticism. A man is shamed either by being openly ridiculed and rejected or by fantasying to himself that he had been made ridiculous. In either case it is a potent sanction. But it requires an audience or at least a man's fantasy of any audience. Guilt does not. (Benedict, 1946: 223)

The Japanese and the Thai are two cultures which are well-known for their orientation toward shame. In such shame-oriented cultures, the effect from the pressure of external sanction from others in order to induce socially accepted behaviour and to dissuade undesired behaviour is often expressed in relation to the word 'face' such as 'losing face' and 'face-saving' (Ting-Toomey, 1985). The loss of 'face' is a powerful sanction for the Thai in encouraging or discouraging certain behaviours (Ukosakul, 1999). One's face is therefore very fragile and sensitive, and a face that is 'broken' would be very difficult to restore (Ukosakul, 1994).

Face is related to a sense of honour. This kind of honour has to do with reputation or recognition of self by others. In other words, honour for the Thai requires an audience; it is social in nature. From the research on Thai 'face' idioms (Ukosakul, 1999), there were thirty-five idioms which convey the notion of honour such as *mii nâa mii taa* 'to have face, to have eyes' which means to have honour, and *sɯ̌w nâa* 'to buy face' meaning to redeem one's honour which was lost. Furthermore, there were twenty-one idioms which describe the emotion of shame or embarrassment, plus other idioms which express the behaviours, reactions and values associated with shame. This strong sense of shame which is an effect of 'face' as the representation of ego affects how social interactions are conducted in the Thai society. A prototypical scenario of shame will be discussed at the end of this chapter.

15.4. The relationship of face to politeness

Brown and Levinson defined 'face' as the 'public self-image that a person wants to claim for himself' (1987: 61). They further added: 'Thus face is something that is emotionally invested, and that can be lost, maintained, or enhanced, and must be constantly attended to in interaction.' (Brown and Levinson, 1987: 61) This definition of 'face' is suited to the Thai situation. However, the Thai notion of face is not so much one's right to act freely (*à la* Brown and Levinson) but rather the acceptance of one's accomplishments and social position in society by others. The Thai notion of face is similar to that of the Japanese (for a discussion of the Japanese concept of face, see Ervin-Tripp, Nakamura and Guo, 1995). However, while the Thai conception of personhood is more socio-centric than egocentric (see discussion in Foley, 1997), it is less socio-centric than that of the Japanese due to the existence of a strong sense of individualism in Thai personality.

Taking the view of politeness as 'socially appropriate behavior' (Meier, 1996: 351), one can see the link between face and politeness. As mentioned above, to preserve one another's self-esteem is the basic rule of all Thai interaction. Furthermore, propriety or appropriateness (*kaláthesà*) is of great importance. Smooth and harmonious relationships are highly valued (Ukosakul, 1994). As a result, to be polite involves strategies to maintain one another's face. Thus, Thai people take great effort not to offend anyone. Politeness strategies involve saying and doing the right thing in the right way and at the right time so as not to hurt another's feelings or ego. In Thai, the expression *ráksăa náam ffaj kan* 'to preserve the water of the heart' which implies to be consciously aware of and not hurt the feelings of others aptly describes this strategy.

Maintaining one another's face involves protecting a person's honour or self-esteem. On the one hand, one must give honour; at the same time, one must avoid behaviours that may cause embarrassment or shame to another. One way to do this is to observe status-consciousness. One's status is usually a blend of both ascribed and achieved statuses. Status in the Thai society is determined by an individual's age, family background, economic standing, political power and connections (associations), education and outlook on life (Moore, 1974: 109). The general hierarchical relationship is that of superior-subordinate or patron-client. Social hierarchy is reflected in many ways in the Thai culture; it is reflected in deferential behaviour patterns, body language, customary greetings, attitudes and expectations, as well as in verbal language. In other words, maintaining one's face implies recognising and accepting another's social status, roles and achievements.

Maintaining face also involves recognising mutual obligations in social relations. Matsumoto (1988) made the point with regard to the Japanese that asking for help is a way of honouring someone by giving them the chance to carry out their role. For the Thai, this is also true but to a lesser degree because the attitude of *kreŋîfaj* 'deference' (which will be discussed in the next section) and the fear of *bunkʰun* 'social indebtedness' can often counteract the impetus to ask for help.

In general, to be polite is to avoid making someone 'lose face' and experience shame. Section 5 describes some politeness strategies used in Thai social interaction.

15.5. Politeness strategies

What are some politeness strategies for maintaining one's face? The first strategy has to do with indirectness. It is necessary to avoid being direct and assertive because the direct approach could be interpreted as a threat to the self-esteem of the addressee. Someone who is too direct and is not considerate of another's esteem could be considered as *mâj hâj nâa* 'not giving face' or *mâj wáj nâa* 'not keeping face'. The indirect approach may appear in the form of hints, beating around the bush, or jokes (Ukosakul, 1994: 215). This approach enables the persons in an interaction to accommodate each other or to withdraw without the loss of 'face' (Stewart, 1972: 52-53). For example, direct refusals of a request may be taken as showing inconsiderateness or disrespect. Therefore, when one is not willing to do what is requested, one could say, 'I am sorry I will not be free at that time', or not say anything at all. The requester will then get the hint.

Indirectness as a politeness strategy is not only utilized in face-to-face interactions but also in written discourse. Chakorn (2006: 103) in her investigation of politeness strategies used in cross-cultural letters of request written in English in the Thai business context observed that

Thai speakers use 'more indirect, deferential and self-effacing strategies' than native English speakers. In the letters of request written by
Thai speakers, 'more hedging (delayed introductions of the actual requests), passive voice, excessive use of "kindly", offers, expressions of
gratitude and the politeness marker "please"' were used.

Ukosakul (1994: 215), in his research on Thai patterns of interpersonal relationships, observed that hints were employed for two
purposes: firstly, to send an indirect message without offending the
receivers; and secondly, to send out feelers to find out if the receivers
were ready for a certain message. In this way, if the response is not
according to expectation, no one will be publicly embarrassed. Hints
are therefore subtle signals sent to people to help them know what
behaviour is expected of them, or that they have done something wrong.
Hints are often used in place of direct requests, advice giving, or outright criticisms and threats, particularly in the presence of a third party.

Another indirect strategy is to 'beat around the bush' which is to talk
around the issue without getting directly to the point. A common Thai
expression *ʔîᵖʰák mɛ̂ɛ náam tʰáŋ hâa* 'to draw from all five rivers' describes the use of this indirect approach. The phrase 'five rivers' refers
to the five major rivers of India. The persons who use this expression
imply that they would try their best to persuade others by telling everything possible they needed to know but not necessarily getting directly
to the point or issue itself. This approach ensures that no one gets
embarrassed and it maintains the smooth and peaceful atmosphere
(*saŋòp râaprɯ̂wn*).

Jokes are also used to distract the attention from the seriousness of a
situation. Joking is used to communicate a message that is sensitive and
could make a person lose face. The listener would then be able to
understand the message from a perspective that is not offensive
(Ukosakul, 1994: 217). However, the indirect approach may not always
convey the intended message.

Another politeness strategy in Thai social interaction which is related to indirectness is the avoidance of confrontation. The idiom *phatᵖʰòn
hâa* 'to confront face' aptly describes a person who is confrontational.
Thus, to avoid the 'I win, you lose' situation, a person who is displeased
with another or has a conflict with another may respond in a few ways:

1.   keep silent about the situation,

2.   avoid the party in conflict altogether (in Thai, the idiom *lòp nâa*
     'to avoid face' means to avoid meeting someone),

3. express his feelings to a third party as a way of releasing his emotional tension, or

4. attempt to resolve the conflict by using mediation through the third party in order to avoid the loss of face for the two negotiating parties.

Not only do the Thai avoid confrontation, avoidance of strong criticism is also keenly observed. Komin (1990) stated that even in academic settings where intellectual criticism has a legitimate place, the Thai will still tone down their criticisms of the ideas by using general and vaguely stated terms because 'it is very difficult for the Thai to dissociate one's ideas and opinions from the "ego" self' (Komin, 1990: 163). In other words, rejection of one's ideas could be taken as rejection of the person maintaining those ideas. It is therefore extremely important not to ʔîkʰîik nâa 'to tear someone's face' or to hàk nâa 'to break someone's face', meaning 'to humiliate' someone in public.

For interactions to be smooth and void of overt conflicts, it is important that there be suppression of negative emotions. The idioms pân sǐi nâa 'to mould the colour of the face' and nâa taaj 'dead face' illustrate the concealment of one's emotions. The value of self-control, of being calm and collected (ʔfaj jen 'cool-hearted') is important for maintaining smooth interpersonal interaction. One who is ʔfaj jen and is able to be polite even while seething on the inside is regarded as a person of strength (Komin, 1990: 181). Again, the aim is to maintain a smooth and harmonious relationship and not make oneself or the other lose face.

Of course, it is not always the case that a person is able to control his emotions. When one is very angry to the point that he does not care for the relationship anymore, he has in his verbal repertoire a host of insults with which to rebuke the offender. Not surprisingly, some of these insults make use of the word 'face' such as 'dog face' nâa mǎa, 'sole of feet face' nâa sôn tiin and 'furry face' nâa kʰǒn. The strength of these insults lie in the extreme negative connotation attributed to animals (dogs are particularly low in the Thai social hierarchy) and the feet which are debased. Of course, if one resorts to the use of such strong insults, the chances for reconciliation with the offended party are very slim.

In general, however, one could say that Thai is a courteous society – *except* when a Thai is behind the steering wheel. Foreigners who have visited Thailand are often amazed at the change of behavior of the Thai behind the wheel. It is interesting to note that on the road, there is no 'face' or interpersonal relationship involved. Thus the politeness strategies described here are thrown out of the window!

An important concept which underlies much of everyday interpersonal behavioural patterns of the Thai is the attitude of *kreŋˆtfaj*. *kreŋˆtfaj* has to do with consideration and respect for another's ego or feelings. It also has the meaning of 'to feel reluctant to impose upon another person ... or to take every measure not to cause discomfort or inconvenience to another person' (Komin, 1990: 164). Richards and Sukwiwat (1982: 12) link the concept of *kreŋˆtfaj* to face by saying that *kreŋˆtfaj* involves 'taking the other person's face needs and feelings into account so that no threat is involved either to speaker or to hearer'. Ide (1982: 382) stated that 'non-imposition is the essence of polite behaviour' for the Japanese. In a similar way, *kreŋˆtfaj* is an appropriate and desirable social mechanism among the Thai. The attitude of *kreŋˆtfaj* helps a person not to take another for granted nor to take advantage of another. It also helps to maintain a smooth and harmonious relationship and to avoid conflicts.

The consequences of *kreŋˆtfaj* are twofold:

1. a person may be obligated to do what he/she does not want to do, and/or

2. a person will not always be able to do what he/she desires to do.

For example, A and B are good friends. A asked to borrow B's car. Because B feels *kreŋˆtfaj* toward his friend, B will let A use the car even though he is not too happy about it. B does not want to cause any ill-feelings between A and himself. However, if A had the attitude of *kreŋˆtfaj* toward B in the first place, A would not have directly asked to use the car even though he needed to use one badly. Doing so makes A appear *nâa nǎa* 'thick faced' or *nâa dâan* 'hardened face', i.e. thick-skinned.

The motivation behind *kreŋˆtfaj* is to avoid intrusion upon one's ego. In the situation described above, B will let A use his car lest he loses face because A would think that B is stingy or that B does not trust A with his car. If A needs the car but feels *kreŋˆtfaj* toward B, A would not ask to borrow B's car in case A loses face when B refuses to help him.

This does not imply that a Thai is not able to request for help. Any request for help is typically presented indirectly in the form of hints (Ukosakul, 1994). Therefore, one may casually mention the need for a car. If the other picks up the hint, he may offer the use of his car. If he does not desire to do so, he will not acknowledge the hint but will casually change the subject. In this case, the requester knows that the other is not willing to lend the car. Neither side will lose face in this encounter.

A Thai knows how far he should go in displaying the degree of *kreŋ̂ʧaj* – it depends on who one is dealing with, the degree of familiarity with that person, as well as the situation (Komin, 1990: 167). To have too much *kreŋ̂ʧaj* makes others feel uncomfortable; too little *kreŋ̂ʧaj* is offensive. But definitely, it is a basic social rule to have the attitude of *kreŋ̂ʧaj*. This concept of *kreŋ̂ʧaj* is not unique to the Thai; the Chinese, Japanese and some other Asian cultures have this concept as well.

15.6. Shame as the effect of loss of 'face'

What happens when the social norms discussed above are violated? The consequence of actions such as being confrontational, being too direct, expressing violent emotions and so on is the loss of 'face' or honour which leads to the experience of negative feelings such as shame or anger. A large number of Thai 'face' idioms that express emotion describe shame and anger. My research on 'face' idioms (Ukosakul, 1999) also reveals an interesting finding: other than the word *aaj* which means 'shame' or 'shyness', every other expression that describes shame or embarrassment contains the word *nâa* 'face', for example, *nâa tɛ̀ɛk* 'broken face'; *nâa ŷʰaa* 'numb face', *nâa ʧ̂ʍʍt* 'tasteless face' and *nâa dɛɛŋ* 'red face'. The relationship of face to shame is therefore very salient.

Noble (1975) described four aspects of shame: honour, failure, covering, and exposure. First, shame is the loss of honour, thus, shame is equivalent to dishonour. Second, shame is associated with several kinds of failure, such as failure to achieve or failure to measure up to a standard. When a person gets caught for misbehaviour, he experiences shame because his wrongdoing has been openly revealed. Third, the state of shame is one of covering. A person who feels shame tries to hide what he really is from others; in other words, he puts on a mask. Fourth, the experience of shame is one of exposure. When something happens to remove that mask, the person's real self is exposed. Then one normally responds to shame by re-covering through diversion via different emotional channels such as anger or humour.

Using Noble's four aspects of shame, I have developed a prototypical scenario for shame for the Thai. This is very much in the same spirit as Kövecses' (1986) well-known model for English 'anger'. This prototypical scenario describes a series of events that take place to bring about shame and the reactions of the person experiencing shame. There are five stages in this scenario:

1. Offending Events,

2. Loss of Honour,

3. Behavioural Reaction,

4. Recovering Honour, and

5. Preservation of Honour (Ukosakul, 1999).

The conceptual framework for shame is graphically portrayed in Figure 15.1.

Offending event(s)

Stage 1 involves events and actions that cause the experience of shame. One can come to experience shame or loss of face in two ways: the first is when an offender commits a face-threatening act that causes another to lose face. The idioms *kʰâam nâa* 'to step over (someone else's) face', *ʔiiik nâa* 'to tear the face', *hàk nâa* 'to break the face', *mâj wáj nâa* 'not spare the face' and *jăam nàam nâa raw* 'to insult the water of our face' depict how others can cause a person to lose face. Notice that the verbs to step over, to tear, to break, not to spare and to insult all reveal

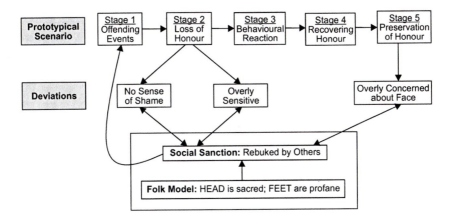

Fig. 15.1.

hurtful actions which show a lack of consideration for the feelings of another.

The second way is when the person does something that causes himself to lose face. The idioms *kʰǎaj nâa* 'sell face' and *sǐa nâa* 'lose face' are two of the idioms which express this way of causing shame to oneself.

Loss of honour

The offending events in Stage 1 cause a loss of honour. This loss of 'face' for the Thai brings about the feeling of shame ranging from slight embarrassment to strong humiliation. These are the *emotional* effects of the loss of honour. Some 'face' idioms which express these emotional effects are *nâa tîʰaa* 'numb face', *nâa tɛ̀ɛk* 'broken face' and *nâa ŋǎaj* 'upturned face'. In these three idioms, we see that the emotional hurt of shame is compared to the physical hurt of being slapped or hit on the face. For example, one feels numb in the face when one is slapped so hard that one is stunned. After the initial feeling of sting of the face, the face will feel numb for a while. One informant explained why *nâa ŋǎaj* refers to being humiliated. He used the illustration from Thai boxing. When one is hit very hard on the face, the head is jerked backwards causing the face to be upturned.

In addition, Thai 'face' idioms reflect the *physiological* effects of shame such as blushing (as expressed by *nâa dɛɛŋ* 'red face') and agitation (as expressed by *mâj rúu tfa ʔaw nâa paj wáaj tʰǐi nǎaj* 'don't know where to put one's face').

It is not always the case that the person experiencing shame will feel that the shame is justified. Sometimes, the offending event may be seen as an injustice and the person will experience anger as well. At other times, even when the offending event is justified, one may still get angry because one's dignity has been violated.

Compared with the other stages in this scenario, this stage contains the highest number of idioms. This is, in fact, not surprising as it is at this stage that the emotion of shame is most intense. Other studies (see Ungerer and Schmid, 1996) have shown that the majority of idiomatic expressions describing emotions characterize this stage of the emotion where physiological and behavioural effects are experienced.

Behavioural reaction

Stage 2 describes the emotional reactions that are the consequences of shame. Stage 3 is the behavioural reaction to this loss of honour. My data reflect five possible behavioural reactions.

The first reaction is *avoidance.* The person experiencing shame would choose to avoid the others who know about the offending events, hoping that they will forget about the matter eventually. Ukosakul (1994) commented that avoidance is one of the most employed strategies in social interaction and conflict management among the Thai. Some 'face' idioms that aptly depict this strategy of avoidance are *mɔɔŋ nâa kan mâj tìt* (literally, 'look at the face but cannot connect') and *mâj klâa sûu nâa* (literally, 'not dare to fight face'), *láp nâa* 'conceal face' and *lòp nâa* 'avoid face'.

The saying *mɔɔŋ nâa kan mâj tìt* 'look at the face but cannot connect' refers to a situation when two persons who have unresolved conflicts avoid each other. The verb *tìt* has numerous senses, such as 'to adhere', 'to append', and 'to stick' (Wit 1977:534). There is the semantic component of two items coming close together. However, in the case where there is conflict between two parties, as in the situation described in this stage, each party will even avoid looking at each other in the eye.

The idiom *mâj klâa sûu nâa* 'not dare to fight face' makes use of the verb *sûu* 'to fight'. Fighting necessitates confronting. Therefore, *mâj klâa sûu nâa* 'not daring to fight face' reveals an act of avoidance (flight, not fight).

The second behavioural reaction to the sense of shame is *to put on a mask* so that others do not realise that the offending event affected the person as much as it did. Several idioms describe this behavioural reaction. They are *sàj nâa kàak* 'put on shell face', *tii nâa taaj* 'to strike a dead face' and *nâa tɕʰɔj taatɕʰɔj* 'still face, still eyes'.

A third way of handling shame would be to use *humour as a diversion.* Even though one may be deeply hurt, one makes light of the matter and laughs it off in order to divert the focus from self. The idiom *nâa tʰalén* 'grinning face' can be used to describe someone who turns an embarrassing situation into a funny episode.

The fourth reaction to the loss of honour is the *retribution of anger.* If the experiencer of shame feels that the action of shaming was unjustified, he (or she) would feel angry. Then he would perform an act of retribution, and the wrongdoer would be the target of the act. In Thai, the idiom *tɔɔk nâa klàp* 'to hammer the face in retaliation' means to 'reproach without sparing the feelings of the other'. When the experiencer *t??k nâa klàp* 'hammers the face in retaliation', he makes the wrongdoer lose face as well.

If the experiencer of shame is very angry, he may insult the offender using various demeaning expressions such as *nâa kʰŏn* 'furry face' or *nâa mǎa* 'dog face' (dogs are considered lowly animals in Thai culture). Sometimes, these derogatory terms are not spoken in front of the wrong-doer but they are used behind the wrongdoer's back with a third party.

The fifth behavioral action is *acceptance*. In this case, the experiencer feels that he deserves what has happened, particularly when he is the one who brought the shame upon himself. He then simply accepts it as his fate. The idiom *kôm nâa* 'bow face' is often paired with the phrase *raìp kam* 'accept fate' to portray this reaction to shame. *kôm nâa ráp kam* means 'to have no choice but to accept the consequences of one's behavior'.

Recovering honour

At stage 4, the experiencer will act to remove the felt shame so that honour can be restored. The loss of honour can be compared to being in a state of disequilibrium. The idioms *kûu nâa* 'to redeem face', *kɛ̂ɛ nâa* 'to correct face' and *sẃṵ nâa* 'to buy face' clearly depict this restoring of equilibrium. The verb *kûu* can mean 'to salvage, to restore, to retrieve, or to re-establish' (Wit, 1977: 132). In all these terms, there is the idea of a change of status from loss to gain. The verb *kɛ̂ɛ* means 'to solve, to mend, to correct, or to save' (Wit, 1977). In these definitions, there is the idea of something wrong being made right. Therefore, the idiom *kɛ̂ɛ nâa* 'to correct face' implies that one's reputation or honour that was wronged is now made right.

Preservation of honour

The final stage in the shame scenario occurs when honour is restored. Two things must take place in order to restore the equilibrium. First, the shame must be removed and the honour re-established. The idiom that describes this stage is *ráksǎa nâa* 'to preserve face'. The verb *raìksǎa* 'to preserve' implies to keep something from getting spoiled or to maintain the present condition. Therefore, one who *raìksǎa nâa* 'pre-serves face' will act to maintain one's reputation.

The second event that must happen is there must be reconciliation (at least partially) with the offending party (if there is a wrongdoer involved). Recall that if the experiencer feels that he has been treated unjustly, he and the offending party will *mɤɤŋ nâa kan mâj tìt* 'look at the face but cannot connect' meaning that the two parties will avoid each other. When that shame is removed and the honour re-established, the two parties can now *mɤɤŋ nâa kan tìt* 'look at the face, can connect' and *hăn nâa kʰâw hăa kan* 'turn the face toward each other' implying that they have reconciled.

A person who highly values reputation can be described as one who *rák nâa* 'loves face'. Whatever one does that is good or right should therefore be done in such a way that others will come to know about it. In this way, one will *dăj nâa dăj taa* 'gain face, gain eyes' and thus receive recognition from others. The aim in all these behaviours is to become someone respected and prominent in society, i.e. someone who *mii nâa mii taa* 'has face, has eyes'. In this way, one's good name will be enhanced and the name of one's family as well. The idiom *tʰ̂ɤ̀ɤt nâa tʰ̂uu taa* 'to lift the face up, to lift the eyes up' describes this aspect of gaining honour.

Deviations from the norm

The scenario described above is by no means the only course that shame can take. There are several deviations from the norm (see Figure 14.1). One deviation which may occur at Stage 2 happens when a person does not feel shame when he ought to. When this happens, others will rebuke that person by using the idioms *nâa dâan* 'hardened face' *or nâa tʰon jaŋka ʔìt ron faj* 'face enduring like fired bricks' or *nâa năa* 'thick face'. These idioms express shamelessness. In rebuking someone verbally by using these idioms, the speaker hopes to make that person feel rightfully ashamed of what he/she has done.

Another deviation from the norm is the other extreme of being shameless, i.e., being embarrassed too easily. To be shameless is to have a 'thick face' *nâa năa*. Conversely, someone who gets embarrassed too easily is labelled as 'thin faced' *nâa baaʔ*.

A third deviation may occur at Stage 5 when a person is overly concerned about one's honour. In this situation, others may rebuke this person by asking sarcastically, *'dâj nâa sák kìi krabuŋ'* 'how many baskets of face can you get?' meaning 'how much recognition do you need?'. Others may also label a person who is overtly trying to gain recognition (even at the expense of others) by using the idiom *îfâw nâa îfâw taa* 'lord of face, lord of eyes'. Furthermore, someone who goes to extremes just to keep up the appearance of being prominent in society is said to *kʰǎaj pʰâa ?aw nâa r??t* 'sell clothes in order to save face'. An example of *kʰǎaj pʰâa ?aw nâa r??t* would be to drive a Mercedes even though one can hardly afford a small car.

15.7. Conclusion

In conclusion, for the Thai, the notion of face is very often equated with ego. To 'lose face' is a social taboo while preserving one's face is the basic rule of all Thai interaction. The concept of face is useful in understanding linguistic politeness in Thai culture. In order to protect the 'face', the Thai has mechanisms to help one maintain smooth relationships with others. These politeness strategies such as indirectness, avoidance of confrontation and criticism, suppression of negative emotions, and the attitude of *kreŋîfaj* help ensure that the honour of a person is protected as much as possible. Overall, the large number of 'face' idioms that have to do with honour and shame is a reflection of the salience of the value of 'face' and its effects on social interaction in Thai society.

References

Benedict, R. (1946) *The Chrysanthemum and the Sword.* Boston: Houghton-Mifflin.

Brown, P. and Levinson, S. C. (1987) *Politeness. Some Universals in Language Use.* Cambridge: Cambridge University Press.

Chakorn, O-O. (2006) Persuasive and politeness strategies in cross-cultural letters of request in the Thai business context. *Journal of Asian Pacific Communication* 16: 103–146.

Ervin-Tripp, S., Nakamura, K. and Guo, J. (1995) Shifting face from Asia to Europe. In M. Shibatani and S. Thompson (eds.) *Essays in Semantics and Pragmatics* 43–71. Amsterdam: John Benjamins.

Foley, W. A (1997) *Anthropological Linguistics: An Introduction.* Mulden, MA: Blackwell.

Ide, S. (1982) Japanese sociolinguistics: politeness and women's language. *Lingua* 57: 357–385.

Ide, S. (1989) Formal forms and discernment: two neglected aspects of universals of linguistic politeness. *Multilingua* 8: 223–248.

Kövecses, Z. (1986) *Metaphors of Anger, Pride and Love: A Lexical Approach to the Structure of Concepts.* Amsterdam: John Benjamins.

Komin, S. (1990) *Psychology of the Thai People: Values and Behavioral Patterns.* Bangkok: NIDA.

Lakoff, G. (1987) *Women, Fire and Dangerous Things: What Categories Reveal about the Mind.* Chicago: University of Chicago Press.

Lakoff, G. and Johnson, M. (1980) *Metaphors We Live By.* Chicago: University of Chicago Press.

Matsumoto, Y. (1988) Reexamination of the universality of face: politeness phenomena in Japanese. *Journal of Pragmatics* 12: 403–426.

Meier, A. J. (1996) Defining politeness: universality in appropriateness. *Language Sciences* 17: 345–356.

Moore, F. J. (1974) *Thailand.* New Haven: HRAF.

Noble, L. L. (1975) *Naked and Not Ashamed: An Anthropological, Biblical and Psychological Study of Shame.* Unpublished manuscript.

Preecha J. (1992) On the semantics of Thai compounds in *hua* head. In C. J. Compton and J. F. Hartmann (eds.) *Papers on Thai Languages, Linguistics and Literature 16* 168–178. Northern Illinois University: Center for South-East Asian Studies.

Richards, J. C. and Suksiwat, M. (1982) Language transfer and conversational competence. *Applied Linguistics* 4: 113–125.

Sanit S. (1975) Concerning the face of Thai people: analysis according to the anthropological linguistics approach. *NIDA Journal* Vol. 4, Year 18.

Stewart, E. C. (1972) *American Cultural Patterns: a Cross-cultural Perspective.* Yarmouth, Maine: Intercultural Press.

Ting-Toomey, S. (1985) Toward a Theory of Conflict and Culture. In W. B. Gudykunet, L. P. Stewart and S. Ting-Toomey (eds.) *Communication, Culture, and Organization Process.* Newbury Park, CA: Sage.

Ukosakul, C. (1994) *A Study of the Patterns of Detachment in Interpersonal Relationships in a Local Thai Church.* Unpublished PhD dissertation, Trinity International University (formerly TEDS).

Ukosakul, M. (1999) *Conceptual Metaphors Motivating the Use of Thai Face.* Unpublished MA thesis, Payap University.

Ungerer F. and Schmid, H. J. (1996) *An Introduction to Cognitive Linguistics.* London: Addinson Wesley Longman.

Wit, T. (1992) *Thai-English Dictionary.* Bangkok: Ruamsasn.

16
Facing the future: some reflections

Francesca Bargiela-Chiappini

> I think of things that conversation analysts study, and the results
> of our work on talk and other conduct in interaction, as being
> studies of culture – culture in the sense of inventories of possible
> actions, of common-sense knowledge about members of the
> society and of other societies organized by reference to categories
> of person, etc, both of which have historically been in the
> province of anthropology (Schegloff 2005: 456)

16.1. Facing the future: some reflections

The variety of perspectives on the concept of face, its place in politeness studies and its manifold functions in interaction as discussed by
the chapters in this volume offer several possible 'leads' for future explorations. The first reassuring consideration is that 'face' and 'politeness', in spite of the lack of agreed definitions on their nature and
characteristics, continue to intrigue scholars around the world; and not
only in pragmatics, where perhaps politeness finds its natural disciplinary home, but also in anthropology, social psychology, communication
studies, philosophy and sociology. To the latter discipline we owe the
first Western elaboration of the concept of face (Erving Goffman).

As a linguist with a passion for anything 'cultural' and 'intercultural',
I am at danger of being lured into many and equally promising discussions flagged up by the chapters: for example, the suggestive power of
idiomatic language in revealing the pervasiveness of face concerns and
their roots in values such as honour, shame and pride (Ho *et al.*, 2004;
Ukosakul; Koutlaki; this volume, Chapters 15 and 6); the centrality of
facework in intercultural negotiations, where ethno-centric bias extends
beyond the dominant negotiation models and pervades also conflict
management approaches, locking individuals and groups of different

cultures in damaging disputes with tangible and lasting consequences on interpersonal and business relations (Ting-Toomey, this volume, Chapter 12); the ontological debates on the very nature of 'face', as constituting and constitutive of social interaction (Arundale, this volume, Chapter 2); or the powerful argument on 'face' as 'a basic structure of sociality and the foundation for the relationship with the Other' expounded by the French phenomenologist Emmanuel Levinas (Kozin, this volume, Chapter 11: 210).

Beside the varied and equally stimulating directions for a future research agenda emerging from this volume, it seems to me that most chapters, more or less explicitly, raise some fundamental issues that deserve special attention and which invoke a self-questioning attitude with respect to ontological and epistemological 'positionings' and desirable disciplinary cross-overs. For example, preference for a social constructionist ontology which sees 'face' as emergent in verbal interaction would presumably be questioning both:

1. an essentialist understanding of 'culture' as pre-existing and influencing interaction, and

2. 'face' as a composite of personal attributes on which the interactants draw upon in mediated or unmediated encounters, and which include, among others, social status, ranking and expertise.

Such a constructionist stance would also be sceptical of treating societal values such as honour, shame and pride – considered 'universal' by some anthropological literature – as essentialist concepts and would seek their locus of realisation and manifestation in the discursive formations in which the interaction is embedded.

In these concluding reflections, I intend to probe the concept that perhaps more than any other affects the discussion of 'face' especially, but not only, in cross- and intercultural research – 'culture'. Closely related to the ontological status of 'culture' and its explanatory import with regards to face, is the issue of what kind of methodologies are best suited to capture the verbal and non-verbal manifestations of 'face'. Not only that: the philosophical interrogation of 'face' (e.g. Kozin, this volume, Chapter 11) leads us into deep questioning of our definitions of the ('cultural') Other. The ruminations that follow are not intended as a scholarly exposition but rather as provocations that poke at our comfortable (Western or Eastern) ethno-centrism, disturb our confidence in the transparency of the 'culture' in which we have grown up, question our knowledge of other 'cultures', and unsettle our confidence in the ability to 'read' the 'face' of the Other in interaction.

16.2. 'Culture' as a determinant of face? A concept lost in debate

Many of us could narrate anecdotes of the manifestations of culture as 'difference in action' witnessable in the intercultural encounters which we have observed as participants. A conference dinner dominated by English as a *lingua franca* would be an event familiar to most academics and a rich source of observable and intriguing intercultural encounters. In such a *locale*, one can notice varying levels of participation, with differences becoming more apparent when the conversations slip into humour and some colleagues seem to be utterly baffled and confused, if not embarrassed, by the not-so general hilarity, often initiated by native speakers. Of course, factors such as prior acquaintanceship, language proficiency, age, gender, (perceived) status differences, personal likes or dislikes, down to mere boredom or jet-lag, to name but few, can all affect the direction and volume of traffic around and across the table. But is it also clear that some people talk less than others, do not talk to the people across the table but only to the neighbours sitting at either side, or are happy to ignore their neighbours completely after they have exchanged 'polite' words with them. Others never seem to (wish to) express a personal opinion on the current topic; others yet use academic titles to refer to particular speakers they have heard at the conference, and the list could go on. It is very tempting, natural almost, to attribute at least some of these behaviours to 'cultural differences' among the dinner guests.

Whether 'culture' is something tangible and observable or whether it is a discursive construction continues to be debated across disciplines (see later in this chapter). The fact that a whole volume could be devoted to analysing definitions of culture harvested exclusively from the literature published in English (Baldwin *et al.*, 2006) is a sign that there is no impending agreement on the essence of the 'thing' scholars are still furiously trying to grapple with. Clearly, different ontologies of 'culture' will offer different perspectives on the phenomenon, which in turn will demand different methodological approaches to the analysis of the 'data'. In our discussions of 'face', these perspectives are very important because they affect our conceptualisations of 'face' and therefore the ways in which we go about analysing it.

Raymond Williams (1983) writing on the history of the word 'culture' concludes that:

> Between languages as within a language, the range and complexity of sense and reference indicate both difference of intellectual position and some blurring or overlapping. These variations, of whatever kind, necessarily involve alternative vies of the activities, relationships and processes which this complex word indicates. The complexity, that is to say, is not finally in the word but in the problems which its variations of use significantly indicate. (1983: 92)

A good way to begin a highly selective and personal investigation of culture is anthropology. The much-quoted 1952 monograph by Kroeber and Kluckhohn, *Culture*, displays the 'propriety attitude' towards the term originally associated with anthropology; half a century later, and 'culture' has migrated to most social sciences and humanities, carrying with it a baggage of ambiguity and contestation (Baldwin *et al.*, 2006). Kroeber and Kluckhohn are probably better known outside of their discipline for their 157 definitions of the term; numbers have doubled according to a recent compilation (Baldwin *et al.*, 2006). The proliferation of definitions is a sign of an elusiveness that has baffled disciplines and scholars for a long time. Influential anthropologist Leslie White in his 1959 paper acknowledges that ontological disputes on 'culture' had already been raging for decades, and recalls the opposition between those who saw culture as 'learned behaviour' and those who considered it an abstraction from behaviour. White's own definition of culture harks back to the 'traditional anthropology' of the American founding father of the discipline when he writes about it in terms of: 'real things and events, observable directly or indirectly in the actual world that we live in' (ibid. 247).

The study of culture remained in the preserve of anthropology until the 1970s; the prestige of cultural anthropology being sealed with the publication of Clifford Geertz's *The Interpretation of Cultures* in 1973. Like Geertz's iconic phrase 'thick description', 'culture' soon began a journey across disciplines, a phenomenon that has been described as 'academic culture mania' (Sewell, 1999). While culture came to occupy centre stage in many disciplines – also following the interest in the French post-structuralists Lacan, Derrida and Foucault – its status in anthropology declined, leaving the discipline in a deep crisis of identity. Significantly for our discussion, and on the wave of post-structuralism and post-modernism, in the 1980s and 1990s 'culture' becomes a contested concept in anthropology for a variety of reasons:

Chapter 14). Perhaps we should be interested in recent critical developments in anthropological theory that have affected the understanding
of 'cultures' in ways that have potential consequences for how we look
at a contextualised, emergent concept of 'face'. For example, the recent
emphasis on social and economic processes affords the re-interpretation of separate and isolated cultures, societies and nations as interconnected in larger regional and global networks. The existence of individual
cultures has also been challenged by a critique of representation that
interprets cultural boundedness and coherence in terms of narrative
devices, resulting in the constructionist reading of 'all associations of
place, people and culture [as] social and historical creations to be explained, not given natural facts' (Gupta and Ferguson, 1997: 4).
Boundedness is not the only classical assumption to be challenged.
Within communities, socially-constructed entities, are far from homogenous and orderly: social agents do not enact culture but, through
political processes, they invent it, transform it and rework it (ibid. 5).

The centrality of the notions of place, identity and power begin to
emerge from this new re-definition of 'cultures'. While in the anthropological study of bounded cultures 'the local' was taken as a given, discursive and historical constructions of locality and community show
how they are constituted within wider social and spatial relations (Gupta
and Ferguson, 1997: 7). Similarly, identity is seen as historically contingent, constituted by 'schemes of categorizations and discourses of difference' and interrogated by them (ibid. 13): 'Identity and alterity are ...
produced simultaneously in the formation of "locality" and "community". "Community" is ... a categorical identity that is premised on various forms of exclusion and constructions of otherness.' (Gupta and
Ferguson, 1997: 13) The construction of 'difference' between communities and identities rests on relations of power and inequality, which
define what can be understood in relation to what. So, for example,
'national' identities can only be understood in relation to supranational
identities and subnational ones (Gupta and Ferguson, 1997: 17). A post-
modern sensitivity colours also the critique of 'culture' in the singular.
Charged with lacking ontological rootedness and a clear referent, culture is seen as being used by powerful actors to legitimise difference
through representation and reification – and obfuscation of connectedness. As a means of 'ordering and defining the world' (Mitchell, 1995:
111), culture has worked as a 'powerful idea' in anthropology by 'bringing the "strange" into the ordinary' (ibid. 111) through ethnographic
processes of localisation, exoticisation and integration, which are
implicated with the expansion of the capitalist economy. The

attractiveness of this powerful conceptualisation of culture could be said to reside precisely in its ethno-centric 'ability to be used to describe, label and carve out activities into stable entities, so that they can be named an attribute of a people' (ibid. 113).

Like the hegemonic discourses of culture just described, the 'politicization of culture' (Wright, 1998) by certain constituencies within and outside academia has serious consequences on people's lives. The example of the 'cultural turn' in organisational studies, inspired by a decontextualised interpretation of Geertz's (1973) work, has led to manipulation of 'culture' as an instrument of managerial control through the vocabulary of 'empowerment': 'managers are deploying both old and new ideas of "culture" in order to gain workers' active participation in new ways of organizing production, profit and power' (Wright, 1998: 12). Authoritative discourses of 'culture' sustain a strong and stable ideology that 'appears hegemonic ... [t]hat is, it becomes naturalized, taken for granted and "true"' (ibid. 9). The apparent unassailable objectivity of this ideology seems to prescribe the impotence of any alternatives. In fact, the contestation of the idea/ideology of culture(s) is ongoing, especially within anthropology (see Hutnyk, 2006); some anthropologists have even dropped culture as the subject matter of their discipline (Street, 1993; Yeongoyan, 1986). Instead, they observe and write the unfolding processes of social practices, a shift in emphasis from the earlier ontology of culture as an object which seems to point to a new and more attractive notion of 'culture as a verb' (Street, 1993: 38).

Following this ontological shift, *practice* becomes one of the two elements, the other being *system,* in a dialectic that attempts to recover culture in its singular and abstract sense. Culture then is 'a dimension of social life autonomous from other such dimensions both in its logical and its spatial configuration, and as a system of symbols possessing a real but thin coherence that is continually put at risk in practice and therefore subject to transformation' (Sewell, 1999: 52). Cultural systems overlap and coexist within geographic boundaries but do not correspond neatly to what we know as 'nations' and 'societies' and often cross them. We may have re-covered some sense of 'culture' in a new processual and dyanamic notion centred on practice but in so doing have we lost 'culture' in the plural? It appears that 'cultural worlds' survive in the discourse of cultural analysis but suffer from the multiple problems of loose integration, contestation, constant change and weak boundedness (ibid. 54-55).

At the end of this rather brief excursus into culture, we have reached a position that is not to far from where we started. It seems that, after the definitional journey that has taken 'cultures' from 'world of mean-ings' to 'ethnoscapes' and, more recently, 'hegemonies' and 'partially coherent landscapes of meaning', the challenge of a cultural analyst to the bewildered rest of us is 'to discern what the shapes and consisten-cies of local meanings actually are and to determine how, why and to what extent they hang together' (ibid. 58).

Japanese anthropology proposes the view that local 'cultures' are constituted through historical processes of continuous dialectics between internal and external factors. For example, the multiple historical en-counters of Japan, first with the 'East' (China) and later with the 'West' (Europe), document how the origins of a distinctive Japanese-self iden-tity are to be found within a complex process of appropriation of a foreign food (rice) and the creation of a powerful mythology based on the transformation of the land from wilderness to abundant rice crops (Ohnuki-Tierny, 2006). Similarly, centuries later, history tells how how Japanese kingship and constitution were modelled on the Prussian sys-tem, to the extent that attempts were made by the Japanese government to raise Shintoism to the level of a state religion (Ohnuki-Tierny, 2006) (presumably copying Christianity as the dominant religion in European nation-states).

These instances of cross-globe, long-term, deep influences, which probably also work in the opposite direction, East to West, show up the East–West dichotomy as not only 'useless and false' (ibid. 13) but as positively dangerous, especially when appeals to its full ontological authority are made to 'justify' differences that lock peoples and commu-nities into essentialist categorisations. The in-between status of Japan, historically oscillating between two dichotomies, 'the West plus Japan vis-à-vis Asia-Pacific, and the West vis-à-vis Japan plus Asia Pacific' (Shimizu, 2006: 19) is a reminder of the ethno-centric bias and political motives beyond the attribution of a substantive and holistic character to entities caught up in the historical flux. At best, we could continue to deploy the East–West as a heuristic tool (Shimizu, 2006), while remain-ing aware that both East and West incorporate dichotomies emerging from cross-overs that date back centuries.

Internal and temporal variation of cultural systems and, consequently, practices, is in evidence in Terkourafi (Chapter 14) while Tao-Seop's (Chapter 13) discussion of similarities across a number of East Asian communities suggest that certain meanings are shared across bound-aries, possibly as a result of shared philosophical traditions and cross-ing historical trajectories. It is more intriguing to find resonances of East Asian practices in the Persian context, which seems to point to possible historical contact through travel, migration or conflict. Perhaps in the future we may wish to concentrate more on what emic concepts of face have in common, what underlying values, norms and categories seem to appear again and again (e.g. shame, honour, status, deference, inner and outer group), the function of ritualised language in facework, which seems very salient in certain languages (Persian and Thai), but that I would suspect is probably present in most languages in different measures.

16.3. Face and understanding the 'other': an interpretative dialogue

We now operate within a cultural paradigm of shifting systems and practices where boundaries, whether historical, geographic, or interpersonal, appear to be less significant in a context of increased, extensive (mediated or unmediated) contact, which far more frequently exposes for (self) examination concepts of personhood, 'other', values and norms. In this unsettled and unsettling space of self- and other discovery, the concept of 'face' is often associated with identity (see Spencer-Oatey, this volume, Chapter 7). It may be objected that 'identity' is only 'an analytical fiction' (Simon 2004, quoted in Spencer-Oatey, this volume) and a western one at it, which makes its use problematic in the study of face in intra- and intercultural interaction. In turn, identity work builds on another troubled concept in psychology, that of 'self'. Originating from within western psychologies, but increasingly finding currency among some Asian scholars (e.g. Lebra, 2004, Gao, 1996; but also see Hamaguchi (1995) for an original critique), implicit and explicit conceptualisations of the 'self' are largely responsible for the body of critical research on 'face' referred to by several authors in this volume.

The aphorism 'Know thyself', attributed in ancient mythology to the Oracle of Delphi, in Greece, echoes across the centuries and informs lay philosophical efforts towards an understanding of one's own mental states and personality traits. Self-reflexivity and self-understanding should also be the basis of intercultural communication: 'All intercultural relations begin with the perception of self, and then extend outward; but to be meaningful it must be knowledgeable.' (Asante, 1983) There has been a tendency in intercultural communication to analyse others rather than self; in business communication this has been attributed to the so-called 'you-attitude' and 'audience adaptation' that dominate communications in business settings (Jameson, 2007: 201). Similarly, intercultural learning concentrates on learning *about* others rather than learning *from* others (Baraldi, 2006), the latter entailing a change of attitude that requires a confident self-opening in genuine curiosity and trust. Many studies in intercultural communication still rely to a large extent on a very narrow concept of cultural identity, i.e. nationality, in spite of earlier calls for a reappraisal of concepts such as self, identity and nation (e.g. Bargiela-Chiappini and Nickerson, 2003). As recent research shows, 'nationality is not the most salient factor in a particular situation or the most central factor in an overall sense of identity' (Jameson, 2007: 205), nor are race and ethnicity 'the most salient elements of cultural identities in minorities' (ibid. 206).

Mapping the multi-dimensional nature of 'cultural identity' requires the deployment of a range of components. A model that attempts to include twenty-three such components (Jameson, 2007: 211), organised in six categories – vocation, class, geography, philosophy, language, and biological traits with cultural aspects – may still fall short on accuracy but acknowledges the importance of self-knowledge in intercultural communication. Too often in our efforts to know who we are, we proceed by describing what we know of ourselves in contrast to (our perceptions of) of the people with whom we come into contact; in other words, we connote our self-identity in terms of *difference from the 'Other(s)'* Stuart Hall (1993: 361) observed that '[t]he capacity to *live with difference* is ... the coming question of the twenty-first century'. The noun 'difference' carries a potentially negative connotation when modified by 'cultural'; while its historical profile is loaded, it is time we concentrated on turning 'difference' into a positively-charged attitude underlying any encounter with another person. Instead of invoking the alleged explanatory powers of 'culture', and its potentially divisive vocabulary – cultural, intercultural, intra-cultural, cross-cultural etc. – we could choose to frame any interpersonal encounter as an opportunity to establish a relation based on similarities *in the presence* of difference(s).

Self-knowledge and self-awareness assist the on-going and often extended process of relation-building and bring to the surface the similarities which provide the first stepping stone on which to inch towards the Other. This initial stage is probably going to be time-consuming in first-time relationships, particularly when vested as well as personal interests are at stake. A classic example is business negotiations with new partners, especially when language issues may intervene as an additional complicating factor, for example when the parties use

English or any other language as a *lingua franca*. Learning *from* the Other becomes possible when a genuine dialogue is established 'as it creates conditions for reciprocity, active participation and empathy' (Baraldi, 2006: 62). Advances in social cognition have demonstrated the human ability to articulate another's view-point as such. Through perspective-taking, 'a higher form of reflexive and reciprocal dialogue through interpretation can be achieved by situated interpreters' (Kögler, 2005: 263). Entering into the Other's world, taking their perspective, is achieved through the reconstruction of their beliefs and the assumptions that they take for granted and that make sense in a specific context of social practices and institutions. In such situations:

> Interpretation is constituted as a dialogue in which I try to understand how the other sees what I take to be at issue; it thus shows itself to be grounded in understanding the self-understanding of another about something we both relate to. (ibid, 264)

When we understand the Other as an agent who can interpret their situation reflexively and take a stand, reification of the Other is avoided; yet, the Other is not elevated above the self, as Emmanuel Levinas would have it, for whom the Other exercises an 'absolute claim' that 'demands total recognition by means of an absolute submission' (Kögler, 2055: 259). According to Levinas (Kozin, this volume, Chapter 11), the subject in relationship is a vulnerable subject, is an emotional subject and therefore 'accessible to us through empathy' (ibid. 212). Scholarly interest in emotions has generated a multi-disciplinary body of literature on their definitions, essence, manifestations and effects on human interaction (e.g. Markus and Kitayama, 1991; Matsumoto, 1989; Fussell, 2002; Bryant and Cantor, 2003; Turner and Stets, 2005). Here the question of how empathy accesses emotional states and how this process and its outcomes become manifested in social interaction, and what the consequences are of this manifestation, seem to me to be inextricably linked to the apprehension of the Other through their 'face'.

If Levinas' ethical, divine face is inaccessible and 'before passion' (Kozin, this volume, Chapter 11: 216), can we in dialogue question the human, everyday 'face' (ibid. 216) about the Other's emotions? Without wishing to reduce 'face' to a metaphor for the emotional self and the Other, studies of negotiation and dispute resolution point to the role and importance of emotions and the dangerous consequences of not paying attention to their influence on human interaction (Hall, 1997). In the context of a dialogue with the Other, we could assume that perception of emotional states might help us guide our interpretation of the

Other (and self) that is conscious of both parties' vulnerability and expresses this consciousness in verbal and non-verbal behaviours that preserve the fragility and sensitivity of the disclosed 'face'.

16.4. Facing the 'Other': a methodological note

As witness the chapters in this volume, the literature on face is vast and multi-disciplinary. The roots of the explanatory power of, and the deep fascination with, this construct in everyday life, are possibly to be found within the depths of philosophical movements around the World. One such movement in Europe, phenomenology, gave us Emmanuel Levinas and his powerful rendering of 'face' sustained by an understanding of morality as the 'elementary given' that resides outside 'the being and the knowledge of being' (Bauman, 1990: 12). A moral relationship, according to Levinas, is established by one mode of existence only, which is 'I being for the Other, I bearing responsibility for the Other' (ibid. 17). Or, to quote the sociologist Zygmunt Bauman's interpretation of Levinas' notion: 'Responsibility is my affair, reciprocity is his. My responsibility is unexceptional and unconditional. The Other need not "prove" anything to "deserve" it.' (ibid. 20) 'Face' in this perspective comes to signify an unexceptional responsibility. In his sociological theory of morality, Bauman (1990) retraces human history in search for the point where responsibility for the Other was lost and finds it where 'the primordial co-ordination between physical and moral proximity is broken' (ibid. 24). In human history, the radius of physical proximity was ordinarily occupied by those we considered neighbours, those who wore a face; the others, the aliens, were those ordinarily living outside of physical and moral proximity and remained faceless. Neighbourhood carried moral significance (ibid. 23). When neighbourhood was invaded by aliens who refused to go away, but stayed – not as visitors or aliens to be fought as those outside the neighbourhood – but as people whose presence we are aware of, with whom we have brief encounters but who are too many for their faces to be remembered, then we learned the practice of indifference. Indifference turns the people new to our neighbourhood into strangers, 'morally distant yet physically close' (ibid. 24–5), a 'faceless crowd' whose units are replaceable and disposable' (ibid. 26). Through indifference, face is lost, or perhaps never even acquired; the Other is denied as a moral object and a moral subject:

> To see, while neither inviting nor justifying reciprocity. To attend, while demonstrating disattention. What is required is a gaze

> masquerading as indifference. A reassuring gaze, informing that nothing will follow the perfunctory scrutiny and no mutual rights and duties are presumed. (Bauman, 1990: 26)

In the light of these considerations, seeking the 'face' of the Other is the first step in making contact with them as a moral subject, an attitude on which dialogue can be established and sustained. There is enough evidence in this volume of the potential of 'face' as a theoretical construct for the interpretation of interaction. But how do we best investigate face-seeking, the workings of reciprocity, the engagement of mutual gaze that precedes the utterance and makes it possible? Kozin (this volume, Chapter 11: 209) mentions ethnomethodology, conversation analysis and Schützian phenomenological sociology. I would like to offer some thoughts on the opportunities offered by ethnomethodology as an approach to the study of face in interaction, even though Kozin concedes that it is a predictable path to follow. Perhaps so for a philosopher like him, or for a sociologist, but ethnomethodology is only beginning to attract the interest of linguists and communication scholars working on face and politeness (Haugh, 2007; Arundale, this volume, Chapter 2).

Within the social sciences, empirical approaches to the study of communication such as conversation analysis, ethnography of communication, and interpretative sociolinguistics have shown that the analysis of 'language in use' can capture the finely-detailed realisation of the construction processes described earlier in the chapter as they unfold. Analysis of real life interaction has been the focus of much politeness research (see Haugh, 2007 for a useful review), but recently debates around the interpretative role of the analyst and the interactants' own understanding of what is going on in talk (Haugh, 2007) have triggered interest in methodological approaches that privilege talk-in-interaction as the site from which agreements on norms and evaluations emerge through which interactants perform action turn-by-turn. These are the tools that are made available to the analyst who wishes to tap into the mechanics of social action. Face concerns are also seen as emergent in verbal and non-verbal processes that are open to the gaze of the interpreters, as well as to their scrutiny. A talk-in-interaction approach focuses on the multiple accomplishments of mediated (and unmediated) talk: 'People talk to each other to construct and order the affairs of their ordinary social activities, to act in social identities and roles, to form and maintain social relationships and group memberships, or formal and recognisable organisations and institutions, or to collaborate for work.' (Nevile and Rendle-Short, 2007)

The impression that one derives when approaching the literature on ethnomethodology (EM) in general and on conversation analysis (CA) in particular is their exclusive focus on data, i.e. everyday, mundane conversations. As a reaction to 'the problems surrounding the tendency for ordinary language descriptions to gloss or idealise the specifics of what they depict' (Heritage, 1984: 234), Harvey Sacks (1992) proposed to focus on every day interactions and avoid interviews, observation methods, contrived data and experimental methodologies. Naturally occurring data were seen as unaffected by idealisation, or a pre-existing research design, or theory, or hypothesis. The fact that early CA data were telephone conversations, selected to eliminate non-verbal behaviour, has not affected the robustness of the findings when compared to later work on face-to-face interaction (Heritage, 1984: 240). Let us remind ourselves of the three basic assumptions of CA: '(1) interaction is structurally organized; (2) contributions to interaction are contextually oriented; and (3) these two properties inhere in the details of interaction so that no order of detail can be dismissed, *a priori*, as disorderly, accidental or irrelevant' (ibid. 241).

The exclusive claim of CA extends to speculations about the orientations and motives of the speakers which are not manifested in the speakers' actions. The analyst's intuition about a particular phenomenon is a starting point but the speakers' orientation to that phenomenon in interaction is what warrants its analytical relevance. Two examples from the recent literature will illustrate the point. The first concerns the different use of membership categorisation devices (MCDs) in the social sciences and humanities and in CA. In the former two, the warrant for a particular categorisation device is its analytical efficacy; in CA such a criterion is insufficient: the analyst will need evidence that 'the parties were oriented to that categorization device in producing and understanding – moment-by-moment – the conduct that composed its progressive realization' (Schegloff, 2007: 475). For an attribute or description to be treated as a MCD as understood by Sacks (1972) we need to look at whether the parties in the conversation make a category out of it, not whether the analyst does (ibid. 477). This requires a re-examination of the role of politeness research analysts when they engage with naturally-occurring data in the ethnomethodological tradition. Incidentally, CA is not an approach to data – '[a]pproaches are ways of getting on a freeway; they don't take you anyplace' (Schegloff interviewed by Wong and Olsher, 2000: 126); CA is engagement with the data, making sense of them, of their orderliness, their underlying and underwriting of human social actions in interaction (ibid.).

The second example is an attempt to persuade Emanuel Schegloff of the benefits of extending the CA's research agenda to include the analysis of what intercultural analysts would call 'native' and 'nonnative' talk (Wong and Olsher, 2000). Schegloff readily admits that he would not advise any analyst to look at data from a language they are not the native speaker of but in the same breath he also resists the pre-analytical categorisation of the data as 'native' 'non-native' unless the data point to the participants' orientation to such categories: 'It is no more transparently relevant that the parties be characterized as 'native' or 'non-native' than it is that they be characterized by gender, by race, age etc.' (Wong and Olsher, 2000: 124) What the analysis should concentrate on is finally dictated by interactional relevance.

The complexity and sophistication of the theoretical apparatus of ethnomethodology and CA as expounded in the work of Harold Garfinkel and Harvey Sacks, has required 'intepretation' by other scholars to make it more accessible to the non-expert (see, for example, Heritage, 1984 and Schegloff, 2007). A recent 'mediating' effort within organisation studies has sought to re-propose EM as one of the most original, though often misunderstood, and for a time even abandoned, attempts at sociological theorising (Samra-Fredericks and Bargiela-Chiappini, 2008), which has had deep resonances in linguistics. Interestingly for some of the discussions in our volume, it has been noted that 'the work of Garfinkel and Sacks who argue for a locally produced order of meaning at the level of talk and mundane action provides a position on language which is compatible with the [Goffman's] idea of an interaction order' (Rawls, 1987: 137). It is tempting to suggest reclaiming Goffman's theorisation of the 'interaction order' and argue for its integration with Sacks' resources for the study of the detailed order and organisation of ordinary activities.

For Goffman, the interaction order is 'a self-ordered and separate domain, depending upon mutual commitment between actors' (Rawls 1987: 146). Interaction is seen as having an orderly and moral character because Goffman attributes to the selves a ritual (i.e. sacred) nature; the face to face contact aims to protect the selves during interaction as well as the interaction order from self-interest (ibid. 139). The sacredness of the interaction order lies precisely in the creation and maintenance of the social self; the fragility of both interaction and social self requires the actors' commitment to act according to the working consensus, and in so doing, to signal adherence to their moral obligations: 'A state where everyone temporarily accepts everyone else's lines is established. This kind of mutual acceptance seems to be a basic structural feature of interaction, especially the interaction of face-to-face talk.' (Goffman, 1967: 11, quoted in Rawls, 1987: 140) Through conversational analysis, access is gained to the practical ways in which 'knowledgeability' and agency accomplish orderly action; moreover, 'analysts can do more than theoretically *claim* identity is reflexively tied to practical undertakings and thus in a permanent state of flux and becoming; they can track such processes second by second' (Llewellyn, 2008: 785).

It is in the encounter between the fragility of the interaction order and of the selves which it sustains, and the fine-grained analysis of action-as-talk using the selves' own resources and 'methods' where perhaps we can start afresh looking at the manifold faces of face(work). Those of us who have worked in organisational contexts, perhaps in different 'cultures', will raise the objection that a conversation analytic approach resists the imposition of contextual constraints on interpretation which are not made relevant by actors in interaction. But Rawls (1989: 166), in her reformulation of Goffman and Sacks, reminds us that 'every action and conversation takes place within an institutional context of some sort, and this context can always be brought to bear at the level of accounts'. Indeed, based on his empirical work in medical contexts, Hak (1995: 135) shows that the achievement of an encounter as 'institutional' is not solely a turn-by-turn accomplishment of participants: 'The latter notion disregards the obvious fact that in most institutional encounters only one party can be considered a practitioner and that the practitioners' point of view will only rarely be made part of a mutual understanding between the participants.' Extending Rawls' insight (on the inclusion of participants' accounts), Hak (1995: 135) suggests that written and spoken reports composed by the practitioners should be integrated in the analysis as 'reportable objects' when they can be considered 'oriented to reporting to specific colleagues on specific occasions' (see also: Seedhouse and Richards, 2007 on 'institutionally relevant artifacts').

Conversation analysis has noted the regularities and commonalities that exist in institutional interaction such as orientation to a core institutional goal, task or identity, constraints on contributions to talk and the use of inferential frameworks and procedures (Drew and Heritage, 1992). The investigation of how actors display the knowledge and understanding they have, how this display makes visible structures of meaning production and their regularities is what ethnomethodology is about. Garfinkel (1967) came to the conclusion that rationality and understandability were achieved through actions themselves, not through the assumption of a shared culture. The consequences of this episte-mology are that we can no longer take for granted commonality of mean-ings and such commonality is not posited for the actors (Sharrock and Anderson, 1986). Ethnomethodology and conversation analysis reject the view of culture as an abstract system; instead they see it as 'witness-able understandings and activities of social interactants' (Lee, 1991: 225).

In view of the ontological shift introduced by ethnomethodology, the position of analysts in the field, be they anthropologists, ethnogra-phers or linguists, is one of a disturbing element. Recalling his experi-ence of a field trip among the Lue people in Thailand in 1959–1961, Moerman (1974: 66) writes:

> By his very presence as someone interested in culture and
> cultures, the social scientist establishes the primary relevance to
> him of ethnic (or kinship, or class, or political) categorization
> schemes as ways of reporting, recording and analysing human
> occurrences. He thus pressures those who would talk to him to
> pay primary attention to these categorizations even when they
> would not otherwise do so.

As observers of situations, if not of 'cultures', linguists working on face and politeness as they become manifested through human interaction, also need to be aware of their tendency to impose categories external to the situation. An ethnomethodological approach to face(work) that zooms into the detail, the systematic and the routine of everyday en-counters could provide new insights on human interaction that do not depend on the super-imposition of 'cultural' constructs but emerge fresh from the sense-making activities of the participants.

References

Arundale, R. B. (2008) Face as emergent in interpersonal communication: an alternative to Goffman, this volume, Chapter 2.

Asante, M. (1983) The ideological significance of Afrocentricity in intercultural communication. *Journal of Black Studies* 14: 3–19.

Baldwin, J., Faulkner, S., Hecht, M. and Lindsley S. (2006) *Redefining Culture: Perspective across Disciplines.* London: Routledge.

Baraldi, C. (2006) New forms of intercultural communication in a globalized world. *The International Communication Gazette* 68: 53–69.

Bargiela-Chiappini, F. and Harris, S. (1997) *The Language of Management. The Discourse of British and Italian meetings.* Amsterdam: John Benjamins.

Bargiela-Chiappini, F. and Nickerson C. (2003) Intercultural business communi-cation: A rich field of studies. *Journal of Intercultural Studies* 24: 3–15.

Bauman, Z. (1990) Effacing the face: on the social management of moral prox-imity. *Theory, Culture & Society,* 7, 5–38.

Bond, M. and collaborators (2004) Culture-level dimensions of social axioms and their correlates across 41 cultures. *Journal of Cross-Cultural Psychology,* 35 (5): 548–570.

Bryant, J. and Cantor, J. (eds. 2003), *Communication and emotion* Mahwah, NJ: Lawrence Erlbaum.

Brislin, R.W. (1981) *Cross-cultural encounters: face-to-face interaction.* New York: Pergamon Press.

Clyne, M. (1994) *Inter-cultural Communication at Work: Cultural Values in Discourse.* Cambridge: Cambridge University Press.

Drew, P. and Heritage J. (eds. 1992) *Talk at Work: Language Use in Institutional and Work-Place Settings,* Cambridge: Cambridge University Press.

Fussell, S. (ed. 2002) *The verbal communication of emotion: Interdisciplinary perspectives,* Mahwah, NJ: Lawrence Erlbaum.

Gao, G. (1996) Self and Other: a Chinese perspective, In W. Gudykunst, S. Ting-Toomey, T. Nishida (eds.) *Communication in Personal Relationships Across Cultures* 81–101. Thousand Oaks, CA: Sage.

Garfinkel, H. (1967) *Studies in Ethnomethodology.* Englewood Cliffs, NJ: Prentice-Hall.

Geertz, C. (1973) *Interpretation of Cultures.* New York: Basic Books

GLOBE, *Global Leadership and Organizational Behavior Effectiveness Research Project,* http://www.thunderbird.edu/wwwfiles/ms/globe/ accessed on 28th January 2008.

Goffman, E. (1967) *Interaction Ritual.* New York: Anchor

Gudykunst, W. and Kim Y. (1997) *Communicating with strangers: An approach to intercultural communication* (3rd ed.), New York: McGraw-Hill

Gupta, A. and Ferguson J. (1997) Culture. Power. Place: Ethnography at the end of an era. In A. Gupta and J. Ferguson (eds.) *Culture. Power. Place* 1–32. Durham, NC: Duke University Press.

Gudykunst, W. and Kim, Y. (1984). *Communicating with strangers: An approach to intercultural communication.* Reading, MA: Addison-Wesley.

Jameson, D. (2007) Reconceptualizing cultural identity and its role in intercultural business communication. *Journal of Business Communication* 44: 199–235.

Kögler, H-H. (2005) Recognition and difference: the power of perspectives in interpretative dialogue. *Social Identities* 11: 247–269.

Koutlaki, S. Two sides of the same coin: how the notion of 'face' is encoded in Persian communication, this volume, Chapter 6.

Kozin, Alexander (2008) In the face of the other: Between Goffman and Levinas, this volume, Chapter 11.

Kroeber, A. and Kluckhohn C. (1952) *Culture.* New York : Meridian Books.

Hak, T. (1995) Ethnomethodology and the institutional context. *Human Studies* 18: 109–137.

Hall, B. (1997) Culture, ethics and communication. In F.L. Casmir (ed.) *Ethics in Intercultural and International Communication* 11–42. Mahwah, New Jersey: Lawrence Erlbaum.

Hall, S. (1993) Culture, communication, nation. *Cultural Studies* 7: 349–363.

Hamaguchi, E. (1985) A contextual model of the Japanese: toward a methodological innovation in Japanese studies. *Journal of Japanese Studies* 11: 289–321.

Haugh, M. (2007) The discursive challenge of politeness research: an interactional alternative. *Journal of Politeness Research,* 3: 295–317.

Heritage, J. (1984) *Garfinkel and Ethnomethodology.* London: Polity Press.

Ho, D.Y-F., Fu, W. and Ng S.M. (2004) Guilt, shame and embarrassment: revelations of face and self. *Culture & Psychology* 10: 64–84.

Hofstede, G. and McCrae, R. (2004) Personality and culture revisited: linking traits and dimensions of culture. *Cross-Cultural Research* 38: 52–88.

House, R.J., Hanges, P.J., Javidan, M., Dorfman, P.W. and Gupta V. (eds) (2004) *Culture, Leadership, and Organizations. The GLOBE Study of 62 Societies.* Sage.

Hutnyk, J. (2006) Culture. *Theory, Culture and Society* 23: 351–38.

Lebra, T.S. (2004) *The Japanese Self In Cultural Logic.* University of Hawaii Press.

Lee, J.R.E. (1991) Language and culture: the linguistic analysis of culture. In G. Button (ed.) *Ethnomethodology and the Human Sciences* 196–226. Cambridge: Cambridge University Press.

Lim, T-S. (2008) Face in the holistic and relativistic society, this volume, Chapter 13.

Llewellyn, N. (2008) Organization in actual episodes of work: Harvey Sacks and organization studies. *Organization Studies* 29: 763-791.

Markus, H.R. and Kitayama S. (1991) Culture and the self: Implications for cognition, emotion, and motivation. *Psychological Review* 98: 224–253.

Matsumoto, D. (1989) Cultural Influences on the Perception of Emotion, *Journal of Cross-Cultural Psychology* 20: 92–105.

Mitchell, D. (1995) There's no such thing as culture: towards a reconceptualization of the idea of culture in geography. *Transactions of the Institute of British Geographers,* 20: 102–116.

Moeraman, Michael (1974) Accomplishing ethnicity. In R. Turner (ed.) *Ethnomethodology* 55-68. Harmodsworth, Middlesex: Penguin Education.

Nevile, M. and Rendle-Short J. (2007) Language as action. *Australian Review of Applied Linguistics,* 30: 1–13.

Ohnuki-Tierney, E. (2006) Against 'hybridity': culture as historical processes. In J. Hendry and H. W. Wong (eds.) *Dismantling the East-West Dichotomy. Essays in honour of Jan van Bremen* 11–16. London: Routledge.

Rawls, A.W. (1987) The interaction order sui generis: Goffman's contribution to social theory. *Sociological Theory,* 5: 136–149.

Rawls, A.W. (1989) Language, self and social order: a reformulation of Goffman and Sacks. *Human Studies* 12: 147–172.

Sacks, H. (1992) *Lectures on Conversation.* Oxford: Basil Blackwell.

Samra-Fredericks, D. and Bargiela-Chiappini, F. (2008) The foundations of organizing: a turn to Garfinkel, Goffman and Sacks. *Organization Studies* 29.

Schegloff, E.A. (2005) On integrity in inquiry ... of the investigated, not the investigator. *Discourse & Society:* 455–480.

Schegloff, E.A. (2007) A tutorial on membership categorization. *Journal of Pragmatics* 39: 462–482.

Seedhouse, P. and Richards, K. (2007) Describing and analysing institutional varieties of interaction. In H. Bowles and P. Seedhouse (eds.) *Conversation Analysis and Language for Specific Purposes* 17–36. Bern: Peter Lang.

Sewell, William H. Jr. (1990) The concept(s) of culture. In V. Bonnell and L. Hunt (eds.) *Beyond the Cultural Turn. New. directions in the study of society and culture* 35–61. Berkeley: University of California Press.

Sharrock, W. and Anderson, R. (1986) *The Ethnomethodologists.* Chichester: Ellis Horwood and London: Tavistock.

Shimizu, A. (2006) West–Japan dichotomy in the context of multiple dichotomies. In J. Hendry and H. W. Wong (eds.) *Dismantling the East–West Dichotomy. Essays in honour of Jan van Bremen* 17–21. London: Routledge.

Simon, B. (2004) *Identity in modern society. A social psychological perspective.* Oxford: Blackwell

Spencer-Oatey, H. (2008) Face, identity and interactional goals, this volume, Chapter 7.

Straub, D., Lock, K., Evaristo, R., Karahanna, E. and Srite, M. (2002) Toward a theory-based measurement of culture. In E.J. Szewczak (ed.) *Human Factors in Information Systems* 61–82. Hersley, PA: Idea Group Publishing.

Street, Brian V. (1993) Culture is a verb: anthropological aspects of language and cultural process. In D. Graddol, L. Thompson and M. Bryman (eds.) *Language and Culture* 23–43. Clevedon: BAAL and Multilingual Matters.

Torkourafi, Marina, (2008) Finding face between *gemeinschaft* and *gesellschaft:* Greek perceptions of the in-group, this volume, Chapter 14.

Trompenaars, F. and Hampden-Turner, C. (1997) *Riding the Waves of Culture: Understanding Diversity in Global Business.* 2nd edn., London: Nicholas Brealey Publishing.

Turner, J.H. and Stets J.E. (2005) *The Sociology of Emotions.* Cambridge, Cambridge University Press.

Ukosakul, M. The significance of 'face' and politeness in social interaction as revealed through Thai 'face' this volume, Chapter 15.

Yeongoyan, A.A. (1986) Theory in anthropology: on the demise of the concept of culture. *Comparative Studies in Society and History* 28: 368–374.

White, L.A. (1959) The concept of culture. *American Anthropologist* 61: 227–251.

Williams, R. (1983). *The Sociology of Culture,* New York, Pantheon.

Wong, J. and Olsher D. (2000) Reflections on conversation analysis and nonnative speaker talk: an interview with Emanuel A. Schegloff. *Issues in Applied Linguistics* 11: 111–128.

Wright, S. (1998) The politicization of 'culture'. *Anthropology Today* 14: 7–15.

Contributors

Eric A. Anchimbe is a lecturer in English linguistics, University of Bayreuth.

Robert B. Arundale is Professor of Communication, University of Alaska Fairbanks.

Francesca Bargiela-Chiappini is currently working as an independent researcher.

Ge Gao is Professor of Communication Studies, San José State University, CA.

Michael Haugh is a lecturer in International English and Linguistics, Griffith University, Brisbane.

Thomas Holtgraves is Professor of Psychological Science, Ball State University, IN.

Sofia Koutlaki graduated with her PhD from the University of Wales College of Cardiff and currently works as an independent researcher and writer.

Alexander Kozin is a Research Fellow at Freie Universität, Berlin.

Tae-Seop Lim is a Professor in the Department of Communication, University of Wisconsin-Milwaukee.

Rosina Márquez Reiter is a senior lecturer in the Department of Culture, Media and Communication Studies, University of Surrey.

Şükriye Ruhi is a Professor of Linguistics in the Department of Foreign Language Education, Middle East Technical University, Ankara.

Helen Spencer-Oatey is Director of the Centre for Applied Linguistics, University of Warwick.

Marina Terkourafi is an Assistant Professor of Linguistics, University of Illinois at Urbana-Champaign.

Stella Ting-Toomey is Professor of Human Communication Studies, California State University at Fullerton.

Margaret Ukosakul is a lecturer in the Department of Linguistics, Payap University, Chiang Mai.

Yasuhisa Watanabe is a lecturer in the Faculty of Business, Queensland University of Technology.

Transcription conventions

These standard transcription conventions are relevant for full interpretation of examples in Chapters 1, 2, 3 and 4

[	beginning of overlapping speech
]	end of overlapping speech
=	latching
-	indicates a cut off of the prior word or sound
<u>underlining</u>	speaker emphasis
::	elongation
CAPITALS	markedly louder speech
↓	marked falling intonation
↑	marked rising intonation
( )	unclear or unintelligible speech
(( ))	extra description of paralinguistic/non-verbal features

Index

Printed in the United States
147841LV00003B/4/P